he Rhetoric of Protest and Reform seeks to
xpand our knowledge and under-
anding of the issues and speechmak-
ig that stirred our nation during the
st three decades of the nineteenth cen-
iry. The fourteen essays written by
:holars of rhetorical criticism and the
istory of American public address,
oncentrate on the political, social, reli-
ious, economic, and intellectual fer-
nent of the "Gilded Age," variously
lubbed as the age of "cynicism," "ex-
ess," "enterprise," and "energy."

Part of the collection examines the
Industrial Protest" with its focus on the
narchers, agitators, union organizers,
ind political orators. Another section
:overs the rural areas, where farmers
istened to populist spellbinders or to
he "calamity howling" of one-gallus
stumpers who proclaimed their peculiar
brands of economic reform. Describing
and evaluating the strategies and platform careers of feminine social reformers brings to life the vitality of the
women's movement. The clash of Christian Socialists and social gospelers with
laissez faire capitalism forms a contrast to
the confrontation of the biblical critics
with their more conservative, evangelical brethren. The last section explores
the efforts of articulate writers and intellectuals to take the message of protest
and reform to the masses through the
lecture platform, the Chautauqua,
Cooper Union, and the Lyceum.

The Rhetoric of

PROTEST
AND
REFORM
1878-1898

Editorial Committee

The Rhetoric of
PROTEST
AND
REFORM
1878-1898

PAUL H. BOASE, *Editor*

ⓟ

OHIO UNIVERSITY PRESS
ATHENS, OHIO

©Copyright 1980 by Ohio University Press
Printed in the United States of America
by Oberlin Printing Company

Library of Congress Cataloging in Publication Data
Main entry under title:

The Rhetoric of protest and reform, 1870-1898.

    Includes bibliographical references and index.
    1. Radicalism—United States—History—
Addresses, essays, lectures. 2. Social movements
—United States—History—Addresses, essays,
lectures. 3. Social reformers—United States—
History—Addresses, essays, lectures.
4. Oratory—Addresses, essays, lectures.
I. Boase, Paul H.
HN90.R3R46   303.4'84   80-11631
ISBN 0-8214-0421-0

Contents

Preface

By 1890, as Samuel Eliot Morison observed, "American Politics lost their equilibrium and began to pitch and toss in an effort to reach stability among wild currents of protest that issued from the caverns of discontent." These currents of protest, with the concurrent voices of reform, inspired the initial editorial committee, headed by Lindsey Perkins, to organize a volume on the history of speechmaking during this era of "Protest and Reform." Ninth in the series, this volume, sponsored by the Speech Communication Association, follows the tradition of earlier studies. Like them it seeks to describe, analyze, and evaluate the issues and the colorful, articulate men and women who used the public platform to help shape our age.

The editorial committee made no attempt to prescribe particular methods of rhetorical analysis. Some of the essays examine the orators independently; others treat the speakers as part of an organized movement. The balance between history and rhetorical criticism varies, but all the studies are analytical and critical. Readers of the volume may note some redundancies in historical narratives. These are difficult to avoid in a volume of independently written studies. Elimination of all repetitions would not serve those who prefer to read selected essays.

The editor expresses thanks to the association and to the many persons who helped prepare the manuscript for publication. Special recognition is given to the following: Lyndon B. Phifer for his careful reading and editing of all the essays; Richard Doolen, the only member of the editorial committee who is not a member of the association, for his perceptive insights as a historian; Robert G. Gunderson and Gregg Phifer, members of the original editorial committee, who read all the essays and provided incisive criticisms. Several graduate students at Ohio University, including Jaime Bryce, Janet Bury, Barbara Graham, and Don Simmons assisted in the editing. Joanne Freeman, Carol Putman, and Lorrie Watson typed the manuscript.

INTRODUCTION

A Setting For Protest And Reform

ROBERT G. GUNDERSON

Naming an age has its perils, particularly naming one as diversified as the period in America that began with "the Gilded Age" and concluded with the so-called "Gay Nineties." Various segments have been called ages of "cynicism," "excess," "enterprise," and "energy." In an inspired frontier image Vernon L. Parrington compared the age to a "great barbecue," where scurrying waiters served choice portions to favored guests while commoners were "put off with the giblets."[1]

Looking beneath the tinsel, historians have found an age of steam and steel and the profound social and economic dislocations that accompany rapid industrial change. "So swift and so basic" were the changes that Ray Ginger concluded "nobody could grasp more than a fraction of what was happening."[2] Arriving in New York City from Warsaw in the winter of 1876, Henry Sienkiewicz the author of *Quo Vadis?*, reacted unfavorably to the "lack of taste in everything"; but he necessarily acknowledged New York's "tremendous industrial development" and the vitality and "energy of its inhabitants."[3] Seizing upon this quality of energy, Howard Mumford Jones selected as its symbol a Double Corliss Engine, the dominating exhibit at the Philadelphia Exposition of 1876.[4]

Arthur M. Schlesinger identified a leading characteristic of the period in *The Rise of the City*, an account of the unparalleled escalation in population from some thirty-nine million in 1870 to seventy-six million in 1900 and of the urban transformations that resulted.[5] An expanding agriculture and the technological innovations of industrialism, to say nothing of the sweat of native-born and immigrant labor, tripled the gross national product between 1870 and 1900.[6] But the rising GNP did little to improve living standards in crowded city tenements or to give comfort to victims of cyclical depression. The cost of living index dropped during the

1

period 1870 to 1896, but so did wages. Blacksmiths who made $2.68 a day in 1870 got $2.31 in 1880. Wages of carpenters dropped from $2.64 to $2.15.[7] Workers in steel, lumber, pottery, mining, and manufacturing made less in 1896 than they did in 1890. Common laborers seldom if ever averaged more than $1.50 a day. Hired hands on farms who worked for "bed and board" in 1870 had not improved their lot by the end of the era.[8] Meanwhile, at Standard Oil, John D. Rockefeller had acquired a fortune exceeding 815 million dollars.[9]

Although Rockefeller's achievement gave considerable substance to the Horatio Alger myth, the disturbing contrast of poverty amid riches severely tested the American dream of a classless society. Even steelmaker Andrew Carnegie admitted that the unequal distribution of wealth was "one of the crying evils" of the day. Confronting this enigma in *Progress and Poverty*, Henry George advocated a single tax to remedy the maldistribution. "So long as all the increased wealth which modern progress brings goes but to . . . make sharper the contrast between the House of Have and the House of Want," George argued, "progress is not real and cannot be permanent."[10]

The economic transformations brought violent strikes, intensified cyclical panics and consequent unemployment, and built bigger "brick Bastilles" in the metaphor of the exiled radical Eugene Pottier—prisons called factories.[11] *Harper's Weekly* provided lurid drawings of the devastating railroad strike of 1877, warned of future strife, and urged that a sufficiently forceful "army of the United States" be prepared to put down "a delirium of crime."[12] Scenes at Haymarket Square, Chicago, in 1886 and at Homestead, Pennsylvania, in 1892 no doubt confirmed the genteel editor in his forebodings.

Financial panics scarred the body politic in 1873 and 1893, each leaving a lingering depression. Jay Cooke & Company, financiers of the Civil War, collapsed in 1873, hauling down its flag on September 18, while depositors besieged the closed doors, muttering about "infernal swindlers and thieves." Soon other banks followed. The diarist George Templeton Strong reported "a seething mob" in New York's financial district on September 20, and by September 24 Wall Street resigned itself to "some great infinite calamity."[13] The postwar boom was over. Agrarians would spend the next generation blaming "The Crime of '73"—the Coinage Act that demonetized silver—for the agricultural slump that followed. Hard times provoke harsh words, as the strident rhetoric of the times demonstrates. After a careful scrutiny of the charges and countercharges Allen Weinstein suggests that the "crime" involves "more than the paranoid fantasies" of contemporary partisans. Using the symbolism of poet Marianne Moore, Weinstein compares the "money-power" myths to "imaginary gardens with real toads in them."[14]

The depression following the Panic of 1893 was, as Carl Degler says, "an earth shaker."[15] Certainly it was the most devastating in American history until the great depression of the 1930s. The bystanders at Parrington's barbecue reflected a grisly realism during the winter of 1893–1894, when the *New York Tribune* headlined "Thousands Cry For Bread," "The Poor Dying From Starvation." A pauper in San Francisco told how he survived by eating barnacles that he chiseled off pilings at a wharf.[16] For the year 1893 *Dun's Review* listed 16,650 bankruptcies. A Police Department survey found 206,701 without means of support in New York City in January, 1894.[17] Clearly the "Nineties" were more somber than the rollicking words and melody of "Ta-ra-ra-ra Boom de-ay" (1892) suggest.

Searching for underlying historical laws to explain anarchical change, Henry Adams "lingered long among the dynamos" at the Chicago Exposition in 1893 for, as he said, they "gave to history a new phase." Adams very reluctantly accepted this disturbing new "force" that "ruthlessly stamped out the life" of the genteel Brahmin class into which he was born. Having observed the gaucheries of the new economic overlords from his strategic vantage point on Lafayette Square across from the White House for almost a generation, he imagined himself as a "purplish-blue and highly venomous hairy tarantula" squatting silently in the "Washington web," devouring "Presidents, senators, diplomats, congressmen and cabinet-officers." The humor inherent in his analogy spares him from being diagnosed as paranoid, but his fantasizing nevertheless reveals a frustrating loss of status. Although the brooding great-grandson of John Adams was more comfortable contemplating Chartres in the thirteenth century, he did find some pleasure in predicting the future. Among other things he recognized the grim inevitability of monopolies, the only force "capable of controlling the new energies that America adored."[18]

Most Americans did not share Adam's gloomy foreboding. Taken in by a rhetoric of quick success, Gilded Age promoters became engrossed with a mania for striking it rich. Mr. Dooley called "th' cash raygister" the "crownin' wurruk iv our civilization."[19] Even the satirist of the age—Mark Twain—succumbed to gold fever. Like his fictional Colonel Beriah Sellers, who daydreamed about making a fortune in eyewash, Twain hoped to make his in gold and silver speculation and in the promotion of a typesetting machine. Andrew Carnegie rationalized materialism in an essay on "Wealth." Preachers spread the joyful word. Russell Conwell, the Baptist minister who founded Temple University, delivered "Acres of Diamonds" some 6,000 times to audiences closely attuned to his materialistic vibrations. To "make money honestly," Conwell once opined, "is to preach the gospel."[20]

To make money was also to win public acclaim. When Commodore Cornelius Vanderbilt died in 1877, *Harper's Weekly* praised him effusively, singling out virtues admired by its readers: "laborious, shrewd, and honest" as well as "frugal, temperate, watchful, and persevering." His charities were, as *Harper's* said, "mostly private, as he had great horror of encouraging pauperism."[21] The public did obeisance to a new breed of heroes—railway monarchs, Viscount James Bryce called them. They were, Bryce said, "among the greatest men . . . perhaps the greatest men in America."[22] While Vanderbilt, James Fisk, Jay Gould, Daniel Drew, Collis Huntington, Leland Stanford, and James J. Hill may have indeed been kingpins of the railway age, other less colorful but somewhat soberer representatives shared sovereignty in the new industrial kingdom: Rockefeller of Standard Oil; Philip Armour and Gustavus Swift, meat packers; Carnegie and Henry Clay Frick, men of steel; J. Pierpont Morgan, financier. Displaced Brahmins made little effort to conceal their contempt for this new "set of mere money-getters and traders." Not one would Charles Francis Adams, Jr., care to meet again "either in this world or the next." But like them, Adams wanted "wealth as the spring-board to influence, consideration, power, and," he added as somewhat of an anti-climax for an Adams, "enjoyment."[23] James Russell Lowell, another Brahmin, deplored the undignified scramble for wealth and the "bar-barizing plutolatry" that converted government into "a game of poker among our millionaires," yet he nevertheless felt exhilarated by America's remarkable "material growth."[24]

The theology of wealth emerged at an expedient moment—and not by coincidence. The Civil War was over; sectional differences were submerged though far from resolved; a complaisant Ulysses S. Grant was President; and a western empire of some one billion acres was up for grabs. The acquisitive lost no time in raising the Jolly Roger. With the connivance of a presidential in-law, Fisk and Gould conspired to corner gold. When the conspiracy failed on Black Friday, September 25, 1869, the perpetrators—warned in advance—bailed out leaving the unsuspecting greedy to suffer the cost. "Let every man carry out his own corpse," advised Fisk, a master of rhetoric as well as of shifty financial footwork. *Les Brigandes*, Jacques Offenbach's operetta, satirized such shenanigans. Fisk brought the production from Europe to his Grand Opera House in New York, playfully referring to himself as a "brigand" in a note to his faithless mistress Josie Mansfield. Fisk's biographer appropriately calls the Prince of Erie "a huge photographic enlargement of the immorality of the time." Certainly Fisk's epigram after his unsuccessful attempt to hijack a rival's railway can serve to characterize a collapse in moral standards: "Nothing is lost save honor."[25]

The catalogue of Gilded Age corruption is familiar, thanks largely to the eloquence and vigor of contemporary reformers. Scandal provided their setting as well as an essential ingredient in their persuasion. A mania for wealth understandably encourages corruption, and this age featured little but "damaged reputation," as Henry Adams put it. George Templeton Strong called things "thoroughly rotten." Noting "a most nasty mess . . . in the custom house," Strong confessed, "I am ashamed to live in a community of Fisks, Tweeds, Vanderbilts. . . ." Illegal railroad money reached every level of government, even the inner sanctums of the White House. Crédit Mobilier smudged Vice-President Schuyler Colfax, Senator James W. Patterson of New Hampshire, and Congressmen James Brooks of New York and Oakes Ames of Massachusetts, among others. The "Mulligan Letters" implicated presidential candidate James G. Blaine. Corruption in the Indian Service involved William W. Belknap, Grant's Secretary of War. Whiskey Ring scandals involved Grant's private secretary, General Orville E. Babcock. In his last annual message to Congress, December 5, 1876, the President acknowledged his "mistakes" but pleaded that the "failures have been errors of judgment, not intent. . . ."[26]

Some state and local governments suffered from a similar misconceived stewardship. William Tweed controlled New York City with the help of the inspired genius of "a gang of rampant scoundrels." The Erie Ring bribed New York state legislators and judges and, when necessary, found hoodlums to administer whatever force might prove necessary in any given situation. In Cincinnati George B. Cox bossed his city with a machine that William Howard Taft described as operating as smoothly "as a nicely adjusted Corliss engine." Lincoln Steffens called Cox's system "one great graft." In Minnesota Kate Donnelly begged her husband to abandon politics. "You are wasting your precious time with scoundrels," she insisted in 1886; "the time is corrupt—there is no virtue." Instead Ignatius Donnelly remained in politics and phrased the eloquent Preamble to the Populist Platform of 1892: ". . . we meet in the midst of a nation brought to the verge of moral, political, and material ruin. Corruption dominates the ballot-box, the Legislatures, the Congress, and touches even the ermine of the bench."[27]

Amorality soon found rationalization in pseudo-Darwinian rhetoric. Making a faulty analogy between biological evolution and *laissez-faire* capitalism, apologists found it easy to exploit so-called evolutionary "laws" like "struggle for existence" and "survival of the fittest" when justifying dog-eat-dog competition. Other spokesmen minimized the mischief of entrepreneurial excesses by emphasizing the benefits of a developing technology and of increased industrial productivity—themes sometimes used by latter-day neo-Whiggish historians.[28] Contemporaries often sanctimoniously condemned the culprit while revering his success.

Their arguments were not unlike praising pirates for redistributing wealth and excusing rapists for promoting fertility—casuistry worthy of the Tweed Ring's Judge George G. Barnard, the legal protector of Fisk and Gould. Treating corruption and waste as inevitable accompaniments of economic expansion, apologists made little effort to demonstrate that unregulated exploitation does in fact lead to constructive innovation in business.

The excesses of exploiters, the agonies of industrial growth, and the derangement of the old order encouraged an energetic rhetoric of dissent—a rhetoric marked by its variety and in some cases its complexity. Among the dissenters were women's rights advocates, organized workers, urban mavericks, Christian Socialists, utopians, intellectuals, economists, good government advocates, and agrarians, who appealed for social change, sometimes even for political and economic equality. Some were intense, gifted, picturesque men and women of vision and imagination. Using the higher criticism, biblical scholars challenged long-standing beliefs, generating friction far outside cloistered schools of theology. In urban pulpits activists like Washington Gladden refused to accept Conwell's acquisitive gospel and instead called for another reformation—for a Social Gospel that applied Christianity to economic and political life. Although dismayed by the failure of the Fourteenth Amendment to grant political rights to women, determined suffragettes like Lucy Stone, Susan B. Anthony, and Carrie Chapman Catt continued their struggle to influence Congress, state legislatures, and party conventions. Victoria C. Woodhull boldly asserted her political rights by running for President on the Equal Rights ticket in 1872. Industrial labor found insistent voices to contest the increasing power of corporations. Leaders ranged from hard-bitten opportunists like Terence V. Powderly and Samuel Gompers to radicals like Eugene V. Debs and the doctrinaire Daniel DeLeon. On farms in the South and West, Grangers and Populists, having survived harassment from nature and from onslaughts of grasshoppers, welcomed a chance to exterminate the oppressive financial domination of the "gold bugs" of the East. Everywhere, as James McBath concludes, the rhetoric of "a small army of lecturers" gave "full throated recognition to the emergent ideas" of protest and reform.

Exploiting all available media of persuasion, reformers argued their various causes in novels, cartoons, pamphlets, songs, parodies, and petitions as well as in speechmaking. Between 1880 and 1900, for example, their rhetoric is found in some 300 social gospel novels and more than 160 utopian or anti-utopian works, including Edward Bellamy's *Looking Backward* and Ignatius Donnelly's *Caesar's Column*.[29] Caricature delineated the faults of the age. Boss Tweed is remembered largely through the vividly penciled hyperbole of Thomas Nast. William H. Harvey's cartoon of the cow being fed in the Middle West and milked in the East epitomized the Populist argument.[30] Songs and rhymes, like pictures, made argument easy to remember. So Populists sang parodies of well known hymns and recited doggerel pleading for "The dollar of our daddies / Of silver coinage free."[31] Pamphleteers spread their dissenting ideas on cheaply printed documents that were hawked at county fairs, union meetings, picnics, party conventions, and holiday gatherings as well as by conventional sales through the usual commercial channels. *Coin's Financial School*, the most popular tract of the 1890s, sold 400,000 copies during its first year of publication and probably more than a million in all its editions.[32] In 1894 the genius of General Jacob S. Coxey put a "petition in boots" to dramatize human misery. In an impressive display of body rhetoric Coxey marshaled his "Army of the Commonwealth" in Massillon, Ohio, for a cross-country march on Washington. Once there, he presented a work-relief program that anticipated some of the New Deal measures of Franklin D. Roosevelt.

It is not easy to generalize about so diverse a group. Their amazing personalities differed as widely as their proposed solutions. Their beliefs can be marked on a continuum from the Marxian socialism of DeLeon through the democratic socialism of Debs, the utopianism of Bellamy, the single tax program of George, the work-relief plan of Coxey, the regulatory reforms and money panacea of Donnelly and the Populists to the social work of Jane Addams, the humanitarian reforms of Gladden and the Social Gospel, and the genteel political tinkering of liberals like George W. Curtis and E. L. Godkin. With the exception of DeLeon they were devoted to political democracy and to individualism. Bellamy, for example, saw no loss of individual freedom in his socialists' utopia.[33] Despite their iconoclasm they embraced the puritanical virtues of thrift, hard work, and honesty. They spoke in a Christian idiom, emphasizing brotherhood and equality of opportunity. They opposed political corruption because it subverted the democratic process. "Bribery is no mere felony," reform Governor Joseph W. Folk of Missouri asserted. "It's treason. . . . Bribery and corruption is a process of revolution."[34] They believed in reason rather than in violence. Debs, a gentle revolutionary, let his membership in the International Workers of the World lapse because of its methods.[35] Reformers hoped to change behavior by "moral suasion," a popular nineteenth-century term now in disuse. Wendell Phillips urged his listeners to shame greedy railway tycoons: "Poison their wealth with the tears and curses of widows and orphans."[36]

There were "misty-minded prophets"; and there were pragmatists with specific, practical remedies like those of Jane Addams—people who "liked to start to heaven from home."[37] A few were flamboyant exhibitionists like Ben Butler and Victoria Woodhull. Some felt a profound sense of alienation, like Donnelly, who has been characterized as a true rebel, "a man on fire." Intense, articulate, and self-assured, the "Sage" of Nininger, Minnesota, was, his biographer says, "easy to admire from a distance, but highly difficult to work with." He regretted that "no great event occurred on the day of his birth." Unlike most zealots, however, Donnelly had a remarkable sense of humor and a caustic wit which relieved tension and perhaps enhanced his persuasion.[38] The more radical Debs harbored an uncompromising hatred for the system, but he never felt alienated from his fellow men or women—even while in jail. He sometimes aroused good feelings among those who opposed him. As James Whitcomb Riley phrased it in a couplet, Debs had "As warm a heart as ever beat / Betwixt here and the Judgment Seat."[39] Few, if any, could match the eloquence of the Brahmin agitator Wendell Phillips, but all tried to satisfy the insatiable nineteenth-century appetite for oratory.

Critics looking for detachment and objectivity among dissenters will look in vain. The vision of political and social evil does not prompt zealots to pussyfoot. Emboldened by the fervor and intensity of Old Testament prophets, they squared off with the world. Convinced that he was "doing the work of his 'Senior Partner' in heaven," William T. Stead told contemporary editors "to take Isaiah as their guide." Stead's devout hope was to "overcome the apathy and ignorance of the masses and immerse them in the great reform movements of the day." His militant exposé of social conditions, *If Christ Came to Chicago*, sold over 100,000 copies in that city alone, but the *Chicago Tribune* denounced this English reformer's findings as "gratuitous" and "offensive." In justifying his emotional appeals Stead observed that some people must "go a great deal too far to get the rest . . . to go half far enough."[40]

Political reformers, as well as exponents of the Social Gospel, used a Manichaean rhetoric that clearly differentiated good and evil. The language was charged with urgency and sometimes with fury born of exasperation. Donnelly, for example, proclaimed that "a wrong has no rights, except the right to die—and die at once." "There are," he announced on one occasion in Minnesota, "really but two parties in this state today—the people and their plunderers."[41] There can be no doubt that reformers created for one another, as Richard Hofstadter says, a "climate of absolutist enthusiasm";[42] but these responses must be measured in the context of the "absolutist" oppressions of their tormentors. Critics clearly fixed the negative stereotypes, calling those seeking change "cranks" who failed to appreciate the blessings of the established order. Altgeld was a "murderer," a "viper," a "blatant Anarchist," and a "half-criminal fool";[43] Phillips a "wild fanatic," a "crazy rhetorical buffoon," whose eloquence, Teddy Roosevelt said, only made his crimes "more heinous." When told of Phillips's funeral one Massachussetts ultra-conservative said that he could not attend but "approved of it."[44]

Senator Roscoe Conkling of New York, a Republican Stalwart, called Civil Service reformers "man-milliners, the dilettanti and carpet knights of politics"—a description that hardly applies to horny-handed Populists like "Sockless" Jerry Simpson, "Pitchfork" Ben Tillman, or "Bloody Bridles" Davis H. Waite.[45] The psychological foibles of Populists have been labored by Hofstadter, who accepted the diagnosis of William Allen White: "neurotics full of hates and ebullient, evanescent enthusiasms."[46] White's implication of their paranoia has been refuted by the Kansas studies of Walter T. K. Nugent, who denies that it was characteristic of their thinking there. "They were bound together," Nugent concludes, "not by common neuroses but by common indebtedness, common price squeezes, common democratic and humanitarian ideals, and common wrath at the infringement of them."[47]

The rhetoric that animates these pages resounds with the cadences of eccentric drummers who are remembered because of their assaults upon bastions of the establishment. They are not befuddled by the "picturesque hallucinations" that deceived Thorstein Veblen's "kept classes."[48] Nor were they enervated by despair. They believed that they could influence the course of events by persuasion. They had faith in education and in the basic goodness of mankind and in the human capacity to learn. They had a romantic notion that even powerful institutions might be changed by their agitation. Skeptics of later generations may dismiss such optimism as naive, but no one should minimize the rhetorical intensity generated by the combined forces of self-confidence and outrage.

* * *

The authors of the following essays find as their energizing ingredient the theme of "protest and reform."[49] They begin with the economic troubles of the 1870s and end with the relative domestic quiet made possible because of the returned prosperity of 1898—a prosperity precipitated by new discoveries of gold and by the inflation brought about by the Spanish American War. They admit that their terminal point is arbitrary but argue that it can be justified by the brief interim that separates Populism from Progressivism. The analysis concentrates on the rhetoric of the political, social, religious, and intellectual revolt: protest against the exploitation of labor; against old political parties; against trusts and monopolies, particularly against the railroads; against traditional patterns in politics, business, education, and religion; and against the political and legal discrimination of women. (A later volume in the series will deal with discrimination against blacks and other minorities.)

The focus is on the rhetoric of those who influence events by what Moses Coit Tyler called "the majestic operation of ideas."[50] The objective of critics, as H. L. Mencken once said, is to "give outward and objective form to ideas that bubble inwardly and have a fascinating lure in them, to get rid of them dramatically and to make an articulate noise in the world."[51] The authors deal broadly with rhetoric in its context, with historical events and issues, as well as with the texts of specific rhetorical appeals. Whatever the method of criticism employed, each author presents a case study of persuasion during a period when the country, like Colonel Sellers, "thrived in the air of indefinite expectation."[52]

NOTES

1. Mark Twain and Charles Dudley Warner, *The Gilded Age: A Tale of Today*, with an Introduction by Justin D. Kaplan (New York: University of Washington Press, 1964); Richard Hofstadter, *The American Political Tradition and the Men Who Made It* (New York: Alfred A. Knopf, 1948), Chapter 7, "The Spoilsmen: an Age of Cynicism," pp. 164–185; Ray Ginger, *Age of Excess: The United States from 1877 to 1914* (New York: Macmillan Co., 1965); Vernon L. Parrington, *The Beginnings of Critical Realism in America: 1860–1920*, Vol. 3, *Main Currents in American Thought* (New York: Harcourt, Brace and Jovanovich, 1958), pp. 23–26; Thomas C. Cochran and William Miller, *The Age of Enterprise* (New York: Harper & Row, 1942).
2. Ginger, *Age of Excess*, p. 328.
3. Charles Morley, ed. and trans., *Portrait of America: Letters of Henry Sienkiewicz* (New York: Columbia University Press, 1959), p. 15.
4. Howard Mumford Jones, *The Age of Energy: Varieties of American Experience, 1865–1915* (New York: Viking Press, 1971), pp. xii, 142-43, and frontispiece.
5. Arthur M. Schlesinger, *The Rise of the City* (New York: Macmillan Co., 1933).
6. Walter T. K. Nugent, *Modern America* (Boston: Houghton Mifflin Co., 1973), p. 81. GNP figures were in current dollars.
7. Clarence D. Long, *Wages and Earnings in the United States, 1860–1890* (Princeton: Princeton University Press, 1960), Appendix A, Table A–11, p. 153, Table A–6, p. 144; Paul H. Douglas, *Real Wages in the United States, 1890–1926* (Boston: Houghton Mifflin Co., 1930), p. 272.
8. Department of Commerce and Labor, *Bulletin of the Bureau of Labor*, 17, No. 77 (July 1908): 61–132; Douglas, *Real Wages in the United States*, Appendix E; Edith Abbott, "Unskilled Labor in the United States," *Journal of Political Economy* 8 (June 1905): 364, 365.

9. Allan Nevins, *Study in Power: John D. Rockefeller, Industrialist and Philanthropist* (New York: Scribner, 1953), 2:404.

10. Henry George, *Progress and Poverty* (New York: D. Appleton & Co., 1879), p. 10.

11. Pottier quoted in Sigmund Diamond, ed., *The Nation Transformed: The Creation of an Industrial Society* (New York: George Brazillier, 1963), p. 5.

12. *Harper's Weekly*, August 11, 1877, pp. 618, 620–21, 624–25, 628–29.

13. Allan Nevins and Milton Halsey Thomas, ed., *The Dairy of George Templeton Strong*, (New York: Macmillan Co., 1952), 4:493–94.

14. Allen Weinstein, "Was There a 'Crime of 1873'? The Case of the Demonetized Dollar," *Journal of American History* 54 (September 1967): 326.

15. Carl Degler, "American Political Parties and the Rise of the City: An Interpretation," *Journal of American History* 51 (June 1964): 47.

16. *New York Tribune*, December 21, 1893; February 11, 1894; January 29, 1894.

17. Ibid., January 2, 1894; February 7, 1894.

18. Henry Adams, *The Education of Henry Adams* (Boston: Houghton Mifflin Co., 1918), pp. 342, 345, 381 ff.; Adams to Sir Robert Cunliffe, January 19, 1899, in Worthington Chauncey Ford, ed., *Letters of Henry Adams (1892–1918)*, (Boston: Houghton Mifflin Co., 1938), 2:204.

19. Quoted in Mark Sullivan, *Our Times: The United States, 1900–1925*, (New York: Charles Scribner's Sons, 1926), 1:290.

20. Ernest J. Wrage and Barnet Baskerville, eds., *American Forum: Speeches on Historic Issues, 1788-1900* (New York: Harper & Brothers, 1960), pp. 256–62, 271.

21. *Harper's Weekly*, January 20, 1877, p. 46.

22. James Bryce, *The American Commonwealth* (London, Macmillan & Co., 1889), 2:515.

23. Adams quoted in Edward Chase Kirkland, *Charles Francis Adams, Jr., 1835–1915: The Patrician at Bay* (Cambridge, Mass.: Harvard University Press, 1965), pp. 80, 128.

24. Lowell quoted in Martin Duberman, *James Russell Lowell* (Boston: Houghton Mifflin Co., 1966), p. 355.

25. *Harper's Weekly*, October 16, 1869, pp. 659, 660, 669; W. A. Swanberg, *Jim Fisk: The Career of An Improbable Rascal* (New York: Scribner, 1959), pp. 107, 205, 282.

26. Strong, *Diary*, 4:409; Gerald W. MacFarland, "Partisan of Nonpartisanship: Dorman B. Eaton and the Genteel Reform Tradition," *Journal of American History* 54 (March 1968): 810; Matthew Josephson, *The Robber Barons* (New York: Harcourt Brace & Co., 1934), pp. 91–93; 163–65; U.S. Grant, Eighth Annual Message to Congress, December 5, 1876 in James D. Richardson, ed., *A Compilation of the Messages and Papers of the Presidents, 1789–1902* (Washington, D.C.: United States Publishing Co., 1903), 7:399–400.

27. Strong, *Diary*, 4:261; Swanberg, *Fisk*, pp. 91–107; Zane L. Miller, "Boss Cox's Cincinnati: A Study in Urbanization and Politics, 1880–1914," *Journal of American History* 54 (March 1968): 823 fn.; Kate Donnelly to Ignatius

Donnelly, September 8, 1886, quoted in Martin Ridge, *Ignatius Donnelly: The Portrait of a Politician* (Chicago: University of Chicago Press, 1962), p. 250. Thomas C. Cochran argues that "the dire condition of state and local government in the 1880s was largely the result of the political abdication of the social elite." "The History of a Business Society," *Journal of American History* 54 (June 1967): 13; Populist Party Platform, July 4, 1892, in Henry Steele Commager, ed., *Documents of American History* (New York: F.S. Crofts & Co., 1934), 2:143.

28. H. Wayne Morgan, ed., *The Gilded Age: A Reappraisal* (Syracuse, N.Y.: Syracuse University Press, 1963), p. 10. In an essay in the same anthology Ari Hoogenboom minimizes the corruption of the period, citing George Washington Plunkitt's distinction "between honest and dishonest graft." He suggests that it may have been "a prim age" that consequently "exaggerated" the scandals. Later, he concludes: "Reformers exaggerated the inefficiency and corruption of the Gilded Age." pp. 70–72.

29. Robert S. Fogarty, review of Kenneth M. Roemer, *The Obsolete Necessity*, in *The Old Northwest* 2 (June 1976): 205–206.

30. William H. Harvey, *Coin's Financial School*, ed. Richard Hofstadter (Cambridge, Mass.: Harvard University Press, Belknap Press, 1963), p. 183.

31. John D. Hicks, *The Populist Revolt: A History of the Farmers' Alliance and the People's Party* (Minneapolis, Minn.: University of Minnesota Press, 1931), p. 204.

32. Jeannette P. Nichols, "Bryan's Benefactor: Coin Harvey and His World," *Ohio Historical Quarterly* 67 (October 1958): 316.

33. Bellamy's emphasis is upon voluntary cooperation and rational behavior. The "system," says Doctor Leete, "depends in no particular upon legislation, but is entirely voluntary, the logical outcome of the operation of human nature under rational conditions." Edward Bellamy, *Looking Backward, 2000–1887*, with a Foreword by Erich Fromm (New York: Signet Books, 1960), p. 89. Robert H. Wiebe also points out that these reformers did not want to return to "a bucolic paradise." "Very few of them despised machinery," he observes, "or pined for a world without factory goods. They simply saw no conflict between popular community control and modern technology. . . ." *The Search for Order, 1877–1920* (New York: Hill & Wang, 1967), pp. 74–75. Daniel Aaron has called Bellamy's utopia a "rather thin and bloodless Nirvana." *Men of Good Hope: A Story of American Progressives* (New York: Oxford University Press, 1951), p. 129.

34. Chester M. Destler emphasizes the debt these radicals and reformers owed to Lockean theory and evangelical Protestantism in *American Radicalism, 1865–1901* (Chicago: Quadrangle, 1966), pp. 3, 19, 212. Henry D. Lloyd, particularly, "harmonized the Lockean political doctrines of the Jeffersonian tradition and the anti-monopolist Populist faith with the collectivist principle." Folk is quoted in Lincoln Steffens, *The Autobiography of Lincoln Steffens* (New York: The Literary Guild, 1931), p. 372.

35. H. Wayne Morgan, "The Utopia of Eugene V. Debs," *American Quarterly* 11

(Summer 1959): 125–126. Charles A. Madison, *Critics and Crusaders* (New York: H. Holt & Co., 1948), p. 502.

36. Phillips quoted in Irving H. Bartlett, *Wendell Phillips, Brahmin Radical* (Boston: Beacon Press, 1961), p. 347.
37. Aaron, *Men of Good Hope*, pp. 94, 218.
38. Ridge, *Donnelly*, pp. 1, 398.
39. Riley quoted in Madison, *Critics and Crusaders*, p. 486.
40. Joseph O. Baylen, "A Victorian's 'Crusade' in Chicago, 1893–1894," *Journal of American History* 51 (December 1964): 418, 423, 429, 433–34.
41. Donnelly quoted in Ridge, *Donnelly*, pp. 245, 278.
42. Richard Hofstadter, *The Age of Reform: From Bryan to F.D.R.* (New York: Knopf and Random House, 1955), p. 17.
43. Quoted in Harry Barnard, *Eagle Forgotten: The Life of John Peter Altgeld* (New York: Bobbs-Merrill, Co., 1938), pp. 300, 385, 394.
44. Quoted in Bartlett, *Phillips*, pp. 332, 398, 400.
45. Conkling quoted in Donald Barr Chidsey, *The Gentleman from New York: A Life of Roscoe Conkling* (New Haven: Yale University Press, 1935), p. 246.
46. William Allen White, *The Autobiography of William Allen White* (New York: Macmillan Co., 1946), pp. 482–83; Hofstadter, *Age of Reform*, pp. 131–32.
47. Walter T. K. Nugent, *The Tolerant Populists: Kansas Populism and Nativism* (Chicago: University of Chicago Press, 1963), p. 242.
48. Veblen quoted in Aaron, *Men of Good Hope*, p. 214.
49. Merle Curti, *The Growth of American Thought* (New York: Harper & Brothers, 1943), pp. 605–632. Curti develops this theme in Chapter 24, "Formulas of Protest and Reform."
50. Moses Coit Tyler, *Literary History of the American Revolution, 1763–1783*, (New York: Ungar, 1957), 1:vii.
51. H. L. Mencken, *A Mencken Chrestomathy* (New York: A. A. Knopf, 1949), p. 429.
52. Twain and Warner, *The Gilded Age*, p. 271.

I

THE INDUSTRIAL PROTEST

1

*The Rhetoric of the Petition in Boots**

MALCOLM O. SILLARS

As the year 1893 drew to a close, the United States was experiencing, as
Robert Gunderson observes in the introduction to this volume, "the most
devastating depression in American history until the great depression of
the 1930s." The federal gold reserve, which at the inauguration of Grover
Cleveland in 1891 had been at a dangerous $100,982,410, had fallen by
November, 1893, to $59,000,000. Six hundred banking institutions failed in
1893. By the end of 1894 over seventy railroad corporations passed into the
hands of receivers; 194 roads, operating 39,000 miles, had failed, including
the Philadelphia and Reading, the Erie, the Northern Pacific, and the
Union Pacific. The year 1893 saw more than 15,000 commercial failures
involving liabilities of $346,000,000.[1] Only partial figures on unemploy-
ment are available but one estimate is that unemployment rose in 1894 to
the total of 4 million, a hitherto unknown number.[2] As the bitter winter
came, cities were faced with the problem of large groups of unemployed
workers. In Chicago, a police census of large factories, wholesale stores,
and lumber yards showed 40.3 percent of the workers unemployed in the
third week of September. Unemployment in San Francisco was estimated
as high as 25,000. The Hartford Common Council, over the Mayor's veto
and "against the public and private protests of many of our best citizens,"
voted to spend $10,000 that winter to employ the unemployed on street
repair. On February 20, 1894, 5,000 men crowded into the Boston State
House and "very fiercely demanded" that the Governor give them
immediate aid. The most conservative figures showed that in the winter of
1893–94 somewhere between four and five percent of the American
population was on relief.[3]

It was in this setting that Carl Browne, in high boots, broad sombrero

17

hat, and buckskin coat buttoned with silver dollars, came to Chicago, (he said) to advertise California at the Columbian exposition. In Chicago, Browne met Jacob S. Coxey, wealthy horse dealer and quarry operator from Massillon, Ohio, who was proposing the employment of the unemployed on a government road-building program by floating non-interest-bearing bonds. Browne convinced Coxey that an army of unemployed men be formed for a march on Washington—a petition "with boots on." Browne believed that the march should begin in unemployment-ridden Chicago but gave in to Coxey's insistence that the historic march begin from Massillon.

The departure was set for Easter Sunday, March 24, when the unemployed were to congregate at Massillon and march to Washington, picking up groups along the way. They planned to have 100,000 men in Washington to demonstrate their need and thus persuade Grover Cleveland and Congress to pass Coxey's bills and save the nation. But few men gathered in Massillon, and many thought it a miracle when a scant one hundred finally departed.

Before Coxey's "Army" moved out, however, under the banner "Peace on Earth Good Will to Men, He Hath Risen, but Death to Interest on Bonds" other armies began preparations to march. Lewis Fry's[4] Los Angeles Army of 600 actually left for the East before Coxey left Massillon. There appears, however, to have been little connection of the Massillon group with Fry's army, with Charles Kelly's San Francisco army of 1,200, or with the many smaller armies, including those of Hogan of Montana, Sanders of Colorado, Jumbo Jim Cantwell of Seattle, Morrison J. Swift of Boston, and Christopher Columbus Jones of Philadelphia.[5]

As an attempt to get results by more effective means of persuasion, the movement was rhetorical in method and object. As this persuasive act moved toward Washington, it had to meet issues about itself and its program. It met those issues with proclamations, general orders, interviews, and frequent speeches.

THE ISSUES

No movement defines itself. It is defined by its friends and, more particularly, by its enemies. The "Petition in Boots" found the issues of its rhetoric in the two major arguments raised against it. The marchers, it was said, are not honest workingmen but tramps. Furthermore, these tramps are trying by threats to force Congress to legislate the impossible: guaranteed employment.[6] But while these popular arguments received the most attention, some concern was also given to the cause and meaning of this spring migration.

The *New York Times*, staunch in its defense of Cleveland Democracy, blamed this migration of "tramps" on Republican demogogues who were trying to use it against the Wilson tariff-reform bill. The Republican *Chicago Inter-Ocean* saw the movement as "an object lesson, illustrating the cruelty of these democratic times." The Republican *Chicago Tribune*, ironically arguing for a solution that was very close to what the marchers wanted, said, "it is a thousand pities that the government did not have some great public work on hand, like the Nicaragua Canal, for instance, and the power to corral the whole crowd and set them to work." James Weaver, 1892 Populist candidate for President, said that the armies "afford us a vivid forecast of the great conflicts and reforms which are to make the closing years of the nineteenth and the early years of the twentieth centuries the most important epoch which has ever dawned upon Christian civilization." It did not matter, he said, whether these men ever got to Washington; the people would apply the remedy of the ballot box.[7] And it was easy to guess what he expected the people to do at the ballot box.

Ray Stannard Baker, then a young reporter for the *Chicago Record*, feeling guilty about some of the derogatory statements he had written in his earlier dispatches, wrote a personal letter to his editor. In part he said:

When such an ugly and grotesque fungus can grow out so prominently on the body politic there must be something wrong. The national blood is out of order, and Coxey, Browne and the other Commonwealers seem, seriously considered, to be but the eruption on the surface. I don't like to think of the army with a sober face, but it seems to me that such a movement must be looked at as something more than a huge joke. It has more meaning than either Coxey or Browne imagines.[8]

In this the young reporter was expressing views similar to those of some more prominent persons. W. T. Stead saw in the America of 1894 the England of 1842. He saw in America a need for the writing of Carlyle and in the Industrial Armies a reflection of the Chartists. "For they are the sandwich-men of Poverty, the peripatetic advertisers of Social Misery. From that point of view they have done their work with notable success, and in that also they resemble their predecessors, the much ridiculed Manchester Insurgents, who killed no one, but merely asserted their grievances and then went home."[9] To Edward Bellamy, labor's support of the armies indicated "that the time is near at hand when the present industrial system will break down and the national system will take its place."[10] A less sure but more astute Thorstein Veblen could see the fundamental meaning of what these "sandwich-men" were selling:

There is a class, shown by the Army of the Commonweal to be larger than was previously apprehended, which is, or has been, drifting away from the old-time holding ground of the constitution. The classic phrase is no longer to read, "life, liberty and the pursuit of happiness"; what is to be insured to every free-born American citizen under the new dispensation is life, liberty and the *means* of happiness.[11]

But insightful analyses like those of Baker, Stead, Bellamy and Veblen were clearly in the minority. And Baker was to see his personal letter appear as an editorial in the *Record* with an added statement converting his guarded sympathy for the Coxeyites to a defense of the established order which dramatized the conflict of the late nineteenth century:

The Correspondent is right. The continual turning of the people to Washington for aid, of which the Coxey army is merely a caricature, is pathetic and portentous. The country is sick just to the extent that its people try to lean on the government instead of standing upright on their own feet.[12]

Democrats blamed Republicans, Republicans blamed Democrats, Populists blamed both, established spokesmen talked of tariff reform and Central American Canals, few understood the significance of the change which was taking place in America. Thus, for Coxey, Browne, Kelly and Fry the immediate issues about the nature of the men and their proposals were central to the success or failure of the movement.

The first charge—that they were tramps—came from all levels of authority. Mayor Solomon of El Paso warned his people of the approach of Fry's Los Angeles Army:

The so-called industrial army, numbering between 900 and 1000 men, will reach El Paso tonight. These men have plundered and robbed the people on their line of march. It is now necessary that the citizens of El Paso prepare for the protection of their property and their families.[13]

As the armies of the Northwest moved on Chicago in late April, James J. Hill of the Northern Pacific Railroad sent a frantic telegram to Grover Cleveland, warning that "there are between four and five thousand men between here and the Pacific Coast in Dakota, Montana, Idaho and Washington in parties of from two to six hundred desiring to go to Washington. They are mainly of the worst class men who do not want to work for a living."[14]

Judge N. M. Hubbard, Attorney for the Chicago Northwestern Railroad, characterized Kelly's army:

In the eyes of the law they are a band of beggars who are organized for an unlawful purpose. They prey on people who are compelled to feed them, . . . we have had men among these people day and night and they have recognized people that have led criminal lives and served time in penal institutions, who are now soldiers in Kelly's army.[15]

Dean Whyland of the Yale Law School hastened to a May 1 meeting of Yale students and told them how he thought they should react to Swift's army coming from Boston: "I guard with jealousy the honor of the Yale Law School, and I hope that none of its members will so far forget his dignity as to join part of the soap-shunning, vermin-haunted rabble which may soon be in this town."[16]

When Fry's army refused employment in St. Louis because they considered the offer an insincere and temporary measure designed to break up the movement, the *New York Times* gave its interpretation of the act:

Now there can be no sort of doubt that the "armies" of Coxey and Fry and Kelly are simply armies of tramps, and of the habitual hardened variety of tramps. There is something of American humor, it must be owned, in the notion of multiplying and embattling tramps until they have passed the limit at which they can be [dealt] with by house dogs and hot water.[17]

All the leaders recognized the tramp charge and took every opportunity to answer it. Restrictions against begging, stealing, and drunkenness were strictly enforced by all the armies. "Of course," said General Kelly, appealing to the middle-class value system of the times, "the boys look hard, but what else could you expect, traveling as we have. Eighty percent of us are American born and one-third married men."[18] Said Jacob Coxey in the speech he was not allowed to deliver on the Capitol steps on May 1: "We stand here to declare by our march of over 5000 miles through difficulties and distress, a march unstained by even the slightest act which would bring the blush of shame to any, that we are lawabiding citizens, and as such our actions speak louder than words."[19]

In point of fact, Coxey was right. With a few minor exceptions the men were amazingly well behaved, and many independent commentators agreed that the armies were, in the great majority, unemployed workingmen who would work if they could.[20]

The most significant defense of the industrials was from General Manager St. John of the Chicago, Rock Island and Pacific Railway. He testified that Kelly's men were "sober," "intelligent," "respectable," "honest," and nine tenths . . . American born."[21]

From such a source the argument was difficult to refute; but the *New York Times* was willing to try:

Authentic evidence that 10 or 5 or 1 percent of the armies was composed of honest and industrious men out of work through misfortune would put a different face on the procedures of the "armies." But no such evidence has been produced, nor is it in the least likely to be produced. The impression that such evidence might, could, would or should be produced has been industriously propagated by interested or deluded persons. Among these are the Republican demagogues, . . . Christian Socialists, . . . [and] the more gullible. . . . These classes [the gullible] have found a spokesman in Mr. St. John, the General Manager of the Chicago, Rock Island and Pacific Railway, who apparently fears violence for the property of that corporation. . . . The best excuse for a railroad man who talks about an army of tramps as Mr. St. John has been talking about Kelly's tramps is that he is frightened out of his wits.[22]

Each day that the armies moved eastward, receiving support from local citizens in towns along the way, was a day that made it increasingly difficult to make the tramp charge stick. The factual issue of the nature of the men perceptibly decreased and the more fundamental issue of value about their proposals increased. Politicians, businessmen, and newspaper editors, the representatives of respectable nineteenth-century society, unable to foresee twentieth-century social liberalism, pointed to the ridiculousness of a petition that violated the very essence of the American system.

Joseph Cook heard Kelly and his lieutenants speak at Ogden, Utah. "Their prevailing idea," he said, "seemed to be that whenever a man cannot for himself find work at two dollars a day, it is the duty of the Federal Government to find it for him and keep him in it. Paternalism in Government was the watchword, and not self-help."[23]

The Catholic Review of New York, seemingly unaware of the implications in the *Rerum novarum* published three years earlier, found Coxeyism a phase of Populism and attacked it because "Populism is another name for paternalism and is based on the supposition that one of the functions of government is to provide a livelihood for all those over whom its sway extends, and that the fact of a man's having been born into the world entitles him *ipso facto* to the means of existence."[24]

Good conduct, statements from leaders, and testimonials from neutrals could blunt the tramp issue, but the debate over the legitimacy of the proposals was a more serious problem of persuasion for the marchers. In the bloodstream of this curious movement ran an assumption in fundamental opposition to the humors of the day. In a larger sense the confrontation of Coxey's proposals and the established social system identified the central domestic issue of the late nineteenth and early twentieth centuries: *Does the government have a responsibility for the economic well-being of the individual citizen?*

Established American values said No; given freedom, reason, and industry, the individual can make his own way. Man's nature gives him reason; the government must guarantee his freedom; industry he must provide for himself. Furthermore, this value system said, the more the government does for a man, the more he loses industry, becomes dependent on the granter of his needs, and thus loses his freedom.

Not only were most opponents unclear on how fundamental was the change in values implied by this movement, but the leaders of the movement were equally unclear. One might argue that it was by design that they chose to build their arguments around the traditional value system. But this is unlikely. It is more probable that, like most American "radical" movements, they did not argue against the traditional value system because they did not believe they were against it!

Jacob Coxey emphasized the acceptability of his programs and procedures. On the steps of the Capitol he would speak in defense of traditional American values—liberty, constitutionality, the will of the people, justice, religion, honest labor, the defense of the middle-class, and the preservation of law and order:

Here rather than at any other spot upon the continent, it is fitting that we should come to mourn over our dead *liberties*, and by our protest arouse the imperiled nation to such action as shall rescue the *Constitution* and resurrect our *liberty*. Upon these steps where we stand has been spread a carpet for the royal feet of a foreign princess, the cost of whose lavish entertainment was taken from the public Treasury without the *consent* and *approval* of the *people*. Up these steps the lobbyists of trusts and corporations have passed unchallenged on their way to committee-rooms to which we, the representatives of the *toiling wealth producers*, have been denied.

We stand here today in behalf of millions of *toilers* whose petitions have been buried in committee rooms, whose *prayers* have been unresponded to, and whose opportunities for *honest remunerative labor* has been taken from them by unjust legislation, which protects idlers, speculators, and gamblers. We come to remind Congress of the declarations of a United States Senator, that for a quarter of a century the rich have been growing richer, the poor poorer, and that by the close of the present century the *middle class* will have disappeared, as the struggle for existence becomes fierce and relentless. . . .

In the name of *justice*, through whose *impartial administration* only the present civilization can be maintained and perpetuated, by the powers of the *constitution* of our country, upon which the *liberties* of the *people* must depend, and in the name of the "Commonweal of Christ," whose representative we are, we enter a most solemn and earnest protest against this unnecessary and cruel act of usurpation and tyranny and thus enforced subjugation of the *rights* and *privileges* of *American citizenship*. We have assembled here in violation of no *just laws* to enjoy the privileges of every *American citizen*.[25]

The main source of America's trouble, Carl Browne said in true Populist fashion, was the international conspiracy of money manipulators, but he linked bankers with the popular folk enemies: thieves and anarchists. "We want," he said, "no thieves or anarchists—boodlers and bankers—to join us."[26]

While opponents argued that bringing large numbers of men to Washington might mean revolution if Congress failed to do as the industrials requested, the leaders preserved to the last an almost childlike faith that Congress would not deny them. It seemed incomprehensible to them that Congress, when confronted with the evidence of need, would deny the specific requests of the petitioners, a further proof of their fundamental faith in the existing American value system.[27]

In response to fears of "anarchy" and violence and in keeping with their acceptance of the traditional value premises of American middle-class rhetoric, the leaders emphasized peacefulness in their speeches and written messages.

The emphasis on peaceful protest was so basic, as a matter of fact, that many of the leaders objected to the use of the term "army" and of military designations for the leaders. While Kelly did not object to being called "General" Kelly of the "California Industrial Army," Coxey and Browne were adamant. Over and over they objected to military terms. Said Carl Browne in General Order No. 1 issued at "Coxiana," Ohio:

All . . . officers will please refrain from the use of titles used by snubocracy of the old dispensation of "general," "captain," "lieutenant," "soldiers," and so on. This is a civic demonstration, and we are all citizens, and the necessary authority of marshal that some of us hold and will be clothed with should not cause any of us to feel big over titles.[28]

Only after all the groups reached Washington in the last days of the movement and the leaders of the Western armies joined with Coxey and Browne did the term "army" come into general use by them. In mid-August a national organization was established with a single constitution. The name of the organization represents a compromise of views: "the Industrial Army Cooperative Commonwealth of the United States," whose first stated object, interestingly enough, was "to preserve peace."[29]

The rhetoric of all the major armies was distinctly peaceful. There was nothing most newspapers would have liked more than some revolutionary speeches. In desperation they may have invented a few. On April 21, camped at Weston, Iowa, just outside of Council Bluffs, with all hope of rail transportation now clearly gone, and possible rebellion brewing in his army, Charles Kelly may have been desperate enough to have told his troops what the newspapers reported:

My comrades, we may have trouble before we reach Washington. Some of us may never return. It may be you or it may be me, but I have no doubt it will be some of us. All revolutions have received a baptism of blood, and I do not expect this one will be any exception to the rule.[30]

But the prevailing powers had their troubles too. With Coxey at Hagerstown, Maryland, Fry in Terre Haute, Indiana, and Kelly about to move on to Des Moines and Chicago, one can build a plausible case for the idea that Kelly's speech was invented by an enterprising newspaperman. It certainly is atypical.

Four days later, on April 25, when the news of the clash between Hogan's Montana Army and federal marshals at Billings reached him, Kelly's response was more true to form:

This is awful. I fear our cause is ruined. Bloodshed is wrong; resistance to the authorities is wrong; it is all wrong. We are reduced to the level of a mob. The militia may be called out at any moment to stop our progress. This gives them an excuse to regard us as lawless. I would have given my life to have this day's work undone.[31]

Coxey's reaction was similar:

Violence has no part in our program. We are simply going to Washington to present a petition to Congress asking them to afford relief for the widely existing distress. I believe that the Constitution has some meaning and that the people have some power, and that when they demand something be done by their servants, something will be done. I do not mean to say that there is no possibility of danger and trouble. I depreciate sincerely any disorders or bloodshed, or the forcible seizure of railroad stock, but the fact that men are obliged to take forcible possession of railroad stock in order to do something that is a matter of life or death to them is a sad commentary on our civilization, and such actions by these private monopolies will only hasten their final downfall.[32]

It was not until the final days of the march on Washington that warlike rhetoric could be heard from Coxey. As the Congress indicated that Coxey would not be allowed to speak and the District Police Chief indicated his intention to restrain Coxey by force, newspapermen badgered him with the question of what he would do if the Congress did not grant his wishes. Still convinced that Congress would agree but now somewhat unsure in his optimism, Coxey was forced into extreme statements, but they were still far less violent than many would have liked:

A copy of the proclamation issued by the District Commissions of Washington, warning the industrial army from invading the capitol, was shown Coxey tonight, and, having perused it carefully, he said, "My answer to it is this, 'the wicked flee when no man persueth.' " It was with a forced smile that he said: "Then my army has struck terror into the hearts of the President and Congressmen."

"Will you heed the proclamation?"

"Emphatically, no."

"If the police arrest yourself and army, what then?"

"Let them dare," snapped the General, his eyes flashing.

"Will you desist from encouraging other industrial armies from storming the Capitol?"

"On the contrary, I shall redouble my efforts to bring every unemployed man, woman, and child to Washington."

"Will not the fear of possible bloodshed deter you?"

"I do not court a resort to arms, but we will demand our rights, even if it takes physical strength to prevail. I shall not commit myself to that, but will repeat my declamation to bring Congress to terms by besieging Washington until justice is done."

"What if the unemployed starve in the streets of Washington?"

"Then the stench of their remains will force Congress to give relief!"[33]

In the perspective of the times and the conditions of the men the leaders of the industrial armies showed amazing restraint in their rhetoric. The nation need not have feared the armies or their intentions. The picture of them as professional tramps, anarchists, and revolutionists was substantially contrived. They were, leaders and followers alike, mostly simple men who, like their opponents, had little understanding of what the movement was or meant.

THE SPEAKERS

Almost nothing is known of the speeches of Lewis Fry. Even the Los Angeles newspapers record little of what he or the other leaders of the Los Angeles Industrial Army said. This is true of most of the minor armies as well. The respected members of the community who spoke for or against the movement were sometimes recorded in the newspapers, but the leaders themselves got scant quotation.

However, the coverage of Coxey's Army and Kelly's Army was sufficient to give a rather good picture of the rhetoric of the "Petition in Boots." The combination represents a fair cross section of the types of men involved. Charles Kelly, a San Francisco printer, fairly well represented the western working-class element of the movement. Jacob Coxey, a respectable businessman, with schemes to solve the problems of the nation's economy, might perhaps (somewhat facetiously) be considered the intellectual of the movement. He may have been, as some charged, just personally ambitious. But all indications are that Coxey was primarily a respectable businessman captured by a naive notion of the workings of the nation's economy and an equally naive view of politics. Carl Browne was a once-in-a-life-time character. When Stead referred to the "sandwich-men of poverty" he must have been able to see that Browne was a sandwich-man to beat all sandwich-men. A closer look at each of these may serve to clarify the dimensions of the rhetoric of the "Petition in Boots."

Charles Kelly, as described by the *Iowa State Register*, does not fit the stereotype of a radical; "he speaks to them [his men] in tones of almost feminine softness, ending his sentences with the little drawl of a southerner. He uses good grammar in his speeches, and is a pleasant-faced, determined looking, undersized man, who rules by tact, good humor and 'horse sense.' "[34]

But while he was not as flamboyant as some (such as Browne), there was a motivational quality to Kelly's speaking which was sentimental and simple in idea and in style. In some ways the preparations for his formal speeches are more obvious in their motivational attempts than the speeches themselves. Kelly used methods he had learned as a member of the Salvation Army. A typical speaking situation was described by one writer as follows:

With the campfires burning all around him and the men preparing their supper, he mounts a flag-adorned wagon and calls the hundreds of curious camp visitors to him. He has a quartet there and at his suggestion it sings "Jesus, Lover of My Soul," and other hymns and revival songs. The exercises assume a decided religious tone, in which Kelly's Salvation Army methods come in good play. He talks of his "Bess and the babies" at home and draws a touching picture of domestic life which appeals to the women in the audience. Then the quartet sings, "Where is My Wandering Boy Tonight?" while the tender-hearted softer sex weeps. This is his chance.

"This meeting," he says in his soft, persuasive voice, "has taken a religious turn. Our meetings always do. I love to talk to a religious people. We understand each other and you know that men who are swayed by the word of God cannot be far wrong. We are right and bent upon performing great and good things. You know that, don't you? I know you do. Now, all of you—all who believe we are honest men—hold up your hands. That's right; that's right; it's unanimous. I knew it would be."

Then for a few moments he talks in a lighter vein, never abandoning religion as his theme, and even going to the length of cracking a joke or two, until he blurts out with:

"And now tell me, what is the most important feature of a religious service? Speak up, don't be afraid. What! You won't tell me! Well, I'll tell you—it's the collection.

"Now, half a dozen of you good-looking citizens take your hats and pass them around the crowd and overlook nobody. You pretty girls, there, you can't use your own hats, but come up and get ours and coax the dimes and dollars out of your lovers' pockets. That's right; that's right. It's in a good cause."

And so on. While the hats are being passed he talks to the hard headed men who want facts by giving statistics as to the number of loaves of bread and pounds of beef and bushels of potatoes and beans necessary for each meal. His manner, more than his words, brings him money.[35]

Despite the expressed establishment fear of the Western Armies, the Massillon group, under the direction of Coxey and Browne, were most criticized as tramps, fools, and revolutionaries. But this picture somehow fails to be convincing when one studies Jacob S. Coxey. He seems more like someone's gentle grandfather than a radical. For the press to paint him in extreme colors was very difficult. When it became clear that Coxey was no wild-man, some speculated that he had somehow "fallen under the spell" of the "evil" Browne.

Coxey's speeches were dull. His plain style was more like that of the local businessman (which he was) speaking on a local clean-up campaign before the Chamber of Commerce than like the utterances of a radical. The complete text of the speech at Williamsport, Maryland, reveals that Coxey spent about one-third of his time reading the bills he was supporting; more than one-third was given to straight exposition of what the bills provided; the remainder was taken up with a defense of the march. The conclusion to that speech illustrates the dull, awkward, archaic style in which he spoke:

To cap the climax, when the money famine was at its height, President Cleveland called an extra session of Congress to repeal the Sherman Act, which act did increase the volume of money at the rate of four million dollars per month. Had it been left upon the statute books, it would have made money a little easier, and by repealing that act business has become worse. There is little hope for the future in a business sense unless the two measures mentioned are passed. These would give immediate relief to the unemployed, in making public improvements and substitute actual money in place of confidence money that has already vanished, thus taking away all possibility of panics and hard times in the future and make it an impossibility for a man to seek work without finding it.[36]

On several occasions Coxey acknowledged that the primary purpose of the movement was to draw attention to the problems. On April 18 at Williamsport he emphasized this function in the introduction:

The aim and object of this march has been to awaken the attention of the whole people. . . . The idea of the march is to attract the attention of the whole people. . . . Believing that the people can only digest one idea at a time, it was necessary to get up some attractions that would overshadow the other matters and have their minds centered upon this one idea and to understand it intelligently.[37]

Since attention was one of Jacob Coxey's primary objectives, the character and rhetoric of Carl Browne, his chief lieutenant, was just what he needed. Contrasted with Coxey's own quiet, didactic, redundant, and flat oratory, Browne's rhetoric was a bell ringer which forced Coxey's Army onto the front pages of the newspapers. Browne was flamboyant in everything: his dress, his religion, and his oratory. In addition to his silver-dollar-buttoned, buck-skinned, sombreroed attire he sported a beard trimmed to make him look amazingly like his favorite picture of Christ. A cartoonist of some talent, he painted huge panoramas on canvas. These were carried on a wagon and unrolled for his evening lectures. He wrote all the general orders that were issued, at least one a day. More column inches were devoted to this eccentric than to anyone else.

He was widely criticized for his divergent religious beliefs (he called it theosophy) but despite the fact that they had nothing to do with the immediate proposals and the issues, he persisted in delivering sermons containing statements like this one:

Do you not see anything strange in the coming together of Brother Coxey and myself? I believe that a part of the soul of Christ happened to come into my being by reincarnation. I believe also that another part of Christ's soul is in Brother Coxey by the same process, and that is what has brought us together closer than two brothers. That prevents all jealousies between us; that strikes down all rivalries. That permits of each according to the other the full measure of credit due and the establishment of an equilibrium of justice between us and mankind that must prevail over all this land eventually, as this principle grows. I also believe that the remainder of the soul of Christ has been fully reincarnated in the thousands of people throughout the United States today, and that accounts for the tremendous response to this call of ours to try and bring about peace and plenty to take the place of panic and poverty. To accomplish it means the second coming of Christ, and I believe in the prophecy that He is to come not in any one single form, but in the whole people.[38]

But substance alone was not what made Browne newsworthy. His style contributed much to the overall picture. Note the weird sense of climax in a general order issued on April 18 at Cumberland, Maryland:

There are events in the lives of men like oases in a desert; green spots that can never be effaced from the memory of man so long as reason holds sway. The past three days of the Commonweal of Christ have been such spots, each succeeding day being more pleasant than the past. Owing to the wonderful harmony existing among us, . . . for the first time since leaving Massillon we left camp on time.[39]

Or listen to Browne's florid attack against the public officials and the press:

Hydra-headed municipality, assisted by the strong file of a corrupt public safety department, has tried to arrest the triumphant progress of the Commonweal of Christ. Several of our noble comrades have been martyred for the cause by the local police. Men who would sell themselves or their country at the back of those argus-eyed hell-hounds of the subsidized press, but the march will go on, for the people are substantially with us.[40]

With disdain Browne repelled the charges against the Commonweal:

If there be any timid persons along the line of march who have become frightened by the press or addlepated mayors in ill-advised interviews that we are Huns and vandals, dispel these fears. We have sufficient food promised us so as not to be as much feared as a state militia, regiment of bankers' clerks and other scions of dudedom, marching through the country. Your daughters are in no danger from us, and your silver and gold are as dross to men who believe [in] legal tender money of paper.[41]

Despite his extravagance of idea, dress, and speech, let no one doubt that

Browne was effective. An anti-Browne newspaper described the mass meeting addressed by Browne on the Monongahela wharf in Pittsburg:

Over 7,000 people stood before Lieutenant Browne when he climbed upon a wagon to speak. There is something wrong with the plumbing inside the commonwealer. He has talked so much that he is hoarse. But he managed to let loose a husky, rasping tirade against the press of the country. "Hit them in the nose," he cried, with a wheeze as he referred to the editors of the newspapers "and send their vile sheets floating down the Monongahela River." The crowd cheered and one man waved his hat. . . . Then the crowd surged toward the wharf. Fifty policemen, in charge of a captain and a lieutenant, could not stop it. The multitude surrounded Commander Coxey's carriage and tore a wheel from its axle. Then it rolled like a black wave against the platform wagon upon which Lieutenant Browne was standing.

The greasy officer of the Commonweal seemed to be pleased with the demonstration. He moved his dirty hands and stood first on one foot and then upon the other. Fiercer and fiercer was his denunciation of what he called the subsidized press until the people, driven mad by his anarchistic utterances, yelled and swung their hats like men at a horse race.[42]

The excesses of Browne's style make credible the plight of the toll-taker over the Monongahela as Browne exhorted him:

"What! Stop a procession with the American flag at its head? Christ died eighteen hundred years ago for just such people as you, and we are willing to die for you now; will you let us pass beneath these flags?" The old toll-keeper thought a moment and then he said; "Boys, go ahead; you may be right."[43]

One might suppose that had there been no Carl Browne and had the public heard only from Coxey, Kelly, and Fry, it might have been much less fearful of the movement; but perhaps had there been no Carl Browne, the people might not have heard much at all of the movement, because it would not have been newsworthy. Perhaps this is the paradox that affects all such movements. Denied the normal channels of publicity they *must* use attention techniques that injure their causes.

The movement was newsworthy and performed its primary function of attracting attention well. It heralded a changing society and value system based on government responsibility for the well being of the individual (a system which neither it nor its opponents really understood) with the rhetorical value system of the established order. As a movement that could give specific workable suggestions to an America in trouble, it was confused and oversimplified. But in mid-August, as the movement found its way to the back pages of the newspapers, the leaders of all the armies gathered in Washington. There they drew up a comprehensive program:

Nationalization of the currency, land, transportation, communication, and all public monopolies . . . ; reduction of the hours of labor . . . , the unabridged right of (labor) combination, . . . repeal of all tramp and sumptuary laws, . . . the unemployed be given employment by the public authorities; silver and gold be coined . . . without limit . . . ; . . . initiative and referendum; compulsory education . . . for children under fifteen; employment of children . . . and girls in occupations detrimental to health and morality be prohibited, and that the convict labor law be abolished.[44]

With the Industrial Armies thus brought in line with the emerging social and economic reform movements of the period, the participants went off, each his own way. Jacob S. Coxey returned to Massillon to receive more votes than any previous Populist candidate for Congress in his district. Thus encouraged, he looked forward to 1896, when he anticipated that he would be elected the first Populist President of the United States.

NOTES

* This paper in substantially the same form was originally published in *Speech Monographs* 39 (June 1972): 92–104. Reprinted here by permission of the Speech Communication Association.

Although it is not specifically quoted in this paper, the reader who wishes more information on the Industrial Army Movement of 1894 will find the best single source to be Donald L. McMurry, *Coxey's Army* (Boston: Little, Brown and Co., 1929).

1. Harold Underwood Faulkner, *American Economic History* (New York: Harper and Bros., 1943), p. 553.
2. Howard R. Smith, *Economic History of the United States* (New York: Ronald Press Co., 1955), p. 403.
3. Carlos C. Closson, Jr., "The Unemployed in American Cities," *Quarterly Journal of Economics* 8 (January 1894): 189 and 212–213; John McCook, "The Unemployed," *Charities Review* 3 (March 1894):236; "Boston's Hungry Unemployed Workingmen," *Locomotive Fireman's Magazine* 18 (April 1894): 401; Frank Parson, "The Relief of the Unemployed in the United States During the Winter of 1893–4," *Journal of Social Science* 32 (November 1894): 6.
4. Variant spellings of Fry's name are Frye and Frey. The spelling selected for this paper is the one used by Donald McMurry in his book *Coxey's Army* and by the *Los Angeles Herald*, the most sympathetic local paper. Perhaps this is a good point to note that there are obvious errors of spelling and language throughout the quotations in this paper. Wherever misspelling can be clearly identified as the fault of the reporter (for instance, where a statement given orally is quoted) I

have corrected the spelling. However, in order to preserve the character of the rhetoric, I have allowed other obvious errors to stand without a scattering of scholarly *sics*.

5. In addition to these armies, various sources mention Grayson of Colorado, Twanley of Oklahoma, Shepherd of Washington, Sweetland of New Jersey, Aubrey of Indiana, Norman of Wisconsin, Randall of Chicago, Charles E. Kain of California. Groups from Ashland and Portland, Oregon, Ottumwa, Iowa, and Monmouth, Illinois, are mentioned. In effect groups from almost every state began to move toward Washington, D.C., and subsequently joined with the main armies, or died. The movement was strongest, however, in the West. *San Francisco Chronicle*, April 14, 1894, p. 2; *New York Times*, April 26, 1894, p. 1; Henry Vincent, *The Story of the Commonweal* (Chicago: W. B. Conkey Co., 1894), p. 17.

6. A third issue, despite its emotive force, did not become as significant as one would expect. Dr. Alvah H. Doty, Chief of the Division of Contagious Diseases of New York City, observed, "There is a fearful menace to the public health in this migration to Washington, for the men following this movement are of a class very susceptible to contracting disease. . . . Chicago is now thoroughly infested with smallpox, . . . these so-called Coxey armies are starting up all over the West. There is a good deal of smallpox in the cities there, and it is almost certain the disease will be carried along with the men." *New York Times*, April 26, 1894, pp. 1–2; "The Danger to Public Health," *North American Review* 158 (June 1894): 701–703.

7. *New York Times*, April 22, 1894, p. 4; *Chicago Inter-Ocean*, April 21, 1894, p. 12; *Chicago Tribune*, April 18, 1894, p. 6; James Weaver, "The Commonweal Crusade," *Midland Monthly* 1 (June 1894): 591, 593–594.

8. Ray Stannard Baker, *American Chronicle* (New York: Charles Scribner's Sons, 1945), pp. 19–20.

9. W. T. Stead, "Coxeyism: A Character Sketch," *American Review of Reviews* 10 (July 1894): 47.

10. *San Francisco Chronicle*, May 6, 1894, p. 14.

11. Thorstein Veblen, "The Army of the Commonweal," *Journal of Political Economy* 2 (1893–94):458.

12. Baker, *American Chronicle*, p. 20.

13. *San Francisco Chronicle*, March 22, 1894, p. 2.

14. Grover Cleveland Papers, Reel 84, (April 24, 1894).

15. *San Francisco Chronicle*, April 20, 1894, p. 1.

16. *New York Times*, May 1, 1894, p. 2.

17. *New York Times*, April 8, 1894, p. 4.

18. *Chicago Herald*, April 17, 1894, p. 1.

19. *Washington* (morning) *Times*, May 2, 1894, p. 1.

20. There is ample evidence from the comments of a number of relatively independent observers of various armies that they were, as a matter of fact, unemployed workingmen and not "Knights of the Road." H. L. Stetson, "The Industrial Army," *Independent* 46 (May 31, 1894):681; Joseph T. Duryea, "The Industrial Army at Omaha," *Outlook* 49 (May 5, 1894): 781–782; Baker,

American Chronicle, pp. 18–19; Henry Frank, "The Crusade of the Unemployed," *Arena* 10 (July 1894):242; Cleveland A. Hall, "An Observer in Coxey's Camp," *Independent* 46 (May 17, 1894): 615; W. T. Stead, *Chicago Today* (London: Review of Reviews Office, 1894), pp. 39–40.

21. *San Francisco Chronicle*, April 22, 1894, p. 13.

22. *New York Times*, April 22, 1894, p. 4.

23. Joseph Cook, "Train Thieves, Tramps and Worthy Poor," *Our Day* 13 (May-June 1894), p. 278.

24. "Cause of Coxeyism," *Public Opinion* 12 (May 24, 1894): 182.

25. *Washington* (morning) *Times*, May 2, 1894, p. 1. [Italics added.]

26. Osman C. Hooper, "The Coxey Movement in Ohio," *Ohio State Archaeological and Historical Society Publications* (Columbus, Ohio 1901), p. 163. This is not the place to go into detail on the charge leveled against Populism that it was anti-British and anti-Semitic. But such a charge is surely not legitimate against the Populist Industrial Army movement. Coxey's undelivered speech on the Capitol steps asked for legislation to "emancipate our beloved country from financial bondage to the descendants of King George" (*Washington* (morning) *Times*, May 2, 1894, p. 1), but this is not a heavily emphasized point. The Rothchilds were mentioned on a few occasions by leaders of the Armies, but there are no strictly anti-Semitic utterances. Except for the western armies' proposals for an end to Chinese immigration no racial or religious bias is revealed by the Industrial Armies. Each had members from all Christian religions, including Roman Catholics. Although they had to defend themselves against the charges of others by noting that most were American-born, foreign-born workers were in the armies. Said Jacob Coxey: "There are no restrictions on recruits, except insistence in the matter of good behavior and American citizenship—nothing in the old lines of Know-Nothingism or bars based on nationality or religion. There is no 'native-born' requisition to be met." (*New York Times*, April 22, 1894, p. 9.) As Coxey moved out of Massillon on March 24, the American flag at the head of the procession was carried by Jaspar Johnson, a Black.

27. On April 20 a letter from Agent Donnella of the Secret Service was brought to President Cleveland by Secretary of the Treasury John G. Carlisle. In part it read: "We have been among the men since [8 am] and are on pretty good terms with several of them, and see no disposition or feeling on their part to violate any law, but they fully believe their presence at Washington will accomplish the purpose for which they go." On April 23 William H. Morrell, a minor New York Democrat, sent a confidential handwritten note to President Cleveland from New York City. His note further showed Coxey's seeming naivete and gave some advice the President should have heeded:

> I have recommended him to *call on you, personally,* on his *arrival in Wash's. He favors "Law"*—not Law-lessness: & seems to be *honest* in the advocacy of his, *non-int't-bearing-Bond-hobby!* Permit me to say, Mr. President; that I think it w'd be *advantageous* to *yourself, and your government* to give him a candid, prompt, and respect hearing. (and let Congress do any "Bluffing" that may become necessary—*later on*). He impressed *me*, somewhat

favorably, and I think he will be able to control his *followers*: and I believe, moreover, that yourself, and Secretary Greshew together, *may easily control him*!

Grover Cleveland Papers, Series 2, Reel 84.
28. Vincent, *Story of Commonweal*, pp. 105–106.
29. *Washington* (morning) *Times*, August 13, 1894, p. 2.
30. *Chicago Tribune*, April 22, 1894, p. 1.
31. *San Francisco Chronicle*, April 26, 1894, p. 1.
32. "Sympathy with the Coxey Movement," *Public Opinion* (May 3, 1894), p. 116.
33. *Chicago Inter-Ocean*, April 24, 1894, p. 2.
34. *Iowa State Register*, April 24, 1894, p. 1.
35. *Chicago Tribune*, May 6, 1894, p. 41.
36. Vincent, *Story of Commonweal*, p. 55.
37. Ibid., pp. 50–51.
38. Hooper, "Coxey Movement in Ohio," pp. 158–159.
39. *Washington* (morning) *Times*, April 19, 1894, p. 1.
40. *Chicago Herald*, April 5, 1894, p. 5.
41. Vincent, *Story of Commonweal*, p. 107.
42. *Chicago Herald*, April 5, 1894, p. 5.
43. Vincent, *Story of Commonweal*, p. 87.
44. *Washington* (morning) *Times*, August 14, 1894, p. 2.

2

Urban Mavericks
And Radicals

CHARLES W. LOMAS

On July 19, 1885, John Swinton issued an appeal to American radicals. Wendell Phillips was dead, and there was no one to replace him:

We need a great orator for this people's battle against capitalism. We need such a man for the impending revolution as Wendell Phillips was for the anti-slavery revolution,—a man of superlative eloquence, of perfect honor, of supreme devotion, of absolute unselfishness, of life-long persistence, caring naught for fame or power, ready to sacrifice himself and all the prizes of life for the cause. Oh, for another Wendell Phillips! . . . . Wanted: An Orator.[1]

For a few weeks Swinton's suggestion brought on a flurry of interest in radical circles. One adolescent reader volunteered himself.[2] Obscure organizers for the Knights of Labor were suggested. Two correspondents found the wanted orator on the plains of Minnesota—the Populist leader of the next decade, Ignatius Donnelly.[3] One suggested Albert Parsons of Chicago, soon to become known as one of the Haymarket anarchists. But several persons took Swinton to task for supposing that a great orator was needed. Oratory was overrated. The truth boldly spoken was enough. When he has something to say, a great orator will come forward.[4] The message must be carried by many men, not by one giant.[5] Teaching is preferable to oratory.[6] One letter writer declared unequivocally that the labor movement was not ready for an orator. There was too much confusion of thought. Until a labor philosopher had clear ideas, no oratory could successfully propagate them.[7]

Of all the suggestions sent to *John Swinton's Paper* perhaps the last came nearest the truth. Certainly a philosopher was needed for the revolutionary radicals who spoke and wrote in American cities in the seventies, eighties, and nineties. Many of them did not know what they wanted; others engaged in baffling changes in direction; but most important, even the most intelligent and consistent among them were so convinced that they alone possessed the truth that they were unable to unite in a powerful and permanent political organization with like minded persons.

The problems were real enough. The irony of want amid plenty could not be refuted. Few bothered to question the common assertion that there were twenty-five thousand millionaires and two million tramps in the country in the 1880s. Radical groups dramatized these facts by staging mock Thanksgiving Day celebrations[8] or parading in rags through the living areas of the rich.[9] The Rev. Hugh Pentecost gave up the ministry for the law and forsook "respectable" company for the society of anarchists and socialists because he was sickened by the sight of "lap dogs driving through Central Park to take the air; children stripping tobacco stems in garrets," and similar brutal contrasts.[10]

Even capitalist newspapers recognized that there was much injustice in the economic order, although they saw no possible solution for the problem. "It is a melancholy fact," the *St. Louis Post-Dispatch* editorialized "that a certain amount of acute poverty and suffering seems to be an inevitable concomitant of our best civilization. The best institutions and the most flourishing trade cannot banish all misfortune and confer universal happiness and content." The editor called upon philanthropists to aid in every possible way but decried the activities of "scheming demagogues" and "misguided but well-meaning fanatics." In America, he concluded, "the only legitimate way to abolish poverty is to work out of it."[11]

Because the problem was obvious to those who cared to look, it was not difficult for radical speakers to make out a "need case," as Henry Bowers, an anarchist, did before the Working People's Debating Club in Pittsburgh.[12] "Just think of the paradoxical society in which we live!" he argued. "There are the farmer, the tailor, the shoemaker, the producers generally, who are very often compelled to be out of employment, and are thereby deprived of the scanty means with which to support themselves and families, simply because there is too much food, clothing, etc.—in short too much of the necessaries of life stocked up." What kind of society was it where parents were "compelled to say to their beloved children: 'The reason, dear children, you have no bread to eat and have to hunger is because there is too much bread in the city!' "? It was self-evident that the "source of poverty and misery is our present unjust economic condition."[13]

The task of the radical orators was thus not to establish need. Nearly all of them argued the same way, pointing out the clear injustice of suffering while storehouses bulged with unused goods. The difficulty was in arriving at a solution that was acceptable even to other radicals. To Dennis Kearney the remedy was simple and certain: Hang the politicians and the Central Pacific "thieves" and run Chinese "lepers" into the sea.[14] But to labor-agitator Joseph Buchanan, Kearney was "simply an ignorant, low-flung, noisy, blatant, impudent blackguard." Any man picked at random on the streets of Denver, Buchanan declared, would have more manhood in a single ounce of his body than could be found in "five tons of Dennis Kearneys."[15] Buchanan and Burnette Haskell also had a solution: the establishment of a socialist society through an elaborate conspiratorial organization—the International Workingmen's Association, or "Red International."[16] But neither of them really believed in revolutionary action. When the excitement of the conspiracy had worn off, Buchanan abandoned it for a comfortable job with the American Press Association, and Haskell embraced a society for forming a utopian colony in the foothills of the Sierra Nevada. Eugene Debs had four solutions in five years as he moved at the end of the century from militant unionism to Bryanism to utopianism to social democracy. Johann Most and his followers in the anarchist International Working People's Association (IWPA) promised an ideal society that would rise through voluntary co-operation after a bloody revolution. As an interim step he offered senseless murder—propaganda of the deed. Yet when Alexander Berkman put the theory into operation by attacking Henry Frick at the time of the Homestead strike, Most repudiated the action, contending that it helped Frick more than it hurt, especially since Berkman bungled the attempt. Berkman's friend Emma Goldman, who had regarded Most as the ideal leader, retaliated by horsewhipping her idol in the midst of one of his speeches.[17] Daniel De Leon offered a carefully reasoned philosophy of scientific socialism, but he consolidated his position by driving away all who differed from him in the smallest particular, alienating the mass movement that might have given his idea reality.

The radical movement in the eighties and nineties had too many ambitious leaders, too much individualism in attempting to attain the co-operative society, and too little co-operation in attempting to attain freedom for the individual. Moreover, most of the radical leaders had little understanding of the inherent conservatism of American workers, who, like Hamlet, found it easier to:

. . . bear those illes we have
Than fly to others that we know not of.

These problems were reflected in oratory characterized by wildly intemperate appeals to violence and only casually related to objective data;

by self-righteous condemnation of deviations from the speaker's or writer's concept of orthodoxy; and by frequent bewildering shifts of methods and goals without abandoning claims to infallibility.

No figure in the radical movement illustrates these problems better than the intellectual leader of the anarchists, Johann Most. It may be of value, therefore, to consider his career in some detail and then to apply these concepts briefly to other leaders of the radical left.

Most arrived in New York, an exile from both Germany and England, in December of 1882. Before this time radicalism in America had been puny and formless. Marxism was only one of many viewpoints about socialism. The anti-capitalist movement was split into many factions, some of them emphasizing economic, some political, some revolutionary action. In San Francisco socialist activity had been almost wiped out by the rantings of Dennis Kearney. When Burnette Haskell gave it energy and direction, he weakened the moral stature of his ideal society by adopting Kearney's ignorant anti-Chinese slogans. The native anarchists of New England owed more to Jefferson and Thoreau than to Marx or Bakunin. In New York and Chicago left wing groups were divided and weak. American Socialists had been reorganized or split four times in the thirteen years since the American branch was started in 1869.[18] The left wing was very much in need of a strong leader.

Johann Most offered such leadership. A forceful writer and speaker, particularly in his native German, he was a disciple of Michael Bakunin rather than of Karl Marx. He brought with him the Bakuninist "conspiratorial form of organization, the cult of violence, the loathing of all authority, the quixotic vision of liberty and equality through destruction and chaos."[19] His reputation preceded him, so the New York newspapers were not slow to give him news coverage. They played up his ugly features, distorted by clumsy surgery in childhood and covered by bushy whiskers. In a day when temperance sentiment was strong they stressed his "beer-sodden" appearance, and noted with distaste that the primary anarchist meeting place was Justus Schwab's saloon. In a day when political cartooning was beginning to be a potent force, Most's grotesque visage was a godsend. Most obliged them further by identifying himself with rifles, poison, and dynamite as political weapons.[20] From this emerged the cartoon sterotype of the bushy-headed anarchist with a bomb in his hand.

But to the confused and often abused German and Slavic immigrants Most appeared to offer a solution for the economic oppression that beset them. When the time came, the workers would overthrow "The Beast of Property."[21] In the meantime they would agitate, sometimes by speaking, sometimes by writing, and sometimes by *attentat* (political murder after the fashion of the European terrorists of Russia, Italy, and Spain).

For a time Most was the undisputed leader of the radical left. A conference in Pittsburgh in 1883 established a union of the anarchists and the most radical of the socialists under the name of the International Working People's Association. For the next three years, until the Haymarket tragedy, IWPA and other radical groups conducted an intense agitation. For the most part IWPA leaders participated in a strike only when a maximum of propaganda could be extracted from it. They invited violence but preferred that it be initiated by the police or the Pinkertons. They talked a great deal about revolution, about retaliation with dynamite, about forming military companies. But, true to the anarchist philosophy they were vague about the form of social organization which was to result from revolution. The right of property in the means of production was to be destroyed. Workers' organizations were to take over and manage the factories. There was to be an interchange of goods between groups of producers, but there was to be no commerce, no governing body, no central planning agency. The anarchist concept of society was as unlike Russian communism of the twentieth century as it was unlike nineteenth-century capitalism.[22]

Most's rhetorical effectiveness was sharply limited by his lack of facility in the English language. As a result much of his speaking was done to immigrant groups, chiefly German socialists. These groups were receptive to anarchist agitation both by European conditioning and by the economic oppression of the factory system and of regular and apparently inevitable cycles of depression. At best, however, they were a small minority of the working class. They little understood the Horatio Alger dream of rags to riches out of which so many American industrialists of the nineteenth century had emerged. Moreover, even in translation the European socialist jargon was incomprehensible to native American laborers.[23] To American workingmen *attentat* was merely senseless murder. However much they might detest the government in power, they could not conceive of a stateless society.[24]

Most himself recognized his limitations. He sought to broaden the base of his movement by attempting to lecture in English, by incorporating into his speeches American themes and images, and by welcoming into the anarchist group the native American eloquence of such leaders as Albert Parsons. He also tried to recruit young people of European background and encourage them to learn to speak to audiences in English.[25]

The most frequently mentioned of the German anarchist's lectures were "The Beast of Property," and "The Deistic Pestilence." Both of these were first written and delivered in German, later in English. Both have been preserved in both languages in pamphlet form. The English language versions, although they bear the marks of translation in some labored constructions and unwieldy sentences, are powerful invective against the evils of the social and economic systems of the late nineteenth century.

There is abundant evidence from both friendly and hostile sources that in German, Most delivered his lectures with a fire that roused his audiences to a high pitch of excitement. He vividly portrayed the wrongs suffered by the masses. It is easy to understand how nervous policemen, hearing him predict the ultimate revolution, would interpret it as an incitement to immediate violent action:

If the people do not crush them, they will crush the people, drown the revolution in the blood of the best, and rivet the chains of slavery more firmly than ever. Kill or be killed is the alternative. Therefore massacres of the people's enemies must be instituted. All free communities enter into an offensive and defensive alliance during the continuance of the combat. The revolutionary communes must incite rebellion in the adjacent districts. The war cannot terminate until the enemy (*the beast of property*) has been pursued to its last lurking place, and totally destroyed.[26]

Yet incitements to violence, even in the future, occupied relatively little time in the *Beast*. Vivid invective was plentiful, however. Here is a partial citing of invective on a single page of the pamphlet version (p.5): "brutal beadle government"; "poor man . . . flayed to complete helplessness by the *beast of property*"; "the *gold tigers* . . . pant for massacres and their thirst for blood is insatiable"; "female labor procures them cheap mistresses"; "the cannibals of modern society continually feast upon juvenile victims."

In *The Deistic Pestilence* sarcastic irony is the key to Most's rhetorical method with language beside which Ingersoll's anti-religious invective pales:

Away with a God invented by preachers of the bloody faith, who, without their important nothing, by means of which they explain everything, could no longer revel in superfluity, no longer glorify poverty, and live in luxury themselves; no longer preach submission and practice arrogance; but who would, through the march of reason, be hurled into the deepest depths of oblivion.

Away then with the malignant trinity—the murderous father—the unnatural son— the lascivious ghost! Away then with all the debasing phantasies in whose name man is degraded to miserable slavery, and through the almighty power of falsehood has been deluded into hoping for the joys of Heaven as an indemnification for the miseries of earth. Away then with those, who with their sanctified hallucinations are the curses of liberty and happiness—the priesthood of all sorts![27]

Most concludes the *Pestilence* with a crescendo of invective, but in the *Beast* he ends with an idyllic picture of the new society of friendly cooperation which would replace the rule of the beast and its ally—government. Men would live in beautiful communities, close to nature. There would be no exploitation, but all would have enough for the good life. Men would work only a few hours a day, the rest of their time devoted to cultural, educational, and intellectual achievement. Heaven could not offer more.

To judge Most's platform effectiveness one must consult those who heard him in German. Buchanan, who did not understand German, but heard Most lecture in English, noted that in Denver he conversed with some of our "best and most conservative citizens, he has been listened to by the most respectable audiences, and all who have seen him or heard him pronounce him a gentleman of rare qualities, a scholar of marked knowledge, and an orator of extraordinary abilities."[28]

Buchanan's Most seems rather tame. On the other hand, the reporter of the *Evening News* (Detroit), heard Most speak in German, which he did not understand, and concentrated on an admiringly hostile report on the agitator's delivery. He described the orator as "an animated windmill," "perpetual motion," "the thrusts of his clenched fists were directed to every subdivision of the compass." He noted that "The gutturals of his dialect, with the vehemence of his utterance, combined to make his delivery a rolling fire of snarls and growls resembling those of a tiger under the whip. . . ."

The reporter found Most's delivery of a "nature to prompt any patriot to deeds of heroic surgery." The speaker was often interrupted by sudden bursts of applause, "which showed that the rough orator came to his points in no roundabout way but flung them naked to the floor and talked on in the midst of the applause."[29]

Young Emma Goldman, already seeking to become an anarchist at twenty was at first repelled by Most's grotesquely twisted face, but as he warmed to his denunciation of the execution of the Haymarket anarchists "He spoke eloquently and picturesquely. As if by magic, his disfigurement disappeared, his lack of physical distinction was forgotten. He seemed transformed into some primitive power, radiating hatred and love, strength and inspiration. The rapid current of his speech, the music of his voice, and his sparkling wit, all combined to produce an effect almost overwhelming. He stirred me to my depths."[30]

Most established the pattern of anarchistic agitation. Although he often took issue with the highly individualistic members of his anarchist group, his influence was dominant in left wing circles in the eighties and continued strong even after he had lost his popularity. Yet, outside of his tiny anarchist circle, he never achieved the status of a leading orator. The anarchist movement was torn by internal struggles and the self-defeating philosophy that denied anyone the right to make decisions binding upon anyone else.

Most never forgave Emma Goldman her attack upon him. As her influence grew, his declined. He was barred from meetings of the Socialist Labor Party of Daniel De Leon. Finally, in 1897, his newspaper bankrupt and his followers dispersed, he left New York and sank into obscurity in his last days.

In part Most's ultimate failure was that of the anarchist philosophy. In part it was his inability to speak to nationalistic Americans on their own terms in an accent that did not bespeak his foreign origin. In part it was that he dealt with the wrong topics for his age. In a day receptive to Horatio Alger he proclaimed the impossibility of class mobility. In a day when evangelists often obtained more newspaper space than presidents, he engaged in violent attacks on religion. In a society that was beginning to be deeply stirred by the social gospel and might have been receptive to Christian socialism he preached the hostility of workers to all forms of religious expression. He proposed a paradoxical society based on extreme individualism, which would somehow result after a bloody revolution in voluntary collective action based on brotherly love. His eclipse was inevitable.

Most's career demonstrates in dramatic fashion many of the failings of the urban radicals of the late nineteenth century. They failed to lead because, often literally and nearly always figuratively, they did not speak the language of American workingmen. Although they did not have the means to execute a violent revolution, they constantly talked of dynamite and guns; but their rhetorical bluster failed to win a mass following. Only when they were driven to desperation, as in the railroad strikes of 1877, would American workmen engage in violent action, and then only for limited ends. The radical leaders failed to organize the masses even for political or economic action because they were so intolerant of deviation from their own version of orthodoxy that they could not work together. Moreover, when one plan of action failed, they turned with equal intolerance to a new set of infallible doctrines. An examination of some of the radicals of the eighties and nineties will illustrate these qualities.

Violent language was early established as the principal rhetorical tool of the radical left. Appeals to violence characterized the speaking of many of the prominent leaders. Only Dennis Kearney succeeded in developing a mass movement by means of this tool, and with minor exceptions his threat never materialized into action. Kearney had no program, but he advocated it with great vigor. Sometimes his speeches merely took the form of abusive epithets; at other times they were filled with lurid threats of hanging, shooting, and burning, but these threats were always conditional. Consider a few typical passages as reported in the *San Francisco Chronicle*:[31]

The Board of Supervisors are the d—est set of thieves that ever disgraced the community. If the municipal authorities continue their persecutions and dare to transgress the law, by heaven! we will meet them half way as a mob. (January 12, 1878)

If we do not get our rights by fair means, we will by powder and ball. . . . The monopolists . . . have built themselves fine residences on Nob Hill, have erected flagstaffs on their roofs. Let them take care that they have not erected their own gallows. (September 23, 1877)

The dignity of labor must be supported, even if we have to kill everyone who opposes us in it. (September 15, 1877)

I have been nice and quiet when I undertake to deliver a speech. . . . When you hear an incendiary speech the Chinese question will be ended. I will turn legions of workingmen loose with their daggers, bayonets, and muskets. They [the monopolists] can avert all this. . . . Let them discharge their Chinamen, open their money bags, build up factories and employ our boys, or, by the eternal God, we will take them by the throat and choke the wind out of them. We are bent on teaching them a lesson they will never forget. (September 15, 1877)

Violent, certainly, but always "tomorrow." Kearney had no plan or program. As economic conditions improved, his empty threats ceased to gain him even a nominal following. Those who had listened drifted away, some because of indifference now that their own economic problems were ended, some to listen to new novelties, some to adhere to more moderate groups like the Greenbackers, Populists, or Single Taxers. If Kearney had any lasting influence it was to force more intelligent and moderate men to consider and seek solutions for the economic and social problems of the day.

Like their mentor—Johann Most—nearly all the members of the anarchists International Working People's Association were addicted to rhetorical violence. The Chicago anarchists who were executed or imprisoned after the Haymarket bombing were never connected in the evidence with the throwing of the bomb.[32] Their real crime was to deliver incendiary speeches and print them in their newspapers, the *Alarm* and the *Arbeiter-Zeitung* along with violent editorials and excerpts from Most's prescriptions for making dynamite bombs. The *Alarm* was filled with rhetorical violence. The police were "bloodhounds of law and order"

(January 9, 1885); the rich were "devils bred in hell and dogs with hearts of stone" (September 24, 1885); the industrial system was "legalized robbery and murder, which was making street walkers of the workingmen's daughters and pimps and thieves of their sons" (December 26, 1885).

Samuel Fielden, one of the anarchists imprisoned for the Haymarket bomb, was regarded by trial judge Gary as a dupe rather than an instigator of violence. Yet even he engaged in wild and lurid denunciation of the exclusion of the anarchists from the Chicago Labor Day celebration:

Comrades: This is a demonstration of workingmen. Tomorrow (the official Labor Day celebration) will be a demonstration of businessmen. Singer and Tallcott, Cribben and Sexton, who shot men through Billy Pinkerton's police, will be present. They have invited Dick Oglesby, the murderer of Lemont, who plunged, through his militia, a sabre into a woman's breast—they have invited him to address laboring men. Also Carter Harrison, who clubbed men, and Jim Bonfield, too I understand. Pinkerton will be there too, I understand, and all the scabs and enemies of labor in order to make you keep down on your knees.[33]

Albert Parsons, the best-educated and most articulate of the Haymarket group,[34] bitterly denounced an industrialist who had given funds to an old people's home, "where after he has exploited you and sucked you dry like an orange, . . . you can go and do a half day's work for a bowl of hot water with a 'bean' in the middle of it. . . . The rich rob the poor and then, like the burglar, toss back a few pennies of the plunder to their victims and call it 'Christian charity.' "[35]

Chicago anarchists talked of blowing up the city, carrying nitroglycerine around in one's pocket, organizing military companies, and establishing a school of chemistry, where Most's manual for making explosives and poison would be the textbook. Parsons and the others argued that dynamite was the great civilizing agent; it made everybody equal.[36] W. S. Gorsuch, reporting his agitational speeches in Baltimore to the readers of the *Alarm*, seemed a little surprised at an adverse reaction from one member of his audience. "When I spoke of the possible advisability of blowing up Turner Hall and the audience with dynamite in order to cause the slaves to 'Revolt now!' one man yelled 'Jesus Christ,' but the balance of the crowd seemed satisfied."[37]

In spite of such incendiary speeches there was little actual violence prior to the Haymarket bomb. At one meeting, where the crowd threatened to sack the mansion of a prominent Chicagoan, the *Alarm* reported that "cooler heads kept the men quiet." This was in spite of the fact that a few moments earlier Parsons, Fielden, and August Spies had been urging the crowd to "agitate, organize, revolt!"[38]

It is quite possible that the anarchists did not really want violence but preferred, at least for the time being, to limit their weapons to loaded words. Speaking at the Haymarket trial in his own defense, Parsons asserted: "Well, possibly I have said some foolish things. Who has not? As a public speaker, probably I have uttered some wild and possibly incoherent assertions. Who, as a public speaker, has not done so?" Parsons contended that he was outraged by seeing "little children suffering, men and women starving," while others were "rolling in luxury and wealth and opulence, out of the unpaid-for labor of the laborers." To make it worse, thirty-thousand men were out of work though no fault of their own, and "the First Regiment is out practicing a street-riot drill for the purpose of mowing down these wretches when they come out of their holes . . . ; . . . the men are drilling . . . to butcher their fellow-men when they demand the right to work and partake of the fruits of their labor! Seeing these things, overwhelmed as it were with indignation and pity, my heart speaks. May I not say some things then that I would not in cooler moments?"[39]

A short time after this statement Albert Parsons, August Spies, George Engel, and Adolph Fisher were hanged on charges of murder growing out of the Haymarket bombing. Though Most continued to speak, and the Chicago group remained in existence, the anarchist movement was discredited, and not even the heroic efforts of Emma Goldman and Alexander Berkman could revive it.

This was not surprising. By its very nature anarchy is doomed to failure. Only its most dedicated adherents can live by its principles; for it depends entirely upon voluntary co-operation. Anarchy cannot be organized with any degree of strength because there can be no party discipline and no effective leadership in the movement. Even without the Haymarket tragedy it is doubtful that the movement could have survived. In the early days of the twentieth century its ablest leaders became involved in militant and disciplined labor movements or joined the Communist Party. Others, disillusioned by the Russian Communist despotism, embraced the liberal wing of one of the major political parties or espoused liberal movements like planned parenthood or the American Civil Liberties Union. In each case the shift required them to give up many of the tenets of their anarchist faith. Except for those who became Communists the doctrine of violence was the first to be abandoned. American workers would not accept a rhetoric that promised only bloody revolution with an outcome so vague that it seemed as remote as the heaven the anarchists rejected.

A second characteristic of the rhetoric of the radical left was intolerance of dissent. As we have seen, this quality appeared even among the anarchists, whose ideal social order was complete and unqualified freedom, in which everyone would wish to co-operate. But it is best exemplified in the career of the ablest of all the nineteenth-century radical leaders, Daniel De Leon, the philosopher and undisputed chief of the Socialist Labor Party. De Leon's affiliation with the party began in 1890. From 1891 until his death in 1914, he was editor of the party newspaper, *The People.* From this central position he vigorously attacked his enemies without and within the labor movement. And he never lacked for enemies. Once he had accepted Marxism, he struck out against Henry George, whom he had supported for mayor of New York in 1886; against the Bellamy Nationalists, who had first introduced him to socialism; against the "labor fakirs" of the American Federation of Labor; against the Social Democrats and the Populists. All these, he thought, were "charlatans," sponsors of "fake movements," who merely diverted the working classes from their revolutionary battle against capitalists. Meanwhile the latter group continued to rob the workers by paying them as wages that portion of their real earnings which they did "not steal along with the other three parts."[40]

De Leon's language was less violent, but not less cutting than that of the anarchists. Because his arguments were carefully thought out and were based on a rational plan for the organization of society, his language did not degenerate into appeals for dynamite and guns. Nevertheless, those who felt the lash of his attack, particularly his rivals for leadership of the labor movement, considered him in Howard Quint's words, "an unmitigated scoundrel who took fiendish delight in character assassination, vituperation, and scurrility." It would be more accurate, however, to describe him as a single-minded idealist, whose fanatic devotion to his cause made him regard those who sought ends short of revolution as heretics and backsliders. Quint appropriately calls De Leon the "late nineteenth-century Grand Inquisitioner of American Socialism."[41]

Quint's description is apt. It indicates the nature of De Leon's speaking and writing as well as the organizing theory on which his rhetoric was based. He argued brilliantly, but then as now American workingmen were more interested in immediate gains than in distant utopias. De Leon's diatribes against Populists, Social Democrats, and "pure and simple" labor leaders came precisely at a time when these groups were beginning to influence American political thought, to modify the harshness of the social order by social legislation on the state level, and to secure a greater share of the producer's dollar through economic pressure by labor unions. The Socialist Labor Party became and remained a loyal, tightly disciplined group of zealots. But intolerance of dissent was contrary to the direction of American politics, and for all his brilliance De Leon was never able to muster sufficient support from the masses to acquire political strength.

Joseph Buchanan once said that the average workingman would not leave his old party as long as its platform contained one plank he approved or join a new party as long as its platform contained one plank he disapproved. De Leon was unable to adjust himself to such popular inconsistencies. He fitted Buchanan's description of the failure of labor leaders: "We have been cranky and crotchety and bigoted; and while we have quarreled and squabbled and split over matters that could just as well as not have been left to the future, the thieves have robbed us, and the voters have left the cranks to fight it out."[42]

Buchanan's criticism of dogmatism in left wing quarters indicates that his brief flirtation with Marxism was only a passing phase. But while Buchanan was pointing up the weakness of one aspect of the radical movement, he was at the same time demonstrating another. Just as De Leon drove away adherents by his fierce orthodoxy, so other leaders, including Buchanan, Haskell, and Debs succeeded in confusing their followers by flitting from one solution to another. At one stage of his career Buchanan was close to the anarchists, sponsoring Most's lectures in Denver and publishing the price of dynamite in his newspaper, the Denver *Labor Enquirer*, in the position where other papers listed stock quotations.[43] At another period he was an aggressive strike leader for the Knights of Labor. At still another time he worked with Burnette Haskell in developing the plan for a conspiratorial organization, the International Workingmen's Association. He supported Ben Butler for President, then Henry George, then became a leader in the Populist Party. Essentially Buchanan was one of those characterized by De Leon:

You will find the reformer ever flying off at a tangent, while the revolutionist sticks to the point. The scatter-brained reformer is ruled by a centrifugal, the revolutionist by a centripetal force. Somebody has aptly said that in social movements an evil principle is like a scorpion; it carries the poison that will kill it. So with the reformers; they carry the poison of disintegration that breaks them up into twos and ones, and thus deprives them in the end of all power for mischief; while the power of the revolutionist to accomplish results grows with the gathering strength that his posture insures to him.[44]

De Leon was wrong about himself, but quite accurate about the group represented by Buchanan.

Yet despite the fact that Buchanan's shifting enthusiasms carried him from one radical group to another, he believed himself to be consistent. He was searching for a formula by which all radical groups could be united. "Paradoxical though it may seem, most of my quarrels with 'leaders' and organizations were results of my desire to see the labor movement unified."[45] At the moment of his enthusiasm for a particular formula his speeches and editorials were served in the language of certainty and flavored with abuse of those who differed with him in solutions, as well as of the common enemies of all radicals. When General Ben Butler was defeated for governor in Massachusetts, Buchanan commented that the "thieves" in Washington had "bought us off with money stolen from us. The day of slavery or revolution is not far distant." The militia who attacked strikers in Leadville were "slum scrapings led by a drunken brute on horseback."[46] In a speech in California he urged a march on Washington years before Coxey's army and declared that if Congress did not respond, the marchers should "dump the whole outfit in the Potomac and organize a good government."[47] In a calmer moment Buchanan recognized this remark as "a fiery oratorical comment, that began and ended nowhere." But he justified his empty rhetoric by the fact that "my heart was full of sorrow for the wrongs that I knew were put upon the toilers of the land." Buchanan's protest was born of emotion rather than reason. Though he stimulated audiences in his role as "Rip-roarer of the Rockies," his inconsistency and lack of firm sense of direction weakened his influence.[48]

In many ways the same comments apply to Eugene Debs prior to the formation of the Socialist Party in 1901.[49] Debs entered the labor movement as a fireman at the age of sixteen. After a brief interruption as a retail clerk and a successful experience in local Democratic politics he returned to the labor movement as national secretary of the Brotherhood of Locomotive Firemen and editor of their *Magazine*. From that point on he was fully identified with the labor movement. He organized the American Railway Union in an effort to bring unity to the feeble Brotherhoods. He lead a disastrous strike against the Pullman Company. Like Buchanan he once endorsed and then rejected dynamite as an instrument of the class struggle.[50] He was successively a leading Populist, a Bryanist, a utopian colonizer, and a founder of the Socialist Party in a four year period at the end of the nineteenth century.

Debs' later career was more consistent, but the Socialist Party he founded was more like Populism than De Leonism, and its ultimate demise was the result of acceptance of its "immediate demands" by other political groups. Its long range Socialist goal was lost as its reform principles were won. But this part of Debs' career belongs to the twentieth century.

Of all the leaders of the radical fringe Debs was the most popular and effective orator. He was far less vindictive in his attack upon the capitalist system than were the anarchists. He did not drive away those on the fringes of socialism as did De Leon. His intense love of humanity in the mass was not diluted by dislike of his fellow men as individuals—a rare attainment. As a result he inspired a large personal following who were able to follow him in his search for the ideal society, in spite of puzzling changes in his announced goals. The rhetoric of Debs was ethical persuasion at its best.

Next to De Leon the most brilliant of left-wing leaders in the late years of the nineteenth century was Burnette G. Haskell. In 1881 Haskell had corresponded with Henry Hyndman, British Socialist leader, and had established the West Coast Division of the International Workingmen's Association, the Red International, which was already in decline in Europe. Buchanan was attracted to the movement. Together they conducted a strong organizing campaign in California and Colorado, winning over many members of the Knights of Labor. When Most called the Pittsburgh Congress that resulted in the formation of the International Working People's Association (the Black International) Haskell made a bid for union of the Red and Black. This document, the original of which is in the Joseph A. Labadie collection at the University of Michigan, was published in the *Pacific Historical Review* by Chester M. Destler, and reprinted in his *American Radicalism, 1861–1901*. In effect it was a bid for unity based on the principles of the Red International, "scientific conspiracy" as opposed to the terrorism of the anarchists. Because it proposed centralized leadership and a temporary dictatorship after the revolution and condemned terror as an instrument prior to complete revolution, it was immediately rejected by Most and his followers.

That Haskell would propose such a union, however, is another example of the shifting trends of the socialist movement. Haskell was an intellectually committed Socialist, whose principles could not possibly harmonize with those of Most. Yet he and Buchanan sought the union. Similarly in California, Haskell accepted the anti-Chinese racism of Kearney, perhaps to win converts from Kearney's Workingmen's Party, but in direct conflict with his socialist concept of the union of all workingmen. Haskell's anti-Chinese speeches, unlike Kearney's, were rationalized into an attack on a form of slavery; but he sought the elimination of the Chinese rather than their emancipation.

After a few years Haskell tired of conspiracy and joined in forming the Kaweah Co-operative Colony in 1886. After its failure in 1891, Haskell lectured for the Bellamy Nationalists and spoke for other radical movements, but his influence was gone.

Like Buchanan and Debs, Haskell was never in public doubt about the truth and justice of the particular solution he happened to be advocating at the moment. In 1885 he addressed an audience in Stockton, California. "Some people," he declared, "cannot understand the reason of this enthusiasm in a moral cause. . . . It is because we, the Socialists, the apostles of the new gospel, are absolutely, positively certain of what we speak; because we know absolutely what will occur within a given time, and because we desire to see these occurrences so controlled as to result, not in the benefit of one or two men, but in the equal benefit of all men for all time.''[51] Whatever effect Haskell may have had upon his audience, he apparently did not convince himself of his own infallibility. Within a year he had abandoned the International for the co-operative colony at Kaweah.

The rhetoric of the radical left was always exciting. It was filled with lurid denunciations of the exploiters and often with equally colorful assaults upon their fellow radicals of even slightly different hue. With the exception of De Leon it was marked by emotional and often irrational portrayal of the woes of the "wage slaves." Except for Debs, radical rhetoric tended to be intolerant of deviation from the brand of orthodoxy supported by the speaker at the moment of utterance. De Leon made this intolerance a virtue. His Socialist Labor Party became and remained a small but disciplined fragment of left-wing thought. Others approached futility by the constant shift in the nature of their enthusiasms.

The major impact of left-wing oratory in the closing decades of the nineteenth century must be assumed to be its dramatizing of the serious economic and social plight of the American workingmen. The solutions they advanced were not suited to the mood of American public opinion, but insistent and unwelcome clamor forced political realists to take notice of intolerable social conditions in America and seek other ways of solving the problems of the day.

NOTES

1. *John Swinton's Paper* (New York), July 19, 1885, p. 1.
2. Ibid., July 26, 1885.
3. Ibid., August 23, 1885; September 6, 1885, p. 2.
4. Ibid., August 2, 1885, p. 2.
5. Ibid.
6. Ibid., November 27, 1885, p. 2.
7. Ibid., September 27, 1885, p. 2.
8. Ibid., December 6, 1885, p. 1.
9. *Freedom* (Chicago), January 1, 1891, p. 2.
10. Ibid., November 11, 1890, pp. 3–4.
11. *St. Louis Post-Dispatch*, November 5, 1886, quoted by *Public Opinion* 2: 31 (November 13, 1886), p. 85.
12. Pittsburgh was not spelled with an *h* until 1911. For ease of reading the *h* has been added.
13. *Freedom*, December 1, 1890, p. 4.
14. In contemporary sources Kearney's given name is sometimes spelled Denis, sometimes Dennis. The spelling used here is from a campaign document of the Workingmen's Party of California. For an extended study of Kearney see Charles W. Lomas, "Dennis Kearney: Case Study in Demagoguery," *Quarterly Journal of Speech* 41 (October 1955): 234–242.

15. *Labor Enquirer* (Denver), July 14, 1883.
16. To be distinguished from the anarchist "Black International," established in Pittsburgh in 1883 (*infra*) and named the International Working People's Association.
17. *New York Times*, December 20, 1892, p. 2. Emma Goldman's account of the incident and the events leading up to it is found in her autobiography, *Living My Life* (New York: Garden City, 1934), pp. 105–107.
18. J. R. Commons et al., *History of Labour in the United States* (New York: Macmillan Co., 1946), 2: 203–300.
19. Theodore Draper, *The Roots of American Communism* (New York: Viking Press, 1957), p. 13.
20. In his newspaper, *Freiheit*, in his speeches, and particularly in a German language pamphlet entitled *Revolutionare Kriegswissenschaft* (no date), Most explained how to make and use nitro-glycerine, dynamite, and poison. Excerpts from the pamphlet, a copy of which is available in the Labadie Collection at the University of Michigan, were translated and published in left wing journals such as the anarchist organ in Chicago, *Alarm*.
21. John [*sic*] Most, *The Beast of Property* (International Workingmen's Association, Group New Haven, undated), pp. 3–15. This speech is reprinted in full in Charles W. Lomas, *The Agitator in American Society* (Englewood Cliffs, N.J.: Prentice-Hall, 1968), pp. 30–41.
22. The conflict between anarchist and socialist philosophies was well illustrated by Burnette Haskell's attempt to provide a basis of union between the IWPA and his own IWA. Like so many attempts at union Haskell's proposals were more nearly a demand for surrender than an attempt at conciliation. He indicated that the united organization should abandon terrorism and organize a central dictatorship to control the production and distribution of goods in the new society. Chester M. Destler, *American Radicalism, 1865–1901* (New York: Octagon Books, 1963), pp. 78–104.
23. Friedrich Engels, who had visited America, urged German immigrant socialists to "doff every remnant of their foreign garb. They will have to become out and out American. They cannot expect Americans to come to them; they, the minority and the immigrants, must go to the Americans, who are the vast majority and the natives. And to do that, they must above all things learn English." Quoted by Theodore Draper, *The Roots of American Communism* (New York: The Viking Press, 1957), p. 32.
24. Richard Drinnon, in his biography of Emma Goldman, reviews the general attitude of incredulity with which American workingmen received Alexander Berkman's attack on Henry Clay Frick. Murder over a "business misunderstanding" they could understand and even sympathize with, but political murder was abhorrent to them. Some even preferred to believe that Berkman's failure proved that he had purposely bungled the attempt, to win sympathy for Frick. *Rebel in Paradise* (Chicago: University of Chicago Press, 1961), p. 52.
25. Goldman, *Living My Life*, pp. 40–53.
26. *Labor Enquirer* (Denver), June 14, 1884, p. 4. Joseph Buchanan, *Enquirer*

editor, said that the Denver lecture was the first time the *Beast* had been presented in English, and the *Enquirer's* text was the first printed in English. The text is identical with an undated pamphlet version in the Library of Congress, printed by the New Haven Group of IWA, to which Most lectured in German in the winter of 1883–1884 on "Idleness Among Workingmen and the Remedy." The English summary of this lecture in the New Haven *Evening Telegram* (quoted by *Labor Enquirer*, February 2, 1884) indicates that it was substantially the same in content as the *Beast*. No doubt on this occasion Most spoke extemporaneously in German.

27. Johann Most, *The Deistic Pestilence*, undated pamphlet, New York Public Library.
28. *Enquirer*, June 7, 1884, p. 2.
29. *Evening News* (Detroit), November 15, 1894 (clipping in Labadie Collection).
30. Goldman, *Living My Life*, pp. 6, 43.
31. The *Chronicle* for a time supported Kearney and probably embellished the speeches in print, but their general character is consistent with versions in other papers. One of his speeches, as reported by the *Chronicle*, is reprinted in Lomas, *Agitator in American Society*, pp. 26–30.
32. The Haymarket tragedy itself is outside the scope of this paper. The best extended account is Henry David, *History of the Haymarket Affair* (New York, 1958). Among many good brief accounts one of the best is in Commons et al., *History of Labour*, 2: 386–394.
33. *Alarm*, September 19, 1885.
34. Allan Pinkerton, eight years before Haymarket, had given grudging praise to Parsons' ability. ". . . it is a notable fact in connection with these communists, that their viciousness and desperation were largely caused by the rantings of a young American communist named Parsons. . . . He is a young man . . . of flippant tongue, and is capable of making a speech that will tingle the blood of that class of characterless rascals that are always standing ready to grasp society by the throat; and while he can excite his auditors, of this class, to the very verge of riot, has that devilish ingenuity in the use of words which has permitted himself to escape deserving punishment." Allan Pinkerton, *Strikers, Communists, Tramps and Detectives* (New York, 1878), pp. 388–389.
35. *Alarm*, December 26, 1885.
36. Lucy Parsons, *Life of Albert Parsons* (Chicago, 1903), p. 155.
37. *Alarm*, May 30, 1885.
38. Ibid., November 29, 1884.
39. Parsons, *Life of Parsons*, pp. 147–148.
40. Daniel De Leon, *Reform or Revolution* (New York: The New York Labor News Publishing Company, 1961), pp. 19–32. This is a pamphlet version of De Leon's speech at Boston, January 26, 1896. For the text of another De Leon speech, see Lomas, *Agitator in American Society*, pp. 59–79.
41. Howard H. Quint, *The Forging of American Socialism* (Columbia: University of South Carolina Press, 1953), pp. 145–146; See also John H. M. Laslett, *Labor and the Left: A Study of Socialist and Radical Influences in the American Labor Movement, 1881–1924* (New York: Basic Books, 1970).

42. Joseph R. Buchanan, *Story of a Labor Agitator* (New York: The Outlook Company, 1903), p. 428. *Labor Enquirer* (Chicago), November 26, 1887, p. 2.
43. *Labor Enquirer* (Denver), June 23, 1883, and subsequent issues.
44. De Leon, *Reform or Revolution*, p. 18.
45. Buchanan, *Story of a Labor Agitator*, p. 438.
46. *Labor Enquirer* (Denver) November 10, and July 28, 1883.
47. *San Francisco Chronicle*, April 27, 1886.
48. Buchanan, *Story of a Labor Agitator*, pp. 287–288.
49. Quint, *The Forging of American Socialism*, pp. 350–388.
50. Ray Ginger, *The Bending Cross* (New Brunswick: Rutgers University Press, 1949), pp. 50–51.
51. *The Evening Mail* (Stockton), October 19, 1885. Clipping in Haskell Collection, Bancroft Library, University of California, Berkeley.

3

Labor in the Age of Protest

J. HAROLD BEATY

The Civil War, followed by expanded agriculture, trade, and industry, stimulated unprecedented economic activity in the United States during the second half of the nineteenth century. Prosperity fluctuated during periodic economic depressions, although the general trend toward economic growth continued. For example, in 1860 more than a billion dollars was invested in factories employing approximately one and a half million workers. In 1900 capital investments exceeded twelve billion, and the number of laborers reached five and one-half million. While the value of manufacturing was increasing elevenfold, population and agricultural output trebled.[1]

THE RISE OF NATIONAL LABOR UNIONS

Almost every socioeconomic group in the United States except farmers and laborers seemed to prosper in the post-Civil War period.[2] Confronted with deterioration in economic and social status,[3] workers banded together for mutual action. Between 1860 and 1869 twenty-four national unions were established, the most prominent of which were the Knights of St. Crispin, the Brotherhood of Locomotive Engineers, and the National Labor Union. Although unions begun in the sixties failed to achieve major gains for workers, they demonstrated the need for action on a national front, brought together scattered trade assemblies, established new interest in industrial relations, and gave America its first prominent labor leader, William H. Sylvis.[4]

The 1870s alerted the public to the fact that the Civil War had "unleashed the demonic in American life" and created a serious labor problem throughout the United States.[5] As the steam-powered turbine replaced the water-powered mill, small investors and craftsmen found it increasingly difficult to compete with corporations. Laborers virtually became pawns in the hands of corporation managers, who looked upon labor as a commodity to be bought as cheaply as possible. When protests brought no tangible results, wage-earners organized for concerted action.

Twenty international unions were established in the decade 1870–1880.[6] Strikes and boycotts brought hardships to the laborer and his family. By the end of the seventies disputes had erupted in almost every state and major industry. Angered by the militancy of striking workers, employers set out to crush all labor organizations. Blacklists, lock-outs, and yellow-dog contracts forced the labor movement underground but failed to halt unionism's growth. Indeed, capital's vigorous counteroffensive stimulated worker interest in unions.[7]

The eighties produced sixty-two international unions, many of which failed by 1889.[8] For a time it appeared that the Knights of Labor would unite the nation's scattered labor bodies. Founded by Uriah S. Stephens in November, 1879, the Noble Order of the Knights of Labor began as a small craft union in Philadelphia, Pennsylvania. Stephens and his colleagues resolved from the outset that the Knights would devote themselves to the general welfare of labor rather than to improving particular working conditions, although the Order endorsed numerous specific reforms in its constitution. The reformist attitude of the Order was idealistic yet impractical, as subsequent events proved. Wage-earners then, as now, wanted immediate tangible gains rather than future reforms.[9]

Stephens and his associates had witnessed the dissolution of the local garment cutters' union in Philadelphia and were persuaded that the primary cause was "blacklisting." To thwart this insidious weapon of management the Knights stressed secrecy and ritual. For twelve years the Order was known by five asterisks and identified publicly as "the Five Stars." Unfortunately the secrecy and mystery aroused antagonism and fear among the public and gave opponents of organized labor a potent weapon with which to attack the Order. In 1881 the secrecy was abolished over the protests of older members. Uriah Stephens resigned as president of the Order and was succeeded by Terence V. Powderly, who served as leader of the Knights until 1893.

Initially organized in local assemblies composed largely of individual workers in separate crafts, the Order later included all workers and former wage-earners.[10] The Order's structure was relatively simple. Local assemblies, composed of individual members, were organized into district assemblies. Each local elected delegates to district assemblies, each district assembly sent delegates to an annual convention called the General Assembly. The General Assembly elected officers and a General Executive Board.[11] Ostensibly the General Assembly was the governing body; while in reality control resided in the district assemblies and the locals.[12]

The phenomenal growth and precipitous collapse of the Order of the Knights of Labor form one of the most incredible chapters of American economic history. Total membership in 1869 consisted of eleven tailors; in 1882 the Order showed a membership of 42,519, and in 1884, 73,326. Between 1884 and 1886 enrollment soared until the official membership crested at 729,677. The sudden increase in membership, for the most part, was a forced influx, workers joining faster than the Order could possibly absorb them.[13] Nevertheless, the spectacular rise of membership in so short a time made the Knights of Labor the most significant labor organization America had yet produced.

Numerous factors contributed to the rapid growth of the Order. The abolition of secrecy, the mood of the times, widespread unemployment, the reformist character of the Order, the dissolution of other unions, aggressive recruitment—all stimulated growth through 1886. Speakers and organizers toured the country, persuading thousands of discontented workers to affiliate with the Knights. Despite the national officers' antipathy to strikes, some spectacular victories in the middle eighties convinced workers that the Order was the militant force labor sorely needed. When strikes against the Gould railroad system in 1885 succeeded, workers stampeded to the Order.[14] "Never in all history has there been such a spectacle as the march of the Order of the Knights of Labor at the present time," wrote labor journalist John Swinton in 1886.[15] Unfortunately the victories of 1884 and 1885 were short-lived. The Knights suffered a disastrous defeat at the hands of the Gould system the following year, and the Order's membership, influence, and strength began to wane.

Reformist objectives, disapproval of strikes, and acceptance of unskilled laborers brought the Order of the Knights of Labor into open warfare with trade unions.[16] When attempts to resolve the conflict between the anti- and pro-trade-union elements failed, trade unionists began a mass exodus from the Order. In a short time it became predominantly an organization of farmers, small-town mechanics, and merchants; creditors took over the Order's property, and membership dwindled to "a few thousand" by 1900.[17]

Despite an ignoble end the Knights of Labor made some significant contributions to the labor movement. After the panic of 1873 it revitalized the labor movement, and awakened the public to the struggle between labor and capital. As the first labor organization to unify divergent social and ethnic groups the Order showed that solidarity was not an impossible ideal. As a formidable enemy of industrial monopoly the Order demonstrated the power of strikes, boycotts, and political action. As an exponent of economic, political, and social reform the Order gave America a lofty democratic tradition to pursue. By no stretch of imagination can these be considered small achievements.

The American Federation of Labor emerged in what may be called the modern era of the American Labor movement. New uses of fuel encouraged greater mechanization in transportation, communications, and industry. Railroads used larger locomotives and more luxurious cars. Sprawling communication systems supplied service over wider geographical areas, and larger and more efficient machinery and tools were introduced into the nation's basic industries. Factories, once located primarily in the East, arose in the South and the West.

Technological improvements in industry affected the American economy in many ways. Networks of transportation and communication changed the United States into a vast economic unit. Large industrial combines were placed in a more strategic position to fight unions. Machines increased productivity, created new social habits, and changed traditional employment patterns.[18] Craft workers, for example, were hard pressed by the ever-growing domination of the machine. Mechanization "threatened their skills" while "the rising tide of semiskilled and unskilled workers threatened their jobs."[19] Since federation seemed the best solution to the craft worker's growing problems, a small group of trade union leaders met in Columbus, Ohio, in December 1886, to bury the floundering Federation of Organized Trades and to organize a new and stronger coalition. Organized in 1881 as a haven for dissident Knights, the Federation of Organized Trades had proven to be a conspicuous failure. It had survived because a small group of trade unionists was determined to establish a rival order to the Knights of Labor.

The conference in Columbus, Ohio, enjoyed a most inauspicious beginning. Forty delegates, representing a small segment of the nation's trade unions, attended. Many other nationals endorsed the idea of a new organization, but sent no official representatives. Samuel Gompers, of the Cigar Makers Union, was elected president; and Peter J. McGuire, of the Carpenters Union, was elected secretary.[20] The Executive Council assumed four major responsibilities: (1) to help organize trade-union groups with strict autonomy, (2) to secure legislation favorable to labor and influence public opinion, (3) to screen boycott proposals of affiliated organizations, (4) and to investigate all strikes and lockouts and issue appeals for financial support of striking workers.[21]

Although the new federation became a reality in 1886, the struggle for survival was long and hard. Conflict with Knights and other rival organizations opened deep wounds. Manufacturers' associations, armed with capital's legislative power and supported by police, militia, and the courts, tenaciously fought the Federation while directing major attention at the Knights. Many trade workers, gripped by the Horatio Alger philosophy of rags to riches, refused to participate in union activity.[22]

Perennial efforts of Socialists to mold the union into a political-action group, strike failures, and economic depressions made the early years of the Federation stormy and difficult. It succeeded for two fundamental reasons: the Federation filled the vacuum created by the Knights' decline; it effectively met the needs of the skilled worker after 1885.[23]

Unlike the Knights of Labor, the American Federation of Labor was more a loose confederation of autonomous unions than a federation. Samuel Gompers described the structure as a "rope of sand and yet the strongest human force—a voluntary association united by the common need and held together by mutual self-interests."[24] Conscious of the inability of previous unions to consolidate both skilled and unskilled workers, the Federation adopted the policy of craft exclusiveness, described by labor historian Norman Ware as "a strategic retreat" rather than an advance of the American labor movement.[25] Gompers, on the other hand, stoutly defended the union's organizational structure, saying that the American Federation of Labor avoided "the fatal rock upon which all previous attempts to affect the unity of the working class have split, by leaving to each body or affiliated organizations the complete management of its own affairs. . . ."[26]

Delegates from individual craft unions met annually to plan policies, endorse programs, and elect general officers. Individual unions were encouraged to form local and regional organizations in each city and state and to establish "departments" in local communities to coordinate activities of all organized workers in the same industry.[27] Ostensibly the executive committee was an administrative body, but in reality Gompers and a coterie of powerful associates controlled the Federation.

Although the Federation supported general labor reforms, it stressed immediate rather than future improvements.[28] "We have no ultimate end. We are going on from day to day. We are fighting only for immediate objects—objects that can be realized in a few years," Adolph Strasser told a congressional committee.[29] The major aim of the Federation, declared Gompers, "is more, more, more, now."[30] Labor preferred to achieve these immediate gains through "collective bargaining" and "trade agreements," leaders insisted. When peaceful means failed, boycotts, strikes, picketing, and any other form of coercion would be used, they added. Since agreements were best negotiated by workers and employers, the Federation vigorously opposed compulsory arbitration. In the beginning leaders publicly disavowed interest in direct political action and fought Socialists, who openly advocated it; yet the Federation became involved in politics numerous times. By 1907 leaders were openly saying: "Stand faithfully by our friends and elect them; oppose our enemies and defeat them. . . ."[31]

As the number of unskilled workers in industry rapidly increased in the

1890s and the Federation continued to reaffirm its policy of craft exclusiveness, industrial wage-earners organized new and stronger industrial unions. In 1890, for example, workers in the mining industry founded the United Mine Workers. When John Mitchell assumed leadership of the organization in 1898, the influence of the United Mine Workers widened and membership soared. In 1894 the American Railway Union, a strong rival of the American Federation of Labor, was organized despite vigorous opposition of railroad brotherhoods. Led by Eugene V. Debs, a dynamic speaker and tenacious crusader, the Railway Union flourished overnight and soon died. In 1896 the Brewery Workers began its long, arduous struggle to unite skilled and unskilled wage-earners. Western miners established the American Labor Union in 1897 and started a class war that shook the entire labor movement. By the turn of the century the army of organized American workers was on the march.

ISSUES

The period from 1870 to 1898 was one of the most turbulent in American history. Conflicts between industry and labor created a storm of debate and violence, shaking the nation to its foundation. Labor's quest for higher wages, shorter hours, improved living and working conditions and union recognition brought a new alignment of forces. It was no longer southerner against northerner but worker against industrialist. When the latter took full advantage of the prevailing *laissez-faire* doctrine to exploit the wage-earner, workers had no recourse except to fight and agitate.

Low income produced greatest unrest among the working class. Employer abuse and harsh working conditions could be endured; not starvation wages. Pauperism was so rampant at times that sizeable segments of the urban population were engulfed.[32] During the depression of the seventies, for example, many factory workers labored twelve to fifteen hours a day for food and lodging; others walked the streets, unemployed and destitute. In the eighties the average per capita earnings of workers declined while the wealth of industrialists appreciably increased. Skilled workers during this decade earned less than two dollars for ten hours' work while unskilled workers received as little as fifty cents a day. These meager wages were even more revealing when one considered that many workers were idle at least a fourth of the time. To avoid starvation entire families, including young children, left their homes to slave at the work bench.[33]

Ruthless employers kept wages low in devious and sometimes fraudulent ways. Labor-saving machinery made it possible for industry to hire thousands of immigrants, even women and children, at whatever wages employers desired. Many families earned as little as $150 a year.[34] Wages were further reduced in some industries by means of excessive fines for minor offenses such as tardiness, humming, singing or talking, loitering in restrooms, and "misconduct"—a catch-all term for anything that displeased management. Where company homes and stores existed, workers paid exorbitant rent and purchased essential commodities at highly inflated prices. Company stores accrued huge annual profits, and workers who rebelled against living in company homes and trading at factory stores were arbitrarily dismissed.[35] Caught in a web from which there seemed no escape, laborers and their families endured severe hardships.

Despite his desperate economic condition, the American laborer resisted deliberate suppression of wages with protests, boycotts, strikes, pickets, demonstrations. His battle cry became "more wages now." Defeated in one skirmish after another, the worker fought with every resource at his command, convinced that employers would never voluntarily improve the wage scale.[36]

Worker agitation for an eight-hour day also produced endless friction between management and labor. The genesis of the struggle for shorter hours can be traced to the pre-Civil War period. The first significant step taken by labor to secure a shorter work schedule, however, occurred in the 1860s when a Boston machinist named Ira Steward persuaded the Machinists and Blacksmiths Union to include an eight-hour plank in the convention's platform.[37] Later, in 1878, the International Labor Union declared in its policy statement: "The first step toward the emancipation of labor is a reduction of the hours of labor. . . ."[38] Almost every new union thereafter adopted a similar plank until the eight-hour movement spread over the United States. In the immediate post-Civil War era laborers, fearful of job opportunity, relied heavily on legislative action for a shorter work-day. Wendell Phillips, in an address delivered at Boston in 1865, urged workers to inform all political candidates: "We mean that the eight hours shall be a day's work, and no man shall go into office who opposes it."[39] But, despite the clamor for shorter hours throughout the ranks of labor, some wage-earners in the eighties were working twelve to fifteen hours a day, seven days a week.

When arbitration and legislative proposals failed to gain shorter work hours, labor resorted to strikes and boycotts. The struggle intensified through the years until May 1, 1886, was set by national unions as the target date for a nation-wide walkout. Although the Haymarket Riot in Chicago brought an abrupt end to the strike, the May Day action revealed the general disillusionment of workers, and subsequent events proved that the loss of particular skirmishes never deterred the American worker in his struggle for shorter work hours.[40]

More tolerable than low income and long hours, yet equally debilitating to the laborer, were the wretched living and working conditions he and his family endured. Numerous families lived in squalor, herded together in overcrowded and unsanitary slums. Laborers toiled long and dreary hours, often from sunrise to sunset, in unhealthful sweatshops, foundries, factories, and mines.[41] Tenement houses in urban centers were used as homes and workshops, where adults, teen-agers, and children (many as young as five years of age) slaved in poorly ventilated, unsafe firetraps, barely subsisting on meager wages. Rent was high, income low, hours long, and conditions deplorable. Of his own experience in a sweatshop, Samuel Gompers declared: "I have never quite forgiven society."[42] Workers in foundries and mines fared no better and perhaps even worse than tenement employees. Many were crippled and injured; some contracted serious physical disorders.

Attempts to remedy these conditions through legislation generally failed. A congressional committee reported that many well-drafted and equitable bills were "killed in committee, emasculated, or killed on the floor of the legislature, or passed with exceptions which rendered them entirely ineffective."[43] Of the legislative measures enacted most were ineffective, having been designed to protect the industrialist and appease the worker. Labor's clamorous demands for improved working conditions continued unabated, although largely ignored. Underpaid and overworked, labor turned to unionization only to find itself bitterly opposed by the press, the church, the courts, and the general public. In his autobiography Terence V. Powderly cynically and realistically observed:

The daily press with few exceptions was against us. Public officials and politicians generally were with us to the door of the voting booth. . . . We had no influential friends, professional and businessmen were not in sympathy with us; the church was almost solidly arrayed on the side of wealth and power.[44]

The daily press was indeed anti-union! A few journalists reported labor activities impartially, but the majority cooperated with employers in opposing labor's basic aims. In an effort to rally public support some unions maintained a labor press. Gompers boasted that in 1896 labor organizations were publishing more than two hundred papers.[45] These weekly journals, largely read by union sympathizers, had little chance, however, to counterbalance the tremendous influence of large metropolitan dailies with much larger circulations.

Newspapers of New York City clearly demonstrate the strong anti-union feeling organized labor had to combat. At the time of the railroad strike of

1877 the *New York Tribune* bluntly declared that "authority ought not to rest until it has swept down every resisting mob with grapeshot . . . though it cost a thousand bloody corpses."[46] Nine years later the *Tribune* described trade unions as organized "despotism" and placed the burden of prolonged industrial depressions upon workingmen.[47] The *New York Evening Post* echoed the anti-union sentiments of the *Tribune*, heartily endorsed the arrest of boycotters, and condemned the strike as a tool of anarchists.[48] The *Sun* and the *Times* vilified unionists in general and the Knights in particular.[49] Not all metropolitan newspapers were as hostile as the New York journals; but most of them were blatantly anti-union. Unquestionably the press molded strong public feeling against organized labor, although it failed to deter unions from pursuing their objectives or their leaders from voicing labor's views.

Powderly's contention that politicians generally were against labor was also true. Legislative support was vocal rather than substantive.[50] Most reform proposals were introduced solely to provide prestige for ambitious legislators seeking the laborer's vote. Where labor successfully obtained favorable legislation, courts, more solicitous of the wealthy than were legislators, nullified gains on the pretext of "unwarranted interferences with freedom of contract."

Powderly's assertion that "businessmen were not in sympathy with us" was no exaggeration. Management's view was best voiced by industrialist Frederick Townsend Martin:

We are the rich; we own America; we got it, God knows how, but we intend to keep it if we can by throwing all the tremendous weight of our support, our influence, our money, our political connections, our purchased senators, our hungry congressmen, our public-speaking demagogues into the scale against any legislature, any political platform, and presidential campaign that threatens our estate.[51]

Motivated by economic self-interest, industry used every weapon in its powerful arsenal to thwart unionization. Blacklisting, lockouts, yellow-dog contracts, bribery, refusal to arbitrate, strikebreakers, spy and "stool pigeon" systems were commonplace.[52] These techniques led Samuel Gompers to declare: "We fought for each gain and with bare hands unaided carried off victories against the protest of a hostile world."[53]

Powderly's statement "the church was almost solidly arrayed on the side of wealth and power" was far from true though Samuel Gompers and many other labor leaders held the same view.[54] Some church leaders denounced unions, others gave tacit approval though few endorsed strikes, boycotts, closed shops and other basic objectives of labor.[55]

ORATORS: POWDERLY AND GOMPERS

Argument and persuasion, always vital in the labor movement, were important to labor leaders in the latter half of the nineteenth century as major weapons in a war of conflicting opinions and causes. The premier labor speakers during the period 1870 to 1898 were Terence V. Powderly and Samuel Gompers, who were dissimilar in appearance, temperament, style, and philosophy. Each delivered hundreds of speeches during his lifetime.

Terence Vincent Powderly, labor's chief spokesman in the 1880s, became a switch tender at thirteen and an apprentice machinist at seventeen. Initiated into the Order of the Knights of Labor in 1876, Powderly served as Grand Master Workman from 1879 to 1893. Chiefly remembered as a pioneer labor leader, Powderly was closely identified with numerous reform movements, including temperance and women's rights. He served three consecutive terms as Mayor of Scranton, Pennsylvania, took an active role in the Greenback-Labor movement, and supported various Democrats or Republicans who he felt were favorable to labor's cause.

A complex, fascinating idealist who lacked the administrative skill to head a large labor organization, Powderly was an indefatigable worker, a prolific writer, a spellbinding orator. The number of speeches delivered, the size of the audiences, the esteem in which he was held as a public speaker by critics and supporters alike attest to Powderly's oratorical skill.

An unlettered man with almost no training in rhetoric, Powderly learned to speak by speaking. From a literary standpoint his speeches do not appear in a favorable light. Powderly regarded speech as largely functional in purpose, not aesthetic. From the standpoint of communication, however, Powderly's speeches were effective. They were obviously prepared and delivered for particular audiences. In keeping with his personality and intellectual limitations Powderly's speech style was simple, direct, and often blunt. He employed language his auditors understood, utilized an emotional appeal they could not resist, and presented arguments they appreciated. For example, addressing himself to the issue of convict labor in 1873, Powderly rhetorically queried working class auditors: "Why should the trades be thus handicapped by prison competition?" He answered:

There are cunning, shrewd, sharp, longheaded, fellows in the state prisons—why not make lawyers of them? . . . There are cut-throats of the sleekest class behind bars—why not make doctors of them and give them a chance of taking life in a legitimate way? . . . There are many bank note experts, many men who have displayed extraordinary financial sharpness in able-bodied swindles—why not make use of their intelligence and send them to join the elegant race of sharks, the bankers?[56]

What Powderly lacked in polish, scholarship, and logic was offset by flamboyant delivery and extraordinary rapport with audiences. Small of stature, partly bald, plagued with poor hearing and even poorer eyesight, Powderly looked more like a poet than a brawny worker. Yet, despite his frail physical appearance, he spoke forcefully. A Canadian reporter said of his platform manner:

He speaks slowly—except when his feelings get intensely interested—but with a loud distinct intonation, gesticulates a great deal and paces backward and forward on the platform when roused in discussing labor's wrongs, like a caged tiger. . . ."[57]

One Chicago journalist said of him:

He kept his audience stirred up from start to finish, and his apt illustrations and dramatic sayings were greatly appreciated, judging from the laughter and applause which frequently interspersed the remarks.[58]

In one sense this report of audience reaction is typical in that the central purpose underlying every Powderly speech was agitation. "I was an agitator and as such did all that lay in my power with voice and pen to agitate against the injustices practiced on workingmen and women," wrote Powderly.[59] In another sense, however, favorable audience reaction to his speech is puzzling when one remembers that most workers disagreed with many of his economic proposals, which seemed radical to them. Apparently wage-earners overlooked Powderly's extreme ideas because he reflected genuine concern for the welfare of America's exploited masses and identified with the suffering of workers and their families. They knew he had experienced the smoke, dirt, grease, sweat, and noise of factory life and was a workingman in purpose and outlook. Whatever the reason, auditors listened when Powderly spoke and were excited by his golden words—a fact clearly evidenced by the huge and enthusiastic audiences that attended the labor, political, and temperance rallies he addressed. During the presidential campaign of 1896 alone it was estimated Powderly addressed more than two hundred thousand persons.[60] One year he received more than four hundred invitations to speak at Labor Day ceremonies.

The range of Powderly's themes was diverse. In a typical labor speech of two hours he would discuss a dozen or more major social and economic issues. Frequent references, of course, were made to organization, education, and co-operation (concepts considered the "first principles" of the platform of the Knights), labor solidarity, more respect for unionism, establishment of the eight-hour day, abolition of child and convict labor, regulation of imported workers, equal pay for equal work, better working conditions, government ownership of railroad, telegraph, and telephone lines, arbitration instead of strikes. Rank-and-file members, concerned with immediate gains rather than future reforms, accepted some of Powderly's proposals and rejected others (particularly his opposition to strikes and abolition of the wage system). Powderly labeled strike agitators "fire-brands" and argued, "You cannot fight cold lead and steel with your finger-ends, and that is just what you must expect to meet when you strike."[61] When peaceful negotiations failed, he reluctantly endorsed boycotts but not strikes, although he was forced on occasion to take over leadership of strikes initiated by Knights against his will.

Undaunted by the inherent conflict between his reformist economic philosophy and that of most wage-earners, Powderly hammered away at replacing the capitalistic system with workers' co-operatives, deploring what he called "the pernicious wage system" and insisting that workers share in management and profits. Strongly influenced by earlier land reformers, he declared: "I do not believe in private property in land and never will. I believe God made the earth for all his children and that only the fruits of the earth belong to men."[62]

A teetotaler, Powderly considered intemperance a "curse," which caused poverty, destroyed self-respect and created a poor image of the worker.[63] "The temperance question is an important one, and I sometimes think it is the main issue," Powderly told delegates to the 1882 General Assembly.[64] "Workingmen, shun strong drink as you would a scorpion. It debases, it weakens, it ruins you. There is not a crime in the calendar that cannot be charged against it."[65]

Of Irish decent yet thoroughly American, Powderly was a strong Jeffersonian, who believed in freedom and equality for all:

The revolution that I would bring about is one based on equality [sic] for all the people of our country; one that will restore natural opportunities to the children of men, one that will make our flag the emblem of all the people and have it stand for industrial worth, not wealth.[66]

He said in the South:

If this land was worthy that brave men should die for it, it is at least worthy that unselfish, thoughtful men should live and work in a grand devotion to the ideas of a real, a true democracy.[67]

In retrospect it appears that reformers like William Sylvis, Uriah Stephens, and Terence Powderly were perhaps more accurate in appraising the basic causes of nineteenth-century economic and social injustice than were trade-unionists. Undisciplined and uncontrolled industry virtually enslaved workers, Powderly and others repeatedly argued. Powderly's greatest mistake, however, was in underestimating the ruthlessness of capitalists and overestimating the vision of workers.

Samuel Gompers, like Terence Vincent Powderly and other successful industrial and union leaders, had a shrewd mind, an aggressive and sometimes ruthless drive, and an insatiable desire for power.[68] After a twelve-hour workday in a sweatshop Gompers as a young man regularly attended night-school classes, debates, lectures, and union meetings. As a union executive he uncomplainingly carried out heavy administrative responsibilities and then spent much of his spare time writing and speaking. In public debate, at which he became a master, Gompers shrewdly outwitted many adversaries, sometimes with logic, sometimes with invective, sometimes with a sheer storm of words. Compelled to scrap for more money, penny by penny, and more leisure, minute by minute, Gompers fought tenaciously.[69] Inordinately ambitious, Gompers served without pay when the Federation's treasury was empty and fought for re-election as president of the American Federation of Labor when the effort hastened his death.

Unquestionably Gompers' drive and ambition grew out of a disadvantaged childhood. Born in the slums of London, where his father worked as a cigarmaker, Samuel dropped out of school at age ten to help support the family. Young Samuel matured quickly. At ten he was a wage-earner; at fourteen, a union activist; at seventeen, a married man; and at nineteen, a father.

The image Gompers reflects varies considerably. Friends considered him a saintly humanitarian; foes regarded him a crass hypocrite. On one score, however, there is universal agreement: Gompers was a persuasive speaker. Like Powderly of the Knights, Gompers also learned to speak effectively by speaking. Endowed with a pleasing voice, yet lacking commanding size (5 feet 3 inches tall) Gompers worked to overcome oratorical weaknesses until he spoke with considerable force and fluency. Squat and stocky, with a head too large for his torso and arms too long for his short legs, Gompers is often described as gnomelike. According to one observer Gompers' most striking physical feature was a histrionic face that spontaneously communicated the emotions he felt.[70]

On occasion Gompers employed picturesque language and dealt with specific ideas.[71] Usually, however, he generalized about labor problems, policies, and objectives in an effective yet unimaginative style. A typical speech went something like this:

For what does organized labor contend if not to improve the standard of life, to uproot ignorance and foster education, to instill character and manhood and an independent spirit among our people, to bring about a recognition of the interdependence in modern life of man and his fellow man? We aim to establish a normal workday, to take the children from the factory and the workshop and to give them the opportunity of the school, the home, and the playground. In a word, the unions of labor, recognizing the duty to toil, strive to educate their members, to make their homes and lives more cheerful in every way, to contribute an earnest effort toward making life the better worth living, to avail their members of their rights as citizens and to bear the duties and responsibilities and perform the obligations they owe to our country and to our fellow men.[72]

When provoked Gompers could be direct and blunt. In an address to the Federation he referred to a critic as "a rag-tail, bob-tailed politician who is eating pap out of the millionaire bag of William Randolph Hearst."[73] Speaking to an audience of businessmen, the diminutive fire-eater shook his fists and said:

I would like to know what you gentlemen have in mind by model mediation and arbitration laws that will limit the rights to which workmen are entitled by God, by nature, and by the laws of the country. . . . You may compress steam, but as sure as nature's law, you will ultimately have an explosion.[74]

At the Federation's 1908 annual convention he listened to the protests of radical critics and then ended a widely publicized speech with this statement: "I want to tell you Socialists . . . economically, you are unsound; socially, you are wrong; industrially, you are an impossibility."[75] Gomper's strength in oral communication lay not so much in style or delivery as in personal magnetism and the ability to catch and express the prevailing spirit of the American workers.[76] Wary of other labor leaders, trade unionists had implicit faith in him. Gompers knew this and took great care to reinforce auditors in the basic interests, goals, and beliefs of workers. Louis Reed, in his study of the labor leader's philosophy says: "He hesitated ever to separate himself from his followers."[77] Gompers himself unapologetically declared: "I represent my side, the side of the toiling wage-earning masses in every act and every utterance."[78] Convinced that workers were embroiled in a titanic and unavoidable struggle with employers, he presented labor's viewpoints cogently, persuasively, and vigorously.

Although some biographers depict him as "a well-read man," conversant in literature, politics, economics, and philosophy, Gompers considered himself an intuitive rather than an objective thinker. Blessed with an extraordinarily retentive mind and averse to speech outlines and manuscripts except on rare occasions, Gompers relied almost completely on personal experience for speech material. His thoughts generally centered around current social and economic problems; his sources were general reading, conversation, letters. This reliance on personal knowledge served to advantage in debates as well as speeches. At Milwaukee in 1902, for instance, he single-handedly engaged a hostile audience of three thousand boycotting brewery workers who had stubbornly refused to obey a return-to-work order issued by the grievance committee of the Federation, patiently listened to their arguments, and offered a rebuttal so persuasive that the protestors unanimously voted to end the boycott.[79]

Although he delivered thousands of speeches at home and abroad, Gompers spent much of his time in personal debates with jurists, industrialists, and Socialists. Despite his disadvantage in discussing judicial matters (most jurists were anti-union), Gompers held his own in forensic encounters. Perhaps his most eloquent public statement was made in a courtroom on December 23, 1908. A vindictive judge, angered by Gompers' refusal to obey a court order he had issued, sentenced him to a twelve-month prison term subsequently reversed by the United States Supreme Court. Asked if he had a statement to make before sentence was passed, the unionist replied:

. . . I do not believe there is a man alive who would chafe more under restraint of his liberty than I would, but if I cannot discuss grave problems, great questions in which the people of this country are interested, . . . if the speeches in furtherance of a great principle, of a great right are to be held against me, I shall not only have to but I shall be willing to bear the consequences.[80]

His bitter experiences with sweeping injunctions and decisions adverse to labor led him to declare: "God save labor from the Courts." As one injunction after another crippled labor's activities, Gompers protested with all the eloquence he could marshal. Convinced that neither courts nor government agencies had sympathy for or an understanding of labor, he resisted reform proposals, including some specifically designed to benefit the worker.

Discomfited by formal courtroom procedures, Gompers was mild, conciliatory, and restrained in debating judicial issues. But this was not so in his battles with employers. He never forgot the exploitation, suffering, humiliation and anguish he had endured as a wage-earner.

During World War I Gompers rose above labor partisanship and joined forces with employers in support of the Allied cause because his dislike for "German autocracy" and his love for American democracy exceeded his animosity for industrialists. This truce with employers was temporary, however, for Gompers deeply resented furtive anti-union tactics of management and he never hesitated to voice his feelings. When industry, supported by the press, the police, and the courts, united in a massive attack upon organized labor shortly before and after 1900, Gompers tenaciously fought back. His caustic barbs cut through the spurious arguments of employers. Managment's tempting offers of "profit-sharing" he described as the paternalistic philosophy of greedy industrialists who want wage-earners "to perform like cows that resignedly chew their cuds and submissively give sweet milk."[81] Welfare proposals in industry were not genuine altruism on the part of benevolent industrialists, he insisted, but the crafty schemes of truculent employers bent on total destruction of trade unions.

The trade-union movement was in fact his religion, his philosophy, and his life. Gompers' persistence and determination in the face of almost insurmountable odds inspired and aroused workers. He debated, hassled, pleaded, and stormed until he gained the loyalty and support of other powerful trade-union leaders. When rhetoric failed, he unhesitatingly ordered boycotts and strikes, although the constitution of the Federation granted him no such authority. He said:

While some may assert that the strike is a relic of barbarism, I answer that the strike is the most highly civilized method which the workers, the wealth producers, have yet devised. . . . A strike will make employers heed and learn when nothing else will avail.[82]

His words were prophetic, for eventually unbending employers broke. And Gompers was the man who stoked the fires of "protest and reform" which ultimately achieved this phenomenal victory.

As the economic, political, and social climate of America changed through the years, Gompers modified his stance on some issues, although he was blind to many fundamental changes. His forceful leadership and leonine courage during the watershed of industrial struggle (1890–1930) earned him the right to be called the Father of the Modern Labor Movement.

NOTES

1. Thomas R. Brooks, *Toil and Trouble* (New York: Delacorte Press, 1971), p. 39.
2. Howard L. Harwitz, *Theodore Roosevelt in New York State, 1880–1900* (New York: Columbia University Press, 1943), pp. 64–74.
3. Brooks, *Toil and Trouble*, pp. 50–51.
4. Foster Rhea Dulles, *The United States Since 1865* (Ann Arbor: The University of Michigan Press, 1959), pp. 76–77.

5. Brooks, *Toil and Trouble*, p. 38.

6. National unions assumed the more imposing title of "International" when Canadian locals joined.

7. George Edwin McNeill, *The Labor Movement, The Problem of Today* (New York: M. W. Hazen Company, 1888), p. 154.

8. Philip Taft, *Organized Labor in American History* (New York: Harper and Row, 1964), p. 84.

9. J. A. Estey, *The Labor Problem* (New York: McGraw Hill, 1928), p. 29.

10. Norman J. Ware, *The Labor Movement of the United States 1860–1895* (New York: Vintage Books, 1964), p. 29.

11. Gerald N. Grob, *Workers and Utopia* (Evanston: Northwestern University Press, 1961), p. 35.

12. Robert R. Brooks, *When Labor Organizes* (New Haven: Yale University Press, 1938), p. 46; Terence Vincent Powderly, *Thirty Years of Labor* (Columbus: Excelsior Publishing House, 1889), pp. 167, 534–535; Ware, *Labor Movement*, p. 164.

13. Robert G. Albion et al. *The Growth of the American Economy*, ed. Harold F. Williamson (New York: Prentice-Hall, 1944), p. 617.

14. Grob, *Workers*, p. 65.

15. Ware, *Labor Movement*, p. 68.

16. Grob, *Workers*, pp. 37–38.

17. Philip S. Foner, *History of the Labor Movement in the United States* (New York: International Publishers, 1955), 2:168.

18. Joseph G. Rayback, *A History of American Labor* (New York: Macmillan Co., 1966), pp. 187–194.

19. Brooks, *Toil and Trouble*, p. 73.

20. John R. Commons, *History of the Labour Movement in the United States* (New York: Macmillan Co., 1918), 2:411–413.

21. Rayback, *American Labor*, p. 194.

22. Anthony Bimba, *The History of the American Working Class* (New York: Greenwood Press, 1968), p. 192.

23. Taft, *Organized Labor*, pp. 121–122.

24. Samuel Gompers, *Seventy Years of Life and Labour* (New York: Augustus M. Kelley, Publishers, 1968), 1:333.

25. Ware, *Labor Movement*, p. xii.

26. Taft, *Organized Labor*, p. 117.

27. Harold U. Faulkner and Mark Starr, *Labor in America* (New York: Harper and Brothers, 1949), pp. 111–112.

28. Harry A. Millis and Royal E. Montgomery, *Organized Labor* (New York: McGraw-Hill Book Company, 1945), pp. 77–78.

29. Faulkner, *Labor in America*, p. 115.

30. Louis S. Reed, *The Labor Philosophy of Samuel Gompers* (New York: Columbia University Press, 1930), p. 12.

31. Patricia Daniels, *Famous Labor Leaders* (New York: Dodd, Mead and Company, 1970), p. 36.

32. Thomas Sewall Adams and Helen H. Sumner, *Labor Problems*, 18th ed. (New York: Macmillan Co., 1911), p. 150.
33. Henry David, *The History of the Haymarket Affair* (New York: Russell and Russell, 1936), pp. 19–20.
34. Ibid., p. 14.
35. Foner, *Labor Movement*, 2:21.
36. Ibid., 1:440, 445, 464–474.
37. David, *Haymarket Affair*, pp. 159, 170; Foner, *Labor Movement*, 1:345, 364.
38. Bimba, *Working Class*, p. 171.
39. Wendell Phillips, *Speeches, Lectures, and Letters*, 2nd Series (Boston: Lee and Shepard, 1891), p. 142.
40. *Proceedings*, A. F. of L. (1889):42.
41. Foner, *Labor Movement*, 1:67, 443; Bernard Mandel, *Samuel Gompers* (Yellow Springs, Ohio: The Antioch Press, 1963), p. 31; Gompers, *Seventy Years*, 1:123–4.
42. Bernard M. Baruch, "My Reminiscences of Samuel Gompers," *The New Leader*, October 30, 1950, p. 18.
43. Foner, *Labor Movement*, 2:24.
44. Terence Vincent Powderly, *The Path I Trod*, ed. Harry J. Carmen, et al. (New York: Columbia University Press, 1940), p. 133.
45. Harwitz, *Theodore Roosevelt*, p. 33.
46. *The New York Tribune*, July 31, 1877. All newspapers are cited from the *Powderly Papers* housed in the Department of Archives and Manuscripts of the Mullin Library of the Catholic University of America in Washington, D.C. The *Powderly Papers* are not indexed. Correspondence and newspaper material are calendared. The remainder of the material, including diaries, documents, manuscripts, notebooks, leaflets, and pamphlets are kept in boxes. The date and place of speeches mentioned in footnotes 63 and 67 were determined by cross referencing and internal evidence.
47. *The New York Tribune*, April 12, 1886, *Powderly Papers*.
48. *The New York Evening Post*, May 13, 1886, p. 392, *Powderly Papers*.
49. Powderly, *Thirty Years*, p. 494; *New York Times*, April 25, 1886, *Powderly Papers*.
50. Don D. Lescakier and Elizabeth Brandies, *History of Labor in the United States, 1896–1932* (New York: Macmillan Co., 1935), pp. 3, 339.
51. Gus Tyler, *The Labor Revolution* (New York: The Viking Press, 1966), p. 22.
52. McNeill, *Labor Movement*, p. 383.
53. Gompers, *Seventy Years*, 1:115–116.
54. Mandel, *Gompers*, pp. 10–11.
55. Grob, *Workers*, pp. 165–166; Ware, *Labor Movement*, pp. 97–102; Taft, *Organized Labor*, p. 88.
56. *Buffalo Courier*, January 18, 1883, *Powderly Papers*.
57. *Toronto News* (Canada), October 14, 1884, *Powderly Papers*.
58. *Chicago Daily Inter Ocean*, October 7, 1889, *Powderly Papers*.
59. Powderly, *The Path*, pp. 38–39.
60. *Scranton Truth*, March 3, 1890, *Powderly Papers*.

61. Daniels, *Famous Leaders*, p. 16.
62. Charles A. Madison, *American Labor Leaders* (New York: Harper and Brothers, 1950), p. 51.
63. *Speech*, Brantford, Ontario, Canada, October 16, 1884, *Powderly Papers*.
64. *Proceedings*, K. of L. (1882):284.
65. Roy Cook, *Leaders of Labor* (Philadelphia: J. B. Lipincott Company, 1966), pp. 29, 30.
66. Madison, *American Leaders*, p. 52.
67. *Speech*, Richmond, Virginia, October 5, 1886, *Powderly Papers*.
68. Eli Ginzberg, *The Labor Leader* (New York: Macmillan Co., 1948), pp. 7–9.
69. Gerald Emmanuel Stearn, ed. *Gompers* (Englewood Cliffs, New Jersey: Prentice-Hall, 1971), pp. 164–165.
70. Benjamin Stolberg, "What Manner of Man Was Gompers?" *Atlantic Monthly* 143 (March 1929): 404–412.
71. In a trade union conference at New York City on 20 August 1893, Gompers delivered an address in which he advanced twenty-two concrete proposals for relief of unemployed workers.
72. *Proceedings*, A. F. of L. (1910):32–33.
73. *Proceedings*, A. F. of L. (1921):401.
74. *New York Times*, January 30, 1913, p. 5.
75. *Proceedings*, A. F. of L. (1903):198.
76. Walter B. Emery, "Samuel Gompers," in *A History and Criticism of American Public Address*, ed. William N. Brigance (New York: McGraw-Hill Book Company, 1943), 2:565–566.
77. Reed, *Philosophy of Gompers*, p. 182.
78. Brooks, *Toil and Trouble*, p. 82.
79. Ralph M. Easley, "What Organized Labor Has Learned," *McClures Magazine* 19 (October 1902):491.
80. Madison, *American Leaders*, p. 94.
81. Mandel, *Gompers*, pp. 220–222.
82. Cook, *Leaders*, p. 41.

4

Labor's Political Allies

DONALD K. SPRINGEN

Men of imagination and diversity of interest periodically ally themselves to fight for what they believe to be a great cause. Such men were Benjamin Butler and Wendell Phillips of Massachusetts, Peter Cooper of New York, and John Altgeld of Illinois. This chapter tells their story—how they fought for political protection for labor through their writing and their speaking.

THE MEN FROM MASSACHUSETTS

Both Benjamin Butler and Wendell Phillips were well-known and effective public speakers in 1870 at the beginning of "the era of protest and reform." They were nearly the same age; both had been trained as lawyers; and both seemed intent on championing labor reform—Butler from the time he was admitted to the bar in 1840 until his death in 1893, and Phillips from the time of the Emancipation Proclamation in 1863 until his death in 1884. They remained lifetime friends.[1]

While the two men were similar in many ways, their dissimilarities were in some instances profound, especially in physical appearance, character, personality, and behavior on the platform. Butler was of medium height and paunchy. He had a large mustache, a bald crown, and a wall eye. He tended to waddle when he walked out to the speaker's stand. On his frequent electioneering trips he was the life of the party. He made four and five, sometimes six and seven speeches daily, of greater or lesser length. When the day was ended, he would become a boy with his jests, his stories, and his side-shaking laughter.[2]

Phillips, tall, lithe, graceful, must have presented an unusual contrast when he joined Butler, as he often did, on the platform. Phillips, unlike Butler, who had to please the electorate to stay in office,[3] was proud, defensive, half-disdainful, and wholly uncompromising on the platform. Phillips was most brilliant as a speaker when most bitter,[4] Butler most effective when playing the part of a low comedian.

Their personality differences and behavior on the platform were probably due to vastly different home situations. Butler, although of "good stock,"[5] was not, like Phillips, a patrician. Phillips felt a responsibility for exemplifying the respectability of his birth and breeding.[6] His speeches were never tainted with vulgarity, envy, or bad manners, as were Butler's. Butler, we must realize, grew up in a boarding house operated by his mother for young girls who worked in textile factories in Lowell, Massachusetts.

Such an environment helped Butler to see factory life from the viewpoint of the worker. He knew their problems and appealed directly and, to the horror of Massachusetts society, ratherly coarsely to their sense of humor. Fairly typical of the personality and style of Butler was what he said to an audience at the City Hall in Lawrence, Massachusetts, to open one of his many political campaigns: "I want to go to Congress again. I have no hesitation in saying so. I am no maiden; I am more like a widow. I know what I want [Laughter and applause]. I am not afraid to ask for it [To the reporters: Put that down]."[7] Phillips never would have talked that way.

It is easy to see why the polite Massachusetts upper classes abhorred Butler. His wit was coarse and blunt. His constituents, however, were mainly fishermen, Irishmen, small farmers, laborers. They enjoyed listening to Butler. As an eminent political historian reminds us, the masses normally choose help and humanity over morality and honesty.[8]

Butler was a man of considerable wealth, especially after the Civil War, and he lived lavishly both in Washington and in Massachusetts. Nevertheless, wage-earners supported him because he continued to work for labor reform throughout his life. He reached the people. Former Congressman Greenhalge put it this way:

There are some public men who never seem to reach the heart of the people. Their services are great, their purpose is high, their lives are pure and stately.

Then there is another type of public man. You can count the number of these on your fingers, in any age, in any nation. . . . There is electric communication between this type and the soul of the people. The difference between these two types cannot logically be explained.[9]

Profound as their dissimilarities may have been in family background, physical appearance, character, personality, and behavior on the platform, Butler and Phillips both agreed in 1870 that the workingman of Massachusetts—the mill worker, the tailor, the shoemaker, the cigar maker, the bricklayer, the plasterer, the painter—was not getting a fair deal from management. Both men also agreed that the way to solve labor-management inequalities of low pay, long hours, and job insecurity was not by striking but by voting for the politician and the party that protected labor instead of money interests.

Both Butler and Phillips were highly skilled speakers who supported their radical ideas with vigor and nerve. They were feared, even hated, by established financiers and industrialists of Massachusetts. Mill owners remembered Butler's success before the Civil War in reducing the working hours of mill workers from fourteen to eleven and a quarter. Owners of industry also remembered Phillips's close affiliation with Ira Steward, a prominent labor leader of the time, sometimes called "the eight-hour monomaniac."[10] Phillips, who had lost friends because of his liberal thinking before 1870, was soon to lose even the friendships of Garrison and Emerson because of his close association with Butler and labor reform. Both men liked a good political fight, however. Phillips was probably amused at the shock and fright he caused in Massachusetts business circles when he announced that Benjamin Butler would run for Governor of Massachusetts on a mixed Republican and Labor Platform and that he, Phillips, was going to help Butler by giving speeches in his behalf. The speeches Wendell Phillips gave in 1871 and 1872 were his most significant addresses as an ally of labor.[11]

Butler's speeches in this campaign were also important ones. They were forerunners of his speeches in the 1884 campaign when, as a candidate for President of the United States, he would make labor reform a national issue. His opening address for the gubernatorial campaign at Springfield, Massachusetts, August 24, 1871, covered most of his ideas on labor at that time.[12] When he began his campaign for governor, Benjamin Butler was a member of the United States House of Representatives. Even then his thinking on labor had a national ring and a foresight that went beyond the state of Massachusetts. His major contention in this 1871 speech was that labor's hours, working conditions, and earnings were grounds for state and national legislation: "Is it not clearly the duty of the State to protect those incapable of protecting themselves?"[13] In discussing the need for labor legislation, Butler made it clear that he was opposed to the Republican Party's policy of subsidies and protection for business and a hands-off attitude toward working class problems. If Republicans had helped emancipate the unpaid slave, he reasoned, why should they now seem reluctant to protect the ill-paid and overworked? Thus Butler appealed to the historical sense of pride of the Republican members of his audience. The problem with this line of reasoning was the fact that few of the Republican delegates who would nominate Butler for governor came to hear him speak; fewer still would be able to read the speech because of the hostility of the press toward Butler. Then, too, the whole idea of a minimum-hour-and-wage law, which Butler was, in fact, proposing in 1871, angered the Brahmins of Massachusetts.

Butler also discussed the need for labor legislation by picturing the plight of women and young children who often suffered physical deformities because of interminable hours spent tending machines. He reminded his audience that the Massachusetts senate had refused to enact even a modest minimum-hour bill for such workers in the last legislative session. He returned to his major contention and concluded that it was the duty of the state to protect children against the avarice of either their employer or their own father. Butler argued thus for state minimum-hour laws, at least for women and children who tended machinery. It was a powerful, logical argument with strong emotional overtones. He was offering workmen action in the state legislature if they helped him win the Republican nomination. Strikes, he told them, were a poor substitute for legislative action. He gave three reasons why: "Strikes are illogical; they are indefensible; they are beneath the dignity of the American workman."[14] Strikes are illogical, Butler asserted, because workers cannot hold out financially long enough to win them. Strikes are indefensible and beneath the dignity of workmen who already have the ballot.

Turning to wages, Butler told his Springfield hearers that they were entitled to more money because increased production through machinery had raised profits. In some instances, such as the newspaper business, profits were up a thousandfold, yet the working printer received scarcely more than before the installation of time-saving machinery. Butler continued by saying that if management found it difficult to raise workers' wages, it could at least let them share in the increased profits by lowering their hours. There was no need for antagonism between capital and labor, he insisted; but if it should develop, the state of Massachusetts should set up an impartial board of arbitration to settle the differences between capital and labor. Twenty-five years later Peter Altgeld recommended a board of arbitration for state and national labor crises, and received praise as a prophet forty years ahead of his time; Benjamin Butler should be recognized as a political figure who advocated a new role for the government in 1871.

Butler's speeches contained labor-reform measures that were mild compared to those of Phillips. Both agreed on the fact that labor was not getting a fair deal from management in an increasingly complex economy. Both also agreed that the way to solve the problem was not the strike but the ballot. Butler, however, recommended government legislation that would protect labor under the capitalist system; Phillips proposed a change in the whole economic structure from capitalism to the socialism of Pierre Joseph Proudhon.[15]

Phillip's first address of significance in the Butler campaign was his speech to the 425 delegates to the third Labor Reform Party convention in South Framingham, Massachusetts, on September 4, 1871. As permanent chairman of the convention he had drawn up the platform and now called for its adoption.[16] The platform advocated a broad program with emphasis on money reform: ". . . labor, the creator of wealth is entitled to all it creates . . . [and] we avow ourselves willing to overthrow the whole profit-making system."[17]

Phillips was astute enough to know that these ideas were too radical to be achieved, as he put it, "in a single leap." So he demanded that at least four steps be taken immediately: (1) a ten-hour day for factory work as a first step and eight hours thereafter, (2) equal pay for equal work for women if employed at public expense, (3) all public debts to be paid at once and no more created, and (4) no more laborers to be imported from China.[18]

In a short speech that accompanied the platform, Phillips praised the labor movement and appealed to the delegates to stay together: ". . . keep the labor-party religiously together."[19] This was an appeal he was to use repeatedly in labor speeches because he believed that he could help labor most by organizing their ranks and revealing their real problems to the public.[20]

Phillips's speech to labor and temperance groups at Salisbury Beach on September 13, 1871, was a strong endorsement of Butler as well as an expression of Phillips's views on labor. It came just before the Republican state convention in Worcester on September 26.

The Salisbury address shook the Brahmins almost as much as the Framingham labor party platform had done days before.[21] Especially galling was Phillips's statement that Butler was the only man in a long list of candidates that year who represented an idea and that if death took all the other candidates the next day, humanity and progress would not be the poorer.[22]

When the Republicans met to choose a candidate, Butler received 464 delegate votes and his opponent 643. Both Butler and Phillips had spoken vigorously. The latter had advocated ideas so radical that many persons believed that Mr. Phillips had himself "lost his head" or "was gone crazy."[23] Phillips probably failed to realize at this time that while the labor leaders and intellectuals interested in labor and temperance reform might listen carefully to a speech advocating radical change in the status quo, rank-and-file laboring men were lukewarm to radical solutions even in times of depression.[24]

When the campaign was over, Butler returned to Congress; but Phillips, who had stirred up a hornet's nest with his labor platform and campaign speeches for Butler, accepted invitations to state his labor views in Boston and New York City. He explained his Framingham platform in detail at the Music Hall in Boston on October 31, 1871, and at the Steinway Hall in New York City on December 7, 1871. In both addresses he constructed a powerful case, using strong ethical, emotional, and statistical proof to show that in both cities three quarters of the people lived in poverty while one quarter or less lived in ease and controlled the three quarters who contributed to that ease without sharing it.[25]

In simple terms Phillips would solve the problems of labor through equalization of property: "What we need is an equalization of property— nothing else."[26] His ideal civilization was "a New England town of some two thousand inhabitants, with no rich man and no poor man in it. . . ."[27] "When we get into power," Phillips concluded, "we'll crumble up wealth by making it unprofitable to be rich. . . . Man is more valuable than money. You say, 'Then capital will go to Europe.' Good heavens, let it go!"[28]

One can imagine the expression on the faces of Boston and New York financiers when they opened their morning papers and read Phillips's "Case for Labor," especially the section recommending the equalization of property by taxing the rich. Reviewing his ideas, one could say that Phillips ably pictured the problem but could not quite mesh the Proudhon economic solution with the vast inequalities that existed in the growing cities of the "gilded age." The social problems existing in Boston and New York City in 1871 could no more be cured by equalizing property, regulating banks, and stopping financial manipulations than those same problems in the identical cities could be cured by similar panaceas today.

Phillips was not, however, all utopian in philosophy; he also rested his hopes on the international solidarity of labor. One of his most noteworthy addresses on the labor problem was delivered to the International Grand Lodge of the Knights of Saint Crispin [Shoemakers] on May 11, 1872, in Boston. He told the shoemakers that they could rally for eight hours, fairer division of the profits, 3 percent interest rates from the government, and almost anything else they wanted, but that they should let the nation hear a united demand from labor: "Only organize and stand together."[29]

Labor listened to Phillips and "stood together," off and on at least, through the remaining years of the nineteenth century. He recognized the problem of unifying labor into a political power when he wrote G. J. Holyoke in England two years after the Crispin address, " . . . the cliques, jealousies, distrust, and ignorance of workingmen are our chief obstacles."[30] It was to take laboring men more than half a century and scores of bitter local and even national labor disputes with management before they recognized the political power of a solid national labor vote. Phillips had at least stimulated labor to think about the political power of the ballot in 1871 and 1872, and he had used all the vigor and skill of great oratory to publicize their cause.

Benjamin Butler agreed with Phillips that workers should organize and use their ballot; but instead of advocating a utopian type of socialism in the place of capitalism or a return to the New England town of fifty years before, Butler urged that labor-management problems be solved through arbitration, thereby avoiding violence and strikes. He also favored strong labor legislation such as minimum-hour laws. He was one of the first political figures in America to represent an industrial district of workingmen, to appeal to labor to vote for him, and then to produce concrete legislative action favorable to his constituents. The labor vote sent Butler to Washington, D.C., as a U.S. Representative from 1866 to 1875 and from 1878 to 1880. It was also labor support that helped elect him Governor of Massachusetts in 1882 and labor support, with the help of the farmers, which gave him the Greenback Party Nomination for President in 1884.

Butler was proud of his labor support, and he liked to brag about his accomplishments for workingmen in Massachusetts. In 1884 he gave scores of campaign speeches across the United States, seeking labor's support. In Providence, Rhode Island, he told his hearers what he had witnessed as a young lawyer in Massachusetts:

. . . men and women working fourteen hours per day with twenty minutes for dinner. . . . God's people were being chewed up like bread for the purpose of making wealth.[31]

Butler explained his sympathy for the laboring man and thus gained close identification with the Providence listeners by telling them how labor clients had sustained him when he was a young lawyer. He told of his accomplishments in Massachusetts: the reduction of the working day from fourteen hours to eleven and a quarter, followed by legislation limiting the work week to sixty hours. Reminding them that Rhode Island had no such law, he won their applause by asking if it would not have been excellent for their workingmen and women if another young lawyer had lived in Rhode Island.

Turning to the national scene, Butler told them of his failure to convince Democrats to think of labor's problems when they wrote their national party platforms. They had spurned his proposal that arbitration settle labor-management difficulties. To illustrate the need for such a tribunal, Butler told his Rhode Island audience the story of a strike at a mill in Fall River, Massachusetts that had occurred after the wages had been cut. The workers had objected because the mills were making money. The mill owners had told them that they would lower wages when they wanted to: "You cannot interfere with our business. We will cut down when we want to." The workers had proposed that the question at issue be submitted to three disinterested men to examine the books; "and if the mills were not making money," Butler went on, "they would go to work at the cut-down, and if they were, then the employees were to be taken back at the old prices." Both parties could have benefited from a tribunal, thought Butler, because it was afterward proved that the owners could not show the books because the majority of the treasurers had been stealing money and "Some are in State prison now."[32]

The example was an effective argument for a board of arbitration, but the idea was a new one to both capital and labor. Butler nevertheless continued to advocate arbitration as a labor-management remedy and thus helped to set the idea in motion. His most forceful exposition of this idea came in a speech to workingmen of Newark, New Jersey, September 19, 1884. He told them in vivid, conversational language how difficult it was to get southern Democrats to recognize labor problems. Southern Democrats wanted to make sure that no Democratic Party Platform would include Negro laboring men:

When I brought this question up, a gentleman from the South said to me, 'Would this tribunal apply to our niggers?' I said, 'Your niggers? Have you got any niggers?' I thought that I marched down with some of my old soldiers some time ago to settle that question [Great applause].[33]

Butler then went on: "If I didn't, we will march again. We are a little older, but I guess we could do some fighting yet [Renewed Applause]." Continuing, he told the group that he knew then he never would succeed in getting the plank approved, because he had suggested equal treatment under the law:

I said yes, that this tribunal would apply to the workingmen of the South as well as of the North. We are to have equal rights, equal powers, equal privileges, equal burdens to all men under the laws, but after I made that declaration I could have no more hope for getting that plank through the Democratic platform than I have of being translated to heaven as Elijah was.[34]

After a study of the Newark address, one easily sees why Butler often changed political parties. Like Wendell Phillips and Peter Cooper he was eventually most comfortable as a Greenbacker. Whatever the party, Butler spoke for workmen everywhere, and his contribution to labor's cause was considerable. With the help of Wendell Phillips, Butler helped Massachusetts develop the first Bureau of Labor Statistics in 1869. For the first time it was possible to picture unemployment with reliable figures. By 1892 Massachusetts had enacted the first effective ten-hour law. Massachusetts was, in fact, "the first recognized leader of all American states in labour legislation."[35] Wendell Phillips and especially Benjamin Butler were largely responsible for these accomplishments for workingmen in Massachusetts. With the passage of time the eight-hour day became law. Health conditions for factory workers improved in other states as well as Massachusetts. Eventually children were no longer allowed to work in factories. Government accepted its role as protector of the weak as Butler had insisted it should in the early 1870s. Butler thus accomplished much in the way of concrete legislation for labor. He also helped to set in motion a flow of labor protest that hastened the day of labor reform. His public speaking irritated men of wealth and position in the United States, but labor loved him. When he died at age seventy-five on January 11, 1893, the *Labor Leader*, a Boston paper, acknowledged labor's debt: "So Ben Butler is dead. He was a man with heart and brain. Kind to the oppressed. Shrewd with competitors. His mark is left on history. It will be many a day before his like is looked upon again."[36]

THE MAN FROM NEW YORK

Peter Cooper, born in the presidency of George Washington, seventy years old when the Civil War broke out, died in New York City on April 4, 1883, at the age of ninety-two years. As someone remarked on his ninetieth birthday, "Mr. Cooper was probably the best living example of a successful American working man."[37] A manufacturer, an inventor of note, and a philanthropist, Cooper is probably best known as the founder of the Cooper Union.[38] A millionaire by 1855, he was determined to found a free-tuition school for men and women who wanted elementary instruction in science and art. Those gentlemen who wanted a classical education could go to Columbia University. The workingman who wanted to know more about mechanics could come to the Union in the evening. Young ladies interested in the arts could study in the School of Design during the day. No mere vocational school, the Union contained, at Cooper's insistence, a large lecture hall to be included on the ground floor for lectures and debates on all subjects and from all points of view. Peter Cooper believed that a citizen could learn from a public speech or a debate. Unused to reading, Cooper, with less than a year of formal schooling, had learned much from lectures during the heyday of the Lyceum.

Cooper liked to give speeches and write letters of advice. Throughout the Civil War he showered Washington with military, economic, and spiritual advice.[39] As soon as the Civil War broke out, he mounted a huge platform in Union Square and called on New Yorkers to unite and sustain the United States government.[40]

Cooper officially retired at seventy-four in 1865. This gave him more time to speak and write letters on the tariff and currency reform. He had occasionally lost small sums of money by backing a small inventor who failed, but he had never lost significantly. By 1870 he was worth several million dollars and probably considered his advice on finance worth noting. His audience, however, was only occasionally composed of respectable bankers and merchants. Those who listened to Peter Cooper most often were the unemployed, dissatisfied workers, and small businessmen—the kind of audience that came to his "Great Hall." They wanted to hear Cooper and other men discuss problems that affected them directly: wages and strikes and tariffs and currency reform. They identified with Peter Cooper, the workingman's friend.

The ethos of Peter Cooper with workingmen increased as he grew richer and older. If not especially skilled in speaking, he was certainly Quintilian's "good man." The secret of his ethos is plain. Essentially he was an honest, generous rich man—an extreme rarity in the age of the robber barons. Moreover, Cooper lived a humble, simple life. He never mixed with the wealthy of his day, for he had nothing in common with them. The importation of cheap goods from Great Britain after the War of 1812 had ruined his small business at that time. As a consequence he thereafter supported a protective tariff and had small liking for British and, later, Chinese labor. American workmen, especially the Irish, were always pleased to hear a word against the British. Cooper paid his own employees well and watched over the welfare of their families. And to the city of New York he was the Benjamin Franklin of the nineteenth century. Cooper urged the Common Council to give New York a great public-school system, fire department, and a clean water supply from upstate. And he gave New York citizens a free education at Cooper Union.

Workingmen eagerly listened to Cooper's logical arguments on money and the tariff after the depression of 1873.[41] He told them that bankers and merchants were taking their money and then strangling them with tight credit. He insisted that the new system of national banks was perpetuating a national debt that caused the federal government to increase taxes to pay the interest. It is the duty of the government, Cooper said to them, to provide an adequate national currency. Cooper's solution closely approximated that of the Greenback Party. In January, 1876, he presided over a huge meeting of workers at Cooper Union and told them not to strike to get what they wanted but to back those who advocated Greenbackism. In New Haven on March 31, 1876, he warned two thousand people in the Music Hall that Wall Street money power was destroying them.[42] On May 18, 1876, Peter Cooper found himself unanimously nominated for President by the Greenback convention at Indianapolis.[43]

In tone Peter Cooper's writing and speaking were usually calm, measured, humorless, and at times banal; but when fired up he could rise to eloquence through vivid imagery and earnest delivery. The Greenback movement of 1876, with its emphasis on the currency question, his favorite subject, ignited him. For the next seven years, until the hour of his death, he wrote and spoke hundreds of thousands of words on his currency views, the volume of words swelling rather than diminishing as he approached and passed ninety.[44] Even more astonishing is the fact that the older he grew, the more radical he became. By the time he had passed ninety, he was advocating a strong paternalistic role for the government in a host of progressive recommendations including a civil-service commission. He advocated governmental industrial schools for workers across the nation and asked for a program of government-sponsored public improvements to help give employment to people. Urging the state to build and own the railroads, he also wanted the unoccupied land in the West given to the people. Even Peter Cooper could not live forever; but had he lived until the 1930s he would certainly have applauded Franklin D. Roosevelt—if he had not found him too conservative.

Cooper, then, was a man of great ethical force whose liberal ideas went even beyond the thoughts of the Greenbackers. Another strong appeal Cooper used, perhaps unaware of its power, was his constant reference to his age. Edward Mack, his chief biographer, believed that Cooper captured audiences for years by telling them what may well have been true: "that this was one of the last times he would ever meet his friends."[45] For example, as far back as 1859, on the day he dedicated Cooper Union, he mentioned in his introduction that his days would soon end: "My time, in the course of nature is rapidly drawing to a close; while you may have many long years to enjoy the benefits of this Institution. . . ."[46]

Cooper also captured attention and held interest because of his appearance and his earnest way of speaking. By 1870 his fringe of beard had whitened, and his hair, which streamed down his back, was light, silky gray. He wore four-lensed spectacles and usually dressed in black. A man of great force, accomplishment, and purpose, he gave almost the opposite impression: that of benignity and simplicity. Not fire but benevolence was in his blue eyes. Many newspaper and other accounts refer to the fact that his presence commanded profound silence and attention. The factor of identification must have been very strong even when Cooper was in his mid-seventies. As one reporter wrote: "He moves like a father among his children."[47] Those who heard Peter Cooper said that he inspired them with awe by his appearance; that when he spoke, the look on his face and the light in his eye gave life and meaning to even banal words.

The career of Peter Cooper was that of an educational ally of labor as well as a political ally. By 1870 fifteen hundred people were coming to the Great Hall every Saturday night to hear such speakers as John Tyndall lecture on electric lights and experimental machines. These Saturday-night audiences were to a great extent composed of thoughtful working people.

Outsiders could rent the Great Hall on other than Saturday evenings, and there were no restrictions on subject or speaker. Thus, Peter Cooper gave New York working people a public forum for mass meetings as early as 1860. This opportunity to hear the views of anyone, no matter how radical, may well have helped place New York laboring men and women in the position of power they occupy today in New York City.[48]

Peter Cooper's success as titular head of the Greenback Party in 1876 was disappointing, but the thousands of young trade unionists and ordinary people who greeted him with deafening cheers at the mass meeting at Cooper Union on August 30, 1876, and on October 20, 1876, and earlier that year in New Haven before his nomination, listened and did not forget.[49] As Cooper's chief biographer stated it:

The old philanthropist . . . was starting, not finishing something. Within two years Greenback votes had swelled to 1,000,000, and later other leaders, with perhaps better ideas than the Greenbackers were to take up the burden of liberalism. Peter was a not insignificant link between the days of Jackson and those of Wilson and Roosevelt.[50]

THE MAN FROM ILLINOIS

Wendell Phillips, Benjamin Butler, and Peter Cooper were all national figures when a young man of twenty-four, named John Peter Altgeld, was admitted to the bar in Missouri in 1871. He was born in the southern German village of Nieder Selters, the son of a wagon maker. When Altgeld was three months old, the family moved from Germany to a farm in Ohio. By the time he was twelve years old, his father decided that he had had enough schooling. The boy did not object, for his schooldays were far from happy. Schoolmates called him "the little Dutchman." He was not a handsome boy and never grew into a very impressive man. He had the coarse, big-boned features of European peasant stock. He reached average height, but his broad shoulders and stumpy legs made him appear short.

Schoolmates jeered at his home-sewn clothing and his heavy German dialect. Know-nothingism was strong in such nearby cities as Cincinnati. The Know-nothingism fever that helped make Altgeld an unhappy boy may also have inspired in him some ambition to leave the farm, enter the professional world, and champion the underdog throughout his life.[51]

The Civil War gave him an opportunity to leave the farm in Ohio. He served only the customary one hundred days, but he saw Washington, D.C., and some of the rest of America. When he returned, he decided that he was going to high school and did so over the objection of his father. After high-school graduation, he taught school and then left Ohio to go West. He worked on farms for his board and keep as he headed West, finally settling down in the little town of Savannah, Missouri. There he taught school during the day, worked on a farm early in the morning and late in the afternoon, and read law late at night.

Altgeld started as a typical small-town lawyer after he passed the bar in 1871. He investigated the Grange movement, strong in Missouri at that time, sympathized with its principles, and became a candidate for county attorney on the People's Party ticket. Those who heard him in that campaign—his first for political office—commented that what he lacked in oratorical finish he made up with his great earnestness.[52]

Within eleven months after Altgeld's election to office in Savannah he resigned and left for Chicago—some say because of failure in courtship. Whatever the reason, he reached Chicago in 1875. He boldly took an office in one of the finest buildings in town and waited for clients. At first, they were laborers, but still he was making a living. He saved some money, returned home to Ohio, and married a childhood sweetheart. It was Emma Ford Altgeld who helped turn this awkward, self-conscious country boy into the self-assured, polite, urbane gentleman who soon became a prosperous Chicago businessman and lawyer.[53] In 1886 he was elected to the Superior Court of Cook County on the Democratic and Labor ticket. On January 10, 1893, he became the Democratic Governor of Illinois, an office he held until his term expired on January 11, 1897. Partly because he controlled the Democratic Party in a powerful state and partly because he recognized the importance of silver as an issue, he became the head of the Democratic Party in 1896 and even in 1900. There is little doubt that Altgeld would have received the Democratic presidential nomination in 1896 except for the one factor he could not control—his German birth.[54]

As Altgeld was rising politically, he also wrote and spoke frequently. First came a book on penal reform in 1884, then two volumes of his views on law, contemporary politics and politicians, and economic and social questions: Volume I, *Live Questions*, in 1890, and Volume II, *Live Questions*, 1899. These two volumes contain most of his important speeches and the gist of his specific goals for reform. *Oratory: Its Requirements and Its Rewards* appeared in 1901, and *The Cost of Something for Nothing* appeared in 1904, published posthumously. Altgeld died of a cerebral hemorrhage at age fifty-five on March 12, 1902, after completing a speech in Joliet, Illinois.

As a lawyer, judge, governor, and powerful member of the Democratic Party, Altgeld gave scores of speeches. Among his more important are those addresses in which he selected labor problems as his principal topic.[55] Several reasons can be advanced to explain Altgeld's interest in the laboring man. He had worked hard as an immigrant boy on his father's farm and later as a hired hand when he was studying law in Missouri. Labor problems had been widespread in large American cities since the depression of 1873 and the riots of 1877. They were widely discussed as important issues of the day. Altgeld had also made friends of men like George A. Schilling, a socialist organizer and national labor leader, through his book on prison reform. It must not be forgotten that, besides being a humanitarian who hated injustice, John Peter Altgeld had a great desire for power. Herndon's description of Abraham Lincoln as a man who was always calculating and always planning ahead could be applied to Altgeld. Like Lincoln, "His ambition was a little engine that knew no rest."[56]

Altgeld's first public speech on labor was remarkably close, in terms of ideas, to that of Wendell Phillips's first talk on the subject in 1865.[57] The occasion was a "revival of the eight-hour movement," a subject Ira Steward had used to interest Phillips twenty-five years before and one George Schilling now used to interest John Altgeld.

Altgeld's speech on February 22, 1890, was longer and more fully developed than Phillips's, but both asked labor to organize and avoid strikes and violence. The speech was especially well received because his audience knew that Judge Altgeld employed a large number of workers on various building projects in downtown Chicago. Labor, through the help of George Schilling, had thus attracted a sympathetic, wealthy man of prominence.[58]

Always calculating, always planning ahead, Altgeld broadcast his name and views as widely as possible. His real-estate empire was growing all the time, and financial success helped him to print and send to politicians and people of influence hundreds of copies of his first book on prison reform. He next collected his speeches, essays, and statements on social problems, published them as *Live Questions*, and mailed this volume by the thousands into southern Illinois. In April, 1892, alone he sent out seventeen thousand copies. Delegates to the Democratic convention for nominating a governor came to know the name Altgeld, and they liked his solutions to social problems. Like Peter Cooper, Altgeld was a living example of a successful American workingman and a sympathetic employer. He had come to Chicago with one hundred dollars and had become a real-estate giant, a builder of office buildings. Workingmen began to listen closely to Altgeld, and the Liberals led by George Schilling worked hard for his election as governor. The vote was 402,672 for former Governor Fifer and 425,558 for Altgeld.

An analysis of Altgeld's speeches and actions during the campaign for governor reveals a man who knew how to please just about everyone but the journalists of Chicago: "Judge Altgeld has visited more families, kissed more babies, inspected more dairies, and helped set more hens than any man before who wanted to be Governor."[59] Altgeld knew when he started campaigning, however, that no resident of Chicago and no one of foreign birth had ever been elected governor of Illinois.

Altgeld used well the available means of persuasion in this campaign. He could address people of German origin in their native language and did so. He strengthened his growing power with labor by making informal little speeches in village halls and stores. Most impressed of all were the coal miners of Illinois, for he met and shook their hands as they came from the mines at the workday's end. He walked down rows of corn to shake the hands of farmers.

The speeches, including those on labor, were cautious utterances. He appealed to labor, for instance, in the Labor Day address at Elgin, but he avoided saying anything considered radical. In short, he acted and talked like a politician running for office. Even Altgeld's inaugural address as governor on January 10, 1893, contained only a suggestion of support for liberal labor policies. Altgeld appeared to be purring good will toward almost everyone in Illinois that day. He had, after all, been careful to visit the town bankers and leading businessmen as well as the workers and farmers in his campaign. He was as assiduous in telling the small businessmen about his "Unity Block" of office buildings in downtown Chicago as he was in shaking the hands of coal miners.

Approximately four months after delivering his inaugural address as governor of Illinois, Altgeld issued a calm, clear, incisive, factual eighteen-thousand-word document that pardoned Fielden, Schwab, and Neebe of any guilt in the Haymarket affair. "Reasons for Pardoning," issued on June 26, 1893, was not a speech, but it provoked hundreds of speeches, especially Fourth of July orations. Altgeld's statement of pardon was so unexpected that it shook America almost as much as the 1886 Haymarket bomb itself. Several reasons can be given for Altgeld's pardoning Fielden, Schwab, and Neebe. The most obvious, as Altgeld himself stated, was that it was right. The men had received an unfair trial. Other motivations were prompted by George Schilling and the workingmen who had elected Altgeld Governor of Illinois. Schilling wanted to hear and see evidence that Altgeld was the friend of labor that he appeared to be in his essays and speeches.[60] Altgeld bent under this pressure. The pardon was issued, and Altgeld was a changed man. A tougher, much more aggressive Altgeld emerged. He spoke with candor now. The compromising politician of weasel words had vanished.

On Labor Day, September 8, 1893, Altgeld accepted an invitation to talk to workingmen of Chicago assembled in Kuhn's Park. The speech struck the right balance with labor and capital, according to all newspaper reports, with the exception of Joseph Medill's *Chicago Tribune*, a paper that vilified Altgeld throughout his lifetime. "Governor Altgeld, at that meeting, was emphatically the right man in the right place," said the St. Louis *Republic* of September 7, 1893.[61]

The 1893 Labor Day address was an excellent speech for several reasons besides its timeliness. In some instances the ideas were forty years ahead of their time. The analyses of the times and the nature of labor-capital difficulties were brilliant. The language, with strong biblical cadence and imagery, was stirring. Altgeld's main purpose in speaking was to caution labor to move along lawful lines and ignore men who advocated violence in labor disputes. Through this address Altgeld succeeded to a remarkable degree in preventing labor violence. He knew that even firebrand workers had implicit confidence in him as governor, and he used his influence well as the principal speaker at their mass meeting.

Foreshadowing the New Deal of 1933, Altgeld declared in 1893 that it was the duty of the state to see that citizens did not starve in Illinois: ". . . let me say it will be the duty of all public officials to see to it that no man is permitted to starve on the soil of Illinois, and provision will be made to that end."[62]

Altgeld, like Roosevelt in 1933, blamed not the workingmen but world conditions for the 1893 depression. Thousands of men in Illinois and even Europe, he said, had been denied work by the policies of men who called themselves statesmen. Thinking of his own role as employer of thousands of workmen who helped erect his office buildings and also considering his reading audience, the governor said that they should pity the employer who was also a victim of world conditions. Hundreds of employers, he stated, sweated by day and walked the floor by night trying to save their businesses from bankruptcy.[63]

This 1893 Labor Day address revealed not only a sympathetic Altgeld but also Altgeld the intellectual.[64] His research into the history of labor was impressive. He may have been thinking of the contribution made by Wendell Phillips when he told his hearers that the nineteenth century had taught the laboring man to look ahead, cooperate with his fellow laborer, organize, investigate, inquire, discuss. Today, he reminded his listeners, labor had respect. Many states had set aside a day to be observed annually in honor of labor.[65]

Speaking as bluntly as Wendell Phillips in the depression of 1873, Altgeld appeared to tell them a lesson he had learned as a politician, and Phillips as an abolitionist: that they must move along lawful lines but that they must demonstrate power. Justice and equity without power will gain you nothing, he reminded them. Governments are created and controlled by power. No one will respect you if you cannot show strength to back your demands. " . . . the earth is covered with the graves of justice and equity that failed to receive recognition, because there was no influence or force to compel it, and it will be so until the millenium," he argued.[66]

Altgeld offered little evidence for his statements in this speech aside from occasional biblical and other historical examples and analogies. Little support was needed. No man exhibited more ethos among laboring men in the country than Altgeld at that moment. He was, in fact, his own authority on the subject. It was a most appropriate address for the occasion.

Altgeld's next address that considered labor questions in detail was given as his biennial message to the Illinois Legislature on January 9, 1895. This address, as opposed to his inaugural, was harshly plain-spoken, uncompromising, and presidential-sounding, because he attacked national problems. He talked of national problems that day because by then President Grover Cleveland, without Altgeld's invitation or consent, had sent federal troops into Illinois to straighten out the Pullman dispute.[67]

The biennial address runs to forty pages even without the inclusion of routine state matters that Altgeld covered in an earlier document instead of including them in the speech; its great length was due, for the most part, to the minute documentation Altgeld offered to explain his actions as governor during the Pullman crisis. Some members of the Illinois Legislature may have squirmed before Altgeld finished his long address, but they heard a figure of importance discuss in depth a new national issue: "Government by Injunction." It was Altgeld who first began to agitate against federal and state courts issuing injunctions. Forty years later the national Congress passed the Norris-La Guardia Act, which removed from the federal courts the power to issue injunctions in labor disputes—the fruit of agitation that Altgeld began on an effective scale with his 1895 message to the Illinois Legislature.

Altgeld was able to state in his biennial message that an act had been passed to stop the sweat shop and child labor by providing for inspection of factories and workshops along with another act creating a board of arbitration for the purpose of adjusting disputes between employers and employees in some cases.[68]

The election year of 1896 arrived. The silver issue soon became as important to Altgeld as the injunction had been in 1895. He studied the silver issue in depth until he became the undisputed authority on money reform in the Democratic Party. He could hold an audience for two hours by the sheer force of his logical presentation and clear organization. He made a great impromptu address at the 1896 convention, an address that stressed "no compromise" on the silver issue and was greeted by yells of unrestrained delight. The oratorical climax at that convention was delivered by another speaker, however, whom few men could match in delivery at that time. Effective as Altgeld was in analyzing issues and documenting his addresses with specific facts and figures, he had difficulty projecting his voice because he lacked pitch control. The result was a rather high-pitched, tense voice, much like that ascribed to Abraham Lincoln.

The United States Constitution denied Altgeld his party's nomination for President, but he had the satisfaction of writing the 1896 and 1900 Democratic Party platforms. He later made as many as seven to eight speeches a day for Bryan. Altgeld thus had an opportunity to articulate the ideas that he had written into the Democratic platform. This German immigrant had become labor's national spokesman.

John Peter Altgeld's rise from a German immigrant farm boy to a man of national prominence created several myths that obscure the real man. Like Abraham Lincoln, Altgeld was neither all saint nor all devil. His early career reveals a clever, ambitious man who used every form of persuasion to win enough votes to become Governor of Illinois. His speeches were cautious and less than candid. One of his more shrewd devices was publishing his essays and speeches and mailing them by the thousands to the prominent citizens of Illinois. After his election as governor and his decision shortly afterward to pardon the Haymarket rioters, he revealed himself as a changed man. He became less the politician seeking office and more the candid spokesman for laboring men everywhere. He urged labor to ignore violent agitators, and he concentrated on labor legislation. He succeeded in passing legislation highly beneficial to labor. His speeches contained ideas for labor-reform measures adopted forty years later by Franklin D. Roosevelt.

CONCLUSION

The last quarter of the nineteenth century produced four men whose careers revolved around a political alliance with labor. All four were instrumental in bringing what were then radical ideas before the public: Wendell Phillips, Benjamin Butler, and Peter Altgeld through their own oratory, and Peter Cooper, to some extent through his own speaking, but primarily through providing a forum for mass meetings at his Cooper Institute.

Starting in 1871, Butler advocated a new role for government as a protector of labor by stating that labor's hours, working conditions, and earnings were grounds for state and federal legislation. He urged laboring men to organize, avoid strikes and violence, and work for lawful means to better their condition. As early as 1871 he was urging arbitration for strikes as well as shorter working hours, especially for women and children. Wendell Phillips during this period was advocating the economic program of Proudhon, the French socialist, that is, a radical change in the capitalistic system. The major contribution of Phillips was urging labor to unite and vote together.

Throughout this period Peter Cooper lent his support to radical ideas and opened his Cooper Institute to all who cared to speak, thus enabling even illiterate laboring men to hear and discuss ideas.

By 1884 Butler could boast of labor reforms written into law in Massachusetts. He focused national attention on the problems of labor in his campaign for President on the Greenbacker ticket.

A generation later Phillips, Butler, and Cooper were dead, and Altgeld became labor's most powerful political ally. First as a judge in Chicago's Municipal Court and later as governor of Illinois and leader of the Democratic Party, Altgeld succeeded in getting the Illinois State Legislature to help laboring men as Butler had done in Massachusetts. By 1896 legislation had been enacted in Illinois to stop the sweat shop and child labor and to create a board of arbitration for certain labor-management disputes. Altgeld had finally been able to put Butler's ideas, such as arbitration, into action; but Altgeld deserves credit for the deep analysis of labor's problems and corresponding solutions. It should be noted that both Butler and Altgeld understood that the United States was becoming industrialized. Populists and men like Bryan never quite comprehended this fact, because their analysis and possibly their intellect never equaled that of Altgeld.

In the total picture of industrial protest there were many men with ideas on labor reform, but these men needed articulate political spokesmen like Benjamin Butler and John Altgeld to see that reforms were written into law. These two political figures were the strongest links between the days of Jackson and those of Woodrow Wilson and Franklin D. Roosevelt.

NOTES

1. An abundance of primary source material is available in the Butler Papers. They are located in the Library of Congress and consist of letters, newspaper clippings, documents, and speech texts in Butler's own hand. These papers are arranged chronologically in 277 manuscript boxes. They will be cited as *Butler Manuscripts*.
   The Library of Congress also holds some valuable letters and speech outlines by Wendell Phillips. Cited hereafter as *Phillips Manuscripts*.

2. J. Q. A. Griffen, "A Portrait of Benjamin F. Butler," *Butler Manuscripts*, 1: 269, W, 59. See also the account by A. Lewis in the *New York Times*, January 14, 1893, p. 2, col. 6.

3. Butler sat almost continuously in the United States House of Representatives for fourteen years after the close of the war in 1865 and ran for Governor of Massachusetts, unsuccessfully, in 1871, 1872, 1878, and 1879. He was elected Governor of Massachusetts in 1882, defeated in 1883, and finally stopped running for office when he was defeated for President on the National (Greenback) Ticket in 1884.

4. See Nora Perry's personal account of Phillips, *Phillips Manuscripts*, 3: 36, L, 1. Also see Irving H. Bartlett, *Wendell Phillips: Brahmin Radical* (Boston: Beacon Press, 1961).

5. See *Butler's Book* (Boston: A. M. Thayer & Co., 1892), Chap. I, on lineage. Also consult Robert S. Holzman, *Stormy Ben Butler* (New York: Collier Books, 1961); Hans Louis Trefousse, *Ben Butler: The South Called Him Beast* (New York: Twayne Publishers, 1957); and Richard S. West, Jr., *Lincoln's Scapegoat General: A Life of Benjamin F. Butler, 1818–1893* (Cambridge: The Riverside Press, 1965).

6. Lorenzo Sears, *Wendell Phillips: Orator and Agitator* (New York: Doubleday, Page, & Co., 1909), p. 12.
   See also an article in the *New York Times*, January 20, 1880, p. 4, col. 7. An intimate friend of Phillips for twenty-five years writes: "His manner in private puts persons at their ease; yet it is the manner of a patrician and men of the common sort who meet him esteem and admire him though they always feel the difference between him and themselves. They cannot understand why he has advocated the cause of the poor and the lowly."

7. *New York Daily Tribune*, August 22, 1876, p. 5, cols. 4 and 5.

8. Richard Hofstadter, *The American Political Tradition* (New York: Alfred A. Knopf, 1948), p. 175.

9. Eulogy on Butler, Tremont Temple, March 15, 1893, *Butler Manuscripts*, 2: 269, W, 59.

10. Ira Steward acquired the nickname because he fought with almost fanatical zeal for this one idea of eight hours from the early 1860s until his death in 1883. It was Steward, in fact, who first attracted Phillips to the labor cause around 1863 and inspired Phillips's first speech on labor in 1865—the speech which

included the famous phrase: "eight hours for labor, eight hours for sleep, and eight hours for his own—his own to use as he pleases." Louis Filler, *Wendell Phillips on Civil Rights and Freedom* (New York: Hill and Want, 1965), p. 193.

11. The finest examples would include: "Speech to the Delegates of the Labor Reform Party," South Framingham, Mass., September 4, 1871; "Speech to Labor and Temperance Groups," Salisbury Beach, Mass., September 13, 1871; "The Foundation of the Labor Movement," Music Hall, Boston, October 31, 1871; and at Steinway Hall, New York City, December 7, 1871, and "The Speech to the International Grand Lodge of St. Crispin," Boston, May 11, 1872. See Wendell Phillips, *Speeches, Lectures, and Letters* (Boston: Lee & Shepard, 1891), 2: 152–167, *New York Times*, December 7, 1871, p. 5, col. 2.

12. The complete thirty-two page text of Butler's Springfield Address is found in *Ephemera*, 1869–1871, 10 p.v.1, New York Public Library. Butler's speeches and public letters outside Congress have not been collected. None of the speech texts and notes in the *Butler Manuscripts* pertain to labor reform.

13. Speech at Springfield, Mass., August 24, 1871, *Ephemera*, 10 p.v.1, p. 16.

14. Ibid.

15. Benjamin R. Tucker, editor of the *Boston Liberty*, was a strict follower of P. J. Proudhon. He had translated Proudhon's *What Is Property?* into English. Tucker's translation was popular with intellectuals like Wendell Phillips who liked Proudhon's scheme of free banking supplemented by the Greenbackers' idea of government money and political action. See John R. Commons, *History of Labor in the United States* (New York: Macmillan Co., 1926), 2: 138–141.

16. His ideas in the platform resembled the thought of the New England Labor Reform League of the late 1860s which went back to Tucker and his translation of Proudhon.

17. George L. Austin, *The Life and Times of Wendell Phillips* (Boston: Lee and Shepard, 1893), pp. 264-267.

18. Ibid., p. 265.

19. Ibid., p. 267.

20. See personal letter from Wendell Phillips to acknowledge support from the Labor Reform Party, September 13, 1870, as given in Austin, *Life of Phillips*, pp. 260–262.

21. If the speech upset and gave offense to Butler's opponents, it was all part of the campaign strategy, according to Carlos Martyn: "The two went into partnership on purpose to rattle the dry bones in Massachusetts. They did it. Under their manipulation, very corpses were galvanized into the semblance of life." Carlos Martyn, *Wendell Phillips: the Agitator* (New York: Funk & Wagnalls Co., 1890), p. 388.

22. Austin, *Life of Phillips*, p. 269.

23. Ibid.

24. See Commons, *History of Labor*, p. 269.

25. Vernon Parrington, after reading the Framingham platform and the Boston and New York addresses of Phillips on labor, said that Phillips called himself a Jeffersonian Democrat but spoke like a socialist: "The man who called himself

'a Jeffersonian democrat in the darkest hour,' wrote down . . . the cardinal plank of the Socialist platform." Vernon Louis Parrington, *Main Currents in American Thought* (New York: Harcourt Brace & Co., 1930), 3:145.

26. Boston Music Hall Address, "The Case for Labor," October 31, 1871. Filler, *Wendell Phillips*, p. 204.

27. Ibid. Phillips had no use for the city. Civilization, he reasoned, rots when too many people gather in one place like Boston or New York.

28. Ibid., p. 207.

29. Wendell Phillips, *Speeches, Lectures, and Letters* (Boston: Lee & Shepard, 1891), 2:176.

30. Letter from Phillips to Holyoke, July 22, 1874, Austin, *Life of Phillips*, p. 305.

31. "Speech to the Workingmen of Providence," *New York Times*, August 20, 1884, p. 5, col. 3.

32. Ibid.

33. "Speech to the Workingmen of Newark," *New York Times*, September 19, 1884, p. 2, col. 2.
    Butler, a Union General during the Civil War, was despised in the South, especially for his high-handed activities as Military Governor of New Orleans in 1862. See Trefousse, The subtitle of the book is "The South Called Him Beast."

34. Ibid.

35. Commons, *History of Labor*, p. 144.

36. *Labor Leader* (Boston), January 14, 1893, p. 1, col. 1.

37. *New York Times*, February 13, 1881, p. 2, col. 7.

38. The rhetorical scholar will find the Cooper Papers at Cooper Union of interest. They contain as many as four copies of his speeches in his own handwriting and many preparatory outlines. These speeches range from commencement addresses, which he gave every year at the Cooper Union, to his favorite economic topics: the tariff and currency reform.

39. The Cooper-Hewitt Papers in the Library of Congress contain many of these letters to prominent figures in Washington.

40. *New York Times*, April 20, 21, 22, 1861.

41. Peter Cooper's great age gave him an advantage even in logical argument. He was in many ways an authority. He had personally observed and analyzed ten financial panics in his life-time. See sketch in *New York Times*, July 7, 1879, p. 1, col. 7.

42. The text of this speech is available in the New Haven *Union*, April 1, 1876, p. 1.

43. The *New York Daily Tribune* is usually a better source for Peter Cooper's addresses than the *New York Times*. The only collection of addresses was published by Peter Cooper the last year of his life in 1883: *Ideas for a Science of Good Government, in Addresses, Letters and Articles on a Strictly National Currency, Tariff and Civil Service.* This collection is available at the Cooper Union Library, but the reader will soon discover that the speeches have been rather carefully edited. During the last decade of his life, Peter Cooper allowed J. C. Zachos, Curator of Cooper Institute, to edit his speeches and writings very

freely, and Zachos occasionally appeared for Cooper and read the address for him after Cooper reached the age of ninety.

44. Edward C. Mack, *Peter Cooper* (New York: Duell, Sloan & Pearce, 1949), p. 373.

45. Ibid., p. 326.

46. Cooper Papers: Printed copy of speech given on November 2, 1859, with corrections in Cooper's own script.

47. *New York Observer* 43 (1865):117.

48. The records of every speaker who ever spoke in the Great Hall are available in the Cooper Union Archives. They show the names of almost every person tied to the interests of labor as having spoken at the Great Hall from 1865 to the present time.

49. Peter Cooper won 82,640 votes out of 8,000,000 cast. See Mack, *Peter Cooper*, p. 369.

50. Ibid.

51. See Harry Barnard, *Eagle Forgotten: The Life of John Peter Altgeld* (New York: Bobbs-Merrill Co., 1938), Chap. I. The Barnard biography is the most complete source on the life of Altgeld. It contains many excerpts from his speeches and interviews with many contemporaries who heard him speak.

52. John K. White of Savannah to Harry Barnard, July 26, 1936. Barnard, *Eagle Forgotten*, p. 37.

53. Emma Ford Altgeld had graduated from Oberlin College, majored in music, painted rather well in oils, and had published several short stories. She frequently listened to and criticized her husband's speeches before they were delivered.

54. "But for this accident of nativity, there seems no doubt that Altgeld would have crowned his platform success by winning for himself the presidential nomination. All that happened at the convention bears out that conclusion—as Professor Nevins, among other keen students of that episode, have attested." Barnard, *Eagle Forgotten*, p. 365, and Allan Nevins, *Grover Cleveland: A Study in Courage* (New York: Dodd, Mead & Co., 1932), p. 701.

55. "The Eight Hour Movement," an address delivered before the Brotherhood of United Labor, at the Armory in Chicago, February 22, 1890. "Elgin Labor Day Speech," delivered at Elgin, Illinois, September 6, 1892. "Inaugural Address," delivered to the General Assembly, January 10, 1893. "Address to the Laboring Men of Chicago," delivered September 8, 1893. "Biennial Message to the General Assembly," January 9, 1895. "Answer to Schurz and Cochran," delivered at Central Music Hall, Chicago, September 19, 1896. "Speech at Cooper Union," New York, October 17, 1896. "Speech at Philadelphia," Labor Day, September 5, 1897. See John Peter Altgeld, *Live Questions*, 2 vols. (Chicago: George S. Bowen and Co., 1899). *New York Times* September 20, 1896, p. 2 col. 6; October 18, 1896, p. 2 col. 1–2.

56. William H. Herndon, *Life of Lincoln* (Cleveland: Fine Editions Press, 1949), p. 304.

57. Altgeld admired Phillips and referred to him as "one of the grandest specimens of noble manhood New England ever produced, a man pure, lofty, noble and cultured. . . ." See "Speech at Brooklyn, New York," *Live Questions*, p. 738.

58. Altgeld's thoughts on labor at this time may also be found in newspaper interviews and long reaction letters that he wrote to articles he read in Chicago papers in the period that he served as Chicago's District Judge: 1886–1891. These are available in both volumes of *Live Questions*.

   Altgeld's ideas on arbitration, which were finally written into law when he was governor, are found in detail not in his speeches but in one of the first newspaper essays he wrote, entitled "Arbitration of Strikes," dated April 26, 1886. See *Live Questions*, pp. 107–116.

59. Chicago *Inter-Ocean*, August 13, 1892, as quoted in Barnard, *Eagle Forgotten*, p. 159.

60. The story of George Schilling's part in Altgeld's decision to pardon Fielden, Schwab, and Neebe is covered in detail in Barnard, *Eagle Forgotten*, Chapter 22.

61. See *Live Questions*, 2: 347–349, for assorted newspaper reactions to this speech.

62. Ibid., p. 343.

63. Ibid. Altgeld did not know in 1893 that by 1900 the sheriff would be at his own door and he would die penniless.

64. Altgeld was considered "brainy" and in 1896 and 1900 the equal of Carl Schurz, the intellectual head of the Republican Party.

65. *Live Questions*, 2:344.

66. Ibid, p. 345.

67. Historians even today write in a biased fashion concerning the facts in the Pullman dispute. The author consulted the Grover Cleveland Papers in the Library of Congress and found them to be of little help. Barnard's exposition of this dispute synthesizes the evidence from all sides. See Barnard, *Eagle Forgotten*, Chaps. 28, 29, and 30. Newspapers of this period are unreliable in reporting the facts.

68. See footnote #58, paragraph 2.

II

THE AGRARIAN REVOLT

5

The Farmer Assesses His Role in Society

PAUL CRAWFORD

RHETORICAL AND HISTORICAL STANCE

Any account of a period or movement is an interpretation. The selection of material is in itself interpretative. Beyond the interpretations of different historians and rhetoricians there is the tendency of the same historians to revise their earlier interpretations. The late Richard Hofstadter admitted in 1955 that in his later writing he was more critical of the Populist-Progressive tradition than he would have been fifteen years earlier.[1] Another leading historian reported in 1963 that if parents came back to the campus to hear the history course lectures presented to their sons and daughters, they would be surprised to learn that some historical heroes and villains of their college courses have exchanged places. "Among the more recent champions of the common man, the Populists and Bryanite Democrats have suffered most from assault and battery by revisionists."[2] As if in an effort to counterbalance an allegedly lenient interpretation by indulgent liberals, some critics drew attention away from the economic distress of the agrarians and toward their "delusions, myths, and foibles."[3] For example, the alleged anti-Semitism in the denunciation of Jewish bankers by some Greenbackers would draw more critical emphasis today than it was likely to receive in most earlier accounts of Greenbackism. However, a review in the *New York Times*, January 4, 1977 by Alden Whitman of Lawrence Goodwyn's *Democratic Promise: The Populist Movement in America* does not emphasize anti-Semitism. Perhaps it is safe to say that anti-Semitism did not loom as large as an issue in the nineteenth century as it did in the twentieth with its emphasis on constitutional rights.

With respect to the Agrarian protest and American history in general a more recent tendency appears to either revise the revisionist historical and biographical interpretations or to stress comparative treatments.[4] Perhaps all this underscores the importance of the historian as reflected in the remark of a leading orator of the Agrarian protest—Ignatius Donnelly—that "history is his-story, and depends on who tells it."[5] When one adds Arthur L. Smith's insightful observation that "a movement is rhetorical in some of its conspicuous characteristics,"[6] it is obvious that the analysis of a movement is indeed a complex undertaking. An interrelation and an interaction of social and rhetorical phenomena make any separatist headings only a convenience of focus for the reader.

Although several thoughtfully conceived plans for analyzing social movements have been introduced into the literature of rhetoric and sociology,[7] the hazards stemming from the imposition of such plans are somewhat analogous to those of imposing the canons of classical rhetoric upon such a study. A framework of categories is preconceived, and it is imposed from the outside without examination; it does not emerge inductively from a study of the movement itself. A given framework in whole or in part may fit one social movement but not all movements.

In an overview of the Agrarian protest, it is no more revealing to speak of the inception of the movement as being in the late 1860s and early 1870s, the experience of mounting dissatisfaction in the late 1870s and 1880s, and the reaching of consummation (and virtual dissolution) in the 1890s than to identify the organizations that became the main vehicles of protest (the Grange, the Greenback Party, the Farmers' Alliance, the People's [Populist] Party, and the fused Democratic and Populist parties). In other words, one might well consider, historically and rhetorically, the successive phases of the Agrarian protest. Before this writer begins that process, he must call attention to certain problems that must be confronted, regardless of the analytic approach used:

(1) The rhetorical critic must so absorb the realities of conflict and the climate of opinion and audience attitudes of the time under consideration that he can mentally place himself in the past under study, yet must not pretend to divorce himself from the advantages that recent scholarship has given to hindsight.

(2) The rhetorical critic must try to identify—and possibly to distinguish—the ideas and attitudes of rank-and-file members of a movement and the views of some of its leaders and spokesmen, particularly as embodied in their private expressions or in remarks to relatively sophisticated hearers who may not be typical of ordinary members.

(3) The rhetorical critic may choose to explore both written and oral discourse and perhaps other forms of symbolic behavior, but he should

keep clear in his own mind what modes of communication were used and the sources of the rhetoric he seeks to characterize; for example, whether his primary concern is speech communication in public address and whether his secondary consideration is the rhetoric of the press.

(4) The rank-and-file members of a movement and perhaps some or all of its leading spokesmen may have been associated with only one or two phases of a movement but may have little or no consciousness of the long-range historical movement as perceived and designated by historians and rhetoricians. Even the chief spokesmen may have held differing perceptions.

In this wider look at the Agrarian protest, perhaps it would be helpful to illustrate in condensed form a historian's summary and an application by a rhetorician of a framework derived from sociological theory. For a historian's summation we may turn to the late Richard Hofstadter, who saw the farmer caught from 1866 to 1897 in a situation of low farm prices, high tariffs, natural disasters, and a need for a long-term credit that conflicted with the banker's need for short-term repayment of loans. Railroads, grain elevators, and meat packers were often capricious in setting prices, and the farmer turned more and more to political remedies, some monetary, including the grasp at free silver that led to a merger with the Democratic Party and ultimate defeat in 1896.[8]

If a rhetorician were to apply the sociological outline of Neil Smelzer to the Agrarian protest, he might draw a summary of conclusions of this nature:[9]

(1) The growing industrialism and correlative decline of agrarianism in American society in the period from 1870 to 1898 gave rise to a struggle for political domination in terms of economic interests that had sectional ramifications, pitting the agrarian West and South, with its large debtor class, against the industrial-financial East, with its centers of capital and money lending. Thus, American society in the last thirty years of the nineteenth century presented a "structural conduciveness" to the development of an agrarian protest movement.

(2) The increasing momentum in the voicing of farmers' grievances produced a "structural strain" in American society, arraigning farmer against industrialist, debtor against banker, homesteader against land speculator, railroad corporation against individual shipper, rustic against city slicker, the horny-handed tiller of the soil against the soft-living plutocrat, the producing masses against the idle rich.

(3) Speakers rallied the farmers and their sympathizers in reform conventions and protest meetings. Editors used the columns of farm journals and newspapers to energize the farmers' behavior at the polls. Together, speakers and writers were leading agents of communication in

fostering the "growth and spread of a generalized belief." This belief was not only that the farmers had just grievances, redressable in part at least, by legislative, judicial, and administrative action, but also the promotion of the quantitative monetary theory and the rejection of the intrinsic (metal) value theory. Underlying the whole philosophy of reformist western agrarians was a belief in the rectitude of genuine popular control of local institutions, including those of government.[10]

(4) Some of the "precipitating factors" were: the financial panics of 1873 and 1893, the increased production of farm crops made possible by the invention of new farm machinery, the dependence of the farmer on foreign markets for disposal of crop surpluses, the contrast between the low prices for farm products and the high prices for the supplies and machinery essential to the farmer, the contraction of the volume of currency in circulation in relation to population growth, the struggle for political control of legislatures, the concentration of corporate power and its influence on courts, legislatures, and regulatory commissions, and gradual disappearance of free and cheap lands in the West.

(5) Through political meetings "outside the gate" after Grange meetings, independent farmer parties, temporary fusion with major political parties, oratory of calamity howling, editorial pleas, reform speaking at conventions spurred by Grangers, Greenbackers, Alliance men, and Populists produced a "mobilization of participants for action."

(6) Divided and eccentric leadership (despite outstanding eloquence), the reluctance of American voters to support a third political party, sectionalism, the rising place of industrialism in American society, and the lack of a perception of a mutuality of interests by individualistic, capitalistic farmers and industrial workers employed by capitalists—all contributed to weaknesses in the "operation of a social control." To the degree that social control was operative, credit, in large measure, must be assigned the various organizations of farmers, who manifested an increasing resort to political action as a remedial instrument, culminating in the formation of the national People's Party in 1892 or perhaps in its fusion with the Democratic Party in 1896, though in suffering defeat with William Jennings Bryan the Populist Party lost and never recovered its identity.

ANTECEDENTS OF THE AGRARIAN REVOLT

Agriculture in the two decades preceding 1870 is not easily characterized, because it exhibited a variety of influences and effects. Even in an age that spoke of the dignity of honest toil the prosperity of the tiller of the soil was equated with status.

Among the hopeful developments was the use of new farm machinery, notably the McCormick reaper. Although Cyrus Hall McCormick first demonstrated his reaper in 1831 and patented it in 1834, it was not until 1847 that the Chicago factory was built. By 1851 McCormick's reaper was known in England and soon thereafter throughout Europe. The reaper and other new farm machinery contributed to that gradual mechanization of American agriculture, which was to produce crop surpluses and problems of glutted markets and low prices.

The interest in the advancement of agriculture and the farmer was reflected in the growth of agricultural societies and fairs. It has been estimated that perhaps 80 percent of the agricultural societies were formed after 1849.[11]

Under way was a series of events that was to become familiar: the abandonment of eastern farm land, the migration westward of the discontented, and the confrontation of the menace of the middleman and the mortgage holder. The spread of land-fever speculation was temporarily halted by the financial panic of 1857, but in the main Americans looked hopefully toward the West.

Though no section of the country was untouched socially and economically by the Civil War, all portions of the Union were not equally affected. Obviously, the South was most radically modified both during the war and in the Reconstruction period.

From 1857 to 1861 the North had been recovering from the panic of 1857 and, except for the darkening political cloud, appeared to be headed for a new era of prosperity. Better prices and ample labor stimulated farmers to produce more foodstuff and raw materials. On the negative side there were already mutterings against the railroads.[12]

When the war came, the need of armies for food increased the use of the mowing machine, the horse-drawn rake, and the reaper. The war resulted in the production of a surplus of wheat that was sent abroad to help maintain the credit of the United States.

One of the important effects of the war was to help give the railroads the upper hand. When the Northwest cast its lot with the Union, the Confederacy closed the Mississippi, and traffic had to be diverted to the railroads. The commanding position of the railroads enabled them to make freight charges that caused farmers to protest that transportation costs absorbed an undue portion of the fruits of their labor. "In no small degree did this extortion add to already existing dissatisfaction with the railroad treatment and precipitate the 'anti-monopoly' revolt which came at the close of the war as precursor to the Granger agitation and legislation of the early seventies."[13]

Not satisfied with the added tonnage and receipts brought by the closing of the Mississippi, the railroads throttled local river transportation by the temporary use of cut-rate charges to drive out competing local carriers. Another of the farmer's problems was the current rate of interest. In 1862 the interest on a $50 loan was 3 percent a month.[14]

Government and private interests joined in promoting the settlement of the West. The new homestead policy of the federal government added to the total available public lands open to settlement. In Minnesota, for example, in 1863 a total of 463,296 acres were taken up in some form; in 1864, 665,750 acres; in 1865, 804,982 acres. Though this rate of increase in the passing of public lands into private hands was not maintained after the war, the total was still significant, being slightly more in 1869 than in 1865. Poor harvests and postwar depression were among the factors that help explain the variations.

Another important influence on the agrarian West was immigration. For example, in Minnesota in 1860 those of foreign birth totaled only 58,728. In 1864 Minnesota passed legislation to "organize a system for the promotion of immigration to the state" in order to "offset the further drain which might result from the Civil War."[15] By 1870 Swedes, Norwegians, and Danes totaled 59,390, and Germans 48,457.

There was, then, a restless rural society composed of native and foreign-born elements who shared a common complaint against the railroads and the money lenders, enjoyed little social intercourse, struggled against the forces of nature, and yearned for a better life. It was to such a society that Oliver Hudson Kelley brought the Patrons of Husbandry, better known as the Grange.

THE GROWTH OF THE GRANGE

In 1866 Kelley, a clerk in the office of the Commissioner of Agriculture, was authorized to make a trip through the South to gather statistical and other information. The deplorable condition of the farmers, especially in the more isolated areas, so impressed Kelley that in 1867 he interested five other minor officials in Washington and one pomologist in establishing the National Grange of the Patrons of Husbandry.[16]

In its inception the Grange aimed to advance agriculture through education rather than legislation. Farm life was to be made more rewarding through knowledge of newer agricultural methods and opportunities for social intercourse to break the monotony of the isolated rural existence.

The growth of the Grange was slow until 1873, when the failure of Jay Cooke & Company touched off a financial panic and depression. Three days after Cooke's collapse, "the New York Stock Exchange took the unprecedented step of closing its doors." Before long the panic became a depression marked by smokeless industrial plants, halted railway construction, bread lines in the cities, and swarms of tramps in rural areas.[17]

The panic struck the farmers with special severity. At best the farmers' margin of profit was low. Having mortgaged their crops to buy farm machinery and other supplies, farmers were at the mercy of their creditors, who were in a position to dictate prices at forced sales.[18] The panic struck in mid-August, 1873. By September 18 the price of wheat fell from one dollar to eighty cents a bushel. Moving farther west along the frontier was already proving an illusory solution. It did not enable the farmers to gain control of their production and transportation costs.

Spurred by economic distress and encouraged by energetic organizers, farmers flocked to the Grange. "By the end of 1873, the Grange had penetrated all but four states—Connecticut, Rhode Island, Delaware, and Nevada—and there were thirty-two state Granges in existence."[19] From the spring of 1873 to the spring of 1874 the number of local Granges increased fourfold, the chief increase occurring in the Middle West.

THE POLITICAL PHASE OF THE GRANGER MOVEMENT

Although the Grange purported to be a nonpartisan and nonpolitical organization, its members were urged to do their political duties as private citizens. Feeling the need for political action, farmers formed independent organizations, as in Illinois and Kansas. Where the Grange had the field virtually to itself, as in Iowa and Minnesota, it simply held unofficial political meetings of Grange members, such meetings being called "outside the gate." At such meetings the tendency developed to adopt resolutions, nominate candidates, and plan county, district, and state conventions.[20]

As professional politicians were disinclined to advocate new and radical proposals that might sweep across party lines and disrupt the established parties, new parties arose in eleven western states in 1873 and 1874:

Known variously as Independent, Reform, Anti-Monopoly, or Farmers' parties, these organizations were all parts of the same general movement, and their platforms were quite similar. The paramount demands were: first, the subjection of corporations, and especially railroad corporations, to the control of the state; and second, reform and economy in government.[21]

THE RHETORIC OF GRANGERISM

The general political aim of the Granger movement was to reduce farmers' cost of supplies and transportation. Its rhetoric was a recitation of alleged wrongs, often set forth in statistics and examples and a demand that the injustices be eradicated.

Facts for the Granges, a pamphlet composed of extracts from the speeches of Ignatius Donnelly, the Lecturer of the Minnesota State Grange, typified this rhetoric. It cited census data that dramatically portrayed the decline in the value of farm lands:

The farms of the United States, during the past twenty years, have increased in value as follows. From 1850 to 1860, one hundred and four per cent. From 1860 to 1870, five per cent. Think of it! New states and new territories have been added to the Union, and yet the increase in the value of farms has been since 1860 but five per cent.[22]

The foregoing was an indication of general economic distress. Specific wrongs included "robbery under the patent laws," which, it was claimed, permitted the charging of excessive prices.

A sewing machine costs for the work and materials twelve dollars. We pay seventy dollars for it. The same machines are exported to Europe and sold for thirty-two dollars, after paying freight across the Atlantic. I found in the *Belfast News* of December 4, 1872, the advertisement of the Singer Sewing Machine for six pounds and ten shillings—about thirty-two dollars and fifty cents of our money.

We pay the difference of nearly forty dollars under our patent laws, for being *the most patient and gullible fools that ever pretended to a capacity for self-government.*[23]

Continuing the recitation of examples, Donnelly cited evidence given in a recent lawsuit, that the McCormick reaper costs $50 to manufacture and sells for nearly $200, that, moreover, the threshing machine that costs $150 to make sells for $750. Donnelly's proposed remedy was legislation to limit the inventor's profit under the patent laws.

The next evil in his catalog of abuses was the high cost of the transportation of farmers' products.

It costs twenty-five cents to carry a bushel of wheat from any inland town in Minnesota to Milwaukee, say two-hundred and fifty miles. It costs the same to carry a bushel of wheat from Milwaukee to Liverpool—3,000 miles *and the cost of transportation the same!*[24]

Charging that transportation costs eat up an unfair share of the price for corn, the Lecturer of the Minnesota Grange said:

In New York in April last there were 4,700,000 bushels of Indian corn. It was worth at the market rates in New York $1,620,000. Now how was it divided? The men that raised the corn got $540,000. The men that carried the corn got $1,080,000.

Yet there were 5,525,000 persons engaged in agriculture in the United States, and only 200,000 engaged in railroading. But the 200,000 got two dollars where the five million got one dollar.[25]

To farmers the remedy seemed obvious—regulating railroad freight rates and providing cheap water transportation. Although farmers usually favored economy in government (presumably to be attained by eradicating corruption), they considered the expenditure of public funds to improve rivers and harbors a legitimate function of government. Farmers urged Congress to repeal duties on materials used to construct steamships and sailing vessels "necessary to cheap freights."[26]

In this period when farmers sought relief through measures designed to lower their costs, the protective tariff was a favorite target. In *Facts for the Granges* it was called "the master thief of all," a system that encouraged certain pursuits by means of "bounties paid to them out of the pockets of the people." Among examples of exorbitant rates cited were: "Hosiery, 96 per cent, nearly double; Blankets, 106 per cent, more than double; Flannels, 113 per cent, that is for $100 worth of flannels you pay $213!!!"[27] Twenty articles in daily use by farmers were shown to have an average tariff rate of 70 percent. Again there was the apparently obvious remedy: the tariff should be lowered.

The Granger program also recommended co-operative buying by farmers in an effort to bring down the prices of their supplies. As events turned out, co-operatives often suffered from inadequate capital and were torn by the demands of manufacturers for prompt payment and of farmers for convenient, long-term credit. Typically farmers needed to borrow money before the planting season and to repay the loan after the crop was harvested and sold. Farmer co-operatives, on the other hand, often were confronted with the manufacturer's and the supplier's demand for payment for machinery and supplies before the farmer could pay the co-operative for the credit the latter had extended.

In the Granger movement the disappointment and disillusionment with other efforts to remedy the economic ills of farmers caused them to resort increasingly to political measures. Ignatius Donnelly thus capsulated a review of the experience of the Grange in a speech at Herman, Minnesota, in 1886: "The old Grange in Minnesota refused to have anything to do with politics; it emasculated itself; it reduced itself to the level of LeDuc's stock farm, which, it was said, consisted of a steer, a gelding, and an Angora goat."[28]

As might be expected, Illinois, the first state in which farmers became well organized in clubs and Granges, pioneered in effective political action. The influence of agricultural interests appeared in the new Illinois constitution of 1870. Specifically it reflected the agitation for the regulation of railroads—an agitation that had been mounting in the 1860s. So strong was the influence of Illinois farmers that they were able to place in this constitution mandatory directions to the state legislature "to pass laws to prevent extortion and unjust discrimination" in railroad rates.[29] In an attempt to implement this constitutional provision the Illinois legislature in 1871 enacted a law prohibiting not only unjust discrimination in railway charges but also all discrimination in railroad rates. Because of the latter sweeping prohibition Chief Justice Lawrence of the Illinois Supreme Court in January, 1873, handed down a ruling that the law of 1871 was unconstitutional.[30] This decision served to encourage the farmers to even more intense political action. They flocked to a protest convention in Springfield on April 2, 1873, and so frightened the legislators that they passed even more stringent laws to regulate railroads.[31] But the farmers' protest had not run its course. In the judicial elections of June, 1873, they not only retired from office Chief Justice Lawrence, who had ruled against them as they interpreted his decision, but also elected their own candidates to fill the two vacancies in the Supreme Court and many of the vacancies in the circuit courts.

This successful action was followed by a strenuous campaign to elect farmers' candidates in the county elections in the fall of 1873. So many farmer-inspired political meetings were held on Independence Day, 1873, that it was called "the Farmers' Fourth of July." A specimen of the more impassioned ceremonial rhetoric Grangerism is afforded by the speaking on that occasion. The usual brand of spread-eagle oratory declaimed on the Fourth of July was supplanted by "impassioned denunciation of corporations." Instead of the customary reading of the American Declaration of Independence, a document modeled after it was recited with vehemence.[32] Besides the obvious fact that the occasion suggested the appropriateness of using such a document it provides a clue to the basic ideology of the Agragrian protest from the Granger period to the reform conventions of 1891 and 1892 culminating in the formation of a National People's (Populist) Party. This ideology embraced the doctrine of natural rights expressed by Thomas Jefferson, himself an agrarian, but it was the officers of corporations, bankers, and the plutocrats generally who were violating the rights of man. In his book *The American People's Money* Ignatius Donnelly includes a graphic illustration of the hog "Plutocracy" uprooting the bricks in the wall of "The Rights of Man."[33] The Farmers' Declaration of Independence began with an adaptation of the familiar words of the American Declaration of Independence to the farmers' complaints:

When in the course of human events, it becomes necessary for a class of people, suffering from long continued systems of oppression and abuse, to rouse themselves from an apathetic indifference to their own interests, which has become habitual . . . a decent respect for the opinions of mankind requires that they should declare the causes that impel them to a course so necessary to their own protection.[34]

This was followed by "a statement of 'self-evident truths,' a catalogue of the sins of the railroads, a denunciation of railroads and Congress for not having redressed these wrongs, and finally this conclusion":[35]

We, therefore, the producers of the state in our several counties assembled . . . do solemnly declare that we will use all lawful and peaceful means to free ourselves from the tyranny of monopoly, and that we will never cease our efforts for reform until every department of our government gives token that the reign of licentious extravagance is over, and something of the purity, honesty, and frugality with which our fathers inaugurated it, has taken its place.

That to this end we hereby declare ourselves absolutely free and independent of all past political connections, and that we will give our suffrage only to such men for office, as we have good reason to believe will use their best endeavors to the promotion of these ends; and for the support of this declaration, with a firm reliance on divine Providence, we mutually pledge to each other our lives, our fortunes, and our sacred honor.[36]

The rhetoric of this early phase of the Agrarian crusade was a catalog of complaints and a demand for state regulation of the abuses wrought by concentrated corporate power. In this demand for government regulation farmers revealed an ideological schizophrenia: They insisted that the economic power of the corporations was a public menace, but they were reluctant to grant government the extensive, positive power requisite to effective regulation. They were inheritors of the Jeffersonian agrarian view "that government is best which governs least," and thus, their advocacy fell short of the concept of government as an affirmative, dynamic agency of public welfare. At best government was an umpire among the contending interests in American society. Farmers' traditional individualism, accented by their relatively isolated rural existence, lessened their ardor for organization whenever crops and prices took an upward turn.

This is not to say that the leading ideas of the Agrarian protest did not evolve and expand during the subsequent Greenback and Populist phases. Indeed, one can find in the minutes of the Gove County, Kansas, Farmers' Alliance an indication that certain Kansas agrarians wished to be identified with the working class;[37] but one hesitates to generalize such data as characteristic of the rank-and-file members of the Populist movement across the West and South. Farmers tended to be political pragmatists, who regarded themselves as included in the Bryanite definition of a businessman, and were reluctant to support any third party, let alone one that would merge industrial workers and farmer-businessmen. The editorial expressions and private correspondence of advanced thinkers such as Henry Demarest Lloyd and Ignatius Donnelly, provides evidence that some Populist leaders endorsed a broadly based, somewhat socialistic reform of society and blamed labor leaders for opposing a genuine union of farmers and industrial workers in a People's Party.[38] How representative such views were and why Donnelly's utterances on the stump to farmer audiences failed to stress a grand coalition of farmers and industrial workers is open to debate.[39] Whether the objection to a united movement of farmers and industrial employees arose among labor leaders or individualistic farmer entrepreneurs, it existed in practice as an obstacle to the success of any attempt to effect unification. Despite his eloquence and ability as a stump speaker—qualities readily testified to by friends and foes—Ignatius Donnelly, while regarded as "The Sage" by his neighbors, was considered an idiosyncratic, unrealistic, eccentric tilter at windmills by most of the general public. A Minneapolis *Journal* cartoon of February 24, 1891, pictured Donnelly as "The Minnesota Don Quixote."[40] Admittedly the *Journal* was a hostile newspaper, but so were most of the major newspapers. The public found Donnelly interesting and entertaining, but aside from local elections to the state legislature the voters failed to give him a majority in any of his many campaigns from 1879 to 1900. To quote only Donnelly's editorial comment and private correspondence, revealing as it is about Donnelly, does not typify the rhetoric of the Agrarian protest. Even in the preface of *Caesar's Column*, Donnelly's pessimistic novel of the prophetic school, he writes of his work "as an instrumentality of good for mankind," expressing the hope that it will "arrest the moving evil"[41] and implying that the novel's way out—a retreat to a semi-socialist utopia in Africa—is to be resorted to if humanitarian reform cannot overcome the evils of plutocratic dominance. Any socialistic proposal ultimately advanced by the Populist Party in 1892, such as government ownership of railroads and telegraph lines, was proposed as a last resort. Agrarians feared big, centralized government. As Professor Ray A. Billington observed, westerners strongly supported popular sovereignty. "They wanted to control their local institutions. This was part of the whole democratic philosophy of the frontier."[42]

Discontent of Grangers was expressed with increasing intensity from 1870 to 1875 and focused on the issue of tariff reform, anti-monopolism, and monetary reform.[43] Grangers proposed somewhat simplistic remedies: lower tariff rates, state regulation of railroads and grain elevators, and an increase in the supply of money in circulation but without causing inflation. The inflationary approach was to come in the second phase of the Agrarian protest: the turning to Greenbackism.

RESULTS OF THE GRANGER MOVEMENT

In the fall campaign of 1873 the agrarian reformers in Illinois succeeded in shattering old party lines and attaining victory in fifty-three of the sixty-six counties where they contested. Though triumphant in the campaign for local offices, the Anti-Monopoly Party was less successful in the contests for state offices.

Most of the third parties of the states of the Middle West had a somewhat spontaneous birth but a short life. They were "heirs of the Liberal Republicans [of 1872] and the precursors of the Greenbackers and Populists . . ."[44] Their most notable legislative achievement was the enactment in five states of laws to regulate railroads. After the passage of these laws the third parties petered out. By 1876 they had disappeared or merged with the Greenbackers.

With the exception of Ignatius Donnelly in Minnesota third-party leaders ceased to be prominent in agrarian-reform movements. For the most part they were successful farmers who had served a term or two in state legislatures. Representative leaders were Willard C. Flagg, president of the Illinois State Farmers Association; Jacob G. Veale, candidate for governor in Iowa; and William R. Taylor, the Granger governor of Wisconsin.

Even Taylor, described by Solon Buck as "typical of the picturesque and forceful figures frontier life so often developed," upon "his defeat for re-election in 1875 returned to his farm and obscurity." Once Governor Taylor had celebrated "a favorable court decision in one of the Granger cases with a salvo of artillery from the capitol," much to the consternation of conventional citizens. Yet even this colorful Granger leader had only a moment on the political stage.

The central political objective of Grangerism in the early 1870s was to place a legislative curb on corporations, particularly railroads, banks, manufacturers of farm machinery, and milling interests. Its economic goal was reduction of the farmer's cost of doing business. To accomplish this the farm organizations and anti-monopoly parties sought state regulation of transportation rates, limitation of interest rates, lower tariff rates, and anti-monopoly protection against allegedly fraudulent and arbitrary practices of the "millers' ring."

Perhaps the most constructive feature of the Granger economic program was the establishment of co-operatives. The capital for these ventures came from the sale of stock to Grange members, who then had the privilege of purchasing goods from co-operative stores at very low prices. Though many of these co-operative stores ultimately failed, many Grangers gained business experience of value in the operation of later farmer co-operatives. Nor were all of the failures attributable to lack of business experience. Often a failure resulted from rival business interests combining to lower prices to a disastrous level in the process of freezing out competition. When a rival store sold below the prices of the co-operative, the members seldom had that degree of organizational loyalty which could resist the lure of lower prices.

Co-operative creameries and elevators fared better than the co-operative stores. In several states they "saved Grange members thousands of dollars." Sometimes the state Grange avoided the financial risk involved in setting up a co-operative enterprise by designating certain firms as Grange agencies and advising the Patrons of Husbandry to sell their products through these agencies. In return for this channeling of Granger business the designated firms gave members of the Grange a favorable marketing arrangement.

In economic experimentation at least the National Grange tended to move more slowly than did the state Granges. By 1876, however, the National Grange sponsored a system of co-operative stores modeled after the English "Rochdale plan." "The stock of these stores was sold only to [Grange members] at five dollars a share and in limited amounts," to encourage widespread ownership. Unlike some of the earlier Grange co-operative ventures, these stores sold at the ordinary prices, paid a small dividend on the stock, and "annually divided the profits among the purchasers according to the amounts purchased." In the East and South sufficient success with this plan demonstrated the wisdom of the National Grange's recommendation. In the Middle West, where experiments by local and state Granges had bred disillusionment about co-operative stores, the plan was not widely adopted.

With respect to co-operative manufacturing the plan of the National Grange proved much less satisfactory. Though the Granger oratory deplored the great power of the manufacturers, the Grange officers underestimated that power when they launched Grange-financed factories to make farm implements. Perhaps the National Grange was misled by the apparent success of Iowa's state Grange. First, the Iowans succeeded in persuading a manufacturer of plows to give a discount to Grangers. Then, when the manufacturers of harvesters refused to sell at wholesale prices to the Iowa Grange, it bought a patent for a harvester and in 1874 manufactured 250 of these machines.

Apparently taking the Iowa experience as proof positive of the success of Grange manufacturing and aroused by what it considered to be the tyranny of monopoly, the National Grange decided to use its accumulated fees, amounting to $250,000, as capital for the manufacture of farm implements. These implements were to be sold to Grange members at very low prices. In pursuit of this objective Grange agents "traveled over the country, buying up patents for farm machinery, but not always investigating the validity of the patents." They planned to establish factories in seven states: Illinois, Indiana, Iowa, Kansas, Kentucky, Missouri, and Wisconsin. They hoped to make all kinds of farm implements including harvesters, plows, wagons, threshing-machines, and even sewing-machines.[45] But these hopes were soon crushed on the rocks of financial failure. When the Iowa harvester factory failed in 1875 it dragged the state Grange of Iowa into bankruptcy. The Grange was inundated by suits over the alleged infringement of patent rights and many local Granges, fearful that they would be held responsible for debts incurred by the state Grange, disbanded. The Northwest, formerly a stronghold of the Grange, saw the order almost vanish.

The rhetoric of Grangerism from 1870 to 1876 arose from genuine economic distress, but it presented an oversimplification of a complex politico-socio-economic situation. It railed against the villainous corporations, alleging that they conspired against the interests of the plain people of the farms. Such remedies as it proposed, with the exception of the ill-fated co-operatives, were largely restrictive. They demonstrated that "calamity howling" alone does not produce constructive programs. Ideationally the agrarians did not plow deep.

On the positive side the era opened the eyes of some farmers not only to the growing power of finance capitalism but also to the possibility that the services of the manufacturer and the middleman are essential to all segments of the economy, not excepting agriculture. Though antagonism between the agricultural and industrial classes did not die, a new respect for one another emerged.

In the long run perhaps the most significant result of the early Granger movement was the social and intellectual stimulus the farmers received. Into the dull, dreary farm life of the 1870s "the Grange came as a liberalizing and uplifting influence." With its agricultural journals, picnics, ritualistic meetings, political gatherings and campaigns, and its admission of women into the order it became a "community servant and gave both men and women a new sense of the dignity of woman." In many communities the coming of the Grange brought an improvement in dress and manners, a note of cheer and hope, and a greater interest in reading and self-improvement.[46]

The limitations of the rhetoric of Grangerism were the limitations of the audience to whom it was addressed—an audience circumscribed by meager opportunity for intellectual and social intercourse in the rural America of the 1870s. At a time when the transportation industry in particular was becoming increasingly interstate in character, the farmers tended to advocate state regulation.

Yet, out of a struggle often viewed in simplistic terms as a sectional contest between the agrarian West and South and the industrial East, there emerged legislative and judicial concepts that helped provide a rationale for the more far-reaching reforms of the late nineteenth and early twentieth century. Not only was the right of government regulation of private business established, but the public interest in the use of private property was defined. In upholding the constitutionality of an Illinois law regulating the charges of grain elevators Chief Justice Morison R. Waite of the Supreme Court enunciated the now famous doctrine that private property when used in a manner that affects the community at large ceases to be *juris privati* only and becomes clothed in a public interest and therefore "must submit to be controlled by the public for the common good. . . ."[47]

THE FARMER TURNS TO GREENBACKISM

Despite his occasional victories in the legislatures and the courts the farmer continued to experience hard times. Having failed to increase his margin of profit through legislative measures designed to reduce the cost of his transportation and supplies, he was ready to turn to a new remedy. If he could not reduce his costs, why not increase the prices of his products? Greenbackism appeared to be the means to this end. In brief, in the late seventies, the farmer turned to currency inflation as the panacea for his economic ills.

In its inception Greenbackism was neither agrarian nor western. Laboring men in the East were the first to engage in organized political activity in behalf of Greenbackism. Indeed, the anti-monopoly parties of the Granger era were generally opposed to inflation. In 1873 Ignatius Donnelly, in a pamphlet of the Minnesota State Grange, which reported excerpts from speeches of its state Lecturer, declared that the farmers had no interest in an inflated money market, going so far as to say: "There is too much paper money. The currency is diluted—watered—weakened . . ."[48] Analyzing the impact of monetary policy on the price of wheat, he argued:

As we have to sell at the world's price, it is our interest that everything we buy should be at the world's price. Specie payments would practically add eighteen cents to the price of every bushel of wheat we have to sell.[49]

As early as 1874, however, the Greenbackers obtained control of the independent agrarian parties in Illinois and Indiana. In response to the call of the Indiana party a conference was held in Indianapolis in November, 1874. It initiated a series of conventions in 1875 and 1876. These culminated in the organization of the National Greenback Party and the launching of a national ticket in the 1876 presidential campaign.[50]

The Greenback Party faced the usual dilemma of new third parties in the United States (except in instances when the new party is the personal extension of a prominent political leader—for example, Theodore Roosevelt's Progressive [Bull Moose] Party of 1912): the choosing of a presidential nominee identified with the actual views of the movement and who at the same time bore a national reputation in order to attract widespread voter support. In 1876 the Greenback Party finally persuaded Peter Cooper, the octogenarian philanthropist and founder of Cooper's Union in New York, to be its presidential nominee. Of course the eighty-five year old Cooper could hardly be expected to conduct a whirlwind campaign. As a matter of fact, the entire speaking burden of the national ticket fell to General Samuel F. Cary, the Greenback Party's vice-presidential nominee, one of the proponents of the "Ohio idea"—that is, that paper money fluctuates in value less than coin and that the volume of currency should be "equal to the demands of business."[51]

If the number of votes received provided the criterion, neither the presidential election year of 1876 nor that of 1880 marked the height of the Greenback movement. In 1876 the Greenback Party polled only about 80,000 votes; in 1880, with General James B. Weaver of Iowa as the Greenback nominee the party received only 308,578 votes in the nation. In the midterm elections of 1878, however, various local and state Greenback candidates garnered about a million votes.[52]

The objectives of the Greenback movement were clearly outlined in the platforms and pronouncements of what came to be officially named the National and then the Independent Greenback Party but popularly called merely the Greenback Party. As in the case of the Granger movement there was a list of wrongs and a series of demands for remedial action. The wrongs included the limiting of the legal tender quality of greenbacks, the changing of currency bonds into coin bonds, the demonetization of the silver dollar, the exempting of government bonds from taxation, the contraction of the circulating medium of exchange (currency), the proposed forced resumption of specie payments, and the waste of public lands.

The demands encompassed the exclusive coinage and creation of money by the federal government accompanied by the suppression of all bank issues of money; the payment of all official salaries, pensions, bonds, and all other debts in legal tender money according to the laws under which the obligations were contracted; the coinage of silver on the same footing as that of gold (not an initial position of the Greenbackers but one at which they eventually arrived); congressional enactment to fix a minimum amount of money per capita; the taxation of government bonds; a graduated income tax; the donation of public lands to actual settlers but prohibiting the sale of public lands to speculators and the grant of public lands to railroads; government encouragement of industry, agriculture, and mining to provide opportunities for employment; rigid economy in every branch of public service; reduction of the hours of the workday; harmonization of the differences in regard to tariff and federal taxation; reduction and equalization of the cost of land and water transportation; combating the system in which a few had overgrown fortunes and many experienced extreme poverty; prohibition of the contract system of prison labor; and legislation to prohibit the importation of cheap Chinese labor.[53]

In brief, the rhetoric of Greenbackism resembled that of Grangerism in reciting a catalogue of complaints derived from genuine economic distress suffered by the farmers and other members of the debtor class. The rhetoric of these two early phases of the Agrarian protest contained what may be said to have been a rather simplistic set of remedial demands, perhaps not always realistic nor wholly consistent. Greenback rhetoric did not give adequate logical consideration to the fact that inflation would raise the prices not merely of the crops the farmer had to sell but also of everything he had to buy.

The rhetoric of Greenbackism differed from that of Grangerism in its designation of the primary villains and also in its more virulent attack upon the politico-economic system as such. In the Greenback rhetoric the honest yeoman and laborer were the victims of a corrupt and inequitable system in which the tentacles of finance capitalism held a strangle hold on politics. Although in voter support Greenbackism gained most of its strength in the agrarian West and South, its rhetoric aimed at the whole debtor class and toward the union of industrial workers and farmers against "the money power," "the moneyed oligarchy," or "bonded aristocracy."[54]

There is some hazard in taking as the view of the rank-and-file of a movement the remarks of a leader, even a keynote address at an official party convention. This is illustrated by the ringing reform rhetoric of Ignatius Donnelly at the Greenback nominating convention at Indianapolis, May 17, 1876. To the assembled 240 delegates from eighteen states Donnelly revealed that he envisioned a party not merely to reform the currency but also to carry the banner for every reform designed to improve the condition of toilers in all sections of the country. In the vigorous style and spirit of the egalitarian rhetoric of his day Donnelly hailed the new party as one "in whose judgment and in whose heart the poorest man who toils in the mines of Pennsylvania or the mills of New England will outweigh in consequence and importance Jay Gould or Cornelius Vanderbilt." Continuing in this vein, the temporary chairman of the Greenback convention declared: "This is a people's country, and we need a people's party. I much mistake the signs of the times if we have not formed it here today."[55] Yet it was not until 1892 that the Northern Alliance and the Southern Alliance, aided and abetted by such reform organizations as the Wheel (which eventually merged with the Alliance), the Knights of Labor, the National Citizens Industrial Alliance, and the National Colored Alliance and Cooperative Union, were able to form a national People's Party capable of gaining twenty-two electoral college votes.[56]

A specific goal of the Greenback Party in the 1870s was repeal of the specie-resumption act. This law, enacted by Congress in January, 1875, designated January 1, 1879, as the date for the government's "redemption of greenbacks at their face value in coin."[57] The fact that this law provided for the "permanent retirement" from circulation "of only a part of the greenbacks"[58] did not deter the Greenbackers from denouncing it as a "suicidal and destructive policy of contraction."

Some indication that the agrarian movement, considered over the long range from 1870 to 1896, failed to advocate a consistent monetary policy is found in another plank in the platform of the 1876 convention of the Independent Party. Although the agrarians were to espouse "free silver" in the 1890s, and, indeed, in 1896 to fuse with the Democrats in support of William Jennings Bryan's advocacy of the free and unlimited coinage of silver at the ratio of sixteen ounces of silver to one of gold, in 1876 they protested against "the sale of bonds for the purpose of purchasing silver to be substituted for the fractional [greenback] currency of [civil] war times . . . [because such a measure] will still further oppress, in taxation, an already overburdened people."

The Greenback movement drew the support of such local and regional reform papers as James Buchanan's *Indianapolis Sun*; Ignatius Donnelly's *Anti-Monopolist* of St. Paul; the *Liberal Reformer* of Morris, Illinois; the *Industrial Press* of Galena, Illinois; the *New Era* of Woodstock, Illinois; the

Independent of Kewanee, Illinois; the *Independent Reformer* of Springfield, Illinois; the *Industrial Age* of Chicago; and the *Standard of Reform* of Lawrence, Kansas.[59] But perhaps the most effective propaganda agencies of the 1876 campaign at least were the Greenback clubs organized by Marcus "Brick" Pomeroy, the editor of *The Great Campaign*, a Greenback paper in Chicago. Pomeroy announced in the first issue of his paper that it would be published every Tuesday from July 18 to November 14, 1876. Under its masthead it carried this statement: "Every Reform Must Begin With the People and Be Won By Agitation and Brave, Patient, Earnest Work."[60]

Attacking the Republican platform pronouncements of 1876, Pomeroy declared:

They give covert sanction to the establishment in our land of a rapacious and unscrupulous money oligarchy whose interests would be subserved by the destruction of our Republic, and in opposition to whose interests we have abundantly seen that neither men, nor States, nor conventions of States can stand valiant and successful battle.[61]

In the Granger period the railroads, manufacturers, and millers were the villains, aided and abetted by the bankers. In the Greenback period more of the rhetorical fire was aimed at the evil force behind the scenes—the "rapacious and unscrupulous money oligarchy."

Farmers were plagued by narrow margins of profit, debts, grasshoppers, and bankruptcies. It is not surprising, therefore, that the bitterness of farmers and laborers often produced a strident note in the Greenback rhetoric. This is illustrated by the following plaintive, graphic passage:

There are two parties in power.
The Republican that holds the head, and the Democratic that holds the tail of the anaconda that is crushing the life out of labor and blighting every industry of the land. The one machine cuts down the farmers' grain; the other is threshing, bagging and carrying it to a foreign market, while the farmer's wife rubs cream on his aching back to heal the scratches made by barley beards and the blisters drawn by the hot sun.[62]

There was no lack of evidence to justify the bemoaning of the increase in bankruptcies. From 1870 to 1875 the number of bankruptcies rose from 3,546 to 7,740, and the amount involved in such failures increased from $88,242,000 to $201,000,000.[63]

With Peter Cooper as the silent octogenarian presidential nominee, General Samuel F. Cary, the nominee for vice-president, and local leaders shouldered the burden of Greenback campaign oratory. The paucity of noteworthy addresses may be indicated by the fact that *The Great Campaign* had to resort to publishing more than once the same speech of General Cary's. Aside from minor adaptations to the occasion this speech was given in Chicago, Indianapolis, and, no doubt, elsewhere. Modern critics might be more impressed by its stress on hard times than by its analysis of causation and remedy. Illustrative of its oversimplification of such analysis was Cary's assertion that "there are two theories about labor. One is dear money and cheap labor, the other is cheap money and dear labor."[64]

On another occasion, speaking to unemployed workingmen in Cincinnati, General Cary remarked with respect to the pressing immediate need of his audience:

I did not come here to propose anything, for the reason that I don't know what to propose to give relief to the starving laborers and their families. If I knew a remedy, I would proclaim it.[65]

Despite the lack of a viable program there were sufficient signs of defection from the old parties' approach to alarm their political leaders, particularly in Illinois and Indiana. Republican orators "waved the bloody shirt" as they verbally refought the Civil War and attempted to ingratiate themselves with the farmers. Although Colonel Robert G. Ingersoll addressed large audiences of farmers in southern Illinois, he often found his effort to identify himself with disgruntled farmers something less than an oratorical triumph. A Greenback paper offered this account of Ingersoll's attempt:

"Yes, gentlemen, I tilled the soil in my youth. Indeed I may say that I was raised between rows of corn in the cornfield." Here a worked up Granger shouted: "A pumpkin, by Jupiter, a pumpkin." The Colonel was fairly overcome and it was some five minutes before he could recover himself and proceed.[66]

Many cross-currents of strong feeling punctuated the presidential campaign of 1876. For the first time since the Civil War the Democratic Party could envision the prospect of national success. Interest in Greenbackism was stimulated by dissatisfaction with hard times for farmers and laborers, resentment over Reconstruction, and disappointment with the national Democratic platform's failure to endorse a strong monetary reform. The Hon. George W. Hauk, a delegate to the Democratic convention, bolted the Tilden ticket and in a speech at the Court House in Dayton, Ohio, declared:

Gentlemen, the repeal of the dollar coinage law was a conspiracy and fraud upon the American people. It was effected in the interests and at the instance of the gold ring and of the holders of the bonded debt of the United States.[67]

In naming the enemy Greenback rhetoricians used not only such terms as the "gold ring," the "money oligarchy," and the "bonded aristocracy," but also the "Jew capitalists." To the charge that his columns were anti-Semitic, editor "Brick" Pomeroy offered this disclaimer and explanation:

We use the term Jew capitalist because the great capitalists of the world happen to be Jews. . . . If these hoarders and lenders of money were Turks, we should call them Turkish capitalists. If they were Chinese, we would call them Celestial capitalists. . . . We have yet to learn that the lending of money has anything to do with religion.[68]

Today's critics might or might not be satisfied with this explanation. It is recorded here as *The Great Campaign's* effort to absolve itself of the charge of anti-Semitism.

It was obvious to even the most ardent Greenbackers that their party had no chance for national victory in 1876. To those negativists one member nevertheless responded positively at a meeting in Joliet, Illinois, on August 30, 1876:

I say to such men and all men who are in the Greenback party and believe in the people's money, that I shall vote for Mr. Cooper, even though I knew that my vote would be the only one cast for him in the entire United States. I would rather vote that one vote, knowing and feeling that I voted as my conscience dictated, than to know that my vote elected the winning candidate, whom I disapproved of.[69]

In the light of William Jennings Bryan's "cross of gold" metaphor in the peroration of his famous speech in the Democratic convention of 1896 it may be of passing interest that the August 29, 1876 issue of *The Great Campaign* featured a cartoon bearing the caption "The Modern Crucifixion" and picturing the overburdened plowholder on a cross made of a plow and being jabbed with spears by the "Bonded Aristocracy" created by the Republican Party. In 1894 the Vox Populi Company of St. Louis copyrighted a cartoon showing Uncle Sam wearing a hat which was really a crown of thorns. The crucifixion of the farmer might be called a major or generative metaphor of the Agrarian protest.

Although a significant element in the agrarian movement was attracted to Greenbackism in 1876, casting more than 6,000 votes in each of five western states—Illinois, Indiana, Iowa, Kansas, and Michigan—the party's entire vote in the country was only 81,737, or less than 1 percent of the total. In the East only Pennsylvania gave the new party any encouragement.

Greenbackism, whose theoretical seeds had been cast upon the winds of public opinion in the Civil War period by relatively obscure New York writers—Edward Kellogg[70] and Eleazar Lord[71]—had begun as a labor cause and evolved into a western agrarian movement.

Perhaps its most substantial achievement in 1876 was the gaining of a balance of power in the Illinois legislature, thus assuring the election of David Davis to the United States Senate.[72] It is perhaps one of the ironies of history that the decisive votes of the Illinois independents that sent Davis to the Senate kept him from serving on the electoral commission and thus prevented Samuel J. Tilden, the Democrat, from becoming President instead of Rutherford B. Hayes, the Republican. The irony lies partly in the fact that where the agrarian Greenbackers in the North tended to fuse with one of the major parties, it was usually the Democratic Party. The ironic situation lay also in the fact that the Northern Republican Party was the chief political target of Greenback propaganda. In the South the Greenbackers usually fused with the party opposed to the establishment, often the weaker Republican Party.

On the whole the election revealed that in 1876 only a small fraction of the farmers of the nation deserted the old parties to cast ballots as Greenbackers. The farmers' primary concern for immediate, tangible problems rather than monetary theory was typified by the theme of a conference held in Omaha near election time and attended by the governors of Minnesota, Iowa, Missouri, Kansas, Dakota, and Nebraska—namely, "practical means based upon experience in the destruction of grasshoppers," including a recommendation that state legislatures offer "a bounty per bushel for the collection and destruction of eggs and unfledged insects."[73]

GREENBACKER ACTIVITIES OF 1877 AND 1878

During the turbulent year of 1877 the Greenback movement surged upward and in 1878 reached its peak. The year of 1877 marked the beginning of a long and bitter industrial conflict. It was precipitated by the unilateral announcement of a 10 percent wage cut for the workers on four eastern trunk-railway lines. Although inadequately organized, the railroad workers, supported by an army of the hungry unemployed, struck. So great was the disturbance that it was denounced by capitalists as a rebellion. The militia was employed freely to suppress the strike. During one week in July traffic on the eastern trunk lines was completely suspended, and it was partly paralyzed elsewhere in the country. In Buffalo, Baltimore, Pittsburgh, Martinsburg, Chicago, San Francisco, and elsewhere pitched battles between the militia and the mob occurred. Only the intervention of federal troops restored order.[74]

Farmers likewise were feeling the pinch of depression. The dollar appreciated in value approximately 148 percent from 1865 to 1878.[75] Greenbackers pointed to the fact that the United States had nearly two billion dollars in circulation at the close of the Civil War, but that the volume of currency had not only failed to keep pace with the increase in population but that the number of dollars in circulation had actually declined. They contended that the overworking of each dollar had given it a fictitious value. The average price of a bushel of wheat in 1866 was $1.52; in 1870, 94 cents; and in 1878, 78 cents. Similarly, the price of a bushel of corn declined from 47 cents in 1866 to 32 cents in 1878. Cotton brought an average price per bale of $97.54 in 1866, $67.25 in 1870 and only $41.40 in 1878.[76]

In attributing the decline in the prices of farm products to an inadequate volume of money in circulation, the currency reformers appear not to have given sufficient consideration to the increase in crop acreage and production. The increase in acreage from 1866 to 1880 was 146 percent in wheat, 81 percent in corn, and 94 percent in cotton. The increase in production, though somewhat less steady as a result of grasshopper plagues and other caprices of nature, was on the whole even greater than the increase in crop acreage. From 1866 to 1880 wheat production increased 221 percent, corn production 98 percent, and cotton production 172 percent.[77]

Be that as it may, the farmer and the industrial worker were suffering financially and were willing to listen to the monetary gospel of Greenbackism. Though some states in which Greenback sentiment was growing did not hold elections in 1877, in those that did the Greenback candidates polled from 5 to 15 percent of the total votes. In most instances the Greenback vote would have been much greater had not one or the other—and in some instances both—of the old parties adopted platform planks favorable to some of the Greenback demands. For example, the difference between the Democrats and the Greenbackers in Wisconsin was insubstantial and the Republican platform in the state leaned toward inflation even if the candidates leaned away from it.[78]

In 1878 the tightening grip of hard times, the spreading influence of the Greenback clubs and press, and the alarm occasioned by the rapidly approaching resumption of specie payment stimulated new efforts to unite the devotees of inflation into a single party. The conference in February, 1878, in Toledo, Ohio, was called expressly to achieve such a union. Attended "by several hundred delegates from twenty-eight states," the conference chose "National" as the party name, although "it was usually known from this time on as the Greenback labor party."

The resolutions adopted in Toledo contained first a set of denunciations and then a list of demands. In addition to condemning the general contracting of the currency, "the limiting of the legal-tender quality of greenbacks, the changing of currency-bonds into coin-bonds," and "the demonetization of the silver dollar," the conference assailed "the exempting of bonds from taxation, . . . the proposed forced resumption of specie payments, and the prodigal waste of public lands."

The demands included "the suppression of bank notes and the issue of all money by the Government, such money to be full legal-tender at its stamped value" and to be issued in such "quantity" as to ensure "the full employment of labor" and a fair interest rate, "the coinage of silver and gold on the same basis," the "reservation of public lands for actual settlers" rather than speculators, and legislation for a shorter working day, the prohibition of Chinese immigration, the "abolition of the contract system of employing convict labor," and the creation of "labor bureaus."[79] Shortly before adjournment the conference adopted two additional resolutions. One was in response to a telegram from General Benjamin F. Butler of Massachusetts. It was a denunciation of the silver bill just enacted by Congress because in its final form the bill limited the amount of silver to be coined. The author of the other resolution was Marcus M. "Brick" Pomeroy. It was a firm declaration against affiliation "in any degree with any of the old parties." It was to prove a vain attempt to prevent political fusion.

In the resolutions adopted in Toledo the demands of labor seem to have been dominant; yet in 1878, a year in which Greenback candidates polled about a million votes, approximately two-thirds of the party's strength lay in the Middle West and one-third in the East. Even in the East the Greenback movement had become agrarian to an appreciable extent. The agrarian tinge found expression in the famous reference of Solon Chase, chairman of the Greenback convention in Maine, to the shrinking value of "them steers" and his double-edged argument: "Inflate the currency, and you raise the price of my steers and at the same time pay the public debt."

The most tangible accomplishment of the Greenback Party in 1878 was the election of fifteen members to Congress. Of these fifteen classified as Nationals, six were from the East, six from the Middle West, and three from the South. In most cases they had won election by a fusion of the Greenbackers with another party or as a result of the willingness of one of the old parties to abstain from making a nomination.

Foremost of the Greenbacker Congressmen elected in 1878 was General James Baird Weaver of Iowa, a gifted orator who was to become the presidential nominee of the Greenback Party in 1880 and of the Populist Party in 1892. His "soldierly bearing, rich voice, and vivid imagination made him a favorite speaker at soldiers' reunions and in political campaigns." His ability, moderation, and freedom from "the eccentricities" that marked many of his "associates" in independent parties won the respect of his colleagues in Congress. Ever sympathetic to the interests of the common people and especially of the farmers, he became the congressional champion of the Oklahoma "boomers," who were opposed by a powerful lobby representing the "cattle barons." Weaver declared that in a battle "between bullocks and babies, he would stand for babies," and his staging of a successful filibuster near the close of a congressional session brought consideration of a bill to open part of Oklahoma to settlement.[80]

THE DECLINE OF GREENBACKISM IN THE 1880's

As events proved, however, political Greenbackism had reached its high-water mark in 1878. By 1880 its decline had set in. Despite Weaver's extensive speaking campaign in which he traveled 20,000 miles, spoke to half a million people, and shook hands with 30,000, he received only 308,578 votes—about 3 percent of the total and less than a third of the votes that the state Greenback parties had polled in 1878. Factional discord within the party and the reluctance of Americans to vote for a third-party candidate who had little or no prospect of winning were among the factors contributing to the poor showing. Another important factor, as demonstrated repeatedly in the history of agrarian politics, was that with the appearance of better times in 1880 the farmers' independent political activity declined. In 1880 American farmers produced more corn, wheat, and oats than they had in any previous year, and for once the price of corn did not fall as production rose. Solon Buck thus sums up the basic cause of the decline of agrarian Greenbackism: "When the farmer had large crops to dispose of at remunerative prices, he lost interest in the inflation of the currency."[81]

By 1882 the Greenback Party was in most states moribund, and 1884 marked its final, feeble appearance in national politics.

SYNTHESIS AND SUMMATION

Thus, while the Greenback rhetoric addressed the ills of the whole debtor class, industrial workers as well as farmers, its strength lay mainly in the agrarian West and South. Continued hard times made farmers turn to inflation of the currency as a way of enhancing the prices of crops and, hopefully, of paying off debts. When hard times struck again in the late

1880s and as a concomitant of the financial panic of 1893, farmers caught the political fever known as "free silver." Ideologically Greenbackism embraced the quantitative monetary theory and advocated an increase in the volume of currency in circulation. As a corollary it rejected the intrinsic value theory, holding that the value of a currency is given by government imprint, not by intrinsic metallic worth. At times Greenback rhetoric became strident and harsh, even anti-Semitic in its denunciation of bankers. Most farmers were not monetary theorists, but pragmatists more concerned with combating grasshoppers than with monetary policy. Underlying the Granger and Greenback rhetoric was the view that the agrarians were merely asking for the restoration of rights set forth in the Declaration of Independence, that the violators of those rights were the giant corporations and the money power.

NOTES

1. *The Age of Reform* (New York: Alfred A. Knopf, 1958), p. 12.
2. C. Vann Woodward, *New York Times Book Review* (July 28, 1963), p. 1.
3. Ibid.
4. Perhaps symptomatic of this tendency are: John A. Garraty, *Interpreting American History: Conversations with Historians* (London: Macmillan, 1970); C. Vann Woodward, ed., *The Comparative Approach to American History* (New York: Basic Books, Inc., 1968); Sidney N. Katz and Stanley I. Kutter, eds., *New Perspectives on the American Past* (Boston: Little, Brown, 1972); W. Koenig, *Bryan: A Political Biography of William Jennings Bryan* (New York: Putnam, 1971).
5. Everett W. Fish, *Donnelliana: An Appendix to Caesar's Column*, Part 2, Extracts and Selections, p. 69; quoted from Ignatius Donnelly's journal (diary) of 1890 (Chicago: F. J. Schulte & Company, 1892).
6. Arthur L. Smith, unpublished paper, "Historical and Social Movements: A Search for Boundaries," read at the sectional meeting, Communication and Social Movements, Speech Communication Association (Chicago, December 30, 1972), p. 2. Quoted by permission of Professor Smith, chairman, department of speech communication, State University of New York at Buffalo, the author of the paper.
7. Some of these thought-provoking schema for the study of movements are suggested by, or derived from: Lloyd Bitzer, "The Rhetorical Situation," *Philosophy & Rhetoric* 1 (January, 1968); Leland Griffin, "The Rhetoric of Historical Movements," *Quarterly Journal of Speech* 38 (April 1952): 184–188; Malcolm Sillars, "Rhetoric as Act," ibid. 50 (October 1964): 277–284; Herbert Simons, "A Theory of Persuasion for Social Movements," ibid. 56 (February 1970): 1–11; Arthur L. Smith, *Rhetoric of Black Revolution* (Boston: Allyn and Bacon, 1969); Neil Smelzer, *Theory of Collective Behavior* (New York: The Free

Press, 1963); Orrin E. Klapp, *Currents of Unrest: An Introduction to Collective Behavior* (New York: Holt, Rinehart and Winston, 1972). See also Herbert W. Simons' challenging article, "Persuasion in Social Conflicts: A Critique of Prevailing Conceptions and a Framework for Future Research," *Speech Monographs* 39 (November 1972): 227–247.

8. Richard Hofstadter, ed., *Great Issues in American History*, 1864–1957, A Documentary Record (New York: Alfred A. Knopf, and Random House, 1958), 2: 131–133.

9. The writer is indebted to Dr. James L. Golden of Ohio State University for introducing the possible use of the Neil Smelzer framework, but only the writer should be held responsible for any application of the schema to the Agrarian protest. Professor Golden's paper, "Social Movements as Rhetorical Situations," was read at the Speech Communication Association Convention in Chicago, December 29, 1972. The outline referred to here is derived from Neil Smelzer, *Theory of Collective Behavior*. The illustrative application is admittedly skeletonized in the interest of brevity.

10. Ray A. Billington in John A. Garraty, *Interpreting American History: Conversations with Historians* (London: Macmillan, 1970), pp. 1–261.

11. Letter to the writer from Kenneth Pauli of Elmira (New York) College, April 8, 1963. Dr. Pauli's dissertation dealt with this period and is on microfilm at the University of Michigan, Ann Arbor.

12. Lester Burrell Shippee, "The Social and Economic Effects of the Civil War with Special Reference to Minnesota," *Minnesota History* 2 (May 1918): 389–412.

13. Shippee, ibid., p. 394. (Another factor was that most railroads in the South ran north and south, not east and west, which would have helped more to hold the South together economically by easing the transport of supplies.)

14. Letter, Schriver to I. Donnelly, November 12, 1862. See *Minnesota History Bulletin* 1 (August, 1915): 133; also cited by Shippee, "Social and Economic Effects," p. 397.

15. Shippee, ibid., pp. 403–404.

16. Edward Winslow Martin (pseudonym of James McCabe), *History of the Grange Movement* (Philadelphia: National Publishing Company, 1873), pp. 402–410; Charles M. Gardiner, *The Grange—Friend of the Farmer* (Washington, D.C.: The National Grange, 1949), pp. 5–6, 24–34. See also Solon Justus Buck, *The Grange Movement* (Cambridge, Massachusetts: Harvard University Press, 1913), pp. 40–44; also, Buck, *The Agrarian Crusade, A Chronicle of the Farmer in Politics* (New Haven: Yale University Press, 1920), pp. 3–4.

17. Samuel Eliot Morison and Henry Steele Commager, *The Growth of the American Republic* (New York: Oxford University Press, 1942), 2:75.

18. Buck, *Agrarian Crusade*, p. 20. See also Martin Ridge, "Ignatius Donnelly and the Granger Movement in Minnesota," *Mississippi Valley Historical Review* 42 (March 1956):701.

19. Ibid., p. 27. For data on the number of Granges, 1873–1876, see table in Buck, *The Granger Movement*, pp. 58–59.

20. Buck, *Agrarian Crusade*, p. 30.
21. Ibid., p. 31. See also Fred E. Haynes, *Third Party Movements Since the Civil War, With Special Reference to Iowa* (Iowa City, Iowa: State Historical Society of Iowa, 1916), pp. 64–65. Haynes says that these were basically anti-monopoly parties, p. 65.
22. Ignatius Donnelly, *Facts for the Granges, Extracts from Speeches Before the Granges of Dakota, Rice, Goodhue, Fillmore, Mower, Olmstead, Winona, and Washington Counties During March, April, May, and June, 1873* (in the Donnelly Papers, Minnesota Historical Society, St. Paul).
23. Ibid., p. 2. See also Earl W. Hayter, "The Patent System and Agrarian Discontent, 1875–1888," *Mississippi Valley Historical Review* 34 (June 1947): 59–82; and Iowa State Grange, *Proceedings*, 4 (1873): 44–45.
24. Donnelly, *Facts for Granges*, p. 3.
25. Ibid.
26. See resolution adopted by Illinois State Farmers' Association in Springfield, Illinois convention, April, 1873, in Hofstadter, ed., *Great Issues in American History*, 2:137 and pamphlet, *Anti-Monopoly Convention* (Rochester, Minnesota) December 2, 1870, p. 45.
27. Donnelly, *Facts for Granges*, p. 4.
28. Everett W. Fish, *Donnelliana* (St. Paul, 1892), Part 2, p. 216. LeDuc was a political rival of Donnelly's who resided in Donnelly's Congressional district. The analogy, while somewhat indelicate, contained a comparison that was abundantly clear to every stock breeder and farmer Donnelly addressed. For an official profession of the nonpolitical character of the Grange see the *Journal of Proceedings* of the National Grange, 7 (February 1874): 58, quoted by Solon J. Buck in *The Granger Movement*, p. 82. Although these sources are old, they are close to realities.
29. Buck, *Agrarian Crusade*, p. 32.
30. Buck, *Granger Movement*, p. 82.
31. Ibid. See also Buck, *Granger Movement*, pp. 84–85. Alfred M. Craig defeated Chief Justice Lawrence.
32. Buck, *Agrarian Crusade*, pp. 32–33, and *Granger Movement*, pp. 86–87.
33. Ignatius Donnelly, *The American People's Money* (Chicago: Laird and Lee, 1895), p. 113. The format of this book is a dialogue between a farmer and a banker on a railroad coach as the train travels from Chicago to the Pacific coast. It was written as a campaign tract for popular instruction prior to the 1896 presidential election.
34. Quoted by Buck, *Agrarian Crusade*, p. 33.
35. Ibid. Unless otherwise noted, the outline here follows Buck, *Agrarian Crusade*.
36. Ibid., pp. 33–34.
37. Norman Pollack, *The Populist Response to Industrial America* (New York: W. W. Norton, 1962), p. 63. Cf. William J. Bryan, *The First Battle* (Chicago: W. B. Conkey, 1896), p. 200.
38. Pollack, *Populist Response*, pp. 63–67.
39. See Paul Crawford, "Ignatius Donnelly, Orator and Agitator" (unpublished

doctoral dissertation, Northwestern University, 1949); and Martin Ridge, *Ignatius Donnelly: The Portrait of a Politician* (Chicago: University of Chicago Press, 1962).

40. The cartoon is reproduced in Martin Ridge, *Ignatius Donnelly: The Portrait of a Politician* (Chicago, 1962), between p. 276 and p. 277.

41. Ignatius Donnelly, *Caesar's Column* (Chicago: J. Reagan & Company, 1894), the preface, "To the Public," p. 5. This novel was first published in 1890 under the pseudonym Edmund Boisgilbert, M.D., but after its success subsequent printings carried in parentheses the name of Ignatius Donnelly as author.

42. Ray A. Billington in Garraty, *Interpreting American History: Conversations with Historians*, pp. 1–261.

43. See a curious combination of prose and verse, Stephen Smith, *Grains for the Grangers* (Philadelphia: John E. Potter & Co., 1873). It contains verse about "All honor to the toiling hand," extracts from essays and addresses, and commentary by the author on such issues as monopoly, the tariff, freedom in trade, the elective franchise, and universal education.

44. Buck, *Agrarian Crusade*, p. 35. To the end of this section the principal source is Buck.

45. Ibid., pp. 66–69.

46. Ibid., p. 73.

47. Munn v. Illinois, U.S. 113 (1877). See also Irving S. Krull, Nell M. Krull, and Stanley H. Friedelbaum, *A Chronological Encyclopedia of American History* (New York: Popular Library, 1969), p. 240.

48. Donnelly, *Facts for the Granges*, p. 10.

49. Ibid. See also Martin Ridge, "Ignatius Donnelly and the Greenback Movement," *Mid-America Historical Review* 39 (July 1957): 156–158.

50. Buck, *Agrarian Crusade*, passim, pp. 80–95.

51. Edward Stanwood, *A History of the Presidency* (Boston: Houghton Mifflin Company, 1893), p. 366. For elaboration of the "Ohio idea," see Irwin Unger, *The Greenback* (Princeton, New Jersey: Princeton University Press, 1916), p. 43; and Robert P. Sharkey, *Money, Class and Party* (Baltimore: The Johns Hopkins Press, 1959), pp. 135–40 and pp. 224–25.

52. Robert C. Cotner, John S. Ezell, and Gilbert C. Fite, ed. *Readings in American History* (Boston: Houghton Mifflin Company, 1952), 2:138. See also Edward McPherson, *A Handbook for Politics for 1878*, 3rd ed. (Washington, D.C.: Solomons and Chapman, 1878), pp. 167–168.

53. *Ibid.* The lists of both the wrongs and the demands are derived from Edward McPherson, *A Handbook of Politics for 1878*, pp. 167–168 (reproduced platform of Greenback Party), in Cotner, et al., *Readings*, 2:138–139.

54. For these typical epithets of the rhetoric of Greenbackism, see the Greenback campaign newspaper, *The Great Campaign* (Chicago), July 18 to November 14, 1876; Ignatius Donnelly's newspaper, the *Anti-Monopolist*, published in St. Paul from July 16, 1874 to December 12, 1878, and its successor, *The Representative*, published in St. Paul from April 19, 1893 to November 28, 1901; Everett W. Fish, *Donnelliana* pp. 244–245; Ignatius Donnelly, *The People's Money* (Chicago), p. 59. Although Donnelly lent his tongue and pen to the free

silver cause in the 1896 campaign, he never regarded free silver as a complete or adequate monetary reform program. Free silver was, in his view, a popular political fever agrarians could not strategically resist, but it was *not* basic, comprehensive Populist monetary theory. Donnelly continued to be a Greenbacker as well as an advocate of free silver. He favored the *international* stabilization of paper money along with bimetallism. Speech by Donnelly at Duluth, Minnesota, reported in *Duluth Evening Herald*, October 8, 1885, in Vol. 38, Memorandum Book and Diary, Book 2, 1885, Donnelly papers, Minnesota Historical Society, St. Paul. In this speech Donnelly advocated the establishment of an international "guaranteed currency."

55. *Anti-Monopolist* (St. Paul), May 25, 1876.

56. Ibid. See also W. Scott Morgan, *History of the Wheel and Alliance* (New York: Burt Franklin, 1891, and reprinted in 1968).

57. Paul Crawford, "Ignatius Donnelly, Orator and Agitator" (unpublished doctoral dissertation, Northwestern University, 1949).

58. Buck, *Agrarian Crusade*, pp. 83–84.

59. Buck, *Granger Movement*, passim, pp. 323–326.

60. *The Great Campaign* (Chicago), July 25, 1876, p. 1.

61. Ibid.

62. Ibid., August 1, 1876, p. 4.

63. Ibid., p. 1.

64. Ibid., October 3, 1876, p. 3.

65. Ibid., August 15, 1876, p. 1.

66. Ibid., August 29, 1876, p. 4.

67. Ibid., August 1, 1876, p. 4.

68. Ibid., August 22, 1876, p. 1.

69. Ibid., September 6, 1876, p. 1.

70. Chester MacArthur Destler, *American Radicalism, 1865–1901* (New London: Connecticut College Monograph No. 3, 1946), pp. 50–77.

71. Vernon Louis Parrington, *Main Currents in American Thought* (New York: Harcourt, Brace and Company, 1930), 3: 273–274.

72. Buck, *Agrarian Crusade*, p. 87.

73. Dixon, Illinois, *Telegraph*, November 9, 1876, p. 2.

74. Morison and Commager, *Growth of the American Republic*, 2: 189–265.

75. Derived from a chart on the appreciation of the dollar from 1865 to 1895 in John Hicks, *The Populist Revolt* (Minneapolis: The University of Minnesota Press, 1931), p. 88.

76. The population of the United States in 1870 was 38,558,731; and in 1880, it was 50,155,783. See the table in Morison and Commager, *Growth of the American Republic*, 2:734–735.

77. See the tables in Buck, *Granger Movement*, pp. 29–32.

78. Buck, *Agrarian Crusade*, pp. 88, 89, 103.

79. Ibid., pp. 88–90.

80. Ibid., pp. 90–93.

81. Ibid., p. 95.

6

The Populist Spellbinders

DONALD H. ECROYD

The period between 1860 and 1890 was one of traumatic economic and social readjustment on many fronts. Industry was expanding under the leadership of men such as Rockefeller, Vanderbilt, and Carnegie. U.S. Steel became the nation's first billion-dollar corporation in 1901. Organizations of working men and women were beginning to demand attention, and the railroad strikes of 1877 began the large-scale labor unrest of the late nineteenth century. Thanks to new methods and better seed, the production of corn and wheat doubled during the years just before 1880. As the western lands began to develop, wheat production in Iowa and Illinois became less profitable and fell off sharply. The raising of dairy cattle, hogs, horses, and corn therefore became more common, bringing about a major shift in agriculture in the older and more stable farm-belt area of the Midwest. The change-over to more scientific and more mechanized farming became general.

This industrial and agricultural expansion and change inevitably meant debts. The rapidly increasing productivity, however, also meant low prices—a devastating combination. To complicate the matter further, even though population increased, the amount of cash actually in circulation was not permitted to rise proportionally. Conditions therefore grew steadily worse year by year. It was not possible for most Midwestern debtors to pay their creditors so long as prices remained low, the amount of money in circulation remained small, and the costs of marketing and transportation remained high. As one contemporary writer put it:

When great heaps of corn lie in [the] fields awaiting sale at twelve cents a bushel, when a mighty crop of wheat brings its possessor but fifty cents a bushel, when cows are worth but fifteen dollars apiece, and good butter sells for eight cents a pound, while thousands in the land are known to be suffering because of the lack of these things, a leanness of pocketbook results which the farmer may understand, but to which he is not easily reconciled.[1]

In Kansas in 1890, for example, nearly every farm in the western two thirds of the state was to some extent encumbered—most of them hopelessly.

Chattel mortgages were drawing from forty to forty-seven per cent annually and farm mortgages nine per cent. In 1890 the farm indebtedness in one county alone amounted to eighty-three per cent of the total farm valuation. Mortgages filed on Kansas farms in the decade totalled $440,000 of which more than one-third were either foreclosed or deeded to the mortgager without litigation.[2]

The same picture could be painted in Illinois, Alabama, Tennessee, Iowa, and Nebraska—to a lesser extent in Georgia, Mississippi, Louisiana, the Carolinas, Indiana, and Colorado. In 1893–1894 a serious crash came, leading to widespread unemployment and even lower prices than ever.

In rural areas the embattled farmers were busily organizing. The largest of their earlier organizations was the Patrons of Husbandry, commonly called the Grange. As it grew weaker, however, a national organization was formed in the middle eighties—The Farmers' Alliance. Very quickly the farmer's economic difficulties, through this organization, became a justification for looking to the government for aid.

The reflex-action type of response aroused by this situation was peculiar to the Middle Border states and in a lesser degree to the South—perhaps in part because both were frontier areas: the one geographic, the other economic.

Frank L. McVey, in a contemporary study of the movement, considers this explanation too simple. His notion is that the formation of agricultural organizations such as the Alliance and the later People's Party that grew out of it was primarily "an effort to stay the decline . . . of prices due to the effect of agricultural and industrial reorganization."[3] This same view is held in the more recent analysis of Communist-line Anna Rochester: "The struggle which culminated in the People's Party was primarily a defensive movement of farmers and other small business interests against the relentless advance of financial capital."[4] From this concept of a defensive motivation it is only a step to the position of Professor James C. Malin of the University of Kansas, who holds that Populism was primarily the result of the rural-urban conflict.[5] Urban people, to the rural Populist, fell into one of two groups—both stereotypes: the capitalists and the laborers. Both were ideas of people who did not exist. In reality the Populist was opposed to all urbanism, particularly because it symbolized the new marketing system that he did not understand. Populism, if we hold this view, was a fight against the new elements in our social structure. It was reactionary as well as progressive. It built upon the narrowness of anti-immigration and anti-trust feeling; it urged a return to "the dollar of our daddies"; it attacked Wall Street, the railroads, and the two old parties as symbolic scapegoats suitable to hang for the crime of creating hard times.

A recent theory of the development of Populism is stated by Richard Hofstadter and is based upon certain assumptions common to the field of social psychology.[6] Hofstadter sees the farmer as downwardly mobile and Populism as an expression of his resentment. As a status-loving group seeking a scapegoat, he argues, the Populists began their attacks upon the money power of the East. Such status resentment and scapegoat-seeking are pervasive. Hence, the Populists even argued an actual conspiracy "of Wall Street" and "the Eastern bankers," became Anglophobic as well, and railed against immigration in general. Hofstadter, Max Lerner, and others, even accuse the Populists of anti-Semitism and account for it as an aspect of this pervasive nativism.[7]

As a result one can follow the long-accepted interpretation of John D. Hicks, who feels that Populism was a political revolt against hard times—a progressive and positive action that was an aspect of ongoing American progressivism: or one can follow Hofstadter and others who consider it to be an irrational attack upon the power elite, akin to the contemporary far Right, or even Fascism.

There can be little question that the Populist movement was an uprising—a revolt if you will—and that it was predicated upon the unfortunate economics of the period. It was progressive in that it urged democratic group action; it was socialistic in that it urged government ownership and operation of the railroads, telephone, telegraph, etc., and in that it looked to the federal government for aid. It was reactionary in that the old days were looked to as an ideal, and much of the agitation was against change rather than for it. With a multiplicity of aggravations it was natural that people should organize for strength, and the frontier influence made the task even easier than it might have been otherwise. Henry George's famous *Progress and Poverty* poured oil on the already towering flames, and, even though they may not actually have read the book, many U.S. citizens were able and eager to discuss the implications of its title. After the publication of Bellamy's collectivist-utopian *Looking Backward* in the early eighties, Bellamy societies sprang up all over the country. The book made a tremendous impression and sold thousands of copies. Thus philosophy, both consciously and unconsciously, began to add to the already-present desire for easement. It added the remedy for economic ills:

agitation toward federal action. To be successful, agitation requires an organization. Thus, both economically and philosophically, a new political action group was indicated.

Populism therefore grew out of the Farmers' Alliance and the labor-reform movement. To quote John B. Clark's *Populism in Alabama*:

With discontent among farmers, it was inevitable that the Grange, or any other farmers' organization, would drift into politics. At most there is only a thin veil between the economical and the political aspect of many vital questions and in such cases they invariably mix.[8]

Both the Grange and the Alliance fully intended to remain nonpartisan in their activities, but this was impossible.

Third parties, however, were not considered respectable. Because of this fact neither the Alliance, which was formed in 1887, nor the Grange, which had a much longer history, intended to work outside the existing party structure. Once the Granger Laws were passed, however, the Grange became less active in the political sphere and lost much of its former influence. As the Alliance became a national organization, its political role quickly became clear, and its efforts to avoid becoming politically active became increasingly futile. At first it limited itself to influencing the program of regular-party candidates. Then it set up a program of its own and bound its members not to vote for any man who refused to endorse it. Finally, it entered politics directly, albeit as a sort of last resort.

First, the party was a party of "little people." Even in their own day, the Populist leaders were not individually accounted to be of any great political importance or power. Some of them were individually known for their literary or military reputations, it is true; but their political impact was a collective one—one in which it is impossible to say that the role of any particular leader was more vital than that of any other. Leaders arose, certainly, but they arose because they were articulate rather than because of their organizational power or prestige. Ignatius P. Donnelly, Tom Watson, "Pitchfork Ben" Tillman, "Bloody Bridles" Waite, Senator William A. Peffer, Mary Elizabeth Lease, General James B. Weaver, "Sockless Jerry" Simpson—who were they before their sounding board appeared? Or, for that matter, who were they when the issues submerged again? Populism can only be studied, therefore, at the local level.

Secondly, Populism was an oral movement. When the historian considers Progressivism in the early twentieth century, he finds that the appeals were largely written. Muckraker novels and articles in magazines and newspapers characterized its propaganda. Even its principal speakers— Teddy Roosevelt, La Follette, Borah—depended heavily on the written word to carry their ideas to the people. The Populists read George and Bellamy, it is true, and they knew their political pamphlets well; but theirs was a rhetorical movement, not a literary one. Along the Middle Border and in the South, where Populist strength was greatest, the power of the spoken word and the appeal of the stump speaker can hardly be discounted. Political rallies, unchallenged as yet by movies, radio, television, or even motor cars, drew big audiences. Politics were partisan to an extent unimaginable in our day, and the political speaker was filling not only his appointed role but the role of entertainer and teacher as well.

It is somewhat difficult to estimate the contribution of the Populist Party to American life as we know it. It is impossible, however, not to recognize the power that undergirded the movement. Large segments of the public were made articulate by the educational work of the Alliance. This new-found voice had an immediate effect upon the doctrines of the established parties. Thus, the Populists made their mark partly through the fear they engendered in the Democrats and the Republicans. To engender such fear was possible, however, only because of the awakened rural electorate and because vital issues had become so similarly identified for both of the old parties. Under such circumstances it was merely a matter of time until one party or the other would be forced to admit Populist principles. That the Democrats did so first was mainly accidental—a side-effect of the bitter battle between the Cleveland and the Bryan wings of the party.[9]

As Nugent puts it in his analysis:

Yet Populism is peculiar in that it may serve either side of the argument. From one viewpoint, it is a mob attempting to bludgeon a respectable elite and a well-ordered society into abject submission. From the other, it is a case study in the democratic process in which a minority, viciously trodden down by certain economic and political evils, struggles manfully to free itself by well-considered institutional correctives. Since the party failed and the program succeeded, it becomes accordingly either a narrow escape from totalitarianism—which threat perdures with the "populistic spirit"—or a notable enrichment of American politics and culture.[10]

Either of these views, as Nugent himself observes, is clearly a caricature. The existential situation as well as the sociopsychological dynamics of the group must be considered. Two factors come through, however, regardless of interpretation.

Kansas was the hotbed of Populism. Her People's Party leaders were the men and women who first led the way to the creation of a new national third party that was broader than the Farmers' Alliance. The Kansas People's Party Manifesto later became the basis of the national platform that was adopted at Omaha in 1892. The Weaver campaign for the presidency was frequently referred to as "Kansas-izing" the nation. Kansas was the source of the movement's greatest strength and the scene of its greatest triumphs. It is because of these reasons that this study concerns itself primarily with the speech making of the Kansas Populists. By concentrating on this crucial local arena we gain insight into the larger movement.

During the early 1890s, hundreds of speakers were active in the Populist movement in Kansas. Each local Alliance had its lecturer. Each district Alliance had its lecturer also, while the state Alliance had a Board of Lecturers. In addition to these elected speakers, every Alliance officer, whether at the local, district, or state level, must be considered as a speechmaker. Local, county, state, and national candidates of the Populist Party itself were active. Also, professional lecturers were hired by the party to stump the state in favor of the cause. In addition to all these, into Kansas came a continuing stream of visiting lecturers and other officers of the Alliance as well as Populist Party big-wigs and candidates from other states.

Obviously, not all these speechmakers received or merited equal attention in the press. Consistently, however, mention is made of William E. Peffer, Jerry Simpson, L. D. Lewelling, Mary Elizabeth Lease, and Annie L. Diggs.[11] Later historians, standard reference works, and articles in contemporary and modern periodicals contain a wealth of material about these five orators, though little about the others. In this period these Kansas Populist speakers were probably the best of the group—certainly the most widely known. By concentrating our attention upon these five, then—whether or not we can in any way consider them to be characteristic or typical—we can learn a great deal about Populist oratory in this period.

Aside from those who worked for the railroads or in the mines, Kansas citizens were almost entirely agrarian. Frontier days were not long behind, and the rural population that predominated in the state had been well trained in the school of direct actionism. Indian raids, county-seat wars, the great cattle drives along the Chisholm Trail, the constant struggle with nature and with one's fellow man, had made many Kansans fiercely self-reliant. Social differentiations were not clear-cut; democracy was the generally accepted way of life. The banker and his wife and perhaps one or two of the ministers, lawyers, doctors, or schoolteachers might be slightly set apart from the rest of the townspeople, but practically everybody else was from the same side of the tracks. Religious faith was largely fundamentalist, whose tenets and evangelism characterized the average Kansan's response to any difficulty. The people's self-reliance, practical democracy, and faith that God was with them and leading them "to the stars through difficulty" just as their state's motto proclaimed, united

Kansans and made it seem natural that where they were under duress, they should band together in an independent party.

The issues upon which national Populism was actually built were primarily three: land, transportation, and money. In Kansas these three issues were also primary.

The land problem was an acute one. In the average Kansas county, according to the eleventh census, 55 percent of the farm families occupied encumbered farms.[12] When it was finally discovered that rain was not going to "follow the plow," literally hundreds of people went broke and were forced to pack their belongings back into their canvas-topped wagons and trek home to Iowa or Illinois and "the wife's folks." Again, according to the the eleventh census 170,000 people left Kansas between 1887 and 1890 alone![13] "In God we trusted, in Kansas we busted" was the motto, almost too tragic to be funny, that was roughly painted on the sides of wagon after wagon that crossed the wide Missouri from west to east. Feeling was bitter toward "the East," where most of the mortgage paper was held. Populist speakers found audiences ready to listen when they proposed laws lowering interest rates from the all-too-common ten to twelve percent level, to one of only three percent; when they urged laws granting longer periods of time for the payment of debt and laws forbidding alien ownership of land.[14]

Transportation was an issue largely because the railroads had the farmers at their mercy. Elevator and stockyard practices were for the most part unregulated, and freight rates were blatantly discriminatory. Railways, elevators, stockyards, meat packers, and grain markets were all lumped together as "big business." Many sincere men felt, and not without some justification, that "big business" was bleeding them dry. Thus the Populists suggested government ownership and operation of the railroads as well as increased control over regulation of the grading, weighing, and care of livestock in the stockyards.[15]

The third major issue was money. Although the population had doubled in the years between the Civil War and 1890, and the volume of business had probably trebled, the number of dollars per capita in circulation had actually declined. The U.S. Department of Commerce gives the per capita circulation for 1865 as $30.35; for 1890 as $23.02. Contrast these figures with the 1945 figure of $191.61, or the 1965 figure of $204.11, and you begin to see why Populist orators were well-nigh unanimous in their demand for an expanded currency.[16]

Populist speakers, then, largely discussed only two or three main issues, and they tended to discuss these in much the same way. One reason for this similarity was undoubtedly the program of education carried on by the Alliance before and during the campaigns of the early nineties. Lecture topics for statewide study and use were published from time to time in state

Alliance papers. Standardized, prepared lesson plans, discussion outlines, and pamphlets were widely disseminated. These materials gave speakers and audiences a common fund of knowledge. This pamphlet material was seemingly endless, and it ranged through endless topics. The writers of these materials were not always experts, and their analyses may not always have been complete or accurate. The pamphlets were well organized, however, and prepared with all possible care and presented without profit. In some instances, where quotations from such material were questioned, their truth was demonstrated by cross-quotations and re-evaluation.[17] The main fallacy in most of the material was its emotional character and its failure to document the sources of information used.

Most famous of all the pamphlets was Mrs. S. E. V. Emery's *Seven Financial Conspiracies which have Enslaved the American People*. The Kansas State Historical Society's copy is gray, paper-bound, and marked "Revised edition, one hundredth thousand. Price per copy 10¢, 2 for 15, 15 for $1.00, or 100 for $6.50." Emery saw the problem of the age much as did Henry George, but the thousands of copies that her little book sold made its influence much more direct than that of *Progress and Poverty*. It is readable, packed with facts, flowing, intensely oral in its style. A typical statement:

But we have not yet completed the enumeration of crimes perpetrated against the people of the country through this infernal system of legalized robbery. Having purchased their bonds with government money, depreciated from 38 to 60 percent (on account of the exemption clause) and having exempted them from taxation, with advanced interest payable in gold, it would seem that the climax of audacity had been reached. But who can fathom the greed of the money shark, or set bounds to the voracity of the civilized brigand?[18]

Several major source books of considerable scope and bulk were also published for the use of the Alliance speaker or People's Party member. *The Farmers' Alliance History and Agricultural Digest*, edited by N. A. Dunning, is one of the more widely used of these volumes. It includes a history of the growth and development of agricultural organizations, particularly the Alliance; brief articles on political subjects, on agriculture and farming, on home-making; and several tables and items of miscellaneous information such as postal rates, farm law, measurement tables for grains, the Declaration of Independence, the Demands of the Farmers' Alliance on U. S. Senators, et al. Sample articles on political subjects in the Dunning volume include C. W. McCune's "The Purposes of the Farmers' Alliance," W. A. Peffer's "Government Control of Money," Jerry Simpson's "The Political Rebellion in Kansas," Bettie Gay's "The

Influence of Women in the Alliance," and the Reverend Isom P. Langley's "Religion in the Alliance." Similar, and more widely advertised, was W. Scott Morgan's *History of the Wheel and Alliance.* Less widely used but much thumbed by Kansas Populist politicians was the Vincent brothers' *Populist Handbook for Kansas,* which included much local material that could be used as evidence in debate.[19]

The facts were known to the listening audience. It is also true that they were understood, for these issues were struck from the bitterness of intense economic despair. Each statistic represented the mortgaged home of a neighbor; each dollar charted as debt represented wheat to be raised and sold from which no personal comfort could be derived; each percentile of inflation tabulated meant extra hours of personal labor. It is no wonder that Populist speeches were emotional. How could it be expected that the facts would not get entangled with the deepest feelings under such circumstances? When Mary Elizabeth Lease trumpeted to the multitudes in one of her mighty perorations,

We will stand by our homes and stay by our fire-sides by force, if necessary, and we will not pay our debts to the shark loan companies until the government pays its debts to us. The people are at bay; let the bloodhounds of money who have dogged them so far beware,[20]

the reaction was undoubtedly immediate and dynamic. Such speechmaking may seem outmoded, but its character should not be unexpected.

In Kansas, as has been pointed out, the principal Populist leaders were Senator William A. Peffer, Governor Lorenzo D. Lewelling, Congressman Jerry Simpson, Annie L. Diggs, and Mary Elizabeth Lease.

Peffer was widely known throughout the state as a writer and lecturer between 1881 and his entrance into the Senate in 1891. While in the Union Army during the Civil War, he read law and finished his bar exams in Tennessee, practicing there awhile. But he finally settled in Kansas, where he served in the state legislature and edited the widely circulated *Kansas Farmer,* published in Topeka. When the 1890 campaign began, he was nearly sixty years old, tall, spare, and with a flowing, wavy, chestnut-brown beard. Grant Harrington, former editor of the Kansas City (Kansas) *Democrat* and a Populist himself during the party's second rise to power, explained:

He could be both tedious and a good talker. He was a slow talker—rather ponderous. But he had facts, and was a clear thinker. But he never got over to the crowd as "one of us"—very deliberate. Sometimes he would fiddle with his beard— of course he *would!* There it was! But the main thing I recall was that he was so deliberate. You didn't have to watch him: you knew what was coming. He was just naturally sedate.[21]

He impressed people with his knowledge of figures and his ability to use them. His dry, statistical style, his notions of finance, and his long beard became trademarks of Populism. He may not have been "magnetic," but he was effective.

Lorenzo D. Lewelling was the son of a Quaker nurseryman and anti-slavery lecturer. In Iowa, Lewelling and his wife became well known for their excellent work as counselors and instructors in the Women's Reform School. Later he was for many years that school's superintendent. He was an Anti-Republican and ran for various offices unsuccessfully. In 1887 he left Iowa for Kansas, moving to Wichita and entering the hatchery business. In Iowa he was a well-known man: liberal, thoughtful, and articulate; in Kansas, however, he was unknown. When the 1892 state convention of the People's Party was held in Wichita, in his capacity as county chairman he gave the speech of welcome. Up to that hour scarcely a delegate had ever seen or heard him. His carefully prepared address and his sincere, gentlemanly delivery stirred his hearers, however. Within twenty-four hours he was nominated as their candidate for governor. His natural Quaker reserve, his sympathy for his fellow men, and his deep religious feeling all contributed to make him a respected man and a sought-after speaker. Even William Allen White, who was among his bitterest critics, could accuse him of nothing save a blind sincerity.[22]

Jerry Simpson was born in Canada. At fourteen he took to the lakes as a cook on a schooner. By the time he was twenty-two, he was master of a large sailing vessel. He followed the lakes twenty-three years in all, his service broken only by the time he spent with the 12th Illinois Infantry in the Civil War. Illness finally caused him to leave the lakes for an Indiana farm, where he became interested in the Grange. Later he moved to Kansas, ending up in the western part of the state as a farmer and stockman. There, because of his lack of political success in third party politics, by 1890 he was generally regarded as a political has-been. When the "Pops" that year nominated him for Congress, his long experience as a radical stump speaker and his personal familiarity with the farmers' problems stood him in good stead. As an old soldier, a farmer, a virile, masculine person who had known hard times, much about him appealed to his audience. His famous broad grin always got the crowd with him. Typically he joined in the fun when his opponents, trying to ridicule him, dubbed him "Sockless Socrates." He never missed a chance to use this nickname to his own advantage, much to everyone's delight. During the campaign of 1890 alone he received more than three hundred pairs of socks. Scarcely a Populist parade was complete without at least one wagon load of pretty girls knitting socks for "Sockless" Jerry.[23]

Annie L. Diggs was also a Canadian. She had the advantage of private tutors and private-school training. She tried newspaper work in

Washington, D.C., in a day when women did not do such things, and was successful. In 1873, her restless, independent spirit led her to Lawrence, Kansas, where she married. She was an avid dry, and took part in the city election of 1877. She also became a lay preacher for the Unitarian Church. She re-entered journalism to write on temperence and religion for several Kansas papers. Interested in the Farmers' Alliance, she served as assistant editor of the *Advocate*, the state Alliance paper. On the platform she remained dainty and feminine. She was only five feet tall and weighed barely ninety-five pounds. Her pictures show her to have been extremely attractive—so attractive, indeed, that we can well understand one editor's comment: "It seems to us that Mrs. Diggs' good looks are somewhat embarrassing to her."[24]

The real "Kansas Tornado" of the group, however, was Mary Elizabeth Lease. Her famed battle phrase urging farmers to "raise more hell and less corn" if they wanted to solve their problems was a ringing challenge to direct action, even though it may well have been apocryphal. She came to Kansas in 1875 from Pennsylvania to teach in the parochial school in Osage Mission. There she met and married Charley Lease, a druggist. During the next ten years Mary Elizabeth bore four children, kept house, and managed in her spare time to study law. She never studied in a law office, but read at home when the day's work was done, sometimes, it was said, even pinning sheets of notes above her wash tub to study while she scrubbed the washings she "took in" at fifty cents a day. A boy who was studying in the office of Wichita lawyer Tom McMeecham helped her some, and she was admitted to the bar in 1885—becoming one of the first woman lawyers in the state of Kansas. She also interested herself in third-party politics, running unsuccessfully for office in 1888. Continual opponent William Allen White wrote categorically, "I have never heard a lovelier voice than Mrs. Lease's. It was a golden voice—a deep, rich contralto, a singing voice that had hypnotic qualities." White went on to comment upon her appearance and effectiveness:

She put into her oratory something which the printed copies of her speech did not reveal. They were dull enough often, but she could recite the multiplication table and set a crowd hooting or hurrahing at her will. She stood nearly six feet tall, with no figure, a thick torso, and long legs. To me, she often looked like a kangaroo pyramided up from the hips to a comparatively small head. . . . She wore her hair in a psyche knot, always neatly combed and topped by the most ungodly hats I ever saw a woman wear. She had no sex appeal—none![25]

Even today, in late August and September, practically every Kansas organization plans a picnic. The lure of the shady grove and the cool breeze along the stream bed is powerful in a land of few trees and great heat. In

1889 the Farmers' Alliance had learned the value of the picnic as a means of reaching the mass of their membership, and in 1890 the Alliance-inspired People's Party used the same technique. At first, in the early summer, the picnics were small, neighborly gatherings; but by late summer many of them were all-day affairs with races, games, and carnival rides. Even with these added attractions, the main feature, of course, was the speechmaking.[26] By September the interest of the people of Kansas in these picnics and "speakin's" was such that the *Barber County Index* carried on page one an article filled with suggestions of what to take along to eat. The writer assured the ladies that three or four boxes of sandwiches to one cake was a good ratio to follow. Also included were recipes for hard-boiled-egg and meat spreads, lemonade, and a few hints on how to keep sardines and salmon from spoiling.[27]

This sort of meeting was a typical Populist occasion for oratory throughout the period of the nineties. When Diggs conducted a series of meetings in Phillips County in July, 1894, the Phillipsburg *Herald* reported that one thousand people gathered in Plummer's Grove to hear her and to applaud the music of the Republican City Ladies' Band "composed of young ladies of that city."[28] At Waushara, August 16, 1890, the various sub-Alliances met "with flags, banners, mottoes, and music at Clingbud's Grove." There, in the afternoon, for more than two hours, Lease "without any apparent effort . . . sent a clear, strong voice to the farthest listener."[29]

September 2, 1890, seven miles northwest of Sun City, out in the hills of Barber County, an enthusiastic crowd gathered to hear Jerry Simpson. "Some families came 50 miles, in covered wagons, and camped there the night before. A barbecued beef was eaten in no time, but hundreds of loaded baskets were equal to the emergency and all were fed."[30] When Peffer spoke at Andale, July 30, 1890, the Andale Brass Band played, and the circular swing whirled the young people around and around just as at the county fair. "The shade was good, but the ground poached up so that the dust was very disagreeable. . . ." Even so, people listened to the music and the speeches from about 9:00 a.m. until 12:00 noon, ate their lunches, went back again, and "listened eagerly until six o'clock."[31] On September 2, 1892, three thousand came to the People's Picnic at Sedgwick. Jerry Simpson, and the famed Quenemo Glee Club were the headline attractions. A band was there, too, and "an organ was brought from a house four miles away" to help with the singing.[32]

Just as common as the picnics, and far larger, were the rallies and camp meetings. Usually these did not stop for the darkness but instead moved into the local opera house or the local courthouse chamber for meetings after supper. Thus, four thousand people heard Diggs speak in the Wichita Auditorium, October 3, 1894;[33] and, when she and Governor Lewelling appeared together on the platform in Pratt, the local paper commented that the crowd was so large that many were "uncomfortably situated."[34] When Lewelling spoke in Ness City, October 31, 1893, so large a crowd gathered that even the local Republican paper admitted that only about one fourth of them could get into the opera house to hear him. A platform was hastily erected in front of the building, and the Governor spoke from there.[35] Similarly, when Lease visited Columbus in early 1891, the crowd overflowed the opera house so completely that the meeting was adjourned to the east steps of the courthouse, where the famous lady orated for over two hours in the afternoon and over three hours in the evening.[36]

People's Party political gatherings were almost always preceded by some sort of parade. Many accounts of these parades are available in newspapers of the period. When Peffer was in Lyons in 1890, the local Republican paper reported that there were 535 teams and 116 men on horseback in the parade. The local drill club marched, bands played, and there were many banners. Some floats were decorated with evergreen to symbolize the "living issue," and some were decorated with bunting, carrying pretty girls dressed in white to represent the states.[37] At Medicine Lodge, a meeting to honor Jerry Simpson in his own home town began with a street procession to the picnic grounds. This included about 450 vehicles and "took an hour and five minutes to pass the Post Office." Flags, mottoes, banners, even a "Bloody Shirt" or two, were waved aloft. The wagons were interspersed with marching singers, bands, a fife and drum corps. There was even a wagon load of children caustically labeled "over production."[38]

At Hutchinson, Lease, Jerry Simpson, and Judge Peffer vied for honors at a monster two-day encampment. Three thousand five hundred people camped on the fair grounds, and more than five thousand heard the speeches. So many came to listen, in fact, that wagons were rolled up, and two speakers were going at once throughout most of the two days. As the editor of the local Republican paper put it, "You had but to sit down almost anyplace and wait, and a speaker would come around and go to making a speech directly." Parades were held, and a milling throng of farm people took over the town. Both the Republican Hutchinson *Daily News* and the *Alliance Gazette* agreed upon one thing: it was an orderly crowd. There were no drunks.[39] This particular comment was made time and again in papers all over the state concerning other meetings as well. Evidently, since the People were sincere, God-fearing farm folk, "demon rum" had no part in their merrymaking or their politicking.

Big as the Hutchinson meeting was, however, the rally at Winfield in 1890 eclipsed it. On September 18-19, from fifteen to twenty thousand people gathered on the fair grounds. There was of course an almost endless parade. All day Wednesday and all Wednesday night the barbecuers were busy roasting beeves, hogs, and sheep. Seven beeves, four hogs, and five sheep were prepared for the first day, and nine beeves for the second, but still there was not enough to go around. "No gambling, dancing, or drinking was in evidence," the *Free Press* commented, despite the fact that a general holiday atmosphere prevailed. An organ was furnished by a local dealer, encouraging a lot of singing. The crowd was so large that much of the time it was necessary to have four orators in operation at one time in order for all to hear.[40]

It cannot be forgotten that this fever pitch was maintained by most Populist speakers for months at a time. Meetings of this sort were their daily lives during most of the summer and early fall. Many of them gave well over a hundred speeches each between the Fourth of July and election day. The typical occasion was one of great excitement, calling for prolonged enthusiasm and much energy on the part of the speaker.

Personal rewards were small indeed compared with the exacting nature of the campaigning. Judge Peffer received no money for his speaking in 1890 above his expenses, "and this may be made up largely, if not wholly by subscriptions to the *Kansas Farmer* when the people are so disposed."[41] Mary Elizabeth Lease solicited subscriptions for the *Nonconformist*, and Jerry Simpson sent in names and dollars to *Commoner*. Annie Diggs was an assistant editor of the *Advocate*. Thus, several of the leading speakers had the additional chore of boosting newspaper subscription lists. Also, there was the task of being pleasant to hundreds of people whom they had never seen before. For example, at the Elk County convention in Howard, July 19, 1894, Diggs not only spoke from the north door of the courthouse, but she also held open house all afternoon at the Metropolitan Hotel for the wives and daughters of delegates.[42]

Consider, moreover, the rigors of speaking outdoors day after day. More than once the papers reported an orator to be "a little hoarse."[43]

Perhaps worst of all was the ordeal of traveling from county-seat town to county-seat town. When Jerry Simpson spoke in Medicine Lodge, September 27, 1890, he had driven his team and wagon all night through the desolate, barren hills from Coldwater to be present. Even today this is a tiring forty-one mile trip.[44] In 1891, after giving five speeches in a day and a half at Westmoreland, Mary Elizabeth Lease traveled more than twenty miles by buggy to Frankfort, where she caught a train to Concordia for her next day's task.[45] August 13, 1894, Annie Diggs spoke in the afternoon in Sedan, though the temperature was 103 degrees in the shade. That night she spoke again and then was driven nineteen miles in a buggy to Moline, where she caught a train for an eighty-mile ride to Wellington, where she was to speak the next day.[46]

Then, too, the weather was a factor. Kansas is extremely hot in August and September, but it can be windy and cold in October. Regardless of what the thermometer might say, the meetings were held. Thus, Lewelling spoke at Ottawa, October 10, 1892, though it was windy and very dusty, "a bad day for farmers to come to hear."[47] He spoke at Sedan, October 22 of the same year, on a cold, raw day, "too windy for banners."[48] It would seem that the crowds as well as the speakers had to be hardy.

All this was good audience psychology, of course. Even the bad weather helped breed *esprit de corps*. The parades and the singing were perfect audience-participation techniques. The bands and glee clubs provided blood-tingling entertainment, and the picnic or barbecue gave the whole affair a festive, wholesome, holiday touch that made the listeners even more receptive. The large numbers that were present always made it seem logical to "climb on the band-wagon." The evangelistic fervor of many of the familiar tunes that were sung and the crusading, evangelistic zeal of the speakers themselves made the audience reaction almost sure-fire.

A typical meeting was likely to be opened with prayer. Then came a glee club or a soloist with a witty or extravagant song to create laughter and break down individual reserve. The song leader then would take the platform, and everyone would join lustily in the singing of new political words to old and well-known revival tunes or to the tunes of well-known popular songs. When the audience was thus unified, the stage was set for the appearance of the speaker of the day, who carried revival psychology to its climax in his or her speech. Everybody listening knew the arguments already; all that was needed was to get an emotional reaction that would produce results. The aim was not a reformed life but a People's Party vote.

To the Populist orator and to his or her audience the basic issues were largely beyond argument, closed by the very course of events themselves. The orator's principal function was one of identifying the problems of the day with the audience and the solution of those problems with the People's Party—of filling the band-wagon and, with it, leading a parade to the polling booths of the state.

Persuasive appeals are the mainstay of rough-and-tumble times, and so it was in the early Populist period in Kansas. At the political meeting anyone could speak, and many took advantage of the opportunity. Genuine debate was common. Mary Elizabeth Lease, for example, almost always asked for questions or debate at the end of one of her speeches.

Once at Waushara a minister rose and spoke against Willits, the Populist candidate for Governor. Lease cross-examined him, wrung from him the fact that he was a Republican, and charged that this was the sole basis of his hatred of Willits. Then, "with withering sarcasm," she made him out to be a fool "amid the wildest cheers from the audience."[49]

Logic, however, as well as emotion was widely and effectively used in Populist argument. Notice the way the two are interwoven in an excerpt from a speech of Senator Peffer:

If you will take the prices of cattle in Chicago in the year 1883, about the beginning of the recent decline, you will find that the average value of cattle in the market was $38.00 a head, while in 1890 the average value of the same class of property was only $18.00 a head, less than one half . . . . It is answered in reply to this particular statement that a dollar buys more today. That is what we are complaining about. It buys more labor, it buys more wheat, it buys more of any kind of property that the producer has to sell. . . .[50]

Almost any speaker could give figures showing the course of debt and poverty, the strength and wealth of Wall Street, or the exorbitancies of railroad and elevator charges. Such use of statistics, together with effective appeals to authority, and a telling use of illustration were the usual logical weapons of the Populist orator. However, when Peffer, in speech after speech, carefully cited the number of millionaires in the country, ending with the statement that sixty thousand people controlled about one fifth of the wealth of the nation while the average wealth of the great mass of people was only $950, the people were not surprised. They had read the same thing in the pamphlet material that was so readily available.[51] Such was the case also when Jerry Simpson attacked the railroads and argued how expensive they had been in terms of municipal and state debts contracted within Kansas in order to subsidize the building and operation of new lines.[52] This was simply an old story to the Alliancemen turned politicians. Since the days of the Grange they had studied the railroads. As Greenbackers they had studied the currency problem. As Alliancemen they had studied the problems of land and marketing. The facts were known.

In a sense this was also true of quotations from authority. Newspaper editors of the period were greatly interested in speechmaking. "Quotable Quotes" were often the subject for editorial comment. Source books of the party included excerpts from Republican speeches that could be used against the then-current stand of that party. Thus, when Annie Diggs quoted Senator Ingalls and made him seem ridiculous, the crowd at Downs applauded and laughed, recognizing the unfortunate ambiguity of the Senator's innocent remarks from materials they had already read and studied.[53] They applauded wildly when Mary Elizabeth Lease rose to refute the discomfited Mr. Brumbaugh at Concordia, using quotations from his own party leaders.[54] They probably recognized the passage from one of Peffer's senatorial speeches which was soberly quoted by their new

governor—L.D. Lewelling—in his somewhat oratorical inaugural address.[55] They laughed, too, at a story that made the rounds about one of
Jerry Simpson's particularly eloquent illustrations. Many remembered
hearing it before, almost word for word. Some of them even asked him
about it. His reported reply was: "I put in the quotation marks, but you
couldn't see them."[56] Most quotations were carefully labeled, however, for
the name of the quoted authority often had a certain rebuttal value of its
own. It was good strategy to take over the remarks of the opposition
whenever possible.

It must not be forgotten that every People's Party speech was in reality a
part of an enormous nonstop debate. Some of the speeches were
constructive, and some were clearly refutation. Most were some of each.
When Jerry Simpson spoke at Medicine Lodge in his 1890 campaign
against Hallowell, the *Barber County Index* observed that:

Jerry's speech cannot be outlined. . . . He cut down everything in front of him
and knocked the old parties into pieces. He played with "Prince Hal" as a cat would
play with a mouse. It was cruel, yet, it was fascinating, and the vast audience
listened with the utmost attention, and as they saw the quick wit, the sharp repartee,
the convincing logic, they laughed and cheered and yelled and clapped their hands
in enthusiastic delight.[57]

The Populist debater was a clever strategist. He did not permit himself to
be forced onto the defensive. He took over the arguments of his opposition
whenever possible—quoting opposition statements and pointing out
inconsistencies in the opposition's point of view. The watchword was
"Attack!" Even the exposition of Populist doctrine was handled as if it
were the solution of an admitted problem, the answer to an anticipated
question.

When considering the effectiveness of such oratory as that of the Kansas
Populist in the early 1890s, the critic must remember that the frontier was
still very close to people. Direct actionism was still an important part of the
political philosophy of the day. Democracy and individualism, to
paraphrase Carl Becker, were not a philosophy but a "way of life."
Religion was firmly interwoven into all thought, and the crusading spirit
was a typical reaction to any prolonged or general evil. Consider the lack of
subtlety with which Mary Elizabeth Lease approaches her argument in this
representative passage:

The moral conscience has been quickened, the heart of the nation aroused, and we
are asking, in all earnestness, "with malice toward none and charity for all," which
of the political parties can best solve the problems of the day? And we answer
unhesitatingly, that party which is most in accord with the teachings of Christ and

in harmony with that safeguard of human liberty, the constitution of the United States.[58]

The rise of the Populist movement was to a large extent the result of the efforts of its speakers. These speakers harmonized with the needs and attitudes of the day and the place and hence were effective. Former Kansas Governor Henry J. Allen said of Mary Elizabeth Lease, in grudging admiration, "She had the real gift of leadership."[59] This "leadership" was one of the most important qualities of the successful Populist orator. It was based on knowing the times, knowing the audience, knowing the subject, and consisted of marching with unembarrassed fervor into battle for uncompromising goals.

NOTES

1. R. B. Russell, "The Independent Party and Money at Cost," *Arena* 4 (August 1891): 341–342.
2. Arch W. Jarrell, "Kansas Portraits—The Populists," *Jayhawk* 2 (April 1929): 117. Jarrell was a long-time Kansas newspaper editor.
3. Frank L. McVey, "The Populist Movement," *Economic Studies* 1 (August 1896): 136.
4. Anna Rochester, *The Populist Movement in the United States* (New York: International Publishing Co., 1943), p. 9.
5. Personal interview: Topeka, Kansas; August 13, 1948.
6. Richard Hofstadter, *The Age of Reform* (New York: Alfred A. Knopf, 1955).
7. For a detailed analysis of the position of Max Lerner, Oscar Handlin, Peter Viereck, Edward A. Shils, Victor C. Ferkis, Hofstadter, and others, see Walter T. K. Nugent, *The Tolerant Populists: Kansas Populism and Nativism* (Chicago: University of Chicago Press, 1963), especially pp. 3–32. The traditional view, with overtones of Frederick Jackson Turner's thesis concerning the dynamic role of the frontier, is probably best understood from John D. Hicks, *The Populist Revolt* (Minneapolis: University of Minnesota Press, 1931). By reading Hicks, the first few pages of Nugent, Hofstadter, and *A Populist Reader*, edited by George B. Tindal (New York: Harper and Row, Publishers, 1966, paperback), one can gain full insight into what is presently known about the history of Populism, as well as becoming acquainted with many of the movement's most important written and oral materials. Other interesting, recent interpretations include those of Norman Pollack, *The Populist Response to Industrial America* (New York: W. W. Norton, 1966), who feels that Populism was a radical, forward-looking movement; and of O. Gene Clanton, *Kansas Populism: Ideas and Men* (Lawrence: The University Press of Kansas, 1969), who argues that the movement had both progressive and retrogressive strains.
8. John B. Clark, *Populism in Alabama*, Ph.D. dissertation, New York

University, 1927 (Auburn, Alabama: Auburn Printing Co., 1927), p. 57.

9. An interesting contemporary analysis of the adoption of Populist principles by the Democrats can be found in Waldo Lincoln Cook, "Present Political Tendencies," *Annals of the American Academy of Political and Social Sciences* 18 (September 1901): 192–195.

10. *The Tolerant Populist*, p. 25.

11. For a thorough discussion of the activities of these men and women, see Donald H. Ecroyd, "An Analysis and Evaluation of Populist Political Campaign Speech Making in Kansas, 1890–1894," unpublished Ph.D. dissertation, The State University of Iowa, 1949. See also, Donald H. Ecroyd, "The Agrarian Protest," in DeWitte Holland, ed., *America in Controversy* (Dubuque: William C. Browne, 1973).

12. Eleventh Census of the U.S., 1890; Report on Farms and Homes, p. 258.

13. Ibid.

14. See *The Populist Revolt*, Chapter 3. Also, Mary Elizabeth Lease at Kansas City in late 1891; Governor Lewelling, Inaugural Address, Topeka, January 9, 1893; Senator Peffer at Lyons, June 7, 1890; Congressman Simpson at Wichita, September 15, 1891; and others. These speeches are included with those collected in the appendix of the Ecroyd dissertation (see above). The original pamphlets, or newspaper sources, are available in the Kansas State Historical Society Collection, Topeka.

15. See *The Populist Revolt*, Chapter 3. Also, Mary Elizabeth Lease at Kansas City in March, 1891; and in the Great Quadrangular Debate, Salina, December 18, 1893; Congressman Simpson at Harper, August 30, 1890; and others collected in the appendix of the Ecroyd dissertation (see above).

16. See *The Populist Revolt*, Chapter 3. Also, Annie Diggs at Osborne, October 30, 1890; Mary Elizabeth Lease in the Lease-Brumbaugh Debate, Concordia, July 20, 1891; Governor Lewelling, Inaugural Address; Senator Peffer at Lyons, June 12, 1890; Congressman Simpson at Wichita, September 3, 1894; and others, collected in the appendix of the Ecroyd dissertation (see above). Currency figures from *World Almanac*.

17. *E.g.*, The Lease-Brumbaugh Debate, Concordia, published by the Concordia *Times*, 1891. (See the appendix of the Ecroyd dissertation. Several copies of the original pamphlet are also collected in the Kansas State Historical Society, Topeka.) A contemporary attack on this pamphlet material can be found in C. W. Wiley, "The People's Party," *American Journal of Politics* 5 (December 1894): 655.

18. (Lansing, Michigan: Robert Smith & Co., Printers and Binders, 1891), p. 46.

19. N. A. Dunning ed., *The Farmers' Alliance Historical and Agricultural Digest* (Washington, D.C.: The Alliance Publishing Company, 1891); W. Scott Morgan, *History of the Wheel and Alliance and the Impending Revolution* (Ft. Scott, Kansas: published by the author and printed by J. H. Rice & Sons, Printers and Publishers, 1889); *Populist Handbook for Kansas* (Indianapolis: Vincent Bros., Publishing Company, 1891).

20. *Kansas City Star*, April 1, 1891.

21. Grant P. Harrington, interviewed in Kansas City, Kansas, August 29, 1948.

22. William Allen White, "A Weak Man in a Strong Position," *The Agora (A Kansas Magazine)* 4 (October 1894); 90.
23. Floyd B. Streeter, *The Kaw* (New York: Farrar & Rinehart, 1941), pp. 306–308. Also, Cecil Howes in the *Kansas City Times,* July 8, 1938.
24. *Seneca Courier-Democrat*, September 14, 1894.
25. William Allen White, *The Autobiography of William Allen White* (New York: The Macmillan Company, 1946), pp. 218–219.
26. Elizabeth N. Barr (Mrs. Elizabeth Barr Arthur), "The Populist Uprising," *A Standard History of Kansas and Kansans* (Chicago: Lewis Publishing Company, 1916), 2: 1148–1149; Hicks, *The Populist Revolt*, pp. 167–170; W. P. Harrington, "Populist Party in Kansas," *Collections of the Kansas State Historical Society*, 16: 413–414.
27. September 17, 1890.
28. August 2, 1894.
29. *The Advocate* (Topeka), August 27, 1890.
30. *Barber County Index* (Medicine Lodge), September 10, 1890.
31. *Kansas Commoner* (Newton), August 7, 1890.
32. *Kansas Commoner* (Wichita), September 8, 1892.
33. Ibid., October 11, 1894.
34. *Pratt County Union* (Pratt), August 9, 1894.
35. *Ness County News* (Ness City), November 4, 1893.
36. *Columbus Modern Light*, June 25, 1891.
37. *Lyons Republican*, June 12, 1890.
38. *Barber County Index*, October 1, 1890.
39. *Hutchinson Daily News*, September 26, 1890; *The Alliance Gazette* (Hutchinson), September 26, 1890.
40. *The Industrial Free Press* (Winfield), September 26, 1890; *The American Non-Conformist* (Winfield), September 25, 1890; see also *The Kaw*, pp. 309–310.
41. This was the phrase that was repeated in issue after issue of the *Kansas Farmer* during the campaign of 1890.
42. *The Elk County Citizen* (Howard), July 19, 1894.
43. *E.g.*, concerning Simpson, *The Wichita Daily Beacon*, October 1, 1890.
44. *The Barber County Index*, October 1, 1890.
45. *The Advocate*, July 17, 1891.
46. *The Lance* (Sedan), August 15, 1894.
47. *Ottawa Journal and Triumph*, October 13, 1892.
48. *The Lance*, November 2, 1892.
49. *The Advocate*, August 27, 1890.
50. *Topeka Daily Capital*, October 2, 1891.
51. At Lyons, June 7, 1890, *Lyons Republican*, June 12, 1890; at Eureka, June 14, 1890, *The Eureka Republican*, June 18, 1890; at the Cincinnati convention, May 20, 1891, see Elizabeth Barr, pp. 1160–1161. Mary Elizabeth Lease used the same figures at Kansas City in late March, 1891, *Kansas City Star*, April 1, 1891; and in her debate with Brumbaugh, July 20, 1891, see the Lease-Brumbaugh Debate pamphlet.
52. *I.e.*, at Kiowa, October 8, 1892; *Kiowa Journal*, October 13, 1892.

53. *Osborne County News* (Osborne), October 30, 1890.
54. See the rebuttal speech in the Lease-Brumbaugh Debate.
55. *Kansas State Governors: Messages*, Vol. 2, 1883-1895, (Topeka: Kansas State Historical Society, 1893).
56. Jarrell, "Kansas Portraits," pp. 117–119.
57. October 1, 1890.
58. "The Great Quadrangular Debate," see Mary Elizabeth Lease's speech, December 18, 1893, Salina, Kansas. (published by *The Open Church*, Salina, 1894). A copy is filed in the Kansas State Historical Society Collection, Topeka.
59. Personal interview: Wichita, Kansas, September 8, 1948.

7

The One-Gallus Uprising: Southern Discontent

ROBERT W. SMITH

There is no charm in agriculture now. The country mansions have gone to decay; the fields are worn to sand, or seamed with gullies; the ditches in the low ground have filled and the meadows, ah! the green, flower-scented meadow we children loved, has become a marsh.[1]

So spoke Thomas E. Watson, fiery Georgia orator, as he pictured the plight of southern farmers in his commencement address at the Milledgeville (Georgia) Academy in June, 1890. He might also have noted the poverty weighing on the small farmer, his disillusionment with state and national government, and his despair (at times) of reform; for these also comprised part of the picture.

Since Appomattox the status of the southern farmer had steadily worsened, yet few in government seemed to care. He had searched his soul, talked with neighbors, listened to speakers, perused agricultural literature (if he could read)—all with the purpose of finding causes and devising solutions. But nothing happened. He not only remained poor, but he grew poorer. He supported the conservative Democratic party but suffered in the process. One Arkansas lecturer told his Washington County audience in April, 1889:

The farmer has no time for thinking, leisure or recreation; he must go back to the treadmills of trifleless toil and work on or starve. He must bow his tired shoulders to carry the increased burdens of his task-masters, while on every side he beholds the sons and daughters of . . . ten thousand Pharoahs passing to and fro. . . . Indeed, I say Egypt and her rulers are here. The Israelites are in bondage and they cry for help! Where is Moses?[2]

What had happened in American agriculture to drive the farmer to such despair? This question can best be answered by tracing the growth and demise of rural southern populism in its pre-twentieth-century milieu.

THE RISE OF DISCONTENT: 1870–1886

In examining the rise of southern discontent during the period immediately after the Civil War one must answer four questions: (1) What economic, political, and social causes prompted farmers to band together? What fostered their militancy to challenge the entrenched Democratic party? (2) What organizations served as vehicles for their challenge to Bourbon democracy? (3) Who agitated for redress? What kind of leaders emerged? And (4), On what topics did the leading spokesmen concentrate? Were the issues the same as those of the 1890s?

Following the War Between the States southern patricians forsook the drab countryside for greener economic pastures in the cities. "The pursuit of agriculture, once a badge of social distinction, suffered a serious loss of prestige."[3] This exodus stemmed from several economic hardships.

Initially the emigration of young men from farms, tired of outdoor drudgery, precipitated a rural labor shortage. Few immigrants from either the North or from abroad replaced them.

Further, southern farms lacked adequate tools for the job. Only on Louisiana's farms did the value of farm implements (in 1880, $112.00 per farm) exceed the national average of $100.00.

Moreover, the value of that poorly equipped land, with its wornout soil and lack of physical improvements, decreased.[4]

Also, the radical change in the relative economic status of farm and city worker stunned and disillusioned many in the countryside. Rural wealth from 1850 to 1890 increased fourfold while urban opulence mushroomed fifteenfold.[5] This imbalance blighted the hopes of southern farmers.

In addition, throughout the South the number of farms increased sharply from 1880 to 1890, the biggest gains coming in farms of less than one hundred acres.[6] So competition drastically increased as prices dropped measurably. Small-time farmers, the one-gallus type, would form the basis for the agrarian protest in the late nineteenth century. Again, cotton, a basic crop, dropped from 13 cents a pound (1874) to 4.6 cents (1894) as improved procedures and machinery nearly doubled the crop from 5.5

million bales (1879) to over 10 million (1894), far outstripping consumption.[7]

Finally, coupled with cotton production, the crop-lien system harnessed 80 to 90 percent of the cotton farmers to the local storekeeper.[8] It permitted loaning of money only on the basis of a cotton harvest—even a future crop. With the price of cotton declining for years, combined with a shrinkage of regional capital, largely destroyed after Appomattox, some men never got out of debt, while the South itself became parasitically dependent on northern and western credit.

Other factors also led to farmers' problems: politics, for example. With the rise of urban industrialization and an increase in city voters politicians yielded to the demands of business and industry and left farmers to shift for themselves. Like the priest and Levite of old, office seekers and legislatures (the latter with a preponderance of urban lawyers) passed by on the other side.

Social elements further compounded the problem. Poor roads and lack of communication, hard work, and long hours isolated families, particularly women, for extended periods. Housewives and lonely farmers welcomed the prospect of some kind of social organization to provide greater contact with the outside world.

The late-nineteenth-century South had essentially two classes. A sixth of the population, composed of merchant, landlord, banker, and capitalist, held all the political power. The other five-sixths of the population, made up of the share-cropper, small farmer and field worker (the common laborer) who lived from empty hand to empty mouth, retained little or no power.[9] It was this lower class white and black that spurred the Populist uprising in the South and kept it alive.

The farmer not only had lost his earlier prestige but also felt a genuine conspiracy at work to destroy his economic and political life. In the dying Jeffersonian tradition "probably no other class of people ever dominated the economical, political, and social life of an American community more completely or exerted a greater influence in national affairs, than did the farmers of the Old South."[10] But now they found themselves helpless, at the mercy of heedless politicians and urban cousins who did not understand them. The white dirt farmers indeed seemed destined to replace the Negro in economic slavery.

Farmers tried many remedies to resolve their difficulties: exchanges, newspapers, and the subtreasury (explained later); but the most important were organizations. In their meetings speakers, both local and national, set aflame the tinderbox of discontent.

The first and least daring of the reform groups was the National

Grange—more accurately, the Patrons of Husbandry. Oliver H. Kelley, a United States Department of Agriculture agent, sought to help President Andrew Johnson's program for farming by touring the South on a fact-finding trip. Though a Yankee Mason, Kelley perceived the psychological lift and the potential help a secret organization would provide the farmer. He kindled an interest in others, no Southerners among them, and established the first Grange in Washington, D.C., in January, 1868. The South got its first charter (Tennessee) in June, 1870. By the end of 1873 some 20,000 Granges within the region's borders were decrying the tyranny of monopolies, high railroad rates, and corporate power.[11] The organization reached its zenith in 1874–75 but not before it had generated within the small-scale farmer a class consciousness that gave him a glimpse of corrective actions he might take.

No enemy of free enterprise, the Grange prohibited club-sponsored political activity but not individual action. The frustration of the farmer, however, continued to rise. By 1886 Israel P. Darden, National Master of the Grange, in his annual message urged the members to "send men to the legislatures, state and national, who will equalize and reduce taxation; restrain corporations from oppressing the people; have finances managed in the interest of the people . . . and extend the same protection to the farmer and to the manufacturer."[12] But Darden urged nothing beyond individual participation in the political arena. The bold idea of collective action would not appear until six years later with the formation of the People's Party.

For several reasons the Grange declined despite its noble purposes of promoting individual efficiency, mutual co-operation, and the maintenance of an adequate standard of living. In the first place, the locals increased so rapidly that members could not develop fraternal feelings among themselves. The resulting social despair weakened the organization. Then, poor communication and the paucity of lecturers prevented members from becoming sufficiently imbued with the organization's potentials. They never really developed an *esprit de corps*. Moreover, dirt farmers had so little money that continued recession swept the Grange and other socio-political groups into virtual oblivion. With the acute shortage of capital, farmers could not trade at exchanges whose very existence presumed a minimum of hard cash. In addition, the inept management of some exchanges led to their bankruptcy. Finally, the Grange could not withstand more attractive competition from the Farmers' Alliance, Agricultural Wheel, and, later, the People's Party.[13]

Unlike the Grange, the Farmers' Alliance originated in the South (Texas). There, in January, 1887, Dr. Charles W. Macune, a 240-pound, largely self-taught lawyer, physician, and farmer, called a meeting at Waco to lay plans for more aggressive action by farmers. The new group, strongly influenced by the earlier Grange, also prohibited local Alliances from direct political action—a political schizophrenia that plagued the Alliance at every level for the next decade. The Waco meeting immediately sent out lecturers and organizers who achieved widespread success in Alabama, Tennessee, and elsewhere in the South. By 1889 Alabama's three thousand lodges had 125,000 members. A year later Texas claimed 150,000 followers.[14]

Under the Alliance the agrarian movement reached its height in the South, though at different times in different states. Essentially conservative, its power lay not in the creation of a third party, but in controlling the Democratic machinery, as it did ably in South Carolina. Also, like its predecessor (the Grange), the Alliance had little quarrel with capital, railroads, or corporations as parts of the free enterprise system, though it deplored their crippling rates and demoralizing prices. Change it welcomed. To spread the good news of reform it used, as had reform movements for centuries, persuasive speakers, but the proposed lecturers' institute seems never to have materialized.[15]

By and large the South maintained a strict color line in the Alliance, seldom admitting blacks to membership despite their attendance at rallies. As blacks could not count on white help, though sometimes it came unexpectedly, they organized the Colored National Alliance and Co-Operative Union in Houston in 1886, and by 1890 had gathered well over a million members, making it the largest black organization of its time. Its purposes, like those of its white counterpart, were to improve the black farmer's financial condition, improve his farming methods, and make him a better citizen.[16] To some extent it succeeded, though its exchange stores usually floundered, often under white management.

Who carried the issues to the people during the early phase of the farmers' revolt? To compile a complete catalog of the orators is impossible. They were found at every level from the humblest suballiance (whose records have since disappeared) to the national organizations. But one could hear the Taylor brothers (Alfred A. and Robert L.) of Tennessee, Benjamin R. ("Pitchfork Ben") Tillman of South Carolina, James S. Hogg of Texas, and Tom Watson of Georgia as each found a wide following in his state. All worked within the major parties as long as possible. Tillman, an intransigent Democrat, never permitted a third party to exist in his state. But, as he clearly showed at a convention in Columbia in April, 1886, he did not oppose the farmers in their support of particular men for public office.[17]

So dissent marched down the roads and streets of southern counties and cities but often to the beat of different drummers. Sometimes it pursued a separatist course; other times it joined one of the major parties. Here and there it replaced ineffective leaders and worked out minor economic and political changes.

DEVELOPMENT OF THE PROTEST: 1887–1891

Farmers in the developing years pondered how best to voice their protests. For the most part the Farmers' Alliance and later Populist Party were made up of lower class, Anglo-Saxon, unredeemed dirt farmers. Sometimes one or both emerging organizations appealed to laboring classes in the city, as happened in Alabama; or they admitted country doctors, ministers, and teachers, as in South Carolina. Yet few joined. Both organizations remained basically agrarian.[18] A few large landowners, like James G. Field of Virginia, were members, but never many. Like their counterparts of the twentieth century, they had little in common with the tenant, the share-cropper, or small landowners.

Yet the southern leadership of the Populists enjoyed significant rhetorical potential. Southern spokesmen, basing their arguments on innumerable examples, could hold their own in oral discourse and frequently even surpassed the spokesmen of established parties. Few dared to challenge Alliance-Lecturer Ben Terrell, or former Methodist missionary Harrison S. P. ("Stump") Ashby (both of Texas) and Marion Butler (North Carolina, especially after Butler gained experience in the early 1890s), or Reuben F. ("Run Forever") Kolb, the well-educated southern blue-blood from Alabama.[19] These were the Moseses called to deliver the enslaved farmer from the shackles of poverty and second-class citizenship. But they were not always easy to recognize or ready to assume the role. Nor were the times always propitious.

Speakers sometimes pictured particular individuals as slave-holding culprits, especially in the 1892–96 era, but at other times it was society or a party generally who felt the brunt of the scorn. Kolb and Terrell, two of the strongest spokesmen, lashed out at the political and social myopia of a reactionary Bourbon democracy whose newspapers could do little more than complain about Terrell's use of "dog-gone," "cusses," and "by golly."[20] And in Charleston, South Carolina, in an August, 1888, debate with the editor of the *News and Courier*, Pitchfork Ben Tillman minced no words about who ran his state:

You [Charlestonians] are a peculiar people. If one-tenth of the reports which come to me are true, you are the most arrant set of cowards that ever drew the fresh air of heaven. You submit to a tyranny in [the local Democratic machine] that is degrading to you as white men . . . [I]f anybody were to attempt this tyranny in Edgefield [Tillman's hometown], I swear . . . we would lynch him.

You people are cringing down in the mire because you are afraid of that newspaper [The Bourbon *News and Courier*] down the street. Its editor bestrides the State . . . [and clings] around the neck of South Carolina, oppressing the people and stifling reform.[21]

His appeal failed. The county responded by sending a solid anti-Tillman delegation to the next Democratic convention. Two years later Colonel Leonidas L. Polk (North Carolina), at the Ocala, Florida, convention, was less specific when he indicted the "discriminating and grossly unjust national legislation" foisted onto hapless America.[22] While the language was indignant, the feelings were even stronger as men simmered in anger.

Several national conventions crystallized reform, but the two in which the South figured most prominently met at Ocala, Florida (December 1890), and Cincinnati, Ohio (May 1891).[23]

Formation of a third party, discussion of unfair national legislation, and consideration of the subtreasury plan dominated the Ocala meeting. The last of these proposals and the one farmers least understood was conceived by the balding, mustached Charles W. Macune. It would permit farmers to deposit produce in large government granaries or storehouses established in counties that marketed $5,000.00 or more per year in farm produce, and then allow them, when prices slumped, to borrow at two percent interest on up to eighty percent of the crop's value. The government could later sell the staples when the market rallied. As with many such schemes, the subtreasury plan plowed a deep furrow between defenders and attackers, some seeing it as a fresh approach to a noxious and perennial problem, others as radical and unconstitutional.

Labor was strongly represented at the Florida meeting but it never significantly influenced southern reform. If a state like Florida was divided between two agricultural regions—North and South—so much that the problems of the one seldom matched those of the other, equally significant differences obtained between the industrial laborer and the rural farmer. Each section recognized the other's distress, but neither could appreciate its counterpart's problems fully nor did it have adequate energies and resources to tackle them.

National Alliance President L. L. Polk, reading his opening address at Ocala, declared that investigation by the best minds for the past two years had led to the general conviction that the economic situation was "due in large measure and in most part, to partial, discriminating and grossly unjust national legislation."[24] But, like Tillman and others, Polk feared any third-party action. He placed his confidence in the socratic doctrine of knowledge: If a people know the right, they will do the right. A man with only ten months of formal education in his entire life and an early defender of the subtreasury, Polk now saw education as the greatest and most urgent need of the order:

If asked what is the greatest and most essential need of our order, as contributing most to its ultimate and triumphant success, I should unhesitatingly answer . . . education. Education in the mutual relations and reciprocal duties between each other, as brethren, as neighbors, as members of society; education in the most responsible duties of citizenship; education in the science of economic government; education for higher aspiration, higher thought, and higher manhood among the masses; education in a broad patriotism, which should bind the conservative masses of the country in the strongest ties of fraternity and union.[25]

Recognizing the need to propagandize, he urged the establishment of a lecture plan, using competent speakers to carry the message far and wide. Further, the country, needing an adequate circulating medium, should restore silver "to its dignity and place as a money metal, with all the rights of coinage and all the qualities of legal tender which gold possesses." Some delegates, like Leonidas F. Livingston, president of the Georgia Alliance, enshrined the political past and thus opposed uniting the variant groups into one organization, while others pushed for a National Union Party, concentrating on money, transportation, and land crises.[26]

The subtreasury plan elicited warm debate at the Florida convention. Sydenham B. Alexander (North Carolina) argued that "any man who opposes the subtreasury bill is either ignorant or has some sinister motive." But W. L. McAllister (Mississippi) withstood the measure in a strong speech declaring that it (1) would not relieve the financial straits of the farmer; (2) was paternalistic, unconstitutional, and impractical; and (3) protected the farmer neither in cost nor price. It should read, he held, "An Act to Ruin and Devastate the Agricultural Interests of the South."[27] Significantly, Reuben Kolb, Alabama's leading reformer in the 1890s, never argued that the subtreasury would relieve the farmer's plight; he simply challenged the Bourbons to propose something better.[28]

Ocala delegates aborted any third-party attempts but inched closer to that goal by resolving to deprive office seekers of Alliance support unless they endorsed the 1889 St. Louis and 1890 Ocala platforms.[29] Fear of a divided white vote, however, intimidated most of those present, binding them yet closer to the traditional major parties.

The Cincinnati convention in May, 1891, had only a few Southern delegates, due to widespread opposition to its intended political action. The recommendations launching a third party and the free coinage of silver confronted the convention. Although the platform approximated those of the St. Louis (1889) and Ocala (1890) meetings, transportation, land, and taxation were insignificant issues. At the close of the reading that called for a third party James H. ("Cyclone") Davis, the loud-mouthed Texan, ran to the stage. After declaring himself an ex-Confederate, he called for adoption of every plank and resolution of the platform. Responding the Rev. Thomas Wadsworth (Indiana), an ex-Union soldier, rushed forward and the two erstwhile foes shook hands. Richard M. Humphrey, the white superintendent of the National Colored Alliance and a vice president of the convention, reacted to the effusive handshakes, and joined the two. Amid exhilaration someone moved to adopt the platform as read. The delegates wildly mounted tables and chairs, longing for higher heights from which to express their feelings.

Thus a third party was born, and, except for Texas, largely without southern help.[30] The move had required nearly a quarter-century to come to fruition. While Grange and Alliance restrictions had long cramped the emergence of a national People's Party, much as Saul's burdensome armor had manacled David from fighting Goliath, they could no longer restrain the political aspirations of the many.

Fearing that a third party would fragment white supremacy, most southern states nonetheless immediately set about to field a slate of candidates in the forthcoming campaign. In all such states the Alliance proved the backbone of the movement.

Convention planks and resolutions did not always coincide with views of orators on the hustings. The former tended to copy national platforms while speakers adapted more to local needs. In Texas, James S. Hogg, the popular and fearless former district attorney, campaigned for governor almost entirely on the issue of a state railroad commission even though he was not an Alliance member. At Mexia, in a four-hour Lincoln-Douglas style debate with Gustave Cook, Hogg argued that since the state had fixed rates at turnpikes, it should also fix railroad rates. Later he indicted bookkeeping principles of the railroads which hid assets (building and rolling stock) as liabilities. He cried out against excessive and discriminatory charges. Denying any desire for an all-powerful commission, he urged that the new one he favored be composed of three men.[31] In front, because of his effective concentration on this one issue to the virtual exclusion of all others, the two-hundred seventy-pound lawyer won the gubernatorial race.

Tom Watson, too, fought the railroads both within and outside legislative halls. In a powerful speech to the Georgia legislature in August, 1891, the raspy-voiced, humorless, and fearless speaker advocated government ownership—a step further than Hogg had gone. It would, he argued, (1) regulate speculative features in railroad management; (2)

remove watered stock and unreal dividends on them; (3) eliminate one of the bulwarks of plutocracy; (4) undercut "that infamous den of thieves known as Wall Street"; and (5) curtail extravagant state salaries and indiscriminate giving of free passes. But just how all these would be effected he did not spell out.[32] Watson's effective speaking prompted Governor William J. Northen to write Grover Cleveland that throughout the state Watson was drawing never less than two thousand and sometimes as many as five thousand listeners—a political fact that frightened party-line Democrats.[33]

Issues in South Carolina were more often characterized by *ad hominem* attacks than by analysis. In Charleston, in late August, 1888, as noted earlier, Tillman declared in a debate with Governor F. W. Dawson, that his middle-class audience was an "arrant set of cowards" for "cringing down in the mire" because of its fear of the local *News and Courier*.[34] And in his 1890 race for governor Tillman ridiculed the same community as "the greedy old city" and scoffed at nearby Beaufort's "niggerdom."[35] At his nomination in March he had indicated his pessimism and "humility," saying "if you ask me to lead the fight, you call me to lead a forlorn hope, but you will have at your head the only man who has the brains, the nerve, and the ability to organize the common people against the aristocracy."[36] He ran a hard race and won by a four-to-one margin. His victory obviously sprang from the despair and growing militance of the common man.

At the South Carolina state Alliance convention (1890) national president L. L. Polk, after a month on the road, pointed up other issues. He (1) denied that crop diversification or overproduction would relieve the farmers' plight (the trouble was underconsumption, he contended); (2) defied any politician to prove the subtreasury unconstitutional and at the same time assert the constitutionality of national banks; and (3) urged the Alliance to wage war on national, not state, matters.[37]

Issues as conceived by the speakers thus ranged over a wide spectrum. Yet spokesmen occasionally lacked the freedom to examine the implications of these issues. For example, when in 1890 Alliance-backed John P. Buchanan (Tennessee) ran for the state house and refused in Lebanon or Lewisburg to debate the subtreasury, it was not because he did not understand it but because the Democratic machine muzzled him. Later, cooling his ties with the straight-outs, he urged its adoption.[38]

Speakers like Watson, Kolb, and "Cyclone" Davis played significant roles in crystallizing the People's Party. Stressing continued agrarian dissatisfaction, they energetically indicted the Democratic machine, scored reactionary policies, and harangued audiences. Clearly the Democratic Party was too laden with the barnacles of intractable policies and corruption to be seaworthy for future voyages, and the speakers seldom tired of picturing the imminent shipwreck of the vessel. If Kolb and Tillman, from political ambition, denounced the status quo, though neither led his state into the third-party movement, Watson and Polk seemed more altruistic and ready to serve if elected.

The formation of a new party in the nineteenth century, as in any modern era, faced enormous obstacles throughout the South: fear of humiliating defeat, dividing the white vote, losing one's place in the majority party, or being scorned as ambitious. The Raleigh *News and Observer* derided North Carolina farmers at the Ninth Congressional District convention (June, 1892) with:

One remarkable thing about all the speakers was the fact that each seemed to suspect that some person unknown and undiscoverable might accuse him of wanting office. It was absolutely painful to watch the crushing blows dealt by each orator against the aforesaid indefinite persons for his [*sic*] possible insinuation . . . . All the gentlemen concurred in the opinion that it would be a mighty big honor to be selected by the People's Party for anything or any place; and, finally, that any man in the party had an undisputed right to aspire to any office.[39]

The Alliance prohibition against political group activity did not discourage individuals, nor did it preclude an Alliance meeting from adjourning and, five minutes later, reconvening as a political rally.[40] Rather it permitted the organization, at any level, to do about anything short of constituting itself as a political party. And the closer the elections came, the bolder grew the locals until the line between legal and illegal business became blurred and academic. No Alliance or sub-alliance ever satisfactorily resolved this ambiguity, though many worried about it from time to time.[41]

Farmers saw Watson, Tillman, Kolb, and, later, Bryan as their deliverers from oppression by city slickers and eastern capitalists. If they respected Polk for his statesmanship and thorough grasp of the issues or Ben Terrell for his rhetorical skills, they looked to the more fiery and belligerent men to hack their way through opposing forces and assault the myopic goals of the established parties. This the early leaders did, providing the necessary impetus to the movement prior to the conventions at St. Louis and Omaha (1892).

FRUITION OF THE MOVEMENT: 1892–1896

The South moved slowly—agonizingly so—toward aggressive political action and complete revolt. Not until after countless local, state, and national meetings did farmers feel sufficiently incensed and independent to take action, even though some had been Greenbackers and come-outers for more than a decade. The taste of new wine could not at first overcome the bitterness of earlier defeat.

Two national farmers' conventions in 1892 propelled the party into the arena. The first, at St. Louis, hammered out a platform dealing with money, land, transportation, and communications.[42] The other, at Omaha, on July 4, heard 1776 delegates (a symbolic number on a symbolic date) herald a "Second Declaration of Independence" and nominate the standard bearers. Although not committed to a third party, southerners participated more actively in the Omaha meeting than one could have thought possible. Joseph C. Manning, Alabama's twenty-two-year-old founder of its third party, nominated for the presidential slot fifty-nine-year-old James B. Weaver, an ex-Greenbacker and Union general from Iowa, who won easily on the first ballot. But considerable disorder reigned for the second spot. Such men as James G. Field (Virginia), Ben Terrell and "Cyclone" Davis (Texas), Tom Watson (Georgia), and John H. McDowell (Tennessee) all could balance a sectional ticket; but Field, the one-legged sixty-six-year-old Baptist landowner (with two thousand acres of "the choicest land") and formerly Virginia's state attorney-general, was finally chosen. While Weaver, Watson, Terrell, and others were equal, socially and economically, to their counterparts in the other parties,[43] the rank-and-file members of the third party were essentially the poor whites and negroes, the ragtag of agrarian society, the one-gallus farmers.

Throughout the South voters responded excitedly to the many stumpers. "The woods are full of orators. There are speeches, and speeches, and speeches," cried one anti-Populist paper.[44] Nationally there were perhaps two thousand orators—calamity howlers some called them—thumping Populist tubs. The South had its share.[45] Only with difficulty however could southerners listen to northerners like Iowa's Weaver or Kansas' Mary Elizabeth Lease (occasionally scorned as "Mary Yellin' Lease") who sometimes accompanied the general and his wife and who was the rhetorical superior of virtually any straight-out Democrat. While many summarily rejected Lease and what she said, others were compelled to listen by the sheer weight of her arguments. In Greensboro, North Carolina, Weaver's concentration on the broad national issues of banking, transportation, land, and money led one friendly reporter to insist that "sick Democracy and Republicanism stood and writhed and squirmed like worms in hot embers while many came to us . . . declaring their conversion to our cause."[46] Weaver's Raleigh audience of perhaps five thousand was partisanly divided, not only because of southern hostility to splinter groups and to Lease, but also because of his alleged misconduct in

Pulaski, Tennessee, during the Civil War. He was accused, among other things, of telling a white man whose house the general occupied that a Negro was the equal of any white man in the South.[47] He spoke only four times in the Tar Heel State where he was more tolerantly received than in Georgia. There his wife was egged. When later he braved the challenges to speak in Pulaski, one hundred mounted sympathizers surrounded the speaker's stand as a protective wall against assault.

Personal feelings also deeply divided listeners and local speakers. At Princeton, North Carolina, when Populist Jack Raines was virtually called a liar he descended from the stand to support his statements. The resulting donnybrook halted a passenger train until the tracks could be cleared.[48] That same month, at Wilson, Marion Butler, the state Alliance president, was egged. In Thomsom, North Carolina, Populists tucked pistols beneath their coats when they attended mass meetings.[49] In Georgia the bitter campaign, the most frightening in the state's history, saw fifteen Negroes and several whites killed.[50] Alabama listened to platform speakers pour out invectives, extreme even by its rough-and-tumble standards. Reuben Kolb, dishonestly defeated in the 1890 gubernatorial election, with Populist backing redoubled his efforts to claim the high office. When the Democratic convention rejected him, he and his followers bolted, set up the rump "Jeffersonian Democrats," and ran anyway, urging immigration and the influx of northern capital to solve the state's financial ills.[51] At Gordon, Alabama, the excitement was so high, heckling so loud, and eggs (a favorite weapon of farmers) so thick that Kolb and his friends were forced from the platform.[52] He was again defeated fraudulently by stuffed ballot boxes and white coercion of blacks.

In North Carolina at least twenty-one reform speakers (less than half the Democrats' number) appeared at no less than 138 speaking occasions during the 1892–93 period.[53] Joint debates were particularly effective in the Tar Heel State. Those between Marion Butler and Charles B. Aycock before crowds in Clinton, Salisbury, and Warrenton, were on a higher intellectual plane than speeches by some others. In the early years Butler's inexperience worked against him, but he developed skill in dodging rhetorical blows as well as handing them out. The two antagonists contrasted vividly: Butler was deliberative, incisive, and dispassionate; Aycock, his Democratic opponent, was logical and articulate; Butler was argumentative; Aycock, simple and direct; Butler sought to convince; Aycock wished to conciliate.[54]

In the 1892 campaign the money issue dominated, followed by the alleged decadence of the Democratic Party, concern for the tariff, and, finally, local issues. Agricultural workers did not wait for the Bryan crusade of 1896 to wave the money banner, nor did they perceive the same issues as did newspaper editors. In North Carolina one paper insisted that the "two great issues in this campaign are the tariff and the Lodge Force Bill," the latter designed to promote Negro rights at the polls. When Populists concentrated on other matters, the paper scorned their efforts as "throw[ing] dust into the eyes of their people."[55] And in Congress the third party's effectiveness caused North Carolina Democrat John Steele Henderson to write to his wife: "The silver question is all the rage. . . . The Republicans and third partyites seem to be having everything their own way."[56]

Georgian populism crested in 1892 and featured some of the ablest southern oratory. Reform stumpers kept progressive fires glowing in Congress and the state, though one active Alliance member, Charles L. Moses, sought to extinguish third-party flames by putting his congressional colleagues on a dilemma: If Congress "were to take away the conservative element represented by the bimetallists on the right, radicals on the left, . . . the Republic would go down in a drama of blood."[57] Either extreme represented a choice that most Populists abhorred, at least at this time.

When Watson spoke on the hustings, sentiments ran high. He loved or hated, and though at times he vacillated, he always did so heatedly. Once when accompanied by H. S. Doyle, an able and intelligent Negro campaigner, forty guards bearing Winchester rifles protected them. In Thomson, Georgia, in August, 1892, Watson spoke for two hours after an exhausting train trip from Washington. To an audience of six thousand people he stressed his own good racial record and elicited a strong affirmative response from the blacks present. Then he appealed for this support:

Now what I want to say is this: I pledge you my word and honor, as a man and as a Representative, that if you stand up for your rights and for your manhood, if you stand shoulder to shoulder with us in this fight, you shall have fair play and fair treatment as men and as citizens, irrespective of your color.[58]

Just how he would deliver was not clear, but it was nonetheless an effective political promise.

The following month in Atlanta, Democrats hissed and hooted until Watson finally left the stand. Many of the several hundred women present were pushed and shoved aside. Some men cursed while others shed tears and mounted tables, pleading for order, but without avail.[59]

In Congress the Georgian enjoyed better decorum but had less success than in rough-and-tumble campaigning. In April, 1892, Watson condemned the tariff's effect on the cotton-grower and scolded William J. Bryan, his future colleague, for avoiding the free-trade issue: "After all the force of his logic, after all the splendor of his rhetoric, after all the driving in the direction of free trade, the gentleman shirked the issue when he got to the actual enunciation of the results of his logic."[60] He rapped timid Democratic knuckles with: "You ought not to ride your horse in this magnificent steeplechase across the country, using free trade whips at every gallop you make, and the moment you reach the wall, instead of lifting your steed for the leap, turn around and walk back to the stable door."[61] His peers listened but did little else, for they opposed most of what Watson stood for.

In 1892 the Populists' fast start brought scattered success throughout the South. Georgia sent fifty third-party men to the legislature while other states elected fewer Populist legislators. No southern state registered a victory for Weaver and Field, and the combined total of Texas's one-hundred thousand votes and Alabama's eighty-five thousand almost equaled the entire remainder of the South. However, the national ticket polled more electoral votes (22) than any third party from 1876 to 1896 and garnered a million popular votes all over the country.[62] Even though only partly successful, the campaign inspired farmers who had long felt powerless.

The number of speeches made cannot be correlated with popular support at the polls. In states like Alabama and Texas the national standard bearers appeared seldom, if ever, yet the third party scored heavily at the polls. In others like North Carolina reform speakers appeared oftener but won less support.

How can we interpret this inverse rhetorical effect? In the first place, Texas, with its many able native speakers, did not need outsiders to round up the mavericks. Local orators handled the situation easily. Further, stumpers avoided some states where they saw little chance of winning. South Carolina, for example, offered few possibilities because of the tight rein held by Tillman. Third-party anti-fusionist representatives were thoroughly baffled when they planned trips to North Carolina and other fusionist communities. Too, southern whites in Georgia, Alabama, Louisiana, and Mississippi, frightened by the prospects of resurgent black power, threw in their lot with racism and white solidarity rather than with freedom from want. While they loathed poverty and the establishment, most voters were too firmly entrenched to see any alternative to white supremacy.

Moreover, some state and local leaders had not developed the necessary *savoir-faire* in handling people. Men like Kolb and Manning could not satisfactorily answer charges that they were dividing the white vote. Others, like Weaver and Lease, both outsiders, repeatedly created hostility in their audiences by their inflamatory statements. Other populist speakers, unable to understand urban problems, could make no progress against the currents of industrial unemployment.

In addition, the choice of James Field did not strengthen the ticket, although he spoke scores of times during the two-month campaign.[63] Out of tune with the dirt farmer, with only modest rhetorical skills, and a "wet" by prohibitionists' standards,[64] he failed to carry his own state; but probably no one else could have swayed Virginia either. In any event the 1892 race was a humbling but learning experience and a rhetorical defeat for the party.

During the 1893–95 period the orators sought to keep the issues alive for the big push in 1896 and to elect as many local and state officials as possible to expedite reform. In some states the Populists joined the party most sympathetic to political reform, even though historically they had been enemies. In Georgia, where strategem and machination ran rampant, frightened Democrats destroyed or hid the 1894 ballots at several polling sites. Realizing the strength of the Populist-Republican consort, one veteran officeholder explained the fraud: "We had to do it! Those damned Populists would have ruined the country."[65] North Carolina's fusion with Republicans sent fifty-nine Populists to the legislature and four to Congress. Alabama elected thirty-six to the state capitol and one to Washington. Lesser gains came in Tennessee, Texas, and elsewhere.[66]

Scandalous fraud again beat Kolb in Alabama in 1894, as it had in 1890 and 1892. He worked hard on ethical appeal—his concern for fairness, his image as a hard and thrifty worker, a war record, and endorsement of respected citizens—yet he could not beat dishonesty at the polls. But he did get himself sworn in by a justice of the peace so that for a while the Cotton State had two avowed governors. Later he bowed out, realizing that he could not muster sufficient support throughout the state. But heavy agrarian backing elected about one-third of the state's legislators sympathetic to farmers. Thirty reform speakers spoke three hundred sixty-five times on one hundred eighty-six occasions in the Cotton State in attempts to pump new blood into a dying carcass, but it was insufficient to dislodge the old parties.[67]

Texan racial and ethnic prejudice in part spelled populism's doom in that state. The third party's spokesmen made little effort to win the Mexican-American vote. County managers in South Texas pleaded for help, but their cries were largely ignored. On the other hand, the Populists made a strong, though unsuccessful, bid for the German vote. The party's fundamentally Protestant and Anglo-Saxon base sometimes even had to answer the charge it was a church-centered political party. At the same time Negro sympathizers played a significant role in the South. John B. Rayner, an educated and articulate mulatto (white father, black mother), commanded wide audiences among both whites and blacks as he crisscrossed the state in his attempts to awaken the support of his own people. But such efforts could not swing the state.[68]

Texan concern for blacks was matched by the campaigning of Watson who strongly supported their rights in his own state. In Georgia thousands of them flocked to his integrated rallies so that never before and only occasionally since have the two races come so close together politically.

TRIUMPH IN DEFEAT: THE 1896 RACE

The final opportunity for agrarian recovery came with the 1896 sprint for the finish line. This was a now-or-never campaign. The Populists would either run the gold standard idolaters into the ground and increase the mints' silver output or die trying. They died trying.

Incomplete records pinpoint nearly three hundred (297) speech occasions during the southern campaign, but the most important single event was the national Populist convention at St. Louis, July 22–25. Unlike in previous years, the South played a significant role in the political deliberations. In an hour-long speech Marion Butler of North Carolina, now the National Chairman, scorned Democratic fusion and saw the campaign's issues as money and transportation. "By the time this question is settled, and before, too, if we don't hurry up, the great transportation question . . . will be upon us." The movement had raised, he declared, "an issue so universal, so great . . . that we have split both of the old parties in twain. Now we have either to save that issue or renounce what we have gained and lay it down in defeat."[69] One straight-out (nonfusion) delegate sought to mangle Bryan's nomination on a trilemma: Dispatch a telegram to him to ascertain if he were a Populist. If he replied *yes*, that made him a traitor to the Democrats, and "we ought not to support a traitor." If he answered *no*, that would turn the Populists against him. If he failed to answer, "that would show him a coward, and we do not want a coward for a candidate." "Cyclone" Davis ominously reminded his audience that three Presidents had been assassinated, leaving the government in the hands of the Vice-President, saying, "Elect Bryan and Sewall, and before March is over Sewall will be made president through the assassination of Bryan . . . and thus you will have a national banker for President."[70]

So the Populists, torn to both the right and the left, often did not know which road to travel. Their rhetoric suffered accordingly.[71]

Assured that the South would not bolt if given the vice-presidency, the Populist convention chose Bryan and Watson as their representatives. The

Georgian, antagonistic to fusion, refused to attend the convention. Bryan, never really sympathetic to dirt-farmer populism, also stayed away.[72]

No plow could move with a strong team when each member pulled in a different direction. So the Bryan-Watson combination, vigorous individually, labored at right angles. They advanced the cause of reform, but each man, weakened and beaten, worked largely alone. The weeds of the political establishment, never really plowed under, nearly killed the seeds of reform. One could see this clearly in the campaign strategy of Bryan as he sought the best of both Democratic and Populist worlds but ultimately lost both.

Following the convention, the Nebraskan spent comparatively little time in the South, though he did speak there on some forty occasions out of nearly four hundred in his six-week tour. At no time did he have anything to do with Watson. Never did he speak a good word for him. He confined himself to the narrow theme that farm prices had declined along with silver and that only by solving money problems could the rural situation improve. He virtually ignored overproduction, improved soil techniques, mechanization, and the larger monetary problems, as well as local or even regional ones.[73] At Knoxville in September he told fifteen thousand people that "a principle paramount in this campaign . . . is the right of seventy millions of people to have just the kind of financial system that they want." At Richmond, repeating parts of an earlier Louisville speech, he saw the struggle as between "democracy on the one side, and plutocracy on the other, and there is no middle ground for any man."[74]

Meanwhile the humorless, hardworking Watson traveled back and forth across the South. Despite his quarrel with Democrats the former college debater supported Bryan in several doubtful states and spoke to thousands in Birmingham, Dallas, Atlanta, and elsewhere. Watson spoke as if fighting his way through approaching hostile forces. By mid-October he had strained his voice box so that his physician doubted if he could return to the circuit before the election.[75] The Georgian avoided North Carolina, deeming its fusion with the Republicans on the state level and with Democrats on the national ticket an impossible situation. "What could I say?" he queried. "I could only repeat the Ten Commandments, say the Lord's Prayer, and dismiss the congregation."[76]

Local orators let no grass grow under their buckboard wagons nor dust settle on their saddles. North Carolina's Dr. Cyrus Thompson, cramped by the awkward arrangement with the two major parties, reportedly divided his speeches on occasion, speaking separately to Democrats, Republicans, and Populists, but with limited success. In all, the Tar Heel State heard sixty-two debates, all by local or state campaigners, as they crisscrossed the area.[77]

Elsewhere Louisiana orators' greater concern with local issues such as race, precipitated violence and bloodshed. Negroes were shot, killed, and whipped in Bourbon attempts to intimidate the blacks. Twice the militia was called out in the April state election.[78] John N. Pharr, the gubernatorial candidate who refused to campaign or even travel on Sunday, spoke to racially integrated audiences. He stressed the silver question, the pervading issue throughout the South.[79] But third-party speakers could not extinguish opposition fires in the Creole State. Agrarian reform in Louisiana was dying out both from fatigue and white fear of black insurgence.

As in Louisiana, with its concern for the bloody-shirt issues of the Civil War and political fraud, so in Georgia and Alabama, the movement harvested its best success prior to the 1896 elections so that Bryan's emphasis on the money question proved largely anti-climactic, at least at the state level. Nonetheless, such states fielded candidates. Shortly before the election Watson told a Sandersville audience that he was out of the race in Georgia, his home state: "There are two tickets you can vote next Tuesday, Bryan and Sewall or McKinley and Hobart, and if you can't stand either, stay at home."[80] In Alabama, while the currency question occupied the time of orators, the issue of a decadent Bourbon democracy also played a part. But the state had no Kolb or Terrell to water the reform seeds. There too the third party had run its course.

During the campaign Bryan rallied farmers but he could not unite the fragmented Democratic Party sufficiently to achieve victory. Though winning every southern state except Kentucky, the Nebraskan lost to McKinley by nearly six hundred thousand votes in the nation at large.[81] Watson, ignored and vilified by nearly all, managed only two hundred seventeen thousand supporters in seventeen scattered states, north and south. The tree of defeat bore bitter fruit for the Georgian, poisoned his spirit, and drove him from politics into a cynical and premature retirement. Even so, hundreds of Populist congressmen, state legislators, and lesser officials assumed new duties. The two major parties were sufficiently frightened to listen to the protests the next several years and to enact into law some of the protesters' demands.

Of the seven issues clearly found in agrarian-reform speaking in 1896, money claimed more time and interest on the stump and in Congress than all others combined. In Alabama, Louisiana, and Georgia political corruption, a favorite theme in all campaigns, consumed orators' time on numerous occasions. The popular election of senators, the graduated income tax, and the initiative and referendum (all credited later to Populist demands) seldom found their way into speeches. Orators leveled their guns at other game. The election, then, saw the last important political efforts by nineteenth-century farmers to revolt against an economy that seemed closed to most of them.

DEMISE OF THE PROTEST: 1897–1898

With the 1896 defeat of Bryan and Watson and many state tickets, southern agrarian reform largely disappeared, for the time being, from the American scene; but it arose now and then in later years. Several factors account for its demise.

First, elections of the 1890s had poured new wine into old wineskins so that parties controlling the states permitted or even initiated changes in ways they opposed. South Carolina's 1897 legislature passed a modestly graduated income tax and an anti-trust bill, gave greater power to the Railroad Commission, and threw out some implacable Democrats.[82] Alabama improved its education and more tightly controlled its railroads—all third-party concerns.

Secondly, poor harvests abroad increased the demand for American farm products, as did the Spanish-American War,[83] so that higher prices brought better farm conditions.

Thirdly, discouragement with general defeat at the polls drove many back into the folds of the mainstream parties. The result was that issues and spokesmen became less clearcut in succeeding years. The bin of fodder for political harangues was at least spoiled if not depleted. Early in the campaign Watson had foreseen this more clearly than most, but few had listened.

Fourthly, reform had run its course. General fatigue had set in. The Congress and state legislatures found Populist demands a trifle boring. Moreover, some areas, like Florida and Virginia, lacked strong leadership and vision, the death knell of any party. Every crusade needs strategists, speakers, promoters, backers, and workers of various kinds. The Populists, limited except for speakers, had little strategy and virtually no financial resources.[84] They were no match for the well-greased political machines of either the Democrats or Republicans on the national level.

Finally, mounting distrust and fear of black power brought dissident whites back under the same umbrella in their efforts to disfranchise Negroes. The Mississippi constitutional convention of 1890 effectively did so. A few years later Tennessee and other southern states stripped blacks and many whites of their vote by adopting the Australian ballot, which eliminated much fraud but required modest literacy skills. Louisiana's infamous "grandfather clause" (1898) was simply one of the more obvious and less subtle attempts to unite the white factions.[85] Where racial camaraderie once prevailed, racism took over.

While Louisiana populists sought black support and fused with the Republicans, they could not swing the state to reform. They, along with other anti-Bourbon forces, did, however, win forty percent of the state legislature's seats. The success, albeit limited, ultimately led to the demise of the third-party movement, for whites feared black political strength. One writer has argued that in the campaigns of 1892, 1894, and 1896 the divided white vote helped to promote a rise of crime in the Creole state. The eighty-three lynchings (1889–1896) were significantly higher in the election years than in the nonelection years of 1893, 1895, and 1897. An absence of unity perhaps encouraged crime.[86]

Southern oratory of the agrarian revolt can also be analyzed in several ways. It was incisive (as with Watson in or out of Congress), eloquent (as Harry Skinner on the hustings), moving (as seen in the L. L. Polk rallies), pedestrian (as James Field at picnics), and aggressive (as Kolb and Manning with Democratic audiences). The third party dissolved, then, not because of incapable speakers, but for other reasons.

Moreover, rallies, picnics, and debates featured gatherings such as the Populists used, but in North Carolina "joint discussions" were commoner. The Tar Heel State hosted at least sixty-two such face-to-face meetings in 1896 alone with Butler as the workhorse. Watson, on the other hand, found few who would match their convictions and skills with his when he spoke. The Democrats wisely avoided him.

Issues in the period 1870–1898 centered mostly on financial reform (increase of the volume of currency, free coinage of silver, and limitations of national banks); but it was never the all-consuming issue at any one time in any single state. Each state had its local problems: In 1892 it was Louisiana's state lottery, Georgia's and Alabama's decadent Democracy, and Texas's alien ownership of land. Four years later Georgia was urging justice for blacks, Alabama was concerned with the tariff, and Louisiana speakers harped on fraud.

The rhetorical style was often colorful and provocative because (1) speakers were able to couch their ideas in striking phraseology; (2) the issues of injustice and unconcern ran deeply; and (3) the many instances of inequity, not always clearly understood (as with the currency problem), afforded the orators ample materials. Delivery was animated so that audiences never complained of not hearing or being bored. Few speakers used more than brief notes in their speaking. If organization of ideas rambled, as it did with some speakers, listeners did not complain about it.

Reform speakers philosophically and nostalgically looked backward during the 1870–1898 period—a fact that strongly suggests that the movement was basically conservative. Not only did candidates and lecturers remind audiences of what the situation had been and what it was now, but Polk had early called for an education "which would bind the conservative masses of the country in the strongest ties of fraternity and union."[87] Charles Moses, congressman from Georgia, had told his fellow Representatives of "the conservative elements represented by the bi-metallists on the right, [and] radicals on the left."[88] The movement saw itself as conservative. Only in the sense of seeking redress by new legislation were they forward-looking. One never saw in them the same vision found in their great-grandfathers a century earlier. Critics called them "radical" only because they differed from the status quo.[89] Thus, when Judge Gustave Cook, Hogg's opponent for the Texas state house, cried "communism" at Hogg's railroad commission, Cook neither understood what communism was nor really knew his opponent's stand. The label revealed less of Hogg's position than it did of Cook's naiveté.

In sum, dozens of southern speakers in more than eight hundred speech situations played a prominent and far-reaching part in shaping the one-gallus revolt of southern farmers in the last part of the nineteenth century. Opponents may have viewed the reformers as monomaniacs on silver, lightheaded in other areas, and the root of political evils (*radix malorum fuerit populismus*), but they brought significant change to the old Confederacy. What would be said of Harvard's Charles W. Eliot in the next century could be said of the Populists. "[They] opened paths for our children's feet to follow. Something of [them] would be a part of us forever."

NOTES

1. Thomas E. Watson, "History of Southern Oratory," in *South in the Building of the Nation* (Richmond, Va.: Southern Historical Publishing Society, 1909), 11:468. Complete text, pp. 454–71.
2. *Fayetteville Arkansas Sentinel*, April 23, 1889, p. 1.
3. Arthur M. Schlesinger, "Rise of the City, 1878–1898," in *History of American Life*, Arthur M. Schlesinger and Dixon R. Fox, ed. (New York: Macmillan, 1933), 10:4.
4. *Compendium of the Tenth Census*, 1880, Pt. 1 (Washington, D.C.: Government Printing Office, 1883), pp. 650 & 659; John B. Clark, *Populism in Alabama* (Auburn: Auburn Printing Co., 1927), pp. 29 f.
5. Charles F. Emerick, "Analysis of Agricultural Discontent in the United States," *Political Science Quarterly* 11 (1896): 439.
6. *Abstract of the Eleventh Census*, 1890, 2nd ed., revised and enlarged (Washington, D.C.; Government Printing Office, 1896), pp. 97 f.
7. Fred A. Shannon, "Farmers' Last Frontier, Agriculture, 1860-1897," in *Economic History of the United States* (New York: Farrar and Rinehart, 1945), 5:415, and William B. Hesseltine and David L. Smiley, *South in American History*, 2nd ed. (Englewood Cliffs, N.J.: Prentice-Hall, 1960), pp. 395 f.
8. Schlesinger, "Rise of the City," p. 7.

9. Shannon, "Farmers' Last Frontier," p. 99.

10. Alex M. Arnett, "Populist Movement in Georgia," in *Studies in History, Economics, and Public Law* (New York: Columbia University, 1922), 104:18.

11. Charles M. Gardner, *Grange, Friend of the Farmer* (Washington, D.C.: National Grange, 1949), pp. 21 ff; and Clark, *Populism in Alabama*, pp. 52 ff.

12. Quoted in Gardner, *Grange*, p. 63.

13. The Wheel started as a debating society in Arkansas in 1882, its chief concerns being the crop-lien system and diversification of crops. But it lacked the impact on the South which the Grange and, later, the Alliance had. Gardner, *Grange*, p. 279.

14. C[omer] Vann Woodward, "Origins of the New South, 1877–1913," in *History of the South* (Baton Rouge: Louisiana State University Press, 1951), 9:191. For a fuller treatment of Macune and his part in the Alliance see Carleton Beals, *Great Revolt and Its Leaders* (New York: Abelard-Schuman, 1968), pp. 75–94. Additional factual data can be found in Wayne Flynt and William Warren Rogers, "Reform Oratory in Alabama, 1890–1896," *Southern Speech Journal* 29 (1963): 94 f., and *Appleton's Annual Cyclopedia and Register of Important Events of the Year 1890* (New York: D. Appleton and Co., 1891), p. 301. Hereafter cited by year.

15. Institutes were suggested for the county, district, state, and finally national levels, each composed of lecturers at the level immediately below. That is, the sub-Alliance lecturers composed the county group; the county lecturers the district group; the district lecturers the state group; and, finally, state lecturers the national lecturers institute. Undated letter in Box 1 Marion Butler Manuscripts, Southern Historical Collection, University of North Carolina, Chapel Hill.

16. *Raleigh, North Carolina Progressive Farmer* (uncertain date), cited in Ina Van Noppen, *South: A Documentary History* (Princeton: Van Nostrand, 1958), p. 405. For a study of the Colored Farmers' Alliance in the South see William F. Holmes, "Demise of the Colored Farmers' Alliance," *Journal of Southern History* 41 (1975): 187–200.

17. Francis B. Simkins, *Tillman Movement in South Carolina* (Durham: Duke University Press, 1926), p. 68.

18. Van Woodward, "Origins," p. 193. "It was the poor, small farmer . . . who constituted together with thousands of his fellows, the rank and file of the People's Party" in Texas, and elsewhere in the South. Roscoe C. Martin, "People's Party in Texas: A Study in Third Party Politics," in *University of Texas Bulletin (Bureau of Research in the Social Sciences*, No. 4) (Austin: University of Texas, 1933), pp. 60 f. This is perhaps the best available monograph treating the agrarian revolt at the state level.

19. Terrell, lecturer of the National Alliance, was the rhetorical workhorse for that organization in the early 1890s. Ashby had gone to Comanche country (Oklahoma) at Fort Sill in 1878 and proved effective as a missionary there. Marion Butler, the Tar Heel Populist organizer, later became the National Chairman of the third party and a forceful speaker. Kolb was graduated from the University of North Carolina (1859) at the age of twenty. He had studied Greek, Latin, rhetoric, and logic. He later served his state as a Confederate

officer. He knew well the joys and sorrows of farming. As state commissioner of agriculture he proved to be a help to other farmers, who greatly respected him. Not as powerful as Bryan on the platform, he was nonetheless effective and in full command of his subject. Hugh D. Corwin, "Protestant Missionary Work among the Comanches and Kiowas," *Chronicles of Oklahoma* 46 (1969): 45; and Charles E. Porterfield, "Rhetorical-Historical Analysis of the Third Party Movement in Alabama, 1890–1894," Ph.D. diss. (Louisiana State University, 1965), pp. 78 ff.

20. Ibid., pp. 35 f.

21. Simkins, *Tillman Movement*, pp. 93f. The *Charleston News and Courier* responded in kind: Tillman led a people "who expectorate upon the floor, who have no tooth brushes, and comb their hair with their fingers."

22. *Jacksonville Florida Times-Union*, December 3, 1890, p. 1.

23. The South gagged the 1889 St. Louis convention by refusing to compromise either its secret order or its color bar in the farm organization.

24. *Florida Times-Union*, December 3, 1890, p. 1. For preparations leading up to the Ocala convention and for the Alliance generally in Florida see *Ocala Banner*, June 27, 1890, p. 1; and James O. Knauss, "Farmer's Alliance in Florida," *South Atlantic Quarterly* 25 (1926): 309–312.

25. *Florida Times-Union*, December 3, 1890, p. 1. Polk also demanded reforms in taxation, alien ownership of land, public transportation, and the popular election of United States senators—needs orators hardly considered over the next half-dozen years.

26. The land issue seldom occupied southern spokesmen, unlike those of the West. True, Congressman William Oats (Alabama) reported to the House (June 1890) a bill noting that certain titled Europeans, chiefly Englishmen, owned some twenty-five million acres in the United States in addition to that held by commoners. But any such measure would help the Great Plains more than the old Confederacy. *Knoxville Daily Journal*, June 10, 1890, p. 1. See John D. Hicks, *Populist Revolt* (Minneapolis: University of Minnesota, 1931), pp. 205–37, for additional information on the party's birth.

27. *Florida Times-Union*, December 9, 1890, p. 1.

28. Porterfield, "Third Party Movement," pp. 240 ff.

29. Some details on the subtreasury plan may be found in Hicks, *Populist Revolt*, pp. 186–204. For a digest of the Florida Assembly see Nelson A. Dunning, ed. *Farmers' Alliance History and Agricultural Digest* (Washington, D.C.: Alliance Publishing Co., 1891), pp. 137 ff.

30. Men came from far and wide to hear "Cyclone" Davis speak in Texas. No Democrat would debate him. Martin, "People's Party in Texas," pp. 121f. "It is said 'Cyclone' Davis' favorite beverage is a round quart of aqua fortis sweetened with brimstone, stirred with a lightening-rod and skimmed by a hurricane." *Clarksville* (Tennessee) *Daily Tobacco Leaf-Chronicle*, September 13, 1892, p. 2; *Columbus* (Georgia) *Enquirer-Sun*, May 21, 1891, p. 1. A full account may be found in *Florida Times-Union*, May 21, 1891, and subsequent issues. Oddly, the *Daily Tobacco Leaf-Chronicle* declared that the platform avoided the

subtreasury and free silver. A simple reading of the documents refutes this. Ibid., May 22, 1891, p. 1.

31. *Dallas Morning News,* June 21, 1890, p. 4; June 22, 1890, p. 10; June 23, 1890, p. 7; June 25, 1890, p. 4; and June 29, 1890, p. 10.

32. Thomas E. Watson Papers, Box-1, Folder-2, Southern Historical Collection, University of North Carolina, Chapel Hill. For a physical description of that "atom of a man; . . . meagre in flesh, and what there is seems laid on grudgingly, as if nature hesitated to make the man at all," etc., see *Clifton Forge* (Virginia) *Review,* July 31, 1896, p. 4. Some would say of Watson what Emerson did of Thoreau, "While we love him, we don't like him."

33. Northen to Cleveland, September 15, 1891, in Grover Cleveland Papers, Library of Congress, cited in Woodward, "Origins," p. 273. When Watson spoke out of doors, "regulations" demanded that (1) the floor of the speaker's stand be six feet above the ground, (2) ten feet separate the platform floor and the canopy overhead, (3) the platform be just large enough for the speaker and six committeemen, and (4) "T-O-M" might be spelled in flowers on the top of the stand or, perhaps, "GOD SAVE THE COUNTRY" painted on the front of the stand. *People's Party Paper,* September 15, 1893, p. 1.

34. Simkins, *Tillman Movement,* p. 93.

35. Ibid., p. 117.

36. Quoted in Simkins, *Tillman Movement,* p. 108.

37. *News and Courier,* July 25, 1890, p. 1.

38. Major Tom McConnell, the state boss, reportedly said of the gag, "If Mr. Buchanan was fool enough to answer all the silly questions put to him by so-called Democrats, he would not deserve to be elected." *Knoxville Journal,* October 13, 1890, p. 2.

39. *Raleigh News and Observer,* June 19, 1892, p. 2.

40. As essentially happened with the Washington County Alliance (Arkansas), June 1892. *Fayetteville Arkansas Sentinel,* July 19, 1892, p. 2.

41. When it closed out its books in 1893, one Virginia sub-Alliance decided "whatsoever is over [should] be donated to the People's party club." William D. Sheldon, *Populism in the Old Dominion: Virginia Farm Politics, 1885–1900* (Princeton: Princeton University Press, 1935), pp. 96 f.

42. For a complete text see Hicks, *Populist Revolt,* pp. 435–39. The issue of reserving land for homesteading found no place in southern oratory except in Texas.

43. For a profile of spokesmen for the period 1832–1956 see Paul T. David, Ralph M. Goldman, and Richard C. Bain, *Politics of National Party Conventions* (Washington, D.C.: Brookings Institution, 1960), pp. 139 ff.

44. *Ocala* (Florida) *Banner,* September 9, 1892, p. 2.

45. Florence E. Smith, "Populist Movement and Its Influence in North Carolina," Ph.D. diss. (University of Chicago, 1929), p. 68. In Alabama Porterfield's research found thirty-five reform speakers who spoke 140 times at 86 places in the 1892 race, and thirty orators with 365 speeches on 186 occasions in the '94 campaign. Porterfield, "Third Party Movement," p. 230. Norman Pollack, ed.

Populist Mind (Indianapolis and New York: Bobbs-Merrill, 1967), pp. 56 f., citing the *Decatur* (Texas) *Times*, March 22, 1893, notes that the Populists did not object to the term "calamity howlers," since that was what they were and would remain "until [our] lost freedom is regained." Robert G. Gunderson's brief study of the Populist orators "Calamity Howlers," *Quarterly Journal of Speech* 26 (October 1940): 401–11. concentrates on Midwestern speakers.

46. *Raleigh Progressive Farmer*, October 4, 1892, p. 2.

47. Ibid. Estimates of the crowd range from ten thousand in Fred E. Haynes, *James Baird Weaver* (Iowa City: State Historical Society of Iowa, 1919), p. 326 to two thousand in the *News and Observer*, September 30, 1892, p. 1, but the Haynes report is too generous in view of space available for the listeners. Significantly the hostile *News and Observer* admitted that the crowd was North Carolina's largest to hear the Weaver-Lease teams. Many southerners never let Weaver forget his statement. *Daily Tobacco Leaf-Chronicle*, September 22, 1892, p. 1. Such stories were magnified in wartime. Anyway, the South was sensitive in such matters.

48. *Wilmington Morning Star*, October 28, 1892, p. 1.

49. *Wilmington Morning Star*, October 25, 1892, p. 1, and October 26, 1892, p. 2.

50. C[omer] Van Woodward, "Populist Heritage and the Intellectual," *American Scholar*, 29 (1959–60): 61 f.

51. Flynt and Rogers, "Reform Oratory," 95 ff. For a helpful sketch of Kolb as an imaginative, successful farmer and speaker see William W. Rogers, "Reuben F. Kolb: Agricultural Leader of the Old South," *Agricultural History* 32 (1958): 109–19; and Porterfield, "Third Party Movement," pp. 78 ff.

52. Clark, *Populism in Alabama*, p. 144.

53. In discussing North Carolina throughout this essay I am leaning heavily on my own previous study: "Rhetorical Analysis of the Populist Movement in North Carolina, 1892–1896," (Unpublished Ph.D. Dissertation University of Wisconsin, 1957), passim.

54. R[obert] D. W. Connor and Clarence Poe, *Life and Speeches of Charles Brantley Aycock* (Garden City, New York: Doubleday, Page and Co., 1912), pp. 64 ff; and Josephus Daniels, *Tar Heel Editor* (Chapel Hill: University of North Carolina Press, 1939), p. 501.

55. *Wilmington Morning Star*, October 11, 1892, p. 2.

56. Henderson to Mrs. Henderson, March 28, 1892, John Steele Henderson Manuscripts, Folder 87, *Southern Historical Collection*, University of North Carolina, Chapel Hill.

57. *Congressional Record*, 53rd Congress, 1st sess., Pt. 1 (1892), p. 417.

58. *People's Party Paper*, August 12, 1892, cited in Pollack, *Populist Mind*, pp. 378 f. After the turn of the twentieth century and his political defeat of 1896 Watson soured on reform; but at this point he was serious in what he wished even if he lacked the muscle to bring it about.

59. *Allardt* (Tennessee) *Gazette*, September 29, 1892, p. 1, and C[omer] Van Woodward, "Tom Watson and the Negro in Agrarian Politics," *Journal of Southern History* 4 (1938): 21 ff. Doyle campaigned extensively in Watson's

behalf in the 1892 race, speaking at least sixty-three times. Ironically the poor white, whatever his political affiliation, more than the Bourbon Democrat, ultimately stripped the black of his franchise. Francis M. Wilhoit, "Interpretation of Populism's Impact on the Georgia Negro," *Journal of Negro History* 52 (1967): 120. By 1892 the Colored Farmers' Alliance, socially and politically starved by the whites who feared the black challenge, had wasted away to a skeleton. Holmes, "Demise of the Colored Farmers' Alliance," pp. 191 ff.

60. *Congressional Record*, 52nd Congress, 1st sess., Pt. 3 (1892), p. 2839.

61. *Congressional Record*, 52nd Congress, 1st sess., Pt. 3 (1892), p. 2841.

62. *Appleton's Annual Cyclopedia* (1892), pp. 308 and 741; U.S. Bureau of Census, *Historical Statistics of the United States, Colonial Times to 1957* (Washington, D.C.: Government Printing Office, 1960), p. 688; and Clark, *Populism in Alabama*, p. 145.

63. The campaign in Field's own state went so badly that Virginia imported Jerry "Sockless" Simpson and others to carry the burden. Sheldon, *Populism in the Old Dominion*, pp. 99 f.

64. Other Populists, like Watson and Polk, had prohibitionist sympathies, but they were unwilling to court prohibition partisans. Political and economic interests claimed their undivided attention. Jack S. Blocker, Jr., "Politics of Reform: Populists, Prohibition, and Woman Suffrage: 1891–1892," *Historian* 34 (1972): 616 f.

65. Arnett, *Populist Movement in Georgia*, p. 184.

66. *Birmingham Age-Herald*, November 8, 1894, p. 5; R. Smith, "Rhetorical Analysis of the Populist Movement," pp. 185 ff; (Columbia) The State, November 10, 1894, p. 1; and *Appleton's Annual Cyclopedia* (1894): p. 739.

67. Porterfield, "Third Party Movement," p. 230.

68. Martin, "People's Party in Texas," pp. 86ff, 95f., 100, 106, and 126f. Prayers, hymns, and amens were commonly heard at Populist conclaves.

69. William J. Bryan, *First Battle* (Chicago: W. B. Conkey Co., 1896), p. 262. See also *St. Louis Globe-Democrat*, July 21, 1896, cited in Robert F. Durden, "Cow-Bird Grounded: The Populist Nomination of Bryan and Tom Watson in 1896," *Mississippi Valley Historical Review* 50 (1963): 410.

70. *New York Times*, July 22, 1896, p. 1; *Superior* (Wisconsin) *Leader*, July 23, 1896, p. 1; and *Atlanta Constitution*, July 21, 1896, cited in Arnett, *Populist Movement in Georgia*, p. 198. Watson described fusion with the Democrats thus: "We play Jonah while they play whale." Most of the listeners were poor and aged yet hopeful. Some men had walked to the convention. At least one slept in the convention hall because of insufficient funds for better communications. Henry D. Lloyd, "Populists at St. Louis," *Review of Reviews* 14 (1896): 299.

71. Congressman and former Alliance lecturer William Talbert (South Carolina) in another context compared the situation to the little boy who one morning put his trousers on backwards, then set out for school. Discovering the situation he burst out crying, "I don't know whether I am going to school or coming home." *Congressional Record*, 53rd Congress, 1st sess., Pt. 1 (1893), pp. 499 ff.

72. In retrospect one can see the opportunism of Bryan, an intransigent Democrat, and his expedient acceptance of the third-party nomination. He was primarily concerned with financial reform and only incidentally with farmers and their problems. That this was true is shown by these facts:
    A. He waited some ten weeks (until October 3) before notifying the Populists of his acceptance.
    B. When he did notify them, he did so by mail, not by telegram or an acceptance speech. The text of the acceptance may be found in *First Battle*, pp. 432f.
    C. The acceptance letter was not particularly warm and did not even thank the convention for its expression of confidence.
    D. He had nothing whatsoever to do with Watson at any point in the campaign.
    E. Populists were never prominent at southern rallies where he spoke.
    F. He seldom spoke for any agrarian reform, believing that all problems were bound up with silver.
73. Gilbert C. Fite, "Republican Strategy and the Farm Vote in the Presidential Campaign of 1896," *American Historical Review* 65 (1960): 788. See also Fite's perceptive "William Jennings Bryan and the Campaign of 1896: Some Views and Problems, *Nebraska History* 47 (1966): 247–64, where he lifts into sharp relief the campaign obstacles of the Nebraskan.
74. *Detroit Free Press*, September 17, 1896, p. 1, and *Clifton Forge* (Virginia) *Review*, September 25, 1896, p. 2. The presidential candidate, despite acute financial limitations, progressed to more regal means of transportation as the race neared the finish line. Initially he travelled in an ordinary coach, then a Pullman sleeper, later a special car, and finally (as in North Carolina) by special train accompanied by secretaries and news correspondents.
75. *Detroit Free Press*, October 13, 1896, p. 2.
76. *Augusta* (Georgia) *Chronicle*, October 31, 1896, cited in C[omer] Van Woodward, *Tom Watson: Agrarian Rebel* (New York: Macmillan Co., 1938), p. 326.
77. F. Smith, "Populist Movement," pp. 152 and 127 ff. After Hal Ayer, State Chairman, heard Dockery at Wadesboro, he wrote Butler that Dockery "burnt the bridges behind him. It was a clean-cut, unmistakable speech . . . creating something of a panic among Republicans." Ayer to Butler, September 1, 1896, Box 3, Marion Butler Manuscripts.
78. Melvin J. White, "Populism in Louisiana During the Nineties," *Mississippi Valley Historical Review* 5 (1918): 14.
79. The Populist press, unlike its Democratic opponents, vindicated Pharr, the "humble Christian who dares to obey the commandment of the most high God" by not working on the Sabbath. *Natchitoches Louisiana Populist*, March 13, 1896, pp. 2 and 3; April 17, 1896, p. 3; and February 21, 1896, p. 2.
80. *Charlottesville Daily Progress*, October 31, 1896, p. 3.
81. Reapportioning about twenty thousand of them in key places would have given fifty-one additional electoral votes to Bryan and hence the White House.

82. *Appleton's Annual Cyclopedia* (1897): p. 733.
83. Clark, *Populism in Alabama*, pp. 176–182, and Paola E. Coletta, "William Jennings Bryan and Currency and Banking Reform," *Nebraska History* 45 (1964): 37.
84. But Watson's *People's Party Campaign Book*, 1892 (Washington, D.C.: National Watchman Publishing Company, 1892) contained stock indictments, in terse style, which third-party speakers could use along with statistical and factual data.
85. For a brief discussion of the loopholes for whites on the Mississippi scene, see James H. Stone, "Note on Voter Registration under the Mississippi Understanding Clause, 1892," *Journal of Southern History* 38 (1972): 293–96. In Tennessee the introduction and extension of the Australian secret ballot had profound effect on voter turnout of both blacks and whites. See J. Morgan Kousser, "Post-Reconstruction Suffrage Restrictions in Tennessee: A New Look at the V. O. Key Thesis," *Political Science Quarterly* 88 (1973): 679.
86. For a fuller sociological analysis of this see Jam M. Inverarity, "Populism and Lynching in Louisiana, 1889–1896: A Test of Erickson's Theory of the Relationship between Boundary Crises and Repressive Justice," *American Sociological Review* 41 (1976): 262–80. This article spawned several attempts to refute the thesis, but the responders were only partially successful in their efforts. For the original thesis which prompted Inverarity's study see Kai T. Erickson, *Wayward Puritans: A Study in the Sociology of Deviance* (New York: Wiley, 1966) where the author argues that when society's solidarity collapses crime increases.
87. *Jacksonville* (Florida) *Times-Union*, December 3, 1890, p. 1.
88. *Congressional Record*, 53rd Congress, 1st sess., Pt. 1 (1892), p. 417.
89. True, one Texas Alliance in 1891 had proposed a scheme whereby the Secretary of the Interior would have been obliged to loan virtually any amount an applicant thought he could use and at a rate of interest the applicant thought fair, but such ideas were never taken seriously. See a fuller account in *Fayetteville Arkansas Sentinel*, November 3, 1891, p. 1.

III

WOMEN TAKE UP THE
CAUSE OF REFORM

8

Women Speak Out
In Protest

FRANCES MCCURDY*

From the July day in 1848 when Elizabeth Cady Stanton rose at the first Woman's Rights Convention and tremblingly read the ninth resolution declaring that women had a duty to secure to themselves the sacred right of franchise, to the present, when liberationists seek full equality, proponents of equal rights for women have heard the argument that men and women are designed for different spheres. In 1873 a justice of the Supreme Court upheld the refusal of the state of Illinois to admit a woman to the practice of law with the assertion that "Civil law, as well as nature herself, has always recognized a wide difference in the respective spheres of man and woman." Because of her "natural and proper timidity" and her innate delicacy, the judge concluded, woman's sphere was in domestic, not in civil affairs.[1] Almost one hundred years later, in March 1972, Senator Sam Ervin "in a voice breaking with emotion" opposed the Equal Rights Amendment on the grounds that it "would repeal the handiwork of God who had created man and woman differently."[2] The senator was not alone in deploring the invasion of women into "practically every activity formerly considered suitable . . . for men only." Other men, also, sighed for some island refuge on the sea of life impregnable to the assaults of the liberated woman.[3]

Though early suffragists differed in many ways from the National Organization for Women and other groups involved in the women's-liberation movement of the 1970s, women of both centuries shared a determination to decide their own sphere of activity. For early leaders the primary objective was winning the right to vote. From 1848, when

Elizabeth Cady Stanton, Lucretia Mott, and a few associates launched the crusade for women's rights, to 1870, the beginning of the period termed "the age of protest and reform," a few victories were won, mostly on the local level. Educational opportunities improved in some degree. Through the Loyal League, anti-slavery societies, and temperance organizations, women proved that they could be effective platform speakers and organizers. In a few communities women voted in school elections, and in New York married women won the right to control of their inherited property and guardianship of minor children; but, over all, few improvements occurred. Women leaders became convinced that the only remedy for the evils they saw about them lay in enfranchisement. The ballot was, in the words of an early temperance lecturer, "a hundred times more important" than any other reform, since through the ballot other reforms could be effected."[4]

Prospects were discouraging in 1870. Despite approval of woman suffrage in Wyoming Territory in 1869 progress toward full political rights for all women had been reversed with the ratification in 1868 and 1870 of the Fourteenth and Fifteenth Amendments to the Constitution. These amendments not only gave a legal basis to sex as a qualification for voting, but also added two million black men to the voting population.[5] Women protested the unfairness of the amendments but were told by old friends with whom they had worked in the Equal Rights Association to stand aside and give the Negro his hour.[6] Believing that the amendments would delay their own enfranchisement for years and perhaps forever, many of the women campaigned against ratification, but to no avail.

Not only were advocates of woman suffrage faced with a new barrier to the ballot in 1870; they were also hopelessly divided by conflicts of personality and on the question of means to the end. A faction led by Elizabeth Cady Stanton and Susan Anthony met in New York on May 15, 1869, and formed the National Woman Suffrage Association. Excluding men from membership, the Nationals chose Stanton as president and Anthony as chairman of the powerful executive committee. Ignoring the National meeting, delegates from twenty-two states gathered in Cleveland on November 16 of the same year at the call of Lucy Stone to form the American Woman Suffrage Association. This group chose Henry Ward Beecher as president and Lucy Stone as chairman of the executive committee. The chief object of the National Association was to persuade Congress to pass a federal amendment guaranteeing suffrage to women; the American Association centered its efforts on the passage of legislation at the state and local level.[7]

Differences between the two associations went beyond opinions on the exclusion of men and the level toward which campaigns should be directed. Although Elizabeth Stanton, Susan Anthony, and Lucy Stone had once worked together for abolition and equal rights, they differed sharply in 1870 on almost everything except rights for women. Stanton and Anthony, who made the decisions for the National Association, were daring and impulsive. Stanton enjoyed wearing the radical image, and Anthony had no gift for diplomacy. They had come into conflict with Lucy Stone and her husband, Henry Blackwell, in Kansas in 1867, when they campaigned in support of the referendum on woman suffrage. Lucy Stone and her husband believed that the campaign should be carried on under the auspices of the Republican Party, which had been closely allied with the Equal Rights Association. Susan Anthony, frustrated by the Republican Party's seeming indifference to women, and always an opportunist, accepted the financial aid and the oratorical efforts of George Francis Train, eccentric and wealthy "copperhead" Democrat, who injected his own ambition to be nominated for President into the campaign. Anthony and Stanton not only appeared with Train on the platform, where he denounced Negro suffrage, but also associated themselves with him in launching the short-lived newspaper *The Revolution*, which Train had promised to finance.[8] Lucy Stone was further alienated when Anthony and Stanton enthusiastically endorsed Victoria Woodhull, whose reputation for free love and spiritualism made her repugnant to conservatives despite her reception by congressional committee men who listened with interest to her argument that the Fourteenth Amendment had, in fact, enfranchised women.

Leaders of the American Association not only disapproved of the break with the Republican Party and the association of woman suffrage with Train and Woodhull; they also disliked the radical policies of the National Association which supported easier divorce laws, denounced with unaccustomed frankness the injustices suffered by married women, took up the cause of working women, and expressed approval of labor unions. Stanton offended some sensibilities by openly flouting clergymen who quoted Scripture in opposition to women's equality. The American Association drew its support primarily from professional and club women. Working diligently but more discreetly for rights for women, it deplored the unfavorable publicity brought to the cause of women by Nationals, who, on the other hand, were inclined to ridicule the "Boston clique" as ultraconservatives too dependent on men to effect the advancement of women. The depth of the antagonism is evident in the characterization of differences by Stanton's daughter as an "internecine war" and in Stone's comment in a private letter to a member of her family that she withdrew in her whole soul from all of the set.[9]

Despite these differences both groups worked tirelessly to advance the cause of women, sometimes differing in methods, more often in style, but united in their determination to break the barrier that limited the sphere of woman by denying her the vote.

LEADERS OF THE MOVEMENT

Many women of the nineteenth century declared themselves perfectly happy in the sphere assigned to them. Strong anti-suffragist sentiment existed among both men and women who deplored woman's attempt to invade the masculine sphere, thus forfeiting her right to chivalry. Clergymen admonished congregations that the woman who did not obey her husband would not obey God, who had enjoined her submission.[10] A columnist of 1870 spoke for many of his fellows as he compared unfavorably women reformers with domestic woman, beautiful and pure, full of grace in body and soul.[11]

The man or woman who spoke for suffrage in the 1870s required courage. Some men who had earlier worked side by side with women for equal rights were unwilling to associate themselves with the unpopular issue of woman suffrage for fear that they would jeopardize the opportunity for the Negro to vote. Woman suffrage did not, however, lack the support of prominent and influential men. Henry Ward Beecher, William E. Channing, Thomas Wentworth Higginson, and John Greenleaf Whittier were among those who publicly supported woman's enfranchisement. Horace Greeley generally published a fair report of the women's meetings in the pages of his *New York Tribune*. Several congressmen regularly presented the women's petitions to Congress and opened committee hearings on suffrage to women speakers. Victoria Woodhull was one of the major speakers before Congress. She was nominated by the People's Party in 1872 as a candidate for President of the United States. Though she was quickly excluded from the councils of the women, she remains a dramatic figure of the period.

Many women however, made significant contributions. Anna Howard Shaw, an ordained minister and a doctor of medicine, spent most of her long life as a lecturer for woman's rights, serving as president of the National American Woman Suffrage Association from 1904 to 1915. Alice Stone Blackwell, daughter of Lucy Stone, devoted her life to reforms of various nature, but especially to woman suffrage in the years under review. Julia Ward Howe, author of "The Battle Hymn of the Republic," was an active force in the New England group. Isabella Beecher Hooker, a member of the Beecher family; Paulina Wright Davis, Mary Livermore, and Matilda Joslyn Gage were among the distinguished women who worked for suffrage. But the unmistakable leaders through most of the period, 1879 to 1898, were Elizabeth Cady Stanton, Susan Anthony, and Lucy Stone.

Elizabeth Cady Stanton (1815-1902) was the source of most of the theoretical basis of the suffrage movement. Her father Judge Daniel Cady of Johnston, New York, allowed her to spend many hours of her childhood in his law office and permitted her the unusual privilege of studying Greek and higher mathematics at the Johnston academy with her brothers. Since no college would accept a woman in 1830, Elizabeth was sent to Miss Willard's academy in Troy, New York, where the curriculum centered around womanly activities such as music, dancing, and embroidery. At the home of her cousin Gerrit Smith, however, Elizabeth met the leading reformers of the day. Among the abolitionists who gathered there was Henry Stanton, a personable young man who was a delegate to the World's Antislavery Convention to be held in London in 1840. Over the objections of her father, who thought that any man engaged in so fanatical a cause as abolition could never support a family, Elizabeth married Henry Stanton and went with him to London. There she met Lucretia Mott, founder of the Female Antislavery Association in the United States and a delegate to the convention. When the men in control of the convention excluded women delegates from the floor, seating them in a gallery behind a curtain, Stanton was indignant. In long talks with Mott she determined to strike a blow for women. The Seneca Falls Convention in 1848 was the first realization of that determination.[12]

Throughout her life, filled with the care of a household and seven children, she was the principal writer for the woman suffrage movement and its most forceful speaker on state occasions. Her articles appeared in newspapers and journals of the day. She it was who shaped the rationale of the suffrage argument and wrote most of the papers presented to congressional committees. Susan Anthony called her the philosopher and statesman of the struggle for rights.[13] Stanton in her reminiscences shared the credit for planning "the coming agitation" with Anthony;[14] the ideas and arguments, however, generally originated with Stanton. Anthony carried them out.

Stanton's interest in women's rights extended beyond suffrage. She wished to see woman realize her full potential in every way possible and was interested in so many reforms that it was sometimes difficult for Susan to persuade her to concentrate on suffrage. She wrote and spoke in favor of improved conditions for working women, for married women's property rights, for reform in woman's dress (she adopted the bloomer costume for a time), for elimination of discrimination in education, for equality in marriage and divorce laws, and for a new interpretation of the Bible which would omit references to the subjection of women, as well as for women's enfranchisement. She was wholehearted in her support of whatever right she was advocating at the time and saw all of them as interconnected. She wrote Martha Wright, one of the Seneca Falls group, "When I think of all the wrongs heaped upon womankind, I am ashamed that I am not forever in a state of chronic wrath, . . . my eyes a fountain of tears, my lips overflowing with curses, and my hand against every man. . . ."[15]

This extravagant statement was characteristic of Stanton's enthusiasm rather than her behavior. She delighted in being controversial. She wrote joyfully of the radical thoughts she had put into the heads of women on one of her speaking tours in the West[16] and confided to Anthony that she had told Theodore Tilton, who had invited her to write for his paper with the qualification that she was not to "shock those good Baptists or say anything about divorce," that she was not to be bought to write at anybody's dictation.[17] Her radical views sometimes embarrassed her husband in his political aspirations and so angered her father that he disinherited her for a time;[18] but she was not to be dissuaded from her convictions.

Stanton had a quick mind and was an omnivorous reader. An entry in her diary for December 15, 1899, when she was eighty-four years old, lists among the books enjoyed in recent weeks: Andrew White's *A History of Warfare of Science with Theology*; Boswell's *Life of Johnson*; Matthew Arnold's *Essay in Criticism*, both series; Bacon's *Essays*; Herbert Spencer's *Education*; Ingersoll's *Great Speeches*; and "several novels of Charlotte Brontë, Thackeray, and George Eliot."[19] She kept up a correspondence with the leading men of her day, including writers, politicians, and reformers.

Plump, rosy, with sparkling blue eyes and white curls that bounced when she nodded her head in vigorous expression of her opinions, she belied the stereotype of the strident, masculine woman seeking to enter man's sphere. Her good humor and daring disarmed even her critics. On one occasion, when the Reverend Robert Collyer chided her for using one of his anecdotes without giving him credit, she wrote over the signature of "your guiltless purloiner" that he should rejoice that he had said something worth quoting. Amused by her reply, he answered that she was of course right and that he was in sackcloth and ashes.[20]

Stanton was the first president of both the National Association of suffragists and of the united group formed in 1890, though her activity in the two years that she served as honorary president of the National American Woman Suffrage Association was confined mostly to writing papers.

Susan Anthony termed Stanton "a word artist" and testified that every state paper presented to Congress or state legislatures in the early days was written by Stanton.[21] Anthony was not alone in considering her one of the finest speakers of her day. For twelve years she was a popular lecturer on the lyceum curcuit, where for eight months of the year she lectured one or two hours every night to diverse audiences. James B. Pond called her the ablest orator and most scholarly woman on the lyceum curcuit.[22] The subjects of her speeches indicate her concern for the rights of women. Among them were "Coeducation," "Home Life," "The Subjection of Women," "Marriage and Divorce," and "Marriage and Maternity."[23] Viewing home and motherhood as only one of the ways in which woman could find fulfillment, she pleaded for the broadening of woman's sphere.

She asked for the suffrage for woman because it was her right and also because it was her right and duty to develop her faculties and escape the bonds of superstition and custom which had held her in subjection. She was uncompromising in her attitude toward removal of obstacles. Woman's happiness and development were of more importance than all of man's institutions, she declared, and "if constitutions and statute laws stand in the way of woman's emancipation, they must be amended to meet her wants and needs," of which she was a better judge than any man could possibly be.[24]

She came to oppose universal suffrage, supporting education as a qualification for voting. Her prejudice against immigrants is perhaps understandable in light of their opposition to emancipated woman, but her harsh adjectives are nonetheless disturbing in a woman who urged the right to full development of every individual. Her belief that right was on her side made her impervious to opposition. Her overwhelming concern for the rights of women sometimes led her to consider any other rights as of minor importance.

Her contribution to women was summed up in a tribute offered to her on her eightieth birthday, a tribute in which it was asserted that "every woman who seeks the legal custody of her children, or the legal control of her property; every woman who finds the doors of a college or university open to her; . . . every woman who enters upon a career of medicine, law or theology" owes her liberty largely to Elizabeth Cady Stanton.[25]

Susan Anthony (1820–1906) told an audience in 1898 that she was not so much a pioneer in woman suffrage as people thought; that her association with the movement did not begin until 1852, when she was made assistant secretary at the Rochester convention. "As I had lots of throat to spare," she told her hearers, "they gave me the task of reading all the resolutions and motions submitted and since that time I've been right busy."[26]

Being "right busy" included serving as chairman of the executive committee of the National Association, as vice-president and president of the National American Woman Suffrage Association, and in speaking for suffrage from New York to California and from Dakota to Georgia.[27]

Born of Quaker stock, with its tradition of equality and free speech for woman, and with a liberal father who supported reform movements and encouraged his wife and daughters to be independent in thought, Anthony had little early experience with injustice to women. She did not seek education beyond that available to both boys and girls in the local schools and thus escaped the bitterness of rejection from a college on the basis of her sex.

When Anthony began teaching, she became indignantly aware of the inequality in pay for women. When she tried to speak out against this injustice, she was met by strong opposition. The arrogance with which men objected to allowing women workers for temperance to speak from the platform further aroused her ire. She was convinced that women must seek reform. Her energies were temporarily diverted to emancipation and support of the war effort, but from 1865 until her death in 1906 the cause to which she gave her undivided devotion was woman suffrage.

Among the leaders of woman suffrage, Anthony most nearly fitted the popular image of the suffragist. She never married and was impatient with others in the movement who allowed marriage to divert them. She scolded them for having babies when they might be making speeches for women's rights. She was tall, angular, sharp-featured, and dictatorial. She gave little attention to enhancing her appearance, though her clothes were always scrupulously neat and clean. She made enemies for herself and her cause by her aggressiveness and lack of tact. When Lucy Stone and others objected to her using their names without their knowledge or consent in statements purporting to represent the Equal Rights Association, she informed them that *she* was the Equal Rights Association.[28] She exercised the same proprietorship of the suffrage association. William Ellery Channing called her the Napoleon of the movement.[29] With the exception of deference to Stanton, to whom she gave unswerving loyalty and devotion, Anthony conducted the affairs of the suffrage association as if she were indeed a general deploying her troops.

Though Susan Anthony was dictatorial and made extraordinary demands upon others, she made even greater demands upon herself. Her energy seemed inexhaustible. Always ready to speak on the suffrage question, she said in 1897 that in her forty-five years on the lecture platform she had spoken in almost every city in the northern and western states and estimated that she had averaged seventy-five to a hundred lectures a year.[30] At the age of eighty-one she reported to suffragists that she and members of the Resolutions Committee had recently signed and sent out four thousand letters to delegates to political conventions, that in the past year she had mailed letters and petitions to more than one hundred other national conventions of various sorts, and that she had written "fully a thousand" letters to suffrage presidents or other individuals in the forty-five states and three territories, asking them to endorse petitions for suffrage.[31]

Anthony was as generous with her funds as with her time. In 1897 she stated that she had never taken one dollar of salary or other support from the suffrage association. Money she earned from speaking or received from various bequests and contributions was appropriated for the cause of suffrage. She gave so generously to other women working for suffrage that when friends wished to provide for her old age, they purchased an annuity so that she could not give it away.[32] When she died, she left her small estate to the suffrage association.

Anthony's courage was legendary in her own lifetime. Jeered at, reviled, burned in effigy, she refused to turn aside from her goal. A contemporary said of her: "No man ever had the courage of his convictions as much as she. It takes a bold spirit to stand up against the dangers of gun-powder, . . . but it is a braver one that withstands ridicule and that mean cunning that makes wit of every act looking toward the advancement of women."[33] She spoke of some of the attacks upon her when she responded to a tribute offered to her on her eightieth birthday: "I have been reviled most of my life; been scoffed and jeered at; I have heard myself called dreadful names and have been the target for every kind of discourtesy." She noted that the tribute was doubly welcome because of the contrast with past experience.[34] If the jeering and name calling made her despondent, she gave no sign to the world. At her death newspapers across the nation commented on her courage in the face of obloquy, ridicule, and even threats. In all the attacks no hint of scandal involving her personal life ever appeared. The rectitude of her character was unassailable.

The greatest influence on Anthony's thought was Elizabeth Cady Stanton. She never thought herself a good speaker, in the early days relying on a friend for the construction of her speeches. Always she turned to Stanton for the source of arguments, but she contributed much to the partnership. Stanton said of their joint efforts: "Through all these years . . . Miss Anthony was the connecting link between me and the outer world—the return scout who went out to see what was going on in the enemy's camp, . . . returning with maps and observations to plan the mode of attack. . . ."[35] Though by Stanton's account they indulged freely in criticism of each other when alone and often had heated differences of opinion, there was never a break of an hour in their friendship.[36] Anthony enjoyed a close friendship with Anna Howard Shaw later in life; but no other person, man or woman, influenced her thought so much as Stanton.

As the years went by, Susan Anthony found herself the center of the suffrage movement. Feted and admired where she had earlier been reviled and insulted, she continued to admonish women, urge congressmen to pass favorable legislation, and to speak for suffrage. Reporters admiringly repeated stories of her earlier adventures. A contemporary averred that men no longer regarded her as the archenemy of domestic peace but now perceived her as the advocate of liberty for all without limitation of sex.[37] For women she was the symbol of their emancipation. When she appeared on the platform at the International Council in 1893, the audience applauded; and when she stood to speak, people climbed upon their chairs and waved hats and handkerchiefs in salute.[38] When she died, however, women were apparently no nearer full political suffrage than they had been in 1870.

Lucy Stone (1818–1893) was an early advocate of woman suffrage. Some thought that she, rather than Stanton or Anthony, should be regarded as the real pioneer. She was the morning star of the women's rights movement, a contemporary said, having lectured for suffrage in 1847 before others began to speak for it and having organized an association in which suffragists could work "who did not wish to have equal suffrage mixed up with free love and other extraneous questions."[39]

As many other women did, she came to suffrage through work against slavery. Her determination, however, to break down the barriers against women in education, the professions, and political affairs was formed in her childhood. The eighth of nine children, she was born on a farm near New Barfield, Massachusetts. From the beginning she was made conscious of the injustices suffered by women. She knew that when she was born her mother had sighed in sorrow that the new baby was a girl because "a woman's life is so hard."[40] In the Stone household women were not encouraged to think themselves equal to men. Her father's will was law in the house. The Bible that she studied as an orthodox Congregationalist told her that women should be submissive to their husbands. When she questioned why this should be so, her mother explained that a curse had been laid upon woman, making her forever subject to man. Rebelling against the wrongs that she observed, Stone determined that she would speak out against injustice to women. She decided that she would go to college. Such an idea seemed insane to her father, though he approved of the plans of two of his sons to attend college. He thought that she had already had enough education and wished her to quit the local school she attended. She pleaded to be allowed to continue. When she had signed a note to repay him, her father advanced her enough money to stay in school until she was sixteen and considered competent enough to teach. She saved what money she could from her meager teaching salary and in 1843, at the age of twenty-five, entered Oberlin College. Having saved barely enough to pay her tuition, she supported herself by teaching in the preparatory school for twelve and a half cents an hour, supplementing this income by doing housework in the Ladies Boarding Hall for three cents an hour.[41]

Finding that Oberlin excluded girls from rhetorical and elocutionary training, Stone organized a debating society for women. She opened the first formal meeting by deploring the lack of rhetorical training for women, "which left them unable to state a question or argue it successfully."[42] Oberlin was in accord with public opinion when it discouraged women from speaking in public. Stone's family shared the aversion to women on the platform. Her mother pleaded with her to give up the idea of lecturing. If she thought that she must speak, her mother added, she should go from house to house and speak with women privately. Stone answered: "I surely would not be a public speaker if I sought a life of ease, for it will be a most laborious one; nor would I do it for the sake of honor, for I know that I shall be disesteemed, nay even hated, . . . but mother . . . if I would be true to myself I must . . . pursue that course of conduct which, to me, appears best calculated to promote the highest good of the world."[43]

Soon after graduation Stone began lecturing for the Massachusetts Antislavery Society but "threw in comments on woman's rights." When leaders of Antislavery Society objected to her mixing the two causes, she arranged with them to speak on abolition on Saturday and Sunday nights, leaving her the rest of the week free to speak on any subject of her choice. She spoke on women's rights, printing notices at her own expense and personally tacking them up on trees and posts in the hopes of attracting an audience. Believing that women should meet to plan the strategy to be used, she called a woman's-suffrage convention in Worcester, Massachusetts, in 1850. Other conventions were held in various cities in the next few years. In 1853 Stone went on a speaking tour of the Midwest and South, speaking for suffrage, temperance, and women's rights.[44]

The tour was managed by Henry Blackwell, whom she had met in Cincinnati when she had called at his hardware store. In 1855 Lucy Stone pioneered in another way when she and Henry Blackwell read at their marriage ceremony a protest against unjust laws that failed to recognize the rights of married women. She did not immediately insist upon being called Lucy Stone but in 1856 expressed a belief that a woman should not give up her name upon marriage and then determinedly became Lucy Stone.[45]

With all of her independence she was far from the mannish creature depicted as the typical suffragist. Though her father had teased her about being plain when she was a girl, contemporaries of her youth and maturity spoke of her charm and attractiveness. She was a small woman with what was often called a sweet face. Her voice was one of her greatest assets. It was frequently termed "silver." Some men declared that, once heard, it was never forgotten. She was tactful. Even when she said disagreeable things, her manner reduced the sting. She generally tried to avoid antagonizing her audiences. She credited men of the opposition with good will, listed their arguments fairly, and then refuted them. She was pointed in her argument and sometimes sarcastic; but she did not scold her audiences, as Anthony sometimes did, or introduce radical ideas along with woman suffrage, as Stanton sometimes did. She was able to appeal to conservative women. Her daughter described a visit made by Lucy Stone to the Mothers Club at Cambridge in 1892, noting that the club was made of "professors' wives" and "various high and mighty people." Though some of the women had objected to hearing a suffragist, they applauded Stone and "made much of her" after her speech. The daughter added that in her white cap, with white things about her neck, her mother was the "sweetest-looking old lady you ever saw and captivates everybody."[46]

Throughout her life Lucy had periodic times of self-doubt and depression. Then she withdrew from the platform and public appearances. Yet she seems never to have questioned the justice of women's rights or the fact that women would one day be granted full suffrage. She made many contributions to suffrage, not the least of them being the persuasion of her husband to give up his business career to devote full time to suffrage. He spoke for women's rights and, with Stone, published *The Woman's Journal,* the most important suffrage newspaper in the United States from 1870 to 1917. He served as editor of the *Journal* most of the time and as manager of the business of the American Suffrage Association. Lucy Stone also persuaded Anna Howard Shaw to lecture for suffrage and converted Julia Ward Howe to the cause. She brought up a daughter to be a devoted advocate of women's rights and continued, herself, to write and speak for suffrage until a few weeks before her death. Policies she had established in the American Association were largely adopted by the united group after 1890, especially in delegate representation and in holding national conventions at various cities other than Washington.

About Lucy Stone there was a touch of self-righteousness and pettiness in personal matters. She had a tendency to depreciate the efforts of others and a willingness to believe any story that discredited Stanton and Anthony or impugned their motives. Nevertheless, she was a shining example of single-hearted and lifelong devotion to suffrage. Her last words to her daughter were: "Make the world better."[47]

METHODS OF PERSUASION

Although women used every available means of persuasion to present their case to the public, several methods seemed more prominent. By addressing the House Judiciary Committee on the behalf of woman's suffrage, Victoria Woodhull initiated legal action as a persuasive technique. Her argument simply proclaimed it the duty of women to vote since the Fourteenth Amendment had authorized enfranchisement. No further legislation was needed. Suffragists had assembled in Washington for the 1871 convention, but when they learned of Victoria Woodhull's appearance before the Congressional Committee, they postponed the opening of their convention to attend the hearing. Following the convention Anthony went on tour with a speech entitled "The New Situation" based on the Woodhull memorial.[48] Woodhull's argument was at least partly responsible for the determination of several women to test their right to vote in the Presidential election of 1872. The editors of *The History of Woman Suffrage* credit Francis Minor, a St. Louis lawyer, with the idea of forcing a legal decision on enfranchisement of women. In 1869 Mr. Minor reported that the Missouri Suffrage Convention had adopted a resolution declaring that the Fourteenth Amendment had enfranchised women and said that his wife would test the theory in the coming election. A similar interpretation had been reached by others in various parts of the country, including the writers of the memorial presented by the glamorous Woodhull in December, 1870, Susan Anthony eagerly endorsed the new interpretation and went on tour; urging women everywhere to vote in the forthcoming presidential election. In several places women attempted to vote, and in a few places their votes were actually counted, but not those of Mrs. Minor or Susan Anthony.[49]

Anthony had made careful preparation for the test. She had assured the fifteen women who accompanied her to the polls in Rochester, New York, that if legal action were taken against them, she would be responsible for court costs. The women were allowed to register and deposit their ballots. Though their votes were not counted, none of the women except Anthony was singled out for punishment. On Thanksgiving Day she was arrested and ordered to appear on a charge of fraudulent voting. In the time that elapsed between her indictment and her trial she toured the country's twenty-nine post-office districts, speaking on woman's right to the ballot. When the irritated district attorney was granted a change of venue to a neighboring county, she spoke in twenty-one of that county's districts in less than a month while her friend Mrs. Gage was speaking in sixteen others. At a trial of questionable justice she was convicted of fraudulent voting and ordered to pay a fine of one hundred dollars.[50]

Mrs. Minor carried her appeal to the Supreme Court, where she lost in a reversal of the Slaughter House decision, which had stated that suffrage followed citizenship.[51] Some suffragists continued to argue that under the Constitution all citizens had the right to vote; but most, faced with the finality of the Supreme Court position, turned to other methods to effect their purpose. The test in the courts was not without value. The women had received widespread publicity, and some sympathy had been aroused for them.

In the days before radio and television, before motion pictures and rapid transportation, groups attempting to persuade others relied chiefly on speaking at local gatherings and on publishing pamphlets and articles. Advocates of a cause hoped to persuade legislative bodies that they had wide popular support by accumulating signatures on petitions. These techniques, used by the temperance and antislavery societies, were also the methods on which the women relied. Suffragists did not organize parades or picket lines until after 1900. Except that the public generally viewed women who held conventions and made public speeches as creatures who had departed from their proper sphere, early suffrage leaders were as genteel in behavior as the most ardent anti-suffragist. An exception was the occasion when Susan Anthony risked the charge of being unladylike to get publicity for the cause she so ardently supported.

Anthony and her friends decided to take matters into their own hands when managers of the Philadelphia exposition held to celebrate the centennial of Independence refused advocates of woman's rights a place on the program. The women waited until the celebration was under way. Then into the midst of the startled crowd gathered to hear the chosen orators—all men—glorifying the virtues of freedom marched Anthony and four faithful followers. They pushed their way through the crowd and thrust into the hands of the astonished presiding officer the women's list of grievances. Retreating, the ladies handed out printed copies of their protest, then moved outside Independence Hall to a platform erected for musicians and there read to the assembled curious crowd their list of women's grievances, including the degradation of disenfranchisement.[52] The demonstrations amused some reporters, who gave considerable publicity to the women, much of it unfavorable; but it won few converts to the cause.

Conventions other than political gatherings received the attention of suffragists. They sought endorsement from the American Federation of Labor, the National Grange, trades councils, schools, and religious gatherings.[53]

Their own conventions were a source of strength, sustaining them for the continuing struggle. Typical programs of the two or three day meetings opened with prayer and song followed by reports of various committees, reading of letters from absent friends, speeches of inspiration and agitation, and discussion of resolutions to be endorsed by the convention. Leaders tried to get the resolutions and some of the speeches published in newspapers.[54]

In lyceums, Chautauqua assemblies, fairs, and privately arranged tours lecturers educated the public on the suffrage question, sometimes openly, sometimes under the pretense of speaking on other subjects.[55] By 1900 many socially prominent women were holding suffrage conversations in their homes. Few men and women could say that they were unaware of the suffrage question. Commonly women depended on political action, using petitions and lobbying in order to persuade. In the forty years following adoption of the Fourteenth Amendment the suffragists poured petitions into congressional and state assemblies.

In the same period they organized 19 campaigns to win support in as many successive Congresses, 480 drives to get state legislatures to submit suffrage amendments, conducted 56 referendums among male voters, 47 campaigns to persuade state constitutional conventions to write in a provision for woman suffrage, and 277 drives to get state party conventions to include a woman-suffrage plank in their party platforms.[56]

In 1886 a senatorial committee reported that suffrage petitions had been coming to Congress since 1865 and that since 1869 they had come from all parts of the country.[57] Sometimes the petitions came from an individual; usually they bore several names, which had been obtained by workers, often at their own expense and at the risk of personal insult. In 1886 Anthony estimated that more than two hundred thousand suffragists had petitioned Congress for the right to vote.[58] The petitions were generally simple and followed a form set up by officials of the suffrage associations. Typical is that circulated in 1876: "The undersigned citizens of the United States, residents of the State of _____, earnestly pray your honorable bodies to adopt measures for so amending the Constitution as to prohibit the several States from disenfranchising United States citizens on account of sex."[59]

Women were painfully aware that petitions of a group powerless to vote could be easily ignored. A Washington newspaper facetiously noted that women were on hand to witness the presentation of their petitions to the Senate committee. The reporter doubted that the results desired by the women would be forthcoming but admitted that they were following a systematic plan.[60]

Susan Anthony believed that petitions and lobbying were of extreme importance. She told convention members in 1893 that the "sole object . . . of this organization is to bring the combined influence of all the States upon Congress to secure national legislation."[61] Under her leadership the National Association consistently held its annual convention in Washington for the express purpose of influencing congressmen. She was usually successful in getting the hearings printed by Congress, enabling financially hard-pressed suffragists to disseminate their propaganda at government expense. The record of congressional action indicates that her plan was in some degree effective. Committees in the House made six favorable majority or minority reports from 1871 to 1898. The Senate returned favorable reports, usually by a minority, from 1882 to 1892, and in 1887 brought a bill to the Senate floor, where it was decisively defeated.[62]

It is doubtful that women expected Congress to pass favorable legislation until woman suffrage had greater public support. Their first goal was to arouse interest in their cause. In 1892 Anthony said, "Wendell Phillips said what he wanted to do on the abolition question was to turn Congress into an antislavery debating society. That is what we have done . . . turned them into debating societies on the woman question."[63]

Whenever a state constitution was being drawn up or a suffrage amendment voted upon, suffragists engaged in state campaigns. They were often frustrated by the lack of respect paid to their pleas. Anna Howard Shaw, addressing the National American convention of 1891, complained bitterly of the treatment of women in the South Dakota campaign of the previous year. Susan Anthony and other eminent women, she said, had been "barely tolerated" while blanketed Indians who could vote were received with the greatest courtesy.[64] The racist premise inherent in the argument is clearly apparent.

Traveling in western states, where many of the campaigns were conducted, meant severe hardships for women unaccustomed to frontier conditions. Mrs. Margaret Campbell, campaigning in Colorado in 1876, wrote Lucy Stone that she had not found a privy, chamber vessel, or washbowl. Added to her woes were the devouring bedbugs that infested the inns.[65] Despite the hardships, the campaigns continued.

Suffragists supplemented campaign speeches with letters, memorials, and pamphlets. They attended to practical political matters by stopping along the way between speaking engagements to persuade respected men in each voting precinct to work with them, and on election day they went to the polls to keep a watchful eye on the proceedings.

Supporters of woman's enfranchisement made repeated attempts to get major parties to put suffrage planks into their platforms. Minor parties usually welcomed women to their ranks and endorsed equal rights, but no group was willing to carry the burden of woman suffrage when it believed that it had a chance for success. Populists, organized on the slogan of "equal rights to all, special privileges to none," seated women as delegates in state and national conventions, employed them as speakers and political organizers; but in 1892, at the time of their greatest national strength, they would not permit suffragists even to appear before the committee on resolutions.[66]

From 1868 suffragists made the rounds of the political conventions, asking for a plank in the party platform endorsing woman suffrage. They sent letters to delegates, enclosing suffrage materials, and addressed a letter to each member of the resolutions committee appropriate to his political affiliation. They believed that they were educating the public in their campaigns. In a speech asking for party recognition of woman suffrage Anthony told her audience that the only way men who were rooted in the old belief of women's inferiority could be educated out of their prejudices was through endorsement of suffrage by the political parties.[67]

Women soon learned that prospects of success were entangled with extraneous issues: party rivalry, internal power struggles, prohibition, immigration, the notion that suffragists were atheists and free lovers; and with demands of other reformers. Suffragists, like other reformers, actually distrusted political parties and politicians. They consoled themselves with their lack of success by condemning the liquor interests, immigrants, and big businessmen who, they believed, blocked their progress.[68] Through the use of legal and political action and by carrying their message to the public, few people could deny the impact the suffragists made by the end of the century.

RHETORIC OF THE SUFFRAGE MOVEMENT: 1870–1898

In the period from 1870 to 1898 the United States was changing from a rural, middle-class, Anglo-Saxon society, with a belief that all men should share equally in the natural rights of life, liberty, and the pursuit of happiness, to an urban nation faced with the problem of big business, the influx of immigrants, the acquisition of colonies inhabited by a people of different culture and different values, and increasing doubt that government could function simply by the consent of the governed.

Suffragist leaders only vaguely understood the changes that were taking place. They continued to base their arguments on the natural-rights theory. An essential part of the argument was the need to establish the common humanity of men and women. It was one thing to accept the belief that all men shared natural rights; it was quite another to accept the equality of women with men. The two sexes were different in nature, in spirit, and in habit of thought, men said. They insisted that domestic women enjoyed superiority over men. "Woman is the queen of the home," a minister admonished his hearers, and ought to remain aloof from the mire of politics. "Imagine Mary voting!" he cried.[69]

Many women protested that they did not want the same rights as men. Typical was the sentiment expressed by a woman who said: "We do not want the ballot. We feel ourselves powerful enough without it—nay, we dread to lose our power, if the ballot is given to us. Where we now have influence, so subtle, so mild, so all-pervading, . . . we will lose it, as soon as men see in us a political creature like themselves."[70] Some said that it would be unwise to impose political duties upon women; that they were utterly devoid of logic and completely lacking in scientific or philosophical spirit. Representative adjectives applied to women who sought suffrage were "noisy," "turbulent," "notoriety-seeking," "ambitious," "egotistical," and "strong-minded." It was said that they were appalling examples of womanhood, revolting against motherhood and wifehood, and urging anarchy of sex and reform against nature.

Fully aware of the adverse sentiment, suffragists argued that by the laws of God and man, woman, as one half the human race, was entitled to her natural rights. Stanton's address "The Solitude of Self," delivered on January 18, 1892, before the House Judiciary Committee, epitomized the natural rights argument of suffragists. She asked for the ballot for woman because it was her right as an individual, her right as a citizen, and her right as a woman. "The point I wish to bring before you on this occasion," she said, "is the individuality of each human soul. . . . In discussing the rights of woman, we are to consider, first, what belongs to her as an individual, in a world of her own . . . Her rights . . . are to use all her faculties for her own safety and happiness." "Secondly," she added, "if we consider her as a citizen, . . . she must have the same rights as all other members, according to the fundamental principles of our government." "Thirdly," she went on, "viewed as a woman, an equal factor in civilization, her rights and duties are still the same—individual happiness and development." She offered as a fourth point what was actually an argument against the inequality of women. "It is only the incidental relations of life," she said, "such as mother, wife, sister, daughter, which may involve some special duties and training. . . . In discussing the sphere of man we do not decide his rights as an individual, as a citizen, as a man, by his duties as a father, a husband, a brother, or a son." She asked for woman's complete emancipation from all forms of bondage, custom, dependence, superstition and fear. Denial of a complete education, her rights of property, political equality, recompense in the world of work, a voice in choosing those who make and administer the law, and a choice of a jury before whom she would be tried was as cruel as putting out her eyes and cutting off her hands, she asserted. She asked that women be given responsibilities. They were not afraid of the burden. "The responsibilities of life rest equally on man and woman," she said, "their destiny is the same, they need the same preparation for time and eternity."[71] Stanton's argument was classical in its natural-rights theory but with the difference that she was not asserting women's present equality before the law but pleading for the opportunity to become equal. To attain the equality she needed education and the vote.

Suffragists adapted to their natural-rights plea the language and the arguments of their revolutionary ancestors. The women's declaration of rights issued at Seneca Falls was an acknowledged paraphrase of the Declaration of Independence, beginning: "When, in the course of human events, it becomes necessary for one portion of the family of man to assume among the people of the earth a position different from that they have long occupied. . . ."[72] Stone echoed the rhythms of Patrick Henry as she deplored the odium attached to the supporters of woman's rights and declared: "If we must incur the hatred of even our dearest friends, let that hatred come, and if we must lose their respect, let that loss of respect come. We will never shrink from the firm avowal of what is truth to us."[73]

Suffragists invoked the Declaration of Independence and the Constitution as authority for their claims. "We have our immortal Declaration of Independence," Lucy Stone told a congressional committee, "and the various bills of rights of the different States . . . and in these nothing is clearer than the basis of the claim that women should have equal rights with men."[74] Suffragists declared that it was not the intention of the founding fathers to deny the franchise to woman. They asked if it were reasonable to suppose that men with "their souls all on fire with newfound freedom" would sit down "like so many little pettifogging lawyers" and draw up an instrument for the express purpose of robbing women of their inalienable rights."[75] Stanton told a congressional committee in 1888 that a fair reading of the Constitution would give women the rights they sought. She supposed that the gentlemen who wrote the adverse reports had read the Constitution, but thought that they "took to a world of speculation" and were ruled by prejudice in their arguments.[76]

Suffragists quoted from the founding fathers in support of their natural rights. George Washington had advised men to recur to first principles, they said. They offered the authority of Benjamin Franklin for the statement that liberty consisted in having an actual share in the choice of those who framed the laws. The names of Thomas Paine, Samuel Adams, Thomas Jefferson, James Madison, and James Otis permeate the speeches of suffragists. They said that "We the people" meant all the people. "Does any one pretend," Stanton said, "that men alone constitute races and peoples? When we say parents, do we not mean mothers as well as fathers? . . . When the race shall spring, Minerva-like, from the brains of their fathers, it will be time enough thus to ignore the fact that one-half the human family are women."[77]

The right of government by consent of the governed was given by God and man's own free nature, the suffragists asserted, and pointed to the word "secure" in the preamble to the Constitution. They interpreted the word to mean that the rights were bestowed by God and that man could not either bestow or withhold this fundamental liberty. They declared that God did not intend men to rule women. Isabella Beecher Hooker told a Senate Committee that God, "sitting between the eternities," had promulgated the doctrine of personal liberty and would see that his doctrines were carried out.[78]

Advocates of suffrage rejected the idea of "virtual representation." No person could represent another, they said. Alice Stone Blackwell recognized the difficulty with virtual representation, pointing out that if a man had a wife, a widowed mother, five unmarried sisters, and five unmarried daughters, his vote counted for no more than that of his bachelor neighbor next door. Further, she asked, how was it possible for one man to represent two women who differed in their opinions?[79] Shaw often observed that unmarried women had no one to represent them. Suffragists doubted that any person could represent another.

If women were denied representation, they asked, why should they be included in taxation? In a country where "no taxation without representation" was a watchword, they said, and where it was universally held that all just governments derived their power from the consent of the governed, it should be unnecessary to plead for the recognition of one half of the people to participate in making the laws by which they were taxed and governed. Women frequently recounted their personal experiences of injustice at the hands of the taxgatherer. They told stories of brave women who refused to pay their taxes as a matter of principle and reported that the very men who came, often apologetically, to collect their taxes said that they would not themselves pay taxes if they could not vote. They reminded hearers that Indians not counted in representation were not taxed, that black men were not taxed before the Fifteenth Amendment, that clergymen were not taxed but that when they died their widows were. If taxation without representation was tyranny under George III, it was just as tyrannical now, the women insisted. A representative statement of the argument was made by Mary Grew, who said: "It is enough for me that the charter of our Nation states that 'taxation without representation is tyranny' and that 'all just government is founded on the consent of the governed.' No woman wrote those words," she added. "They were written by men."[80]

Women spoke of the degradation they felt at being denied the ballot along with criminals, idiots, and the insane. They pointed out distinguished members of their sex who could not vote in contrast to the most ignorant, drunken, and bought men. Troubled by their continued defeat in their quest for the vote, they blamed the immigrants and the black men, who, they thought, were easy tools of the liquor interests and party bosses. Though the attitude of the women may have reflected widely held prejudices of some leading men of the day, the apparent racism and arrogant wish to deny other individuals the right they sought is nevertheless a dark chapter in their history. They spoke of the "refuse of the old world thrown upon our shores," of the ignorant foreigner "who would burn your barn or break into your house" going to the polls on election day side by side with the first man in the land or, if too drunk to walk, riding in a carriage while native-born refined American women were denied the vote. They compared the treatment of women with that given to former slaves. They spoke of the "ignorant Negro," the "half-civilized and blanketed Indian," of Mexican "greasers," of "Patrick, Sambo, Hans and Yung Tung" all legislating for the daughters and deciding the moral code for the mothers of America.[81]

To the argument that with the right to vote went the duty of fighting, women answered that the mother who "gives birth to the children, gathers their rations, does picket duty for them," and watches over them until they are old enough to do military duty has rendered quite as important service to the country as the men who go to war.[82] Sometimes suffragists dismissed the argument with the comment that the ballot and the bullet required different functions. Sometimes they scoffed that the very men who used the argument had themselves sent substitutes in the late war.

Suffragists defended their plea for the ballot against the charge that a majority of women, especially the "better class," did not want the vote by offering thousands of names on petitions for enfranchisement. They further reminded their hearers that no other class of voters had been required to show a universal desire for suffrage in order to have it granted..

Less confidently than they argued the natural right to the ballot, the women argued the expedience of suffrage. The primary argument advanced in the name of expedience was that women would be a moral force in government. Suffragists prophesied that women would exert an influence for religion, purity, temperance, and peace. Prostitution, the saloon, and war would not flourish if women were in power, they predicted. They held that the influence of women was needed to balance the large number of corrupt and ignorant voters who had been added to the population. In a typical speech the suffragist said: "You have before you a great problem as to whether republican government itself is to be successful at this time. . . . We believe that women have in their possession what is needed to make it a success. . . . We can supply what is lacking, not because women are better than men but because they are other than men; . . . and it is their mission to guard most sacredly and closely those things which protect home life."[83] Shaw was more specific when she told her audience: "The millennium will not come as soon as women vote, but it will not come until they do vote." She listed some of the functions women could be expected to perform. They were concerned with keeping their children healthy. This necessitated the provision of pure water. She asked: "Is there any reason why women should not have a vote in regard to water works? A woman knows as much about water as a man. Generally, she drinks more of it." She noted that street cleaners swept the dirt up on Monday and left it to blow about until Saturday, commenting that any housekeeper would know better.[84]

A second form of the expedience argument was insistent that woman needed the ballot to protect herself.[85] Speakers declared that low wages paid to women and poor working conditions were related to the fact that women lacked the power to vote. They declared that women needed the vote to protect her property and her earnings from the unjust laws that men had made, to protect her rights in her children that man's law gave to the father, against unjust laws that bound her to an intolerable marriage, against light punishment meted out for sex crimes, against health hazards, and other injustices she suffered. Advocates of suffrage pointed out that no bad effects had resulted in the states and local communities where women had voted; that, on the contrary, most of the people in those areas agreed that woman suffrage had been beneficial.

The arguments and the methods changed little from 1870 to 1898. The titles of the speeches heard in convention and from the platform were new, but the content was familiar. Anthony, ever optimistic, resigned from the presidency of the association in 1900 with the statement that "Suffrage is no longer a theory, but an actual condition."[86] Her statement was debatable. By 1898 twenty-three states permitted women to vote in school elections, and Kansas had municipal suffrage. Only the four western states of Wyoming, Utah, Idaho, and Colorado permitted women to vote on an equal basis with men. Some reforms had been made in state laws. Woman had control of her property in most states. Many colleges were open to her. She could enter law, medicine, the ministry, science, or business. The call in 1898 for the thirtieth annual convention of the National American Woman Suffrage Association exulted that "in this half-century a new world has been created for woman. In home and school, in church and State, in the courts and industries and professions, a reformation has been effected."[87]

The very progress in the condition of women made the prospect of full enfranchisement even more remote. Congressmen declared that the ballot was not needed. They saw no reason to impose the burden of voting upon the great mass of women who did not wish for it in order to gratify the "comparatively few" that did. Women were to wait another twenty years for total victory, and no other state extended the franchise until 1910.

Suffragists were not idle, however. They continued to campaign in state and party conventions, to seek hearings in Congress, and to try to influence public opinion to accept the idea of a wider sphere for women than tradition had allowed her. Proliferation of women's clubs, an increasing number of women who received college degrees and made careers for themselves in the professions or industry, and the improvements that made life easier for woman in the home all contributed to her final achievement of equal voting rights.

Much of the credit for the final victory should go to the liberationists of the nineteenth century. They suffered ridicule and insults; they underwent almost unbelievable hardships; they gave unsparingly of time and energy, making financial and personal sacrifices for the cause. If they could speak to the women of the twentieth century who enjoy full political rights and a large measure of personal freedom, they might well repeat the words of Abby Kelly: "Sisters, bloody feet have worn smooth the path by which you come up here."[88]

NOTES

* Betty Boyd Caroli, author of the following essay and Janet Bury and Barbara Graham, graduate students at Ohio University, helped prepare this essay for publication.

1. Opinion in Bradwell v. Illinois, cited in U.S. Congress, Judiciary Committee, *Hearings on H. R. 196*, 92d Cong., 1st Sess., Cumulative Issue, no. 3, p. 57.
2. *St. Louis Post Dispatch*, March 23, 1972, p. 1.
3. These sentiments are quoted in Bernard Schwarts, *Rights of the Person*, introduced as testimony in U.S. Congress, Judiciary Committee, *Hearings on H. R. 196*, 92d Cong., 1st Sess., Cumulative Issue, no. 3, p. 61.
4. Anna Howard Shaw, Letter to Lucy Stone, July 18, 1888, Blackwell Family Papers, Manuscript Division, Library of Congress, Washington, D.C.
5. Carrie Chapman Catt and Nettie Rogers Shuler, *Woman Suffrage and Politics* (New York: Charles Scribner's Sons, 1923), p. 164. Hereafter referred to as Catt and Shuler, *Woman Suffrage*.
6. The split in the suffrage movement over the fourteenth and fifteenth amendments is discussed by several authors, including: Page Smith, *Daughters of the Promised Land* (Boston: Little, Brown and Company, 1970), pp. 142 ff; Andrew Sinclair, *The Emancipation of The American Woman* (New York: Harper and Row, 1965), pp. 189 ff; William L. O'Neill, *Everyone Was Brave* (New York: Quadrangle, 1969), pp. 18–21.
7. Ida Husted Harper, "The Winning of the Vote," unpublished history of the woman suffrage movement, Alphabetical file, National American Woman

Suffrage Records, Manuscript Division, Library of Congress, Washington, D.C., Box 257.

8. Catt and Shuler, *Woman Suffrage* pp. 61–63. See also: Andrew Sinclair, *The Emancipation of the American Woman* (New York: Harper & Row, 1965), pp. 187–9.

9. Harriott Stanton Blatch and Alma Lutz, *Challenging Years* (New York: G. P. Putnam's Sons, 1940), p. 61; Lucy Stone to Antoinette Blackwell, *circa* 1887, Blackwell Family Papers, Box 44.

10. For a summary of the arguments of anti-suffragists, see Aileen S. Kraditor, "The Rationale of Antisuffragism," *The Ideas of the Woman Suffrage Movement: 1890–1920* (Garden City, New York: Doubleday and Company, 1971), pp. 12–27.
    Although the period covered by Miss Kraditor is primarily that listed in the title, she reviews earlier history. Arguments of anti-suffragists changed little from 1870 to 1920.

11. *New York Daily Tribune*, February 12, 1870, p. 6, col. 5.

12. Elizabeth Cady Stanton, *Eighty Years and More: Reminiscences, 1815–1897* (New York: European Publishing Company, 1898), pp. 1–153, hereafter referred to as *Reminiscences*; Alma Lutz, *Created Equal: A Biography of Elizabeth Cady Stanton* (New York: The John Day Company, 1940), pp. 3–43.

13. Clipping from unidentified newspaper, October 27, 1902, Susan B. Anthony Scrapbooks, 5 vols., Manuscript Division, Library of Congress, Washington, D.C., III.

14. Stanton, *Reminiscences*, pp. 166–167.

15. From Tenafly, New York, March 21, 1871, Theodore Stanton and Harriot Stanton Blatch, ed., *Elizabeth Cady Stanton as Revealed in Her Letters, Diary, and Reminiscences*, (New York: Harper and Brothers, 1922), 2:131.

16. Letter to Elizabeth Smith Miller from Des Moines, Iowa, June 12, 1871 in Stanton and Blatch, *Stanton Letters*, 2:132–133.

17. Letter to Susan Anthony from Tenafly, New York, May 30, 1870, Stanton and Blatch, *Stanton Letters*, 2:126–127.

18. Ibid., 2:61.

19. Ibid., 2:347.

20. Letter to the Reverend Robert Collyer from Tenafly, New York, February 22, 1880 and footnote, Stanton and Blatch, *Stanton Letters*, 2:167.

21. Unidentified newspaper clipping of October 27, 1902, Susan B. Anthony Scrapbooks, III.

22. James B. Pond, "Great Orators and the Lyceum," *The Cosmopolitan* 21 (July 1896): 243–256.

23. Blatch and Lutz, *Challenging Years*, pp. 193–196.

24. Excerpt from speech, Susan B. Anthony and Ida Husted Harper, ed., *The History of Woman Suffrage*, 1902, 4:176–178. Volumes 1–3 are edited by Elizabeth Cady Stanton, Susan B. Anthony, and Matilda Joslyn Gage and published in Rochester, New York by Charles Mann, 1881–1886. Ida H. Harper edited volumes 5 and 6, published by the National American Woman Suffrage Association and printed in New York by J. J. Ives and Company, 1922. Volume 1 covers the record of the years 1848–1861; 2 from 1861–1876; 3 from 1876 to

1885; 4 from the years 1883 to 1900; 5 and 6 cover the years 1900–1920. Cited hereafter as *HWS*.

25. Ida Husted Harper, *The Life and Work of Susan B. Anthony* (Indianapolis: The Hollenbeck Press, 1890–1908), 2:848. Hereafter referred to as *Life and Work*.

26. Clipping from *The Washington Post*, February 15, 1898, Susan B. Anthony Scrapbooks, II.

27. Harper, *Life and Work*, passim.

28. Elinor Rice Hays, *Lucy Stone: One of America's First and Greatest Feminists* (New York: Tower Publications, 1961), p. 211. Hereafter referred to as *Lucy Stone*.

29. Harper, *Life and Work*, 3:1547. Cited in *Boston Traveler*.

30. Ibid., 2:925.

31. *HWS*, 4:440, 449.

32. Harper, *Life and Work*, 1:459, 2:694–695; and 813, 892, 925; *HWS*, 4:250.

33. Harriet E. Grim, "Susan B. Anthony: Exponent of Freedom," (Unpublished Ph.D. Dissertation University of Wisconsin, 1938), 2:447.

34. *Life and Work*, 3:1175, quoting the *Washington Star*.

35. *New York Daily Tribune*, February 16, 1870.

36. Stanton, *Reminiscences*, p. 166.

37. Harper *Life and Work*, 2:752, quoting from Chicago Interocean.

38. Ibid., 3:xli and 746; Grim, "Anthony," 2:905.

39. W. A. Allen, "Down Memory Lane," undated clipping in Blackwell Family Papers, Box 5.

40. Hays, *Lucy Stone*, pp. 26–27.

41. Alice Stone Blackwell, *Lucy Stone: Pioneer of Woman's Rights* (2nd ed.; Boston: Little, Brown and Company, 1930), pp. 3–49. Hereafter referred to as *Lucy Stone: Pioneer*.

42. Blackwell *Lucy Stone: Pioneer*, p. 6; *The Woman's Column* October 28, 1893, p. 1, Blackwell Family Papers.

43. Blackwell, *Lucy Stone: Pioneer*, pp. 64–66.

44. Handwritten manuscript of a speech by Lucy Stone, Blackwell Family Papers.

45. Hays, *Lucy Stone*, pp. 150–154.

46. Letter written by Alice Stone Blackwell, March 13, 1892, Blackwell Family Papers.

47. Allen, "Down Memory Lane," Blackwell Family Papers, Box 5.

48. Harper *Life and Work*, 1:381.

49. Lucy Stone had walked quietly with her husband's mother to the polls in November 1868, where Mrs. Blackwell had cast her ballot, voting a straight Republican ticket. The inspectors of the polls received it respectfully, but declined to let it be deposited in the ballot box. Hays, *Lucy Stone*, p. 214. On attempts to vote, see: Alma Lutz, "Susan Brownell Anthony," *Notable American Woman*, ed. Edward T. James et al., (Cambridge, Mass.: Harvard University Press, 1973), 1:55. Helen R. Pinckrey, "Virginia Louisa Minor," *Notable American Woman*, ed. Edward T. James et al., (Cambridge, Mass: Harvard University Press, 1973), 2:550–1.

50. Katherine Anthony, *Susan B. Anthony: Her Personal History and Her Era*

(Garden City, New York: Doubleday and Co., 1954), pp. 277–301; Harper *Life and Work*, I:423-453; *HWS*, 2:407–410, 586–715, 934–950.

51. *HWS*, 2:715–755, 950–952; *Life and Work*, 1:453–454.
52. *HWS*, 3:16–53.
53. Edith M. Phelps, *Selected Articles on Woman Suffrage*, 2nd ed. (Minneapolis: H. W. Wilson Co., 1912), pp. 76, 110–111, 103. See also *HWS*, 4:446–447.
54. Harper, *Life and Work*, 1:87–88.
55. See the concluding essay in this volume by James McBath.
56. Catt and Shuler, *Woman Suffrage*, p. 107.
57. U.S. Congress, Select Committee on Woman Suffrage, *Majority Report on S.R. 5*, 49th Cong., 1st Sess., p. 5.
58. U.S. Congress, Select Committee on Woman Suffrage, *Hearings on S. R. 5*, 49th Cong., 1st Sess., p. 6.
59. *HWS*, 3:59.
60. *HWS*, 3:67, quoting the *National Republican, circa* 1877.
61. *HWS*, 4:218.
62. Catt and Shuler, *Woman Suffrage*, p. 229.
63. *HWS*, 4:207.
64. *HWS*, 4:182.
65. The account is reported in a letter from Lucy Stone to Alice Stone Blackwell from St. Louis, August 24, 1877, Blackwell Family Papers, Box 44.
66. *HWS*, 4:437–438.
67. Harper, *Life and Work*, 2:1019.
68. Rheta Child Dorr, *Susan B. Anthony: The Woman That Changed the Mind of a Nation* (New York: Frederick A. Stokes Co., 1928), pp. 57–58, 72–76. See also Phelps, *Articles on Suffrage*, p. 58.
69. Newspaper clippings from unidentified newspaper, Susan B. Anthony Scrapbooks, I. The writer of the article was the Reverend Charles Parkhurst of the Madison Avenue Presbyterian Church.
70. *New York Daily Tribune*, February 21, 1870, p. 5, col. 4.
71. *HWS*, 4:189–191; Kraditor, "Rationale of Antisuffragism," pp. 38–43; U.S. Congress, House Judiciary Committee, *Hearings*, 52d Cong., 1st Sess., pp. 1–5.
72. *HWS*; 1:68–70.
73. Lucy Stone, handwritten manuscript, Blackwell Family Papers.
74. *HWS*, 4:191.
75. *HWS*, 2:506–512.
76. U.S. Congress, Senate Committee on Woman Suffrage, *Report No. 2543*, 50th Cong., 2d Sess., Appendix I., pp. 9–16.
77. *HWS*, 3:81.
78. *Report No. 2543*, Appendix II.
79. *Report No. 2543*, Appendix II, pp. 51–52.
80. *HWS*, 2:814.
81. The argument against black men and immigrants is summarized in Catt and Shuler, *Woman Suffrage and Politics*, pp. 160–64.
82. The popular argument is a part of a manuscript in the handwriting of Lucy Stone in the Blackwell Family Papers. The manuscript written on the back of municipal ballots begins with page 8.

83. *HWS*, 4:266.
84. *HWS*, 4:278.
85. Aileen S. Kraditor, *The Ideas of the Woman Suffrage Movement, 1890–1920*. (New York: Columbia University Press, 1965), pp. 43–5.
86. *HWS*, 4:388.
87. Susan B. Anthony Scrapbooks, II.
88. Quoted in a manuscript in the handwriting of Lucy Stone, Blackwell Family Papers.

9

Women Speak Out
For Reform

BETTY BOYD CAROLI

Historians frequently attribute the American outburst of protest between
1870 and 1898 to dissatisfaction with industrialism, especially among a
displaced middle class. Other scholars connect its genesis to various
economic swings in both directions.[1] Whatever their motivation, women
emerged in the period following the Civil War as highly visible
participants in various reform groups, often organizing and controlling
them. Formerly content with the role of a submissive and innocent
homemaker, women involved themselves in closing saloons, opening
kindergartens, ameliorating life in prisons, slums, and factories. Their new
roles forced them to shed both their submissiveness and their innocence. An
analysis of the activities of Anna Dickinson, Carry Nation, Frances
Willard, Charlotte Perkins Gilman, Mary Livermore, Josephine Shaw
Lowell, and Ida Barnett Wells, all prominent in reform, shows the extent to
which women added new tactics, new concerns, and new kinds of
justifications to their old roles.

Generalizations on women reformers of the late nineteenth century
should not obscure differences between those working for the same cause.
Carry Nation, the outspoken religious fanatic who advocated violence
when necessary to close the hated saloons, appealed to a rural, midwestern
audience when she talked of "hatchetations" and "jointists."[2] Frances
Willard, the genteel lady from Illinois, eschewed Nation's methods when
she spoke to audiences in England, as well as the United States, on a long
list of subjects besides temperance.[3] Both women had found their cause
through conversion, not birth. Nation's grandfather, James Campbell,

started each day with a drink. His famous granddaughter wrote of him: "Every morning my grandfather would put in a glass some sugar, butter and brandy, then pour hot water over it, and while the family were sitting around the room waiting for breakfast, he would go to each and give to those who wished a spoonful of this toddy, saying, 'Will you have a taste, my daughter or my son?' "[4] Nation's conversion to the temperance cause followed her marriage to Charles Gloyd, an alcoholic physician whose proclivities for drink were not discovered by his bride until after their marriage on November 21, 1867.[5]

Frances Willard admitted that she hardly knew what a saloon was before the eruption of the temperance crusade in 1874. "I thought the queer looking places with blinds and screens were barber shops," she wrote.[6] Not a teetotaler herself, she acknowledged that the crusade found her "with a keg of beer in the cellar."[7] Beyond their midwestern origins and their conversion to temperance at about the same time, Nation and Willard shared very little.

Despite individual variations female social reformers of the late nineteenth century introduced an approach to their work that set them apart from their antebellum predecessors. They shared less with the Grimké sisters, Frances Wright and Ernestine Rose, whose reputations bloomed in the prewar decades, than with the professional organizers who labored in the mainstream of twentieth-century reform. Late nineteenth-century women formed the bridge between the pioneering efforts of individual women who hesitatingly spoke at random meetings in the 1830s and 1840s and twentieth-century women who proudly took their places, as equals, in courtrooms and legislatures, in Presidents' cabinets and union offices. The women discussed here increased the sphere of activity acceptable for their sex by speaking publicly to audiences that included men and by forming organizations to achieve reform. They added new concerns to the reforms their antebellum predecessors had sought, and they substituted pragmatic and logical justifications for the emotional, religion-based appeals favored by earlier women.

THE RIGHT TO SPEAK

The antebellum decades never conceded the propriety of women speaking at public gatherings. Members of both sexes typically dismissed addressing mixed audiences as "unladylike." Even Hannah Mather Crocker, granddaughter of Cotton Mather and one of the women credited with initiating the American feminist movement, wrote in 1818:

It would be morally wrong and physically imprudent for any woman to attempt pleading at the bar of justice as no law can give her the right of deviating from the strictest rules of rectitude and decorum. . . . There can be no doubt that, in most cases, [women's] judgment may be equal with the other sex, perhaps even on the subject of law, politics or religion they may form good judgment, but it would be morally improper and physically very incorrect for the female character to claim the statesman's berth, or ascend the rostrum to gain the loud applause of men, although their powers of mind may be equal to the task.[8]

Restrictions against women speaking in public resulted, in part, from biblical injunctions against women teaching or preaching to men. Among the oftenest quoted were I Corinthians 14:34–35: "The women should keep silence in the churches. For they are not permitted to speak, but should be subordinate, as even the law says. If there is anything they desire to know, let them ask their husbands at home." Another frequently cited injunction came from I Timothy 2:11–12: "Let a woman learn in silence with all submissiveness. I permit no woman to teach or have authority over men; for she is to keep silent."

The antebellum decades even enlarged the list of objections to women speaking in public by adding appeals to nature to the older biblical advice. Historian Barbara Welter has documented the rise between 1820 and 1860 of a "cult of true womanhood" which demanded of women a list of childlike virtues: piety, purity, submissiveness and domesticity.[9] Wives and mothers were too good to risk exposure to the real world of practical concerns. Nature had assigned to them a separate sphere. This sentencing to a limited arena debilitated women as William Taylor and Christopher Lasch have observed: "It was [woman's] purity contrasted with the coarseness of men that made woman the head of the Home (though not of the family) and the guardian of public morality. But the same purity made intercourse between men and women at last almost literally impossible and drove women to retreat almost exclusively into the society of their own sex, to abandon the very Home which it was their appointed mission to preserve."[10]

Both the biblical injunctions and the "limited sphere" concept of the antebellum years came under powerful attack in the late decades of the nineteenth century as women began to speak out on a variety of reforms besides suffrage. Their right to ascend rostrums had begun to gain acceptance because of the efforts of the Grimké sisters, Frances Wright, Abby Kelly Foster, Lucretia Mott, Ernestine Rose and others in the 1830s and 1840s.[11] But full approval came after the Civil War as a result of adulation heaped on Anna Dickinson. According to James B. Pond, her manager, she was "from her first appearance until she retired from the lecture field, the 'Queen of the Lyceum.' "[12]

Born to the Quaker tradition, which approved of women speaking in public, Anna Dickinson first attracted attention outside her own circle of friends when she was only seventeen. At a meeting of "Friends of Progress" in Philadelphia in 1860 she became incensed when a man, respected in the community, explained his feelings on education for women. "My daughters," he argued, "can do as much as any man's daughters. . . . But they cannot be doctors, nor lawyers, nor preachers, nor bank presidents, nor college professors. . . . If my daughters cannot be, *no* man's daughters can."[13]

Although not scheduled to speak, young Anna Dickinson disagreed with such ability and enthusiasm that several in the audience remarked on her talent.[14] Invitations came for her to speak in neighboring towns. Soon William Lloyd Garrison offered her the chance to join his lecture series. Only nineteen years old, she delighted in associating with such famous orators as Henry Ward Beecher and Wendell Phillips. She wrote her family: "I have made an opening which will be worth hundreds to me next winter and probably thousands afterwards. I have already an engagement to speak in the Fraternity Course—the highest honor that could be given to any lecturer with the price of one hundred dollars."[15]

Honors continued to arrive. In late 1863 members of the United States Congress invited Anna Dickinson to speak in their hall. In her address there on January 16, 1864, entitled "Words for the Hour," she both attacked President Lincoln's war policies and defended his intentions.[16] This appearance gained her a national reputation. One New York newspaper marveled at her ability: "The lecturer and the lecture were enthusiastically received and the general opinion was of wonderment at the versatility, admiration of the eloquence and the enthusiasm at the patriotism of the lady."[17]

After the war's end Dickinson continued to lecture on numerous topics, including women's rights, immigration, and unions. Rather than associate herself with a specific cause she spoke on a variety of subjects. In the 1871–72 winter she addressed one hundred and fifty different audiences for fees ranging from 150 to 400 dollars.[18] Her income totaled $23,090 in 1872, a year in which the President of the United States earned $25,000.[19]

Objections raised to women speakers before the war did not deter audiences from going to hear Dickinson. The novelty of hearing a lady speak may have enhanced her reputation and that of other women who embarked on lecturing careers. James Pond, who managed speaking tours for several professional orators in the late nineteenth century, noted that demands to hear women decreased after a peak of enthusiasm in the early 1870s.[20]

Although Dickinson occasionally encountered attacks that men would not have faced, she responded with wit and grace. She was particularly vulnerable to harassment because she remained single. In a speech to a predominantly male California audience she had just finished her plea for greater justice for Chinese immigrants when a male heckler interrupted, "Would you marry a Chinaman?"

Dickinson replied with a question: "If you were poor and oppressed, wouldn't you like to hear me, or someone else, defend you?"

The man answered that he would.

Then she had her moment. "And I would defend you," she said, "but oppress you by marrying you, never, not if you got down on your knees would I marry you."[21]

In the spring of 1874 Dickinson agreed to speak on prostitution, a subject considered by many to be unfit for a lady. One newspaper commented:

Miss Dickinson is a young, unmarried woman—the last person in the world to have any knowledge of the social evil, unless she has made it a special study, and this is the last study in the world which a young, unmarried woman should make a specialty.[22]

Anna Dickinson did not shun criticism. She met it openly and directly. Speaking to a large audience in Cooper Union, New York City, on April 19, 1872, she heard hissing when she criticized the Grant administration. "Let any hiss who please and let those applaud who choose," she said. "I will utter the truth despite censure or applause and will maintain it though I stand alone."[23] The hisses turned to applause.

Other women who invaded formerly male arenas exposed themselves to dangers more serious than verbal assaults. Evidence indicates that their sex may have given them special protection. Carry Nation faced many attacks from opponents who pelted her with eggs and fought back against her hatchet and her tongue. Genuine martyrdom demanded more serious assault, however, and she often begged to be shot. "How glorious to be a martyr to the cause," she told friends.[24] At least one biographer attributed her failure to die at the hands of a mob to western chivalry or to her own bad luck.[25]

Settlement-house workers, responding to requests to confront drunken and abusive husbands and fathers, also exposed themselves to danger. Mary McDowell, the middle-class Ohio woman who moved to a Chicago slum in 1894 with her housekeeper, often faced erring husbands in behalf of women whose pleas lacked effect.[26] Although they may have resented her intrusion into their affairs, the men rarely responded with physical violence. Instead they named her the "Angel of the Stockyards."[27]

Anna Dickinson's lectures on controversial subjects exposed her to more than one wrathful audience. In 1863, when the Republican Party could find few friends in Pennsylvania mining towns, anyone speaking for its cause faced special danger. Dickinson, barely twenty years old, seemed the best choice to carry the Republican banner. One friend wrote that she would get a rough reception but that she could manage: "Your sex will gain for you an attentive audience and your genius will do the rest."[28]

During this speaking tour, a miner shot a curl off her head. Dickinson did not move. After a brief silence somebody called out, "Oh but she's a brave girl, boys; let's hear what she has to say."[29]

Anna Dickinson's popularity diminished after 1872, when she spoke in behalf of Horace Greeley against the more popular Grant. Several famous women suffragists, including Susan B. Anthony and Elizabeth Cady Stanton, had favored a Grant victory as more helpful in advancing their cause.[30] Dickinson's disagreements with suffrage leaders, her association with the eccentric Greeley, and her personal feud with the powerful newspaperman Whitelaw Reid all combined to diminish her standing with the public. She tried acting and writing but never achieved the popularity she had enjoyed as a lecturer.[31]

Anna Dickinson helped establish permanently women's right to lecture on important, controversial topics to audiences including men. By demanding and receiving fees equal to those paid the most famous male orators she showed that women lecturers were to be judged by *what* they said, not *that* they said it, and she paved the way for twentieth-century women who did not even question their possession of this important right.

THE RIGHT TO ORGANIZE

Late nineteenth-century women used their public speaking abilities to form and control organizations. Civil War efforts had already initiated them in the advantages of cooperation. In late 1861, wives, mothers, and sisters of Union soldiers started the Sanitary Commission to support their men by gathering supplies, ministering to the wounded, and communicating with families of the ill and dead.[32]

Another war-inspired organization—the Loyal Women's National League—grew out of a mass meeting in New York City on May 14, 1863.[33] The League sought to extend abolition to areas not covered by President Lincoln's Emancipation Proclamation of January 1, 1863. To attain their objective women in the League enrolled five thousand members, whose work became educating and persuading the nation.[34] A network of canvassers branched out across the continent and brought back, in the first phase of their efforts, one hundred thousand signatures on petitions.[35]

Activities of the Sanitary Commission and the Loyal League marked an important departure from the unorganized, individual reform efforts of antebellum women and prepared for further changes after 1870. In the 1830s and 1840s women had participated in abolitionist, pacifist, and temperance groups, even attended the World Anti-Slavery Convention in London in 1840; but their roles had been limited to women's groups or observers, as in the London conference. Local sewing clubs and church circles met for discussion and pleasure, but most of their members perceived little efficacy in combining their efforts on matters of national interest.

While antebellum women appealed to individuals as individuals, late nineteenth-century women attempted to influence institutions through organizations. Frances Willard, whose leadership of the Woman's Christian Temperance Union helped make it one of the largest clubs in the country, noted the importance of cooperative activity:

The sober second thought (after prayer) of the WCTU was organization. The voice of God called to them from the lips of his prophet: "Make a chain, for the land is full of bloody crimes and the city is full of violence." And so in every town and village we are forming these chains of light and loving helpfulness which we call "Woman's Christian Temperance Unions." We have already 23 states organized, with thousands of local auxiliaries. Every day brings fresh accessions of women, translated out of the passive and into the active voice on this great question of the protection of their homes.[36]

Women's national organizations proliferated after the Civil War. Sorosis began in New York in 1868 with a charter claiming that it formed "for promotion of useful relations among women, the discussion of principles which promise to exert a salutary effect upon women and society, and the establishing of an order which would render women helpful to each other and actively benevolent to the world."[37]

The formation of two national organizations—the Women's Suffrage Association in 1869 and the Woman's Christian Temperance Union in 1874—marked a new optimism. Women had learned the advantages of co-operation, and a new generation of college-educated women responded enthusiastically to the club movement.[38] Between 1870 and 1898 the "Age of Protest and Reform" witnessed a mushrooming of clubs: American National Red Cross Society, 1881; American Association of University Women, originally the Association of Collegiate Alumnae, 1882; National Society of the Daughters of the American Revolution, 1890; Colonial Dames of America, 1890; National Council of Jewish Women, 1893; National Association of Colored Women's Clubs, 1896; International Sunshine Society, 1896; National Congress of Parents and Teachers, originally the National Congress of Mothers, 1897; and many others.[39]

Total membership in these organizations reached thousands. By 1894 the General Federation of Women's Clubs reported that it included 355 individual organizations and four state federations.[40] The range of objectives in Federation clubs shows the diversity of their activities: art, philanthropy, educational work including kindergartens, household economics, municipal and legislative work. Women in the Federation founded and supported three hospitals, four public libraries, and several free kindergartens.

The organization impulse may help explain the faith its founders held in the settlement house as a way to improve society. Jane Addams, whose Hull House was not the earliest example but remains the most famous, explained in a speech in Plymouth, Massachusetts in 1892: "Hull House endeavors to make social intercourse express the growing sense of economic unity of society. It is an effort to add the social function to democracy. It was opened on the theory that the dependence of classes on each other is reciprocal."[41] Addams helped start a Dante Club, a Women's Club, an Italian Club, and two labor unions, all at Hull House.[42]

The club movement of the post-Civil War period did not belong to women alone. Men's organizations and others open to both sexes also multiplied.[43] The myriad of women's clubs shows, however, the change that had occurred in women's attitudes toward themselves and their role in society. Their sphere (that much-used word to describe a limited circle of accepted activity) had broadened to include several concerns formerly reserved for men. The clubs proved the existence of leadership abilities among women and at the same time furnished opportunities for developing additional expertise in forming and altering public opinion and action.

NEW CONCERNS

Settlement work, performed by Mary McDowell, Jane Addams, Ellen Gates Starr, Lillian Wald, and others in the 1880s and 1890s, emphasizes the extent to which that period linked antebellum reform and twentieth-century efforts. Women's work broadened to include economic, political, and social concerns of their communities. In this respect reform efforts foreshadowed the work of Rose Schneiderman, Frances Perkins, Margaret Sanger, and others in the years following 1900. Yet women continued to approach reform through the home, echoing the "cult of true womanhood," which their mothers and grandmothers had embraced.[44] While they sought to improve their communities they declared they defended home and family.

Few of the late nineteenth-century women reformers questioned prevailing ideas on woman's role in the family—a role which assigned to the wife and mother the primary responsibility for overseeing the food, clothing, and housing needs of her family. In this division of labor, the husband's responsibility stopped at providing money to buy materials. Even Mary "Mother" Jones, the outspoken Irish-born labor organizer, urged women to support unions so that their men could earn enough to keep them at home, where they belonged.[45]

Charlotte Perkins Gilman, one of the most original thinkers of the late nineteenth-century feminists, did not attack the wisdom of the typical family unit. She insisted, however, on woman's independence within that unit, a situation not possible, she argued, so long as cooking and child care remained unpaid chores performed separately in each household.[46]

After a short, unhappy marriage, Charlotte Perkins Gilman began speaking on a list of topics, including "human nature, nationalism and religion."[47] She attributed her debut on the lecture circuit to the seedbed of new ideas and cults that she encountered in California in 1890 and to a chance meeting, at about the same time, with a woman on a bus. The stranger invited Gilman to speak to the Nationalist Club of Pasadena, an experience she later described:

This was an entirely new proposition. I had never given a public address or expected to. But here was an opportunity, not wrong, and I accepted it. All I knew of the art of oratory was something I had read in a newspaper when I was a child—that a public speaker should address the farthest person in the room, then everyone could hear. That had struck me as good sense, and I had laid it up, to prove most useful now.[48]

Charlotte Gilman's career gained attention in the decade that followed. Her pay came from the collection plate passed among the listeners. In the early days four or five dollars was not unusual for an evening's work. Topics varied with the audience and the situation, but many dealt with the economic status of women. She wrote of these years: "My main interest then was in the position of women and the need for more scientific care for young children. As to women, the basic need of economic independence seemed to me of far more importance than the ballot, though that of course was a belated and legitimate claim, for which I always worked as opportunity offered."[49]

Charlotte Gilman gathered her ideas on the need for women's financial independence into a book, *Women and Economics*, a draft of which she finished in seventeen days while living in five different houses. She wrote:

Economic independence for women necessarily involves a change in the home and family relation. But, if that change is for the advantage of individual and race, we need not fear it. It does not involve a change in the marriage relation except in withdrawing the element of economic dependence, nor in the relation of mother to child save to improve it. But it does involve the exercise of human faculty in women, in social service and exchange rather than in domestic service solely. This will, of course, require the introduction of some other forms of living than that which now obtains.[50]

The author recommended that household chores, particularly cooking and child care, be performed by people who would be compensated. Community kitchens would serve families, who could sit down and eat together as paying guests. Children would be cared for by professionals, thus freeing their mothers for other work. After she remarried in 1900, Gilman introduced her recommendations into her own household.[51] Her daughter came to live with the Gilmans in their New York City apartment, and the family took meals together at a boarding house down the street. Gilman continued with her writing and lecturing until her death in 1935.

The reforms Gilman sought did not involve changing the family unit but merely altering the economic status of women in the marriage arrangement. "My socialism was of the early humanitarian kind," she wrote, "based on the first exponents, French and English, with the American enthusiasm of Bellamy. The narrow and rigid 'economic determinism' of Marx with its 'class consciousness' and 'class struggle' I never accepted, nor the political methods pursued by Marxians."[52]

Frances Willard's career also emphasizes how women's concerns extended to new areas in the last decades of the nineteenth century. After her death her name was linked primarily to prohibitionism; but her life was devoted to many causes, and she related each of them to improvements in the home and family.[53] She even urged the replacement of temperance with "home protection" as a name for that cause. "But the old name was endeared to those who had suffered for it," she wrote, "and they were not disposed to give it up. In this, I then and always believed them to be unwise."[54]

Willard embraced feminism well before she spoke out on liquor, and her interest in women's rights brought her to the lecture platform. Travel in Europe and the Middle East in the late 1860s convinced her that both sexes suffered from women's inferior treatment. When she returned to the United States she accepted invitations to speak on what she had observed in Turkey, Italy, Germany, and Egypt.[55] Willard wrote that her lecture career blossomed soon after she refused to speak:

While I would rejoice to speak, were I a man, such a beatitude was not for women and I would not face the grim visage of public prejudice. Something less than four years later, I was glad . . . to speak for an hour and a quarter in Centenary Church,

Chicago, without manuscript. So goes the world. It is always broader and better farther on.[56]

Once initiated into the feminist cause, Willard soon moved to other reforms. In 1874, after resigning from her prestigious position of Dean of the Women's College at Northwestern University, she joined the temperance movement, which had rejuvenated itself the previous winter.[57] Willard served as National Corresponding Secretary of the WCTU until 1879, when she assumed the presidency. This office she held until her death in 1898. From the beginning of her association with the WCTU she insisted that the organization work for a long list of reforms. At the 1874 convention she said: "We believe in the living wage; in an eight-hour day; in courts of conciliation and arbitration; in justice as opposed to greed in gain; in 'Peace on Earth and Good Will to Men'."[58] After 1879 Willard sought to enlarge the scope of the organization's work with her "Do All Policy," which included thirty-nine departments working to achieve better health and hygiene, establish kindergartens, improve working conditions, open savings banks, institute fashion reform, obliterate prostitution, and prohibit the sale of alcoholic beverages.[59] As head of a large national organization, she spoke publicly on many subjects formerly thought unacceptable for consideration by women.

PRAGMATIC, LOGICAL JUSTIFICATIONS

In her attempts to institute reform Frances Willard and other women of her time relied heavily on pragmatic, logical justifications to convince their audiences. Willard claimed to reject Elizabeth Cady Stanton's "futile arguments based on reason"[60] but she shrewdly advised her own followers to combine prayer with persuasion and petition in order to influence legislation. The petition she presented to four national nominating conventions on behalf of the WCTU included this explanation:

We members of the WCTU . . . believe that while the poison habits of the nation can be largely restrained by an appeal to the intellect through argument, to the heart through sympathy and to the conscience through the motives of religion, the traffic in these poisons will be best controlled by prohibitory law. We believe the teachings of science, experience and the Golden Rule combine to testify against the traffic in alcoholic liquors as a drink and that the homes of America, which are the citadels of patriotism, purity and happiness, have no enemy so relentless as the American saloon.[61]

Willard's speeches sometimes included biblical references or pleas for divine guidance, but her emphasis remained on this world. In this respect she reflected the social-gospel movement of her time more than the antebellum harbingers who warned of theological retributions for drinking and wrongdoing. In her speech to the Woman's National Council of the United States in 1891 she quoted James Martineau: " 'Of nothing can we be more sure than this; that if we cannot sanctify our present lot, we could sanctify no other.' "[62]

Mary Livermore's reform career parallels Willard's in several respects. Mary Livermore was born in 1820 to parents who, like Frances Willard's, traced their American roots back to New England in the 1630s.[63] After the Chicago branch of the Sanitary Commission took on the task of coordinating national efforts during the Civil War, Livermore became a full-time agent.[64] Dedication to the commission took her to the public platform. This move she says she made reluctantly. She wrote:

It has been my fortune, during the last quarter of a century to occupy the position of public lecturer on the Lyceum platform. It was not of my seeking . . . But my acceptance of an active membership in the Sanitary Commission carried me inevitably into methods of work different from any that I had known before. It was necessary for me to organize women into Soldiers' Aid Societies, to induct them into ways and means of work which should meet the imperative needs of the hour, to go to the front of hospital nurses and place them where they were needed, or accompany boatloads of supplies, the proper distribution of which I was responsible. I was obliged to narrate publicly my experiences and observations while engaged in this work, to quicken the activity of other workers and stimulate the collection of hospital supplies. And when some great enterprise like a colossal Sanitary Fair was to be inaugurated, it was necessary to arouse the enthusiasm of the people and mass the various forces into solidarity. All this called for public speech; I could not escape it.[65]

After the war's end Livermore continued to accept speaking engagements on a wide range of topics.[66] One of the most famous of her lectures, delivered eight hundred times in twenty-five years, entitled "What Shall We Do With Our Daughters?" advocated physical training, dress reform, and improved education so that women could be self-reliant. Livermore noted that these changes would benefit men as well as women: "Not only for the daughters' sakes, but for the sake of the human family, of which women make one half, should we look carefully to the training of our daughters."[67]

Livermore's speaking career was successful and profitable. James Pond, organizer of several lecture series, wrote: "Mrs. Livermore . . . is the most successful woman on the platform I have ever known."[68] Although she delivered the same lecture hundreds of times, she spoke extemporaneously and attempted to fit her material to the particular audience and situation. She wrote:

While I have always written out my lectures most carefully when preparing them I have never used a manuscript nor notes even when delivering them. I have had the reputation of speaking extemporaneously, but unless called on unexpectedly I have always made preparation for even brief addresses. Speaking without manuscript and never memorizing my lectures, I have gradually departed not only from the text but from the order observed in their composition and very soon the manuscript lectures become valueless to me . . . . A manuscript interposed between speaker and his audience becomes, at times, a veritable non-conductor.[69]

Livermore often appealed, well armed with statistics, directly to the self interest of her listener. In one of her famous speeches "Does Liquor Pay?" she argued that it did not. She noted that the Chief of the National Bureau of Statistics had reported that Americans spent nine hundred million dollars every year on liquor. This amount equaled, she calculated, four times the cost of the 1871 Chicago fire with one hundred million dollars left over. Besides the direct cost of drinking, Livermore pointed to the amount spent indirectly on alcohol. In her visits to thirteen state prisons she had been told that 80 to 90 percent of the inmates were in their present situation because of liquor.[70] Adding up the cost of these incarcerations, the harm done to children of drinking parents, and the dollars spent directly on liquor, she estimated that Americans wasted two billion dollars each year on alcohol or its effects.[71]

Arguing that woman's suffrage could stop this misuse of money and human energy, Livermore predicted that women would use their votes for the good of society:

Illiterate foreign peasants, who can neither read, write nor understand the English language and whose moral sense is deadened by alcoholic indulgence and by an appetite for strong drink inherited from generations of brutish ancestors are marshalled to the polls by tens of thousands to cast their vote in favor of saloons, the brewery and the distillery. But the self-governed, Christian, cultivated women of the land, its wives and mothers, are denied the right to voice or a vote in the settlement of this mighty question. . . . The ballot in the hands of women will prove the most powerful enginery for temperance reform the world has ever seen.[72]

Although many late nineteenth-century women reformers, besides Frances Willard and Mary Livermore, typically used pragmatic, logical justifications, none exemplifies this approach more clearly than Josephine Shaw Lowell. Her abolitionist family, which traced its New England roots back five generations, moved to Staten Island in 1855 when she was twelve.[73] In 1863 she married Charles Russell Lowell. Within one year she became his widow and the mother of his daughter.[74] She devoted the rest of her life to philanthropic and charitable work. In 1876 Governor Tilden appointed her the first female member of the New York State Board of Charities. This job she held for thirteen years.[75]

Josephine Lowell's reports to the state board included many appeals to the head, fewer to the heart. In her 1878 report she wrote:

The examination (of poorhouses in New York State in 1874–75) has made it clear that by far the greater number of paupers have reached that condition by idleness, improvidence, drunkenness or some form of vicious indulgence. It is equally clear that these vices and weaknesses are very frequently, if not universally, the result of tendencies which are to a greater or less degree hereditary. . . . There are a large number of families throughout the state which are kept together by public and private charity, the sole end of whose existence seems to be rearing of children like themselves. It is in the highest contrary to sound policy to keep such families together; in fact, the sooner they can be separated and broken up the better it will be for children and for society at large.[76]

Lowell expressed bluntly her feelings on charity:

My own opinion is that the only justification for the expenditure of public money is in the public good, that is the good of the whole mass of people. No government is authorized to levy taxes on one part of the community for the benefit of another part; the honest working portion of the people should not be deprived against their will of their hard-earned money for the care of that portion which is shiftless, incompetent and vicious, unless, in the end, the result is to be for the advantage of the taxpayers themselves.[77]

Lowell continually urged that better prisons and asylums would improve life for all, not just those incarcerated. "For *self* protection," she wrote, "the State should care for these human beings who, having been born must be supported to the end; but every motive of humanity, justice and *self interest* should lead to the extinction of the line as soon as possible."[78] (Emphasis added.)

Ida Barnett Wells also relied heavily on logical appeals to convert her listeners. Born to former slaves in Holly Springs, Mississippi, in 1862, Wells studied at nearby Rust College.[79] When both her parents died in an epidemic of yellow fever in 1878, she determined to keep her five younger brothers and sisters together by teaching at a local school. She later moved to Memphis to work near a widowed aunt, who offered to care for the younger sisters.

An interruption in Ida Wells's trip to Tennessee resulted in her embarking on a life dedicated to improving conditions for her race. A conductor on the Chesapeake and Ohio Railroad ordered the young woman to ride in a smoking car with other Negroes. Insisting that her ticket entitled her to a seat in the regular passenger section, she left the train rather than sit in the smoker. She sued the railroad company. The court ruled in her favor, awarding damages of five hundred dollars.[80] When a higher court reversed the decision, she recorded her disappointment in her diary: "I had hoped such great things from my suit for my people generally. I have firmly believed all along that the law was on our side and would, when we appealed to it, give us justice."[81]

Wells did not, however, abandon her faith in reason. In 1889 she became one-third owner of the newspaper *Memphis Free Speech*.[82] Continuing with her teaching job, she used the paper to publicize her views on the poor quality of Negro schools. After the local board of education refused to rehire her because of her critical editorials, she wrote: "Of course I had rather feared that might be the result, but I had taken a chance in the interest of the children of our race and had lost out. . . . But I thought it was right to strike a blow against a glaring evil and I did not regret it."[83]

Turning her attention to the effect on her people of lynching hysteria in the 1890s, Wells helped organize black women into the Women's Era Club in Boston to assist her.[84] In her struggle to end law by the lynch rope she insisted on specific, provable details. She objected, for example, when Dr. E. E. Hoss, editor of the *Christian Advocate* in Nashville, defended lynching as a response to assaults Negro men made on white women. As a result of her own research into lynch victims' cases, Wells showed that, in the majority of cases, attacks on white women had not even been charged. Of the twenty–seven lynchings in one year in Alabama, for example, only seven involved charges of assaults on white women.[85] Of the two hundred lynch cases recorded in the United States in 1893 fewer than half involved any allegation of attacks on white women, and several of the victims were black women.[86] Wells's carefully documented speeches and articles appealed to the logic of her audiences and eventually convinced many people to reject the unsupported claims made by the defenders of lynching.

CONCLUSIONS

The careers of Ida Barnett Wells, Carry Nation, Frances Willard, Anna Dickinson, Charlotte Perkins Gilman, Mary Livermore, and Josephine Shaw Lowell illustrate the extent to which women enlarged the sphere of activity acceptable for their sex between 1870 and 1898. Each of them reached audiences through public speaking, a tactic not conceded to women in the antebellum decades. Activities during the Civil War had convinced them of the power of national organization. The clubs and settlement houses they formed in the postwar years illustrate both their faith in cooperation and their ability to lead reform groups. Formerly restricted to their own kitchens and churches, wives and mothers redrew the lines to include concern for the quality of other people's lives. Women who had never entered a saloon, visited a prison, seen a prostitute, lived in a slum, or belonged to a labor union directed their attention to ameliorating life through reforms in these areas. Rather than deserting their traditional role in the family unit, they insisted that they improved it. Rejecting as insufficient the emotional, religion-based appeals of their antebellum predecessors, female social reformers in the last decades of the nineteenth century armed themselves with statistics and emphasized pragmatic, logical justifications to convert their audiences. By adopting new tactics, new concerns, and new kinds of appeals women in the "Age of Protest and Reform" decreased the distance between the spheres of the two sexes and moved much closer to the twentieth century.

NOTES

1. Among the many interpretations of the reform impulse, see Samuel P. Hays, *The Response to Industrialism* (Chicago: University of Chicago, 1957); Harold U. Faulkner, *Politics, Reform and Expansion, 1890–1900* (New York: Harper and Brother, 1959); and Richard Hofstadter, *The Age of Reform* (New York: Random House, 1955).
2. Carry A. Nation, *The Use and Need of the Life of Carry A. Nation* (Topeka, F. M. Stevens & Sons, 1909), passim.
3. Frances Willard, *My Happy Half Century* (London: Ward, Lock & Bowden, Ltd., 1894), passim.
4. Nation, *The Use and Need*, pp. 25–6.
5. Ibid., p. 62.
6. Annie T. Wittenmyer, *History of the Woman's Temperance Crusade* (Philadelphia: National Temperance, 1878), Introduction by Frances Willard, p. 14.
7. Frances Willard, *Home Protection Manual* (New York: The Independent Office, 1879), p. 6.
8. H. Mather Crocker, *Observations on the Real Rights of Woman with their Appropriate Duties, Agreeable to the Scripture, Reason and Common Sense* (Boston: Printed for the Author, 1818). pp. 15–16 and 20.
9. Barbara Welter, "The Cult of True Womanhood: 1820–1860," *American Quarterly* 18 (Summer 1966): 151–174.
10. William R. Taylor and Christopher Lasch, "Two 'Kindred Spirits': Sorority and Family in New England, 1839–1846," *New England Quarterly* 36 (March 1963): 35.
11. For a discussion of women speakers in the antebellum period, see Doris Yoakam, "Women's Introduction to the American Platform," in William N.

228 WOMEN TAKE UP THE CAUSE OF REFORM

Brigance, ed. *History and Criticism of American Public Address*, 2 vols. (New York: McGraw-Hill, 1943), 1: 153–192. Marie Kathryn Hochmuth edited a third volume of *History and Criticism of American Public Address* (New York: McGraw-Hill, 1955).

12. James B. Pond, *Eccentricities of Genius* (New York: Dillingham Co., 1900), p. 152.

13. Cited in Judith Anderson, "Anna Dickinson, AntiSlavery Radical," *Pennsylvania History* 3 (July 1936): 150.

14. Giraud Chester, *Embattled Maiden* (New York: Putnam, 1951), p. 17.

15. Ibid., 40.

16. Ibid., 5–7.

17. *New York Tribune*, January 18, 1864, p. 6.

18. Chester, *Embattled Maiden*, 86.

19. Joseph Nathan Kane, *Facts about the Presidents*, 2nd edition (New York: H. W. Wilson, Co., 1968), p. 353. According to James B. Pond, lyceum manager, Anna Elizabeth Young, nineteenth wife of Brigham Young, earned $20,000 narrating the story of her life in 1873.

20. Pond, *Eccentricities of Genius*, p. 143.

21. Cited in Chester, *Embattled Maiden*, p. 100.

22. Ibid., 154.

23. *The New York Sun*, April 20, 1872, p. 1.

24. Cited in Robert Lewis Taylor, *Vessel of Wrath* (New York: The New American Library, 1966), p. 15.

25. Ibid.

26. Howard E. Wilson, *Mary McDowell, Neighbor* (Chicago: University of Chicago Press, 1928), p. 38.

27. Mary Anderson, *Woman at Work* (Minneapolis: University of Minnesota Press, 1951), p. 34.

28. Chester, *Embattled Maiden*, p. 71.

29. Ibid., 71.

30. Elizabeth Cady Stanton, Susan B. Anthony and Matilda Joslyn Gage, eds. *History of Woman Suffrage* 3 vols., (Rochester: Fowler & W., 1881–1886), 2: 518–9. The entire six-volume *History of Woman Suffrage* is the work of multiple authors. Anthony worked with Ida Husted Harper on Volume IV published in 1902. The last two volumes, edited by Ida Husted Harper, were published in New York in 1922.

31. In February 1891, Susan Dickinson, Anna's sister, applied to have her committed to the State Hospital for the Insane in Danville, Pennsylvania. Anna fought in the courts and in the press for vindication of her sister's charges,—and the first trial in 1895 resulted in a split jury. Two years later another jury compromised its own internal dissension by agreeing to declare her sane at the time of her incarceration but to award her damages of only six and one-quarter cents. She thus had to pay all court costs, about 3500 dollars. She lived until October 22, 1932, almost forgotten in her later years.

32. L. P. Brockett and Mary C. Vaughan, *Woman's Work in the Civil War: A Record of Heroism, Patriotism and Patience* (Philadelphia: Zeigler, McC. & Co., 1867), p. 580.

33. Stanton, Anthony and Gage, *History of Woman's Suffrage*, 2:50–53.
34. Ibid., 2:81.
35. Ibid.
36. Willard, *Home Protection Manual*, p. 6.
37. Mary I. Wood, *The History of the General Federation of Women's Clubs* (Norwood, Mass.: The History Dept., General Federation of Women's Clubs, 1912), p. 27.
38. William L. O'Neill, *Everyone Was Brave: A History of Feminism in America* (New York: Quadrangle Books, 1969), p. 79. O'Neill cites one woman's enthusiastic response: "I felt as if I had been flung out into space (after college), and the notices of those meetings were the only threads that connected me with the things I had known."
39. Margaret Fisk, ed. *Encyclopedia of Associations*, 3 vols. (Detroit: Book Tower, 1973), passim.
40. For a list of objectives and membership, see Wood, *History of the General Federation*, passim.
41. Jane Addams, *Philanthropy and Social Progress* (New York: T. Y. Crowell & Co., 1893), p. 1.
42. See both Addams, *Philanthropy and Social Progress*, 50; and Jane Addams, *Democracy and Social Ethics*, edited by Anne Firor Scott (Cambridge: Belknap Press, 1964).
43. Fisk, *Encyclopedia of Associations*, passim.
44. Ann Douglas, in *The Feminization of American Culture* (New York: Alfred A. Knopf, 1977), emphasizes a different development in nineteenth century United States. Between 1820 and 1875, Douglas argues, women and ministers combined to sentimentalize American culture. Tragedy resulted: "Feminization inevitably guaranteed, not simply the loss of the finest values contained in Calvinism, but the continuation of male hegemony in different guises. The triumph of the "feminizing" sentimental forces that would generate mass culture redefined and perhaps limited the possibilities for change in American society. Sentimentalism, with its tendency to obfuscate the visible dynamics of development, heralded the cultural sprawl that has increasingly characterized post-Victorian life." (p. 13)
45. Mary Harris Jones, *The Autobiography of Mother Jones*, edited by Mary Field Parton (Chicago: Charles H. Kerr & Co., 1925), p. 238.
46. Charlotte Perkins Gilman detailed her ideas in two books: *Women and Economics: A Study of the Economic Relations Between Men and Women as a Factor in Social Evolution* (Boston: Small, Maynard & Company, 1898) and *The Living of Charlotte Perkins Gilman* (New York: D. Appleton-Century Company, Inc., 1935). She was born in 1860 to a family whose ancestors helped settle Massachusetts in the 1630s and whose nineteenth-century offspring included such famous reformers as Catharine Beecher, Harriet Beecher Stowe and Henry Ward Beecher. Although she was married to Charles Stetson for a few years, she used her maiden name, Perkins, and the name of her second husband, Gilman, on her published work.
47. Gilman, *The Living*, p. 167.
48. Ibid., p. 122.

49. Ibid., p. 131.
50. Gilman, *Women and Economics*, pp. 210–211.
51. Gilman, *The Living*, p. 283.
52. Ibid., p. 131.
53. For an excellent discussion of Frances Willard's involvement in many causes, see Mary Earhart Dillon. *Frances Willard, from Prayers to Politics* (Chicago: University of Chicago Press, 1944). Dillon attributes Willard's association in most people's minds with temperance to her secretary, Anna Gordon. After Willard's death, Gordon destroyed papers showing Willard's interest in unionism and socialism.
54. Willard, *My Happy Half Century*, p. 306.
55. Ibid., p. 204.
56. Ibid., p. 195.
57. For Willard's description of her resignation from Northwestern, see her book, *My Happy Half Century*, p. 247. Annie Wittenmyer describes the eruption of the temperance crusade in *History of Woman's Temperance Crusade*, p. 26.
58. Joseph R. Gusfield, *Symbolic Crusade* (Urbana: University of Illinois Press, 1963), p. 76.
59. Frances Willard, *Glimpses of Fifty Years* (Chicago: Woman's Temp., 1889), pp. 411–22.
60. Dillon, *Frances Willard*, p. 152.
61. Willard, *My Happy Half Century*, pp. 293–4.
62. Frances Willard, "Address to the First Triennial Meeting of the Woman's National Council of the United States," Washington, D.C., February 22, 1891, p. 37.
63. Mary A. Livermore, *The Story of My Life* (Hartford: A. D. Worthington & Co., 1897), pp. 38–39.
64. Ibid., p. 469–471.
65. Ibid., pp. 483–4.
66. Ibid., p. 491–494.
67. Ibid., p. 619–620.
68. Pond, *Eccentricities of Genius*, p. 155.
69. Livermore, *The Story*, p. 614.
70. Ibid., p. 701.
71. Ibid., p. 704.
72. Mary Livermore, "Should Women Have a Vote on the Liquor Traffic?" Speech delivered in Melrose, Massachusetts. Copy, with no date, is at New York Public Library.
73. William Rhinelander Steward, *The Philanthropic Work of Josephine Shaw Lowell* (New York: Macmillan Co., 1911), pp. 1, 6.
74. Ibid., pp. 45–8.
75. Ibid., p. 52.
76. C. S. Hoyt, "Extracts from a Report on Pauperism with Suggestions by Mrs. C. R. Lowell," Presented to the State Board of Charities, January 3, 1878, p. 1. Copy in New York Public Library.

77. Josephine Shaw Lowell, "Considerations upon a Better System of Public Charities and Corrections for Cities," no date, pp. 1–2. Copy of paper in New York Public Library.

78. Cited in Stewart, *The Philanthropic Work*, p. 101.

79. Ida B. Wells, *Crusade for Justice: The Autobiography of Ida B. Wells* edited by Alfreda M. Duster (Chicago: University of Chicago Press, 1970), xv. Mrs. Duster, who was Ida B. Wells's daughter, uses her mother's maiden name throughout but other historians, including Eleanor Flexner, refer to her as Mrs. Wells-Barnett. Ida Bell Wells married Ferdinand Lee Barnett in 1895 after she had achieved a national reputation as speaker and writer. See Eleanor Flexner's short biography of Mrs. Wells-Barnett in *Notable American Women*, edited by Edward T. James et al. (Cambridge: Harvard University Press, 1971), 3:565–6.

80. Wells, *Crusade for Justice*, xvi.

81. Ibid., xvii.

82. Ibid., p. 35.

83. Ibid., p. 37.

84. Ibid., p. 81.

85. Ibid., p. 195.

86. Ibid., p. 193.

IV

THE REVOLT
IN RELIGION

10

Christian Socialism and the Social Gospel*

PAUL H. BOASE

In 1895 George D. Herron, the dynamic apostle of Christian Socialism, his "Tongue touched with fire,"[1] warned Bostonians that "Revolution of some sort is not far off," and "Blood such as never flowed will remit the sins of the existing order."[2] The Congregational "Jeremiah" from Grinnell, Iowa, pleaded with his upper middle-class listeners to forsake the "greedy maxims of Benjamin Franklin," and to suppress "the gross and hideous lust of money." He implored them instead to join in a passionate crusade to rescue the nation from the holocaust he envisioned.

The social-reform movement Herron helped to propagate gradually gathered momentum during Reconstruction and in the 1890s caught the imagination and stirred the conscience of a small band of religious reformers.[3] Then, interlaced with "Progressivism" the protest achieved maturity as the Social Gospel, a popular theological stance of many Protestant denominations in the first half of the twentieth century.[4]

Many of Herron's followers and ministerial colleagues, who had lived through the Civil War had watched their nation's dramatic industrial machine in operation—a feat fully as amazing to them as space probes and moon landings to us. But just as many concerned dissidents and agitators of the 1970s found poverty and pollution in the midst of plenty, so, too, the nineteenth-century religious protesters and reformers saw their land bursting with economic potential but plagued with industrial strife and still unable or unwilling to yield the good life to the farmer or to the laboring masses. They saw their cities, filled with mansions and "heaven-piercing, turreted temples . . . within cannon shot" of "frightful

235

wretchedness." With rising indignation they watched the wealthy and politically powerful (many of them devout attendants at divine worship) "grind the faces of the poor," engage brother merchants in deadly combat, and ravish the nation's natural resources.[5]

To examine the rhetorical strategies of these spokesmen for Christian Socialism and the Social Gospel constitutes the primary focus of this essay.

ORIGINS OF SOCIAL CHRISTIANITY

Protesters and reformers who embraced Christian Socialism and the Social Gospel proclaimed an ancient message. The roots stretch back to Mosaic law and to the preaching of the Hebrew prophets, to Amos and Isaiah and, of course, to Jesus and the concept of the kingdom of heaven on earth. Some churchmen in nearly every century and in most denominations and sects have attempted with varying degrees of success to apply the ethical teachings of the Judeo-Christian tradition to social as well as individual sins.

Students of the Bible are familiar with the unsuccessful attempt of the apostolic church to establish a voluntary form of communism. And in America in the first half of the nineteenth century both religious and nonreligious enthusiasts dotted the frontier landscape with utopian socialistic communities. The best-known of each type was exemplified at Brook Farm and New Harmony. Analyzing these frontier communal experiments, John H. Noyes, founder of the so-called "free love" community at Oneida, New York, and an early historian of American socialism, made an important discovery for students of the social-gospel movement. He sensed an intimate relationship between religious revivalism in the antebellum period and the mushrooming communal experiments. "The Revivalists failed for want of regeneration of society," he observed, "and Socialists failed for want of regeneration of the heart."[6] Religious reformers have always faced this perplexing dilemma in their struggle with evil. Should they concentrate on the system or on the individual within the system? They have found no easy answer. Perhaps none exists.

Whether reformers were bent on changing society or individuals, they have uniformly depended on what Saint Paul called the "foolishness of preaching." Social gospelers were no exception. They were men and women with remarkable laryngeal stamina. Although they used every available means of persuasion, including their own newspapers and journals as well as church and secular publications, they relied most heavily on the spoken word. As happens with the rhetoric of most movements, some of the eloquence was never recorded, but fortunately many of the leaders preserved their speeches. For example, Washington Gladden, remembered as the father of the Social Gospel, admitted that all but six of his thirty-one published volumes were "printed as they were preached, with almost no revision."[7] Joseph Cook, representing the conservative wing of the Social Gospel, achieved widespread fame for his immensely popular "Boston Monday lectures," which appeared regularly in British and American newspapers and were later published in eleven volumes.[8] The speech-to-print pattern also held true for Richard T. Ely, professor of economics at the University of Wisconsin, probably the most influential of many laymen associated with the Social Gospel, whose widely publicized *Social Aspects of Christianity* was first presented as a lay sermon.[9] The radical George D. Herron's several volumes published during the 1890s were nearly all sermons or lectures.[10] Few of the outstanding Social Gospel leaders failed to leave a permanent record of their public addresses.

Indeed, a frequent criticism of the social-gospel prophet was that he talked too much, frequently making speech an end in itself and thereby falling short of the Greek classic model: "a speaker of words and a doer of deeds." Although such agitators as Walter Rauschenbusch managed to establish political and activist ties, most were essentially propagandists, preachers, exhorters, educators, and proclaimers. Early in his career, Rauschenbusch, whose name is habitually related to the Social Gospel, recognized that speech had to be combined with political activism; therefore, he vigorously supported Henry George for mayor of New York City in 1886.[11] He was not alone in this crusade, joining other exponents of social concern, including R. Heber Newton, Rabbi Gustave Gottheil, and Father Edward McGlynn, Catholic priest of St. Stephen's Church, who was censured by his superiors for his political activity. In 1897, by the time George ran for mayor a second time, the writers, speakers, and active propagandists for the Social Gospel had increased many fold. Religious newspapers, journals, and books poured upon the scene in unprecedented numbers.

In spite of this enthusiasm, Ely wrote to Gladden at the turn of the century that "we who write on economics and social questions reach a comparatively small audience."[12] And Walter Rauschenbusch remembered the "Gay Nineties" as lonesome days, when "we were few, and we shouted in the wilderness. . . . Our older friends remonstrated with us for wrecking our career. We ourselves saw the lions' den plainly before us, and only wondered how the beasts would act this time." To a challenge by Terence V. Powderly, head of the Knights of Labor, to produce ten preachers who took any interest in labor problems, William Dwight Porter

Bliss, then editor of the Christian Socialists' newspaper, *The Dawn*, could find only sixty-two bona fide representatives.[13]

POST-CIVIL WAR SOCIAL COMPLACENCY

The prophets and reformers were confronted with a complacency whose roots were nourished in Protestant theology, Social Darwinism, and the cultural mores of middle- and upper-class nineteenth-century Americans. The forces that awakened a few socially sensitive individuals to the need for social Christianity stemmed from the industrial revolution that struck America with devastating force following the Civil War. As an awkward, industrial adolescent, America was suffering from all kinds of growing pains, indiscretions, and contradictions and from the vitality commonly associated with youth. Factory furnaces, tended by immigrants housed in miserable slums, belched smoke, darkening the horizon and symbolizing the industrial empires that dotted the North and East. Ribbons of steel spanned the nation, bringing a mixture of blessing and disaster to the western farmers. By the turn of the century, the lad was no longer the quiet pastoral swain of bygone days but a smart sophisticate who had moved into the city.

America was, on the one hand, rich, powerful, cold, impersonal, corporate, and ruthless and, on the other, depressed, underpaid, overworked, alienated, and bitter. Somewhere between were the clerics and churchmen, who had also come a long way from the Puritan heritage of Cotton Mather and Jonathan Edwards and even from the camp-meeting revivals of Peter Cartwright. Indeed, the Church itself, though hardly an adolescent, was experiencing either growing pains or ague as a result of its confrontations with Darwinism, the new liberal theology of Horace Bushnell, and the devastating attacks of Robert Ingersoll. But its complacent reaction to post-Civil War suffering and industrial greed, impressed few observers as Christ-like.

Not that the church closed its eyes to evil or that it was totally unaccustomed to speaking against social as well as personal sin. Even the revivalists, whose primary aim was to prepare souls for eternity, were not unmindful of the necessity for social salvation. They had spoken eloquently for universal, state-supported education, liquor laws, and political morality; they had reached the heights of oratorical sublimity in their homilies for the abolition of slavery.[14]

Optimism ran high in northern Protestant circles immediately following the war. Protestants had seen "the glory of the coming of the

Lord." Many pious adherents devoutly believed that the church, through God's grace or as His agent, had single-handedly won the day.

In his New Year's Day sermon in 1865, Gilbert Haven, Methodism's best-known abolitionist, sensing that victory was nigh, declared that "no equal reform was every so speedily effected. . . . Hallelujah! the Lord God omnipotent reigneth! His right arm hath gotten Him the victory!" In his Civil War sermons Haven, who became a bishop in 1872, consistently spoke the language of reform, advocating, in addition to the usual temperance theme, the establishment of universal education, social equality, economic security for all, and even women's suffrage and racial intermarriage. "Amalgamation is God's word," Haven assured his listeners. "Who art thou that fightest against God?"[15] Little wonder that Washington Gladden described Haven as "a fresh and piquant per-sonality . . . with whom it was delightful to disagree."[16]

Charles G. Finney, the greatest evangelist of the antebellum period, whose preaching inspired scores of abolition agitators, never lost his buoyant, fervent conviction that those "saved for service" would reform and purify the world. When he revised his *Lectures on Revivals* in 1868, he left unaltered his optimistic prediction that "If the church will do all her duty, the millennium may come in this country in three years."[17]

The eloquent Henry Ward Beecher also turned his powerful oratory toward the rhetoric of reform. Although he adhered to a conservative economic philosophy and never developed a sympathetic rapport with labor, he urged ministers in 1862 "to preach on every side of political life. I do not say he may; I say that he must. That man is not a shepherd of his flock who fails to teach that flock how to apply moral truth to every phase of ordinary practical duty."[18]

But as the guns cooled after the mighty four-year struggle, so too did a preacher's enthusiasm for mixing politics with religion. Even as Appomattox silenced the drums of rebellion and the cry of the slave, it also muted and distorted the ecclesiastical voice for social reform. In his opening remarks in a sermon preached on November 3, 1878, Washington Gladden recalled a friend's comment made at the close of the Civil War "that with the destruction of slavery moral issues were likely to disappear from our politics; that the political parties would divide upon the simple question of finance and economy; and that religion and politics were no longer likely to be brought into such close relations." Gladden himself looked for "no such dissolution of the partnership between religion and politics . . . until the millennium."[19]

The vast majority sided with Gladden's friend. To them the chief business of the Church was to save individuals from sin and prepare them for eternal life. Somehow politics, economics, and industrial strife seemed far removed from the pulpit or the gospel.

Of course, a few temperance reformers talked about exorcising demon rum through governmental adjuration, perhaps even through granting the franchise to females. "The wives of drunkards," Gilbert Haven declared, "will not vote as they do."[20] And Joseph Cook, following the same argument, drew applause from his Monday noon audience when he said, "Women's vote would be, to city vices depending on intemperance, what lightning is to the oak. God send us that lightning!"[21] Indeed, one of the few movements that gave hope to a nascent social gospel was the continuing struggle of the average cleric to dethrone King Alcohol. The earliest crusades of the Woman's Christian Temperance Union (WCTU) and the Prohibition Party were intimately tied to the objectives of the labor unions, the Populists, and the Christian Socialists. The scandals attending Grant's administration received appropriate condemnation from the pulpit and the religious press, but most of these sins, like intemperance, seemed to blend with themes the revivalists had always used to encourage individual sinners to head for the mourner's bench and the altar. Gambling, card playing, polygamy, free love, vicious literature, and amusements—principally the ball and the theater, those "twin sisters of vice, exciting every lustful passion and giving unbridled liberty to the lowest animal desires"[22]—continued to inspire fire-and-brimstone rhetoric.

Perhaps the greatest shortcoming of the Church and chief cause of its post-Civil War complacency toward social and industrial evils was that it became gloriously contented. It had arrived. It had become popular, prosperous, and proud. Methodist preachers no longer "went with their elbows out, and wore blankets instead of coats, peeling bark with their teeth; and sleeping in the woods. . . ."[23] Their bishop—Mathew Simpson—who delivered Lincoln's funeral address, was a friend and associate of Presidents Grant, Hayes, Arthur, and Garfield.[24] The churches, content to blend comfortably with the prevailing social and economic mores, generally misinterpreted Saint Paul's timeless injunction and became instead "conformed to this world."

In its self-confidence, the church and its leaders may have underestimated the role that Union cannons and bayonets had played in winning the victory for the Lord. It certainly remained impotent to appraise the impact of the new, boisterous, industrial delinquent spawned during the Civil War. Indeed, most churchmen could neither evaluate the war baby nor discipline him during his adolescent years. Rural churchmen and their pastors often remained blithely unaware of any possible connection between the Church and the problems of the city. Many of the typical American churches—the Methodists for example—were themselves only coming into adolescence, and they often joined the industrial giants as they romped together toward the industrial trough. The most successful of the "robber barons" spent their Sundays worshipping in the increasingly plush sanctuaries and contributing to an increasingly affluent Church. Trapped by her own middle-to-upper-class culture, the church did little more than attempt to sanctify the *status quo*.

Both the pastors and their flocks were either children of the farm or very recent urban settlers. They understood the rugged individual who swung the ax or guided the horse-drawn plow. They could live comfortably with the small shopkeeper at the general store, the skilled artisan, and the professional man. But as the "amber waves of grain" receded before blazing factory furnaces, neither the preachers nor their congregations grasped the economic or social implications for Church and society. Sympathetic rapport with the sweating, faceless laborer who toiled at the machine and a proper evaluation of his employer came slowly and to relatively few churchmen.[25] The man in the blue overalls, who carried a lunch bucket, lived on the other side of the tracks, often spoke with a foreign accent, and more than likely attended a Roman Catholic church, if any. His economic and social misery seemed far removed from the old-time religion, and neither the "poor" nor the "poor in spirit" were "blessed." Indeed, the laborer's wretched condition merely furnished grist from the homilies linking poverty to the worker's own willful sins.

Russell Herman Conwell, undefatigable evangelist of the gospel of wealth, assured his listeners that "there is not a poor person in the United States who was not made poor by his own shortcomings, or the shortcomings of someone else." And, since Conwell detected sin in a mere 2 percent of the wealthy, the basic cause of poverty must lie at the door-step of the poor. Misery and poverty could in no way be linked to the economic system. It stemmed directly from weaknesses in the character of man—flaws he could correct through adherence to the Calvinistic virtues of thrift, hard work, and diligent stewardship. Goodness inevitably produced success even as destruction followed wickedness.[26] The rascals who succeeded during Grant's administration presumably furnished the exceptions to prove Conwell's rule. Even the liberal Washington Gladden in a "Plain Talk with Workingmen," blamed much of the laboring man's distress on his "own doing or misdoing, or not doing. Laziness, incompetency, vice, unthrift, are the sources. . . ." But, unlike most of his ministerial colleagues, at this early date he was also able to deliver an equally stern rebuke to employers who would not recognize the rights of labor.[27]

SOCIAL DARWINISM

Throughout the postwar era the sons of the Puritans in the East and of the camp meetings in the West had found a new deity, whom William James dubbed "the bitch goddess Success" and who reigned majestically at the "great barbecue." But they needed to show the world a less malignant figure and to convince themselves of the righteousness of their behavior. They found this rationalization, strangely enough, in the theory of evolution as adapted to social and economic life by Herbert Spencer. Indeed, Spencer's Social Darwinism furnished a central issue and the battleground where the social-gospel spokesmen and their conservative opponents struggled for the mind and heart of America. An understanding of the issues of reform is impossible without an appreciation of Social Darwinism as it was preached and taught by William Graham Sumner.

A somber, lantern-jawed, magnificently bald, keen-eyed, gruff-voiced professor who had forsaken the pulpit in 1872 to accept a newly created chair of political and social science at Yale, Sumner was highly popular with students and was an effective platform speaker. The same year that Sumner came to Yale, he also discovered Herbert Spencer's *The Study of Sociology*, which led him to delve more deeply into the complete doctrine of evolution. From his research he concluded that nature was not only unreasoning and brutal but niggardly as well. Man, therefore, enjoyed no alternative other than to struggle valiantly to exist. Sumner was positive that not enough of this world's goods existed for everyone—that many lacked the moral fiber, the perseverance, and the competitive drive to survive. As in the animal world, only the keenest competitors would endure. The laws governing the social structure were as fixed and inexorable as those in the biological sciences. But if this natural competition were allowed to operate freely, without any outside interference, the best of the race would persevere and progress would inevitably occur. Any outside tampering with natural competition, however, would lead to disaster.

Free enterprise to Sumner was exactly that. He had no more sympathy for the tycoon who sought governmental grants or preferential tariffs than he had for the reformer who wished to substitute cooperation or socialism for competitive capitalism. Combinations and trusts, even labor unions, were acceptable; and a strike, if successfully negotiated without violence, fitted his concept of freedom. During the last third of the nineteenth century he carried on unrelenting warfare with the forces of reform, protectionism, socialism (Christian and secular), and governmental intervention in economics.

Sumner also discovered in his study of evolution that if the best were to survive, it followed that those who perished were less than good. The natural rights of man, a premise long precious to the reformers, was to Sumner patently false. Man may have been born free, *but never equal*; and in his struggle against nature, he enjoyed no natural rights. If society were to be improved and poverty eliminated the credit for such an achievement rested with Sumner's "forgotten man": the frugal, hard-working, independent citizen who paid his taxes, raised a respectable family, asked for no handouts, and established the moral tone of the community. To ask this God fearing, honest man to worry about the plight of the ne'er-do-well or, worse yet, to support him through taxation, was to place him in a forgotten position.[28] Sumner's essay "The Absurd Effort to Make the World Over" was his gruff answer to the "Essay on Ethics" by Richart T. Ely, one of the founders of the American Economic Association, who had gone on record in favor of economic reform through the ministrations of church, state, and science.[29]

Typical of Sumner's rhetoric was his assertion that "It would be hard to find a single instance of a direct assault by positive effort upon poverty, vice and misery which has not either failed or . . . entailed other evils greater than the one which it removed." Even the drunk in the gutter, Sumner insisted, "is just where he ought to be. Nature is working away at him to get him out of the way, just as she sets up her processes of dissolution to remove whatever is a failure in its line. Gambling and less mentionable vices all cure themselves by the ruin and dissolution of their victims."[30]

Although many good churchmen would never have abandoned Sumner's drunk to the gutter and would have struggled valiantly to remove the bottle from his lips, the pulpit giants of the "gilded age" became staunch defenders of Social Darwinism. At first glance evolution seemed to shatter the very foundations of the Church and to destroy the authority of the Bible, the concept of sin, and a belief in God. Even today some groups retain this view. During the 1860s and 1870s the clerics raged against these "atheistic" pronouncements. But as passions cooled and the resilient powers of rationalization took over, many of the intellectuals, such as John Fiske, could see the hand of God in the processes of evolution. And, interestingly enough, the doctrine ably served the disciples of Christian Socialism and the Social Gospel as well as the apologists of Social Darwinism and *laissez faire*.

But probably the most eloquent and important spokesman for the economically conservative and reactionary Christian in the nineteenth century was Henry Ward Beecher. Paradoxically, Beecher not only gave aid and comfort to the privileged classes but also popularized the new theology of Horace Bushnell and Theodore Munger, which later became the theology of Washington Gladden, Lyman Abbott, and many of the social-gospel advocates. Beecher successfully rejected the harsh Calvinistic theology of his youth and reached the pinnacle of sublimity in his sermons on love—love of God and love of man—but he also identified strongly with the burgeoning bourgeois society and spoke the language of the aristocracy.

Preaching the gospel of wealth even before Andrew Carnegie and Russell Conwell popularized it, Beecher comforted rich and poor alike during the catastrophic railroad strike of 1877 by declaring: "God has intended the great to be great and the little to be little." While enjoying an income close to $40,000 a year he belittled the assertion of the unions that a man could not support a wife and five or six children on a dollar a day. "No," said he, "not if the man smokes or drinks beer. . . . But is not a dollar a day enough to buy bread with? Water costs nothing; and a man who cannot live on bread is not fit to live."[31]

Beecher's economic rhetoric was, by and large, the rhetoric of the Church, echoed in the less-eloquent voices of ministers who accepted the Spencerian doctrine of fang and claw. Inconsistently they condemned the less-sophisticated violence of the unions. Strikes were considered senseless and subversive, leading toward the more deadly sins of socialism, anarchy, and communism. Nevertheless, labor discontent and violence mounted during the closing years of the century and climaxed finally in the Haymarket bombing of 1886, the depression of 1893, the Carnegie and Pullman strikes of 1892 and 1894, and a host of violent, bloody labor wars that shook the nation.

Most churchmen reacted to labor's plight and to its use of strikes in a fashion designed to warm the hearts of big business. As unemployed men roamed the streets in the 1870s, the railroad companies slashed wages by 10 percent, precipitating the bloody strike of 1877. In scenes not unlike the city riots of the 1960s, troops battled angry mobs of workmen amid blazing freight cars while the followers of the Prince of Peace joined the rich in a declaration of war on the poor. Two leading church papers—the *Congregationalist* and Beecher's *Independent*—recommended that the "club of the policeman" knock "out the brains" of the lazy, lawless labor gang. If the club did not quell the riot "then bullets and bayonets, canister and grape—with no sham or pretense. . . . Napoleon was right when he said that the way to deal with a mob was to exterminate it."[32]

RISE OF THE SOCIAL GOSPEL

While the average churchman and his pastor remained blissfully ignorant of the plight of the laborer, an increasingly influential, rhetorically powerful group of Christian prophets raised their voices against this unholy competition. Unhappily the pulpit giants of the era—Henry Ward Beecher and Phillips Brooks—spoke the language of the aristocracy; and Dwight L. Moody was so busy selling salvation to millions of individual sinners that he had little time left for social concerns. He did lend his support to a number of worthy causes, and his evangelical appeal to the love of God rather than to the terrors of the law was compatible with the social-gospel message.

The prophets of the Social Gospel began to sense the contradictions between their conception of Christ's law of love, the brotherhood of man, and the kingdom of heaven and the industrial world of hatred, suffering, and violence they observed on every hand. In his *Recollections* Washington Gladden recalled his earliest series of lectures on social issues delivered in 1875, *Working People and Their Employers*. Although they seemed radical at the time, Gladden later recognized their weaknesses. Still they helped to bring him and his associates in the Social Gospel to face, frankly and honestly, three questions: (1) Is the current theology of personal salvation failing to solve the contemporary problems? (2) Are social and industrial subjects legitimate for a religious audience? (3) Is the minister of the gospel competent to speak on social, economic, and political questions?[33] With mounting vehemence Gladden and other Social Gospel preachers defended the affirmative on all three issues.

C. M. Morse probably shocked many readers of *The Methodist Review* in 1891 by declaring "that if every individual in the United States should be 'regenerated' in an hour this wholesale conversion of the community— under present methods—would not result in a single reform in the industrial and social world." In his evaluation of the industrial community he found about the same number of "wicked men" and "regenerated men" engaged with equal ferocity in the unholy race for riches. Employing a somewhat earthy metaphor, Morse noted that "all classes of men now sit under the droppings of the sanctuary," but "the teachings from the pulpit have no appreciable influence upon the social movements of the day."[34] Washington Gladden tended to agree. Early in his pulpit career he rejected the premise that a "saved" man would automatically turn his attention to social injustice or that a group of "saved" men would seek to establish Christian relationships in industry. The "regenerated" capitalist, he feared, would more likely embrace the law of supply and demand than Christ's law of love.[35]

Meanwhile the exponents of social Christianity continued to seek the salvation of individual sinners; and even the radical Christian Socialists in the first issue of *The Dawn* admitted that the beginning must be "with the inner and working toward the outer."[36] Yet they doubted the quality of a conversion that enabled a capitalistic "pillar" to buy his way to heaven with tainted money. John Wesley's celebrated formula "Gain all you can, save all you can, give all you can" no longer provided a satisfactory rationalization for church-patronizing but ruthless tycoons—men like Daniel Drew, whose industrial sins were as scarlet but who could weep for joy in a Methodist class meeting for his personal salvation and then contribute his ill-gotten wealth to a theological school. It smacked of gross hypocrisy in the clergy as well as the laity. "Are we really saving souls," Gladden asked, "when we permit men like the packinghouse proprietors and insurance wreckers to sit comfortably in our pews and enjoy our ministrations? I fear that some of these men may have grave accusations to bring against us . . . for (our) having failed to tell them the truth about their own conduct." Since the so-called saved were not establishing right relationships in the industrial world, it followed that the minister must speak directly to the issue.

The third question, dealing with clerical competence in the realm of economic and political problems, continues to plague clerical spokesmen today. To Gladden the plea of incompetence was "a fearful self-accusation" but one that no minister could legitimately claim. "Here is the field on which the battle of Gog and Magog is being fought out today."[37] It is not surprising, therefore, that throughout his ministry he labored in conferences and seminars, responding to requests for help from ministers who were indeed incompetent to preach on social questions. A minister from Massillon, Ohio, wrote a frantic note to Gladden for assistance because he and his colleagues were "not sufficiently conversant" with the Social Gospel to accept the invitation of the labor unions to speak about problems facing the workingman. Eugene Debs had recently addressed Massillon workers with "a masterly presentation of his cause," and local preachers hoped to set up a course of lectures that would correct their own deficiencies.[38]

In every stage of competence and from nearly all denominations prophets of the Social Gospel set forth on their crusade with less concern for the sweet bye and bye and more for the sour here-and-now. Their God was immanent—not off in the clouds, but in the world, working out His purposes through men. Sin was no longer limited to persons but infected society and, therefore, had to be attacked directly on the social and industrial level and swept from the economic and political systems. *Laissez faire* economics, which permitted pagan competition, must yield to Christian brotherhood and give way to social and industrial planning and cooperation. Like the prophets of old the social gospelers operated at a crisis level; but, unlike their predecessors, they were buoyantly optimistic, convinced that, with destiny, heaven, and the "stars" on their side, the long awaited kingdom of God was at hand.[39]

THE CONSERVATIVE APPEAL

Spokesmen for the Social Gospel ranged along a continuum from right-wing to radical. They were firmly united in seeking a Christian "solution" for social and economic problems. In method, plan, and specific program, however, they differed widely; but, as brothers in Christ and as members of both orthodox and liberal denominations, and in view of their common objective, they often met for discussions and planning sessions. Reactionaries found the doctrines of William Graham Sumner comforting, but most conservatives, like A. J. F. Behrends, Minot J. Savage, and Joseph Cook, advanced well beyond *laissez faire* to advocate specific social and economic reforms.

A born reformer, Cook championed the cause of labor early in his career in a series of debates at Lynn, Massachusetts. Four years later, in 1875, as the popular orator for the Boston Monday Lectures, he addressed overflow crowds at Tremont Temple and, later, at Old South Meeting House. A large, burly figure with reddish hair and beard, he thrilled audiences with his dramatic, epigram-filled analyses, oracular utterances, and amazing "facts."[40] Praised fulsomely by many of the intellectuals of his day, he was severely castigated by others such as John Fiske for his "bellicose . . . floods of tawdry rhetoric," his inaccuracies, sensationalism, and demagogic techniques.[41]

Cook unashamedly praised himself as an independent, unfettered by any church ties, who would bend his "knees neither to capital nor to labor, but only to justice." Actually he personified the conservative position, supporting reforms, in part at least, to stave off violent revolution. His oratory treated such diverse social-gospel topics as "Secret Socialistic Societies," "Sex in Industry," "Wages and Children's Rights," and "Infidel Attack on Property." Deeply suspicious of secret societies and afraid of Socialists, he searched for a Christian solution to economic problems to save the nation from "windy socialistic philosophies."

But were socialism or communism to go beyond mere elocution, Cook, amid applause, assured his audience that America had yet to see "a day so red with blood as will be that day when socialism attempts spoliation here by force of arms. . . . Caesar was Rome's escape from Communism; and the day that a socialist revolution shall succeed in the United States, you will find on our map a Rubicon, and a man on horseback ready to cross it."

Yet Cook was well ahead of the average cleric of the day. He rejected the classic wage-fund theory used by generations of ministers to demonstrate the impossibility of raising wages. Although opposed to strikes, he urged arbitration of labor disputes, supported Rochdale cooperatives, urged liquor controls, and demanded legislation to protect women and children. Typical of his style and prophetic of subsequent Social Gospel rhetoric was his repeated assertion that only "the Golden Rule . . . can lead New England out of painful social and political crisis on the questions of capital and labor . . . [and] can bring the golden age."[42]

RADICAL SPOKESMEN

To Cook's extreme left were the Christian Socialists, best represented rhetorically by George D. Herron, the popular professor of sociology at Grinnell College, and William Dwight Porter Bliss, founder of the Society of Christian Socialists in 1889. During the 1890s both attempted, with moderate success, to promote a number of socialistic organizations and propagandistic organs. The radicals of the gay nineties cut across most denominational lines, including in their ranks such diverse figures as Hamlin Garland, Mary A. Livermore, Edward Bellamy, Father J. O. S. Huntington, and Frances E. Willard. As early as 1874, Willard and her ladies of the WCTU endorsed labor's demands for a living wage and the eight-hour day; and in 1889 she became an associate editor of *The Dawn*, the principal propaganda weapon of the Christian Socialists.[43]

Karl Marx wielded little influence with these radicals, who got their inspiration from England's Christian Socialists, from the economic doctrines of single-taxer Henry George, and from reading Edward Bellamy's novel *Looking Backward*. That best-selling utopian novel inspired a spate of Nationalist clubs, which in turn helped to promote Christian Socialism. Although they disagreed on some points, Bellamy's Nationalists and Bliss's Socialists were in basic agreement.[44] Christian Socialist preaching was often vague and sentimental, ignoring, by and large, the basic doctrines of scientific socialism, class struggle, and economic determinism.[45] Still, a sharp distinction set the radicals apart from the conservatives, represented by Cook, and moderate leaders of the Social Gospel, such as Gladden. The radicals demanded more than a reform of the economic and political system; capitalism contained inherent evils necessitating a complete revolution. Although the overhauling was to take place with Fabian deliberation, devoid of violence, it would nonetheless be a thorough change. Bliss served as the missionary of this revolution and Herron as the evangelist.

Few leaders of Christian social concern equaled Bliss in devotion and actual participation in the cause he pursued relentlessly until his death in 1926. A missionary's son born in Turkey, Bliss received a standard theological education and served in the Congregational Church before switching to the Protestant Episcopal Church in 1886. Early in his career he witnessed the terrible human suffering in the manufacturing cities of

Massachusetts. With Bishops Henry Potter and Frederic D. Huntington he helped organize the American branch of the Church Association for the Advancement of the Interests of Labor (CAIL), the first and most effective Social Gospel organization. In spite of abuse heaped on him from left- and right-wing extremists and meager support from the masses within and outside the Church, his failures only drove him to new publishing ventures and speaking missions that carried him to nearly every state in the union and to Canada and England as well. As the Saint Paul of the Christian Socialistic crusade, Bliss is best remembered for his indomitable zeal, the purity of his motives, and his passion for justice. "Unaggressive, but persistent, he preached his gospel of social salvation to all who would listen or read, and did it with a sheer disregard of personal consequences."[46]

During the last ten years of the nineteenth century Herron, unquestionably the most colorful figure in the Social Gospel movement, blazed his way across the nation as the evangelist of the radical left. His admirers referred to him variously as a "nineteenth-century Ezekiel," and "John the Baptist . . . to applied Christianity."[47] Self-educated for the most part, he entered the Congregational ministry in 1884 and six years later lifted himself from obscurity to national fame through a sermon he delivered to his brethren in Minneapolis. The note he sounded in 1890 as he delivered "The Message of Jesus to Men of Wealth" was the one he rang consistently for the next decade. A somber yet hopeful melody, uncomplicated by theological dogmas, it was a sharp condemnation of the social and religious *status quo* and its glorification of competition and self-interest.

In his stirring peroration at Minneapolis he personalized the appeal by asking: "Is the Gospel of Jesus livable?" Obviously it was. Then, fortifying his remedy with divine authority, he issued a new kind of altar call. Using the language and imagery of the camp-meeting evangelist, he urged his listeners to substitute Christ's law of love for capitalistic competition and to sacrifice themselves utterly to bring in the kingdom of heaven on earth. Instead of appealing to individual sinners to forsake the sins of the flesh and "flee from the wrath to come" he called "for able men who are willing to be financially crucified in order to establish the world's market place on the Golden Rule basis." Lest they stand unrepentant in this "new day of judgment" that "is surely and swiftly dawning," he begged his audience to grasp life's richest reward by joining God's annointed in making "the market place as sacred as the church." Cognizant of the imminent, sometimes attractive martyrdom that ever confronts the reformer, and perhaps sensing his own ultimate tragic end, he summoned the "new John Baptist . . . who will speak truth and justice to the Herods of finance, though their ecclesiastical heads be the price of the message." William

Graham Sumner's doctrines he compared to "the seductive whisper of the serpent in Eve's ear,"[48] and Russell Conwell's gospel of wealth he denounced as darkest heresy. Whereas Conwell, in "Acres of Diamonds," exhorted his audiences to accumulate riches, Herron urged them to spend themselves in God's service.

His words, widely circulated, soon inspired an enthusiastic following, including a wealthy widow, Mrs. E. D. Rand, who was willing to spend some of her fortune to endow a "chair of Applied Christianity" for him at Iowa (later Grinnell) College. The president—George Gates, himself an eager disciple of the new prophet—soon helped turn his institution into the nucleus of the Social Gospel for a few years. Mrs. Rand also endowed a lectureship that brought to the campus the leading figures in social Christianity. In the meantime Herron's powerful oratory attracted students and outsiders to his classes in such numbers that he soon moved them to the college chapel. He was in constant demand as a lecturer at universities and in churches and often spoke two or three times a day. In addition to being speakers, Herron and Gates were also the leading figures in the establishment of *The Kingdom*, an important Social Gospel paper of the period.[49]

In 1892, before his arrival at Grinnell, Herron had organized an institute of Christian sociology through the Young Men's Christian Social Union of his church at Burlington, Iowa. Later he joined with prominent Social Gospel leaders, including Richard T. Ely, John R. Commons, and Bishop John H. Vincent, to develop institutes at Chautauqua, New York, Oberlin College, and other centers where social concern was of paramount interest. As the Principal of Instruction and Organization for the American Institute of Christian Sociology, Herron wrote the introduction for a brochure that described procedures and methods for setting up an institute. "There must be entire freedom and candor of speech" in the sessions, Herron advised, and "above all . . . frank questioning, intellectual honesty, moral candor."[50] Closely allied to the institute idea were "retreats of the kingdom" and "Schools of the Kingdom," which were held at Grinnell during the early 1890s.[51]

These fervent evangelical ministrations under the direction of a man who believed that "God has sent me with this message of a new redemption" naturally created sensational effects, both positive and negative.[52] Herron received credit for inspiring a best-selling novel and for stimulating a fascinating experiment in communal living—the Christian Commonwealth Colony in Georgia. In 1898 Charles M. Sheldon wrote *In His Steps*, the most popular of several Social Gospel novels that appeared near the turn of the century. Sheldon's book not only sold 15 million copies and became the most widely read volume during the early years of the twentieth century but ranked with *Uncle Tom's Cabin* and *Ten Nights in a Bar Room* as a classic social tract.[53] The plot was Sheldon's, but the message was Herron's. So, too, when Ralph Albertson and his colleagues set out for Georgia "to obey the teachings of Jesus Christ in all matters of life and labor in the use of property," they were attempting to put Herron's teaching into practice. During the four years of its existence, from 1896 to 1900, the Commonwealth Colony published its own lively journal: the *Social Gospel,* and won the admiration and support of the leading figures in social Christianity. The colony failed for several reasons, the chief being an epidemic of typhoid fever; but interestingly enough a modern community named Koinonia Farm, very similar in organization and purpose, was established in 1942 only a few miles from the site of the original colony.

By the time the Commonwealth Colony closed its doors, Herron found many doors, Christian and secular, slammed in his face. His radical message naturally inspired vigorous protest from the right. No lesser figure than the governor of Nebraska rebuked Herron for his commencement address in 1894 at the University of Nebraska.[54] Invited to commission the graduating cadets, the governor stepped to the lectern and used his time instead to castigate Herron as an anarchist. Like most name-calling, the epithet hurled at Herron contained little or no truth, yet it aroused morbid anxiety in an audience still fearfully aware of the Haymarket bombing eight years earlier. A year after the Nebraska episode Herron launched a speaking crusade in California, sharply polarizing his disciples and his detractors.

A clash occurred at the first of fifteen appearances Herron made in California. Speaking before the Congregational Club of San Francisco, he was confronted during the discussion period by the Rev. Dr. C. O. Brown, pastor of the First Congregational Church, who bitterly denounced the crusader "as an anarchist, whose teachings meant destruction to all established institutions." The chairman finally forced Brown from the floor for his "rambling irrelevancies" but not before he promised to direct his Sunday sermon "against this man." Brown kept his word. As Herron's defenders observed scornfully, the attacks were "systematic," based on "calumny, misrepresentation, injustice, unfairness. . . ."[55]

Brown's published denunciation supported by testimonials from thirty-eight backers soon received wide circulation in the press. David Starr Jordan, President of Stanford University, wrote to express his gratitude for Brown's analyses of Herron's doctrines. "I thought at first you were a little too severe in your objection to him," Jordan noted, "but I have been forced to the conclusion that he is not a fanatic, but a rank humbug." The conservative Joseph Cook understandably ridiculed Herron, assuring

Brown's flock that "the best thought of this country . . . from Plymouth Rock to the Golden Gate, commends the position of your pastor."[56]

Herron's disciples quickly sprang to his defense, attributing to him the qualities of a prophet not unlike Isaiah, Amos, Joel, and even Jesus Himself. Accusing Brown and his cohorts of faulty logic and misquotation, seven leading west-coast preachers published their rebuttals in *The Arena*. To document Brown's "unfairness" Elder M. J. Ferguson, pastor of the First Christian Church in San Francisco, showed that one of Brown's oft-quoted statements he attributed to Herron was actually a fragment torn out of context. Providing the complete quotation with all its qualifiers, Ferguson then asked, "What fair-minded man, capable of understanding plain speech, would single out a part of this sentence as a 'deliberate intention to stir up mob violence,' or as the ground of 'a charge of inciting a riot?' "[57]

The mystic, messianic Herron certainly propagated a vague, sometimes contradictory message that confused even his own supporters. Frankly unconcerned about the unscientific nature of his work, he declared on one occasion that "Great spiritual facts and principles are not apprehended but distorted by the intellect. Not the clear in head, but the pure in heart shall see God."[58] One of his admiring contemporaries branded him an impressionist whose "loving and forgiving nature . . . charms and captivates even the most critical" but who is "so erratic and unreliable as to lose the confidence of accurate thinkers."[59]

Herron probably could have surmounted these criticisms had he not become so violently anti-institutional and had he not attacked with vehemence the church, the state, and finally the institution of marriage. When Mrs. Rand went to Grinnell, her daughter Carrie accompanied her and assumed a position as dean of women and teacher of social and physical culture. As Herron spent more and more time at the Rand residence, he furnished the village gossips with more and more to talk about. Under intense pressure from the conservative board of trustees at Grinnell, Herron finally submitted his resignation in 1899. Two years later his wife divorced him, and two months after that he married Carrie Rand in a ceremony designed to dramatize his opposition to "all coercive institutions."[60] Convinced that Herron had confused the law of love with the love of sex, the Congregational Church expelled him.

THE MODERATE SPOKESMEN

About a year before Herron's divorce, J. Pierpont Morgan's pastor— W. S. Rainsford, one of the early leaders of the Social Gospel movement and rector of the wealthy St. George's Church in New York—invited Herron to speak to his congregation. What Rainsford heard distressed him. Three days later he wrote to Washington Gladden in Columbus, expressing his gratitude that the Ohioan would also be able to address the affluent New York audience. As a dedicated liberal Rainsford expressed no sorrow that Herron had spoken. "The Church," said the Manhattan rector, "was strong enough to let every honest man say his say." But he branded Herron's speech "sad nonsense almost from the beginning to the end. Indeed, I do not think it is exaggeration to call most of it incoherent rant, full of muddling inconsistency, nay, contradiction, and leading no whither."[61]

In his address to the New Yorkers, Gladden may or may not have unraveled Herron's inconsistencies. Gladden's reasonable rhetoric, however, was typical of the moderates in the Social Gospel movement and probably influenced the largest number of citizens to reexamine their economic, social, and religious tenets.

During his lifetime, from 1836 to 1919, the growth of Gladden's religious, political, and economic philosophies closely approximated the evolutionary development of the Social Gospel in American Protestantism. Son of a Methodist farmer-teacher-preacher and raised in an intensely religious atmosphere, he attended church "as regularly as . . . dinner," read the Bible from beginning to end many times, listened to evangelical appeals and polemical disputations, and struggled in vain to achieve the kind of religious experience then deemed necessary for eternal life. Happily, in his eighteenth year "a clear-headed minister lifted me out of this pit, and made me see that it was perfectly safe to trust the Heavenly Father's love . . . waiting for no raptures. . . ."

The farm lad's introduction to politics coincided with his informal training in public speaking and forensics. In the winter of 1852 Gladden was selected to lead the affirmative side in a debate at the country school on the repeal of the Fugitive Slave Law. He secured the speeches of William H. Seward, Benjamin Wade, John P. Hale, Joshua R. Giddings, and others. He said that "every morning for three or four weeks, I was up as early as four o'clock, digging into the Constitution . . . getting all the light I could from every quarter." Gladden defeated the schoolmaster who led the negative side, and received "a strenuous lesson in forensics, the value of which I never forgot."

Young Gladden's religious, social, and political conscience developed as he watched his own small, rural Presbyterian Church struggle with the slavery question, saw the faces of the elders flush with anger when a young minister dared to pray for the slaves, and, with dismay, observed the congregation fire the suspected abolitionist for his "incendiary praying." The socially sensitive members, however, withdrew, formed a Congregational Church "in the front rank of this ethical movement," and invited the radical to return.

Gladden also witnessed the rising concern of his church for social reform and political action. At sixteen he listened to a "rousing speech" by the temperance orator Neal Dow, fell victim to his "fluent and fervid rhetoric," and joined the Good Templars two years later. As secretary of his local temperance lodge, the young enthusiast helped secure the election of a prohibition candidate to the legislature and the passage of the New York Prohibition Law of 1855. "There was keen satisfaction in playing the game," wrote Gladden. "It was good to be in it, and to know that you were helping to bring things to pass."

Nourished in this soil of reform, Gladden's impulse to enter the ministry readily took root. The "individualistic pietism" held no attraction for him, but "a religion that laid hold upon life with both hands, and proposed, first and foremost, to realize the Kingdom of God in this world" became his life's passion. After a year in the Owego (New York) Academy, Gladden turned to Williams College to complete his formal education and then returned to his home in 1859 to take up duties as a teacher in the public school. "Schoolmastering, however, was not my trade," he confessed, and soon the pastor of the Congregational Church—Moses Coit Tyler, whose room at the boarding house was next to Gladden's—directed the young teacher's thoughts once more toward the ministry.

Although at Williams he had studied theology with Mark Hopkins and had received rigorous rhetorical training from John Bascom, Gladden confessed that his license to preach was granted by the Susquehanna Association of Congregational Ministers only because Henry Ward Beecher's brother Thomas "was not a stickler for ecclesiastical proprieties." Gladden branded his early preaching "crude," his theology "raw," and his rhetoric "ragged." Nevertheless, nine months after graduation from Williams he accepted a call to a church in Brooklyn, where for the first time he witnessed Josiah Strong's "Problem of the City."[62] It was, said Gladden, a thing stupendous and overpowering, a mighty monster. . . . The impersonality and brutality . . . the lack of coordinating intelligence" filled him with awe. Even as he wrote in 1910, he wondered whether the nation could control the unleashed economic and political powers. After a half-century of struggle with the Social Gospel, he still confessed his bewilderment and doubt about the city and man's ability to conquer the related social, industrial, and political problems.[63]

Gladden's experiences in Brooklyn threw him into contact with the pulpit giants of the period, including Henry Ward Beecher, Horace Bushnell, and Theodore Munger. Although none of these figures fully understood the relationship of industry and economics to the church, the change in theological climate they inspired did much to destroy the rigid Calvinistic doctrines and opened the way to the humanistic philosophies inherent in the Social Gospel.

Gladden's apprenticeship for the Social Gospel kept him in positions where his contacts with industrial, political, and attendant ethical concerns were paramount. In North Adams, Massachusetts, he witnessed the strife created by the importation of Chinese labor. Returning to New York City in 1871 as religious editor of the *Independent*, he arrived at the height of Boss Tweed's reign and observed with keen perception the scandals of the Grant administration. Moreover, the ethical and business practices of his own paper continuously tormented his sensitive conscience. A year and a half before his resignation he complained bitterly in a letter to the editor about the paper's business ethics and warned that "between the religion which seeks first the Kingdom of God, and the greed which makes everything subserviant to gain, there is a great gulf fixed and they who try to straddle it will go to the bottom of it."[64] In November, 1874, following the consummation of an advertising contract with Jay Cooke, Gladden, no longer able to abide the *Independent's* business ethics, submitted his resignation and explained his action by an analogy that he felt was "not much overstrained." To his friend Lyman Abbott, later a moderate Social Gospel advocate, he wrote in magnificent understatement that "a church which lets out one corner of its basement for a brothel is likely to find that its preaching upstairs is somewhat discredited."[65]

Returning to New England and a church at Springfield, Massachusetts, Gladden found a city still suffering from the economic collapse of 1873 and filled with the angry unemployed. When an impulsive Irish labor leader asked Gladden to address the jobless, he faced the turbulent group with words that he later admitted were naive and less than persuasive. Still, he managed to convince some of the men and the leader to attend church the following Sunday night to hear what he had to say to their employers. Those who attended were at least assured that "the pulpit was not prejudiced against them," and their leader became one of his "loyal parishioners."[66]

In 1882, when Gladden moved permanently to Columbus, he found himself once again embroiled in the industrial conflict. He was in constant demand as a lecturer on social questions and on the "new theology." Throughout his sermons appeared the recurring themes of the Social Gospel—namely, the immanence and transcendence of God, the dignity and divine possibilities of man, the kingdom of heaven on earth, a fervent concern for social justice, and a buoyant optimism that seemed to see the millennium just around the corner. Eulogizing John Bascom, his Williams College professor who later served as president of the University of Wisconsin (1874–1887), Gladden declared that Bascom would have changed Browning's refrain in *Pippa Passes* to "God's in his world and heaven cannot be far away."[67] Even though Gladden was distressed by World War I and died four months before the armistice, he never lost faith in his conviction "that human progress is moving in the direction of the emancipation and enthronement of man. The whole thrust of history goes that way."[68]

SOCIAL GOSPEL MATURITY

Only three weeks after the death of Washington Gladden the Social Gospel lost the greatest of its prophets. Unlike the aged Gladden, Walter Rauschenbusch, not yet fifty-seven years old, died at the height of his career. The recognized leader of social Christianity, he was acclaimed then and now as "its most brilliant and generally satisfying exponent."[69] In his life and work he seemed to combine the virtues of Bliss, Herron, and Gladden without their attendant weaknesses. A powerful rhetorician, he preached the Social Gospel persuasively from the pulpit, the platform, and the teacher's desk. From his pen came *Christianity and the Social Crisis*, an inspiration for Martin Luther King, Jr., and Norman Thomas. As Harry Emerson Fosdick observed, Rauschenbusch became the inspiring word for a whole generation of preachers.[70]

Like the other disciples of the Social Gospel, Rauschenbusch received his motivation largely from secular rather than religious sources. Early in his ministerial career he was thrust into a Baptist church near Hell's Kitchen in New York City. He had already absorbed the social philosophy of Henry George. As he watched misery explode around him during the depression-ridden 1890s, despite a hearing loss that plagued him most of his life, he "could hear human virtue cracking and crumbling all around."[71] Immersing himself in the works of Jacob Riis, Edward Bellamy, Henry D. Lloyd, and other reformers, he also joined a group of like-minded crusaders who organized the Brotherhood of the Kingdom, a fascinating Social Gospel discussion group. They founded one of the early papers, *For the Right*, a monthly devoted to propagating Christian Socialism.

Pursuing the Kingdom ideal through an analysis of historic Christianity, Rauschenbusch concluded that it was central to Jesus's teaching, but through the centuries had been lost amid the machinations of theologians and ecclesiastics. The kingdom of evil, on the other hand, was all too evident in the diabolical greed of the capitalistic overlord who ruthlessly crushed the weak. The struggle for ascendancy, bitter and never ending, found the prophets of social justice always in the front line, seeking to establish, through cooperation, justice for all men. "If we can trust the Bible," he wrote, "God is against capitalism, its methods, spirit and results. The bourgeois theologians have misrepresented our revolutionary God."[72] Socialism furnished the answer, but it was a very special brand of Christian Socialism, which rejected class warfare and the materialistic philosophy of Karl Marx. The Kingdom of God had in some measure already come to America and would continue to come, as demonstrated in the chain of reforms evident in history.

One of Rauschenbusch's addresses: "The New Apostolate," probably delivered at the Amity Missionary Conference in 1896[73] shows clearly the marked contrasts in his rhetoric as compared with the jeremiads of Herron and Cook. "Written," said Rauschenbusch, "with malice toward none" and "without any hate in it,"[74] the rhetoric exhibited a patient optimism and quiet logic that tended to increase rather than dampen the ardor of a potential reformer. Later the address was included in Rauschenbusch's compellingly persuasive volume *Christianity and the Social Crisis*. It was "put together," as one critic expressed it, "with the skills of a platform orator."[75]

Interlaced with a multitude of vivid, apt metaphors, Rauschenbusch pictured Jesus as the first apostolate, "born from a deep fellow-feeling for social misery" sensing the ripe harvest without the reapers. Drawing the analogy to his own times, he pleads with his hearers to champion the cause of social justice, directing his challenge to the "strong" man with "heroic stuff in him" to follow the only course now open to a Christian "to gain the crown of martyrdom." Fully aware of the obstacles, he held forth no promise of "Utopian delusion" but nevertheless implored his listeners "to seek what is unattainable. . . . There will always be death and the empty chair and heart. There will always be the agony of love unreturned. Women will long for children and never press baby lips to their breast. Men will long for fame and miss it." But in his moving peroration he metaphorically portrayed the nineteen Christian centuries as the "long preliminary stage of growth" which always precedes "the flower and fruit." "Generations unborn," he predicted, "will mark this as that great day of the Lord for which the ages waited, and count us blessed for sharing in the apostolate that proclaimed it."[76]

Fortunately for Rauschenbusch and his cohorts, the Social Gospel agitation coincided with the Progressive movement, each drawing inspiration from the other. Descendants of mugwump reformers, now called muckrakers, marched jubilantly with "Fighting Bob" La Follette, the silver-tongued Bryan, the dynamic Teddy Roosevelt, or the scholarly reformer from Princeton, Woodrow Wilson. People listened eagerly to the exposés of Ida M. Tarbell, Lincoln Steffens, and Upton Sinclair. When T.

R. shouted, "we stand at Armageddon and we battle for the Lord," the average layman had only the foggiest of notions where he stood. But Walter Rauschenbusch and the disciples of the Social Gospel knew.[77] In 1908, a year after the appearance of his epoch-making volume, representatives from nearly all the major denominations formed the Federal Council of Churches. It was a Social Gospel-inspired organization whose membership contained the nineteenth-century prophets and the younger men who were to carry on the crusade.

During the twentieth century the passion of the reformers passed through periods of lofty optimism and deepest pessimism brought on by two world wars, a noble but disappointing experiment in national prohibition, another depression, a fundamentalist reaction to Social Gospel liberalism, and a different approach to theology expressed in the neo-orthodoxy of Reinhold Niebuhr, himself one of the early disciples of Christian Socialism and the Social Gospel.[78] But these involutions and transitions, modifying the social thrust of Christendom during the twentieth century, are beyond the scope of this discussion.

RHETORICAL EVALUATION

For a variety of reasons the preachers of protest and reform faced nearly insuperable odds in their struggles to adapt the message of the Social Gospel to their respectable, middle-class congregations. Most of their listeners and many of their own conservative colleagues showed unmistakable symptoms of suffering from the Horatio Alger syndrome. Divinely sanctioned inequities in wealth appeared nearly everywhere throughout the country, but the pious and ambitious were bound to win. Capitalism might contain a flaw or two, but the door to success was open wide to all but the impious and slothful. Moreover, the new evolutionary doctrines of Social Darwinism seemed to provide a comforting rationalization of *laissez-faire*.

Conservative leaders like G. Frederick Wright of Oberlin helped establish the enthymemes and maxims that were inimical to the Social Gospel. Reminding the reformers that even Jesus was resigned to the continuing and inevitable presence of the poor, Wright cautioned them that "the cares and responsibilities and rewards of riches can belong only to the few." Many readers likewise shared his conviction that the "few rich" increased only as the "many poor" developed habits of thrift, temperance, hard work, and piety. And in a nation with abundant resources and land one or two Carnegies provided ample evidence to justify the gospel of wealth as absolute truth. Moreover, any attempt to distribute the wealth more equitably raised the frightful specters of socialism and communism, rarely condemned by the liberal spokesmen for the Social Gospel. Instead of attempting to turn theological students into political economists and social reformers which he considered a "dangerous thing," best left to lawyers, judges and "business men and statemen of large calibre," Wright urged the clergy to expend its energies "in building up the true moral fibre of their young men and women, in rousing their dormant spiritual energies. . . ."[79]

These conservative attitudes, hostile to the social message, rendered audience adaptation, never an easy task, a constant plague to the reformers. Messages that might have moved the absent poor often fell on the deaf ears of the attending rich. Daniel DeLeon, an acid-tongued socialist agitator, smiled wryly as he watched William Dwight Porter Bliss try to sell Christian Socialism and trade unionism to a well-heeled Episcopal audience in Boston. "It seemed like pouring water on a duck's back to ask them to give up their wealth. . . . Asking God and landlords and speculators to change their tactics is more absurd than trying to make the hungry lion lay [*sic*] down in peace besides a lamb!"[80]

Many landlords and speculators, also church laymen, harbored a deep suspicion of a preacher's competence to speak authoritatively in economic and political spheres. Lord Bryce in his perceptive two-volume classic *The American Commonwealth*, wrote understandingly of the religious reformer's dilemma, pointing out that as Church and state separated, the minister whose authority at the beginning of the nineteenth century was akin to the bishops in western Europe had by the last quarter of the century lost his ethical appeal in the realm of politics. Citing Henry Ward Beecher as an exceptional case when he joined the mugwumps in the presidential canvass of 1884, Bryce concluded that "It is only on platforms or in conventions where some moral cause is to be advocated, such as Abolitionism was thirty years ago or temperance is now, that clergymen can with impunity appear."[81]

When clergymen did appear in the pulpit or the public platform, the finding of viable solutions to social and economic problems proved difficult and their addresses often suffered from an overexpanded "problem" step and an underdeveloped "program." They were stimulators rather than activists, and their diagnosis of the problem was more perceptive than their prescriptions, which often sounded sentimental or utopian. The complex economic and political chaos and suffering they portrayed so vividly would vanish if men simply followed the Golden Rule. And, strangely enough, a few idealists like "Golden Rule" Jones, mayor of Toledo and "Golden Rule" Nash of Cincinnati came very near to proving it. Echoing Gladden, the reformers could point to the sky and watch the stars in their courses lead mankind toward a brighter tomorrow, but they were not always able to find an immediate earthly solution. The editor of *The Nation* criticized

Gladden for the vagueness of the program outlined in his *Tools and the Man*, charging him with fuzzy thinking in treating abstract, complex organizations like the state, society, and the government as though they were subject to the same kind of persuasion as the individual. "No careful thinker will permit himself to reason in this way any more than deliberately to attribute sex to a war-vessel."[82]

Many exponents of the Social Gospel suffered myopic vision in other spheres, particularly in the realm of race—a fault more apparent today than in the nineteenth century. Although not totally unaware of the race problem, the nineteenth-century social prophets perhaps thought that they had solved that one on the battlefield. A few spokesmen, such as Josiah Strong, even preached the inherent superiority of the Anglo-Saxon.[83] Yet, the dominant issues of the Social Gospel led reformers and protestors inexorably to the present confrontation with racial injustice and to the eradication of the ghetto. In his "Pilgrimage to Nonviolence" Martin Luther King, Jr., recognized his debt to Walter Rauschenbusch, who "left an indelible imprint on my thinking" and "gave to American Protestantism a sense of social responsibility that it should never lose."[84]

Near the close of the nineteenth century Shailer Mathews, a recognized leader of the Social Gospel, capsulized the central issue of the struggle within organized Christianity for the appropriate approach to reform. Writing in *The American Journal of Sociology* he outlined the duty of the Church, to try to accomplish two interrelated and integral functions. Appealing to both the evangelicals and the reformers, he stressed a timeless truth in the hypothetical assertion: "If there can be no regenerate society without regenerate men, neither can there be regenerate men without a regenerate society."[85] This basic, fundamental issue of Church and individual involvement with social evil—moral, political, and economic— is as potent and explosive as ever. The conflict between capital and labor may have eased, but the poor and oppressed are still with us; and world peace seems farther off than ever. Problems of the inner city continue to plague the nation. Still, reminiscent of an earlier period, amid the chaos and oppression, a minority of conscience-stricken Christians, still being stoned or ignored, pick away incessantly at the mind and heart of a complacent majority.

NOTES

*This paper contains some materials originally published in *The Rhetoric of Christian Socialism*, ed. by Paul H. Boase (New York: Random House, 1969), pp. 3–39 and *America in Controversy: History of American Public Address*, ed. by DeWitte Holland (Dubuque, Iowa: Wm. C. Brown Co., 1973), pp. 185–202.

1. Charles Beardsley, "Professor Herron," *Arena* 15 (April 1896): 784.

2. George D. Herron, "The Opportunity of the Church," *Arena* 15 (December 1895): 42. The edited address is in Paul H. Boase, ed., *The Rhetoric of Christian Socialism* (New York: Random House, 1969), pp. 94–104.

3. Robert T. Handy, "George D. Herron and the Kingdom Movement," *Church History* 19 (1950): 105.

4. In an address early in 1962 Dr. Kyle Haselden, the editor of *The Christian Century*, acknowledged, with mixed emotions, the death of the "Social Gospel." For many years the paper was the universally recognized "voice" of the Social Gospel. Although many sophisticated theologians have laid the name to rest, the issues that gave life to the Social Gospel and its radical relative—Christian Socialism—are as lively as ever. See *Christian Advocate* 6 (February 15, 1962): 2.

5. "The Power and Responsibility of the Christian Ministry," *Arena* 4 (November 1891): 767–768.

6. John Humphrey Noyes, *History of American Socialisms* (New York: Hillary House, 1870; reprinted in 1961), p. 27.

7. Washington Gladden, *Recollections* (Boston: Houghton Mifflin, 1909), p. 411.

8. *Dictionary of American Biography*, 4: 371–372.

9. Robert T. Handy, ed., *The Social Gospel in America, 1870–1920: Gladden, Ely, Rauschenbusch* (New York: Oxford University Press, 1966), pp. 180–184.

10. Charles H. Hopkins, *The Rise of the Social Gospel in American Protestantism: 1865–1915* (New Haven: Yale University Press, 1940), pp. 186–187.

11. Donald B. Meyer, *The Protestant Search for Political Realism, 1919–1941* (Berkeley: University of California Press, 1960), p. 19; Handy, *Social Gospel in America*, p. 11.

12. Ely to Gladden August 28, 1900, Washington Gladden Papers, Box 4 (Ohio Historical Society Library, Columbus, Ohio).

13. Walter Rauschenbusch, *Christianizing the Social Order* (New York: Macmillan, 1912), p. 9.

14. Paul H. Boase, "Slavery and the Ohio Circuit Rider," *The Ohio Historical Quarterly* 64 (April 1955): 195–205; "Moral Policemen on the Ohio Frontier," 68 (January 1959): 3–18.

15. Gilbert Haven, *Sermons, Speeches and Letters on Slavery and Its War* (Boston: Lee and Shepard, 1869), pp. 387, 503–504, 601, 626–627; Timothy L. Smith, *Revivalism and Social Reform* (New York: Abingdon, 1957), pp. 225–237.

16. Gladden *Recollections*, pp. 189.

17. Charles G. Finney, *Lectures on Revivals of Religion* (Oberlin, Ohio: E. J. Goodrich, 1868), p. 290.

18. Henry F. May, *Protestant Church and Industrial America* (New York: Harper & Row, 1949), p. 40.

19. "The Duties of Citizens," November 3, 1878 (unpublished sermon), Washington Gladden Papers, Box 28.

20. *Zion's Herald*, June 17, 1869, p. 280; cited in Emory Stevens Bucke ed., *The History of American Methodism* (New York: Abingdon, 1964), 2: 327.

21. Joseph Cook, *Boston Monday Lectures: Labor, with Preludes on Current Events* (Boston: Houghton Mifflin, 1880), p. 196.

22. D. R. Dungan, "The Evangelist," *Christian Standard*, April 30, 1881.

23. James B. Finley, *Sketches of Western Methodism* (Cincinnati: Methodist Book Concern, 1855), p. 502.

24. Robert D. Clark, *The Life of Matthew Simpson* (New York: Macmillan, 1956), pp. 293–303.

25. H. Francis Perry, "The Workingman's Alienation from the Church," *The American Journal of Sociology* 4 (March 1899): 621–629.

26. Russell H. Conwell, "Acres of Diamonds," in Ernest J. Wrage and Barnet Baskerville ed., *American Forum: Speeches on Historic Issues, 1870–1900* (New York: Harper & Row, 1960), pp. 263–275.

27. "A Plain Talk with Workingmen," *The Christian Union*, July 30, 1885, p. 8; "A Plain Talk with Employers," July 23, 1885, pp. 8–9.

28. William G. Sumner, "The Forgotten Man," in Wrage and Baskerville, *American Forum*, pp. 229-243.

29. Ralph H. Gabriel, *The Course of American Democratic Thought* (New York: Ronald, 1956), p. 248.

30. *Social Darwinism: Selected Essays of William Graham Sumner* (Englewood Cliffs, N.J.: Prentice-Hall, 1963), pp. 24, 122–123.

31. James Dombrowski, *The Early Days of Christian Socialism in America* (New York: Columbia University Press, 1936), p. 5; May, *Protestant Churches*, p. 94.

32. May, *Protestant Churches*, pp. 92–93.

33. Gladden, *Recollections*, pp. 250–258.

34. C. M. Morse, "Regeneration as a Force in Reform Movements," *Methodist Review* 73 (November 1891): 929; Reply by R. F. Bishop in 74 (March 1892): 303–304; a second article by Morse 74 (November 1892): 876-883.

35. Gladden, *Recollections*, p. 251.

36. *The Dawn*, May 15, 1889, p. 1.

37. Gladden, *Recollections*, pp. 253–254.

38. C. M. Roberts to Gladden, February 22, 1900. Washington Gladden Papers, Box 4.

39. Gladden, *Recollections*, p. 431.

40. *Dictionary of American Biography*, 4:371–372.

41. John Fiske, *A Century of Science* (Boston: Houghton Mifflin, 1899), pp. 333–349.

42. Joseph Cook, *Boston Monday Lectures: Labor with Preludes on Current Events* (Boston: Houghton Mifflin, 1880), pp. 83–84, 241, 287; and *Boston Monday Lectures: Socialism with Preludes on Current Events* (Boston: Houghton Mifflin, 1880), pp. 51-57.

43. Mary Earhart, *Frances Willard: From Prayers to Politics* (Chicago: University of Chicago Press, 1944), pp. 245–259.

44. Howard H. Quint, *The Forging of American Socialism* (Indianapolis: Bobbs-Merrill, 1964), p. 126.

45. Dombrowski, *Christian Socialism*, p. 104.

46. *Dictionary of American Biography*, 2:378.

47. Adeline Knapp et al., "Prof. George D. Herron: The Man and His Work in California," *Arena* 4 (September 1895): 110–128.

48. Wrage and Baskerville, *American Forum*, pp. 276–282.
49. Robert T. Handy, "George D. Herron and the Kingdom Movement." *Church History* 19 (June 1950):97–115.
50. *The American Institute of Christian Sociology*, Labadie Collection, University of Michigan, Ann Arbor (1893), p. 3.
51. Handy, "Herron and the Kingdom," pp. 101, 109.
52. Beardsley, "Professor Herron," p. 793.
53. Gabriel, *American Democratic Thought*, p. 270; Hopkins, *Rise of Social Gospel*, p. 143, puts the sale at 23,000,000.
54. Dombrowski, *Christian Socialism*, p. 178.
55. Knapp et al., "Prof. George D. Herron," p. 111.
56. C. O. Brown, *The Kingdom's Extra Edition—A Rejoinder* (Pamphlet: San Francisco, 1895). See also *The Oberlin News*, June 13, 1895, p. 4; June 20, 1895, p. 4.
57. Brown repeatedly quoted Herron as saying: "The politicians will be fuel to the burning that is coming." The full quotation was: "The politics that remains insensible to the waking social consciousness, the politicians who ignore the social conscience and make the holy watchwords of the past the hypocrisy and traffic of the present, will be but fuel for burning in the day of wrath that is coming to consume our trade politics and false social philosophies as stubble." Knapp et al., "Prof. George D. Herron," p. 120.
58. May, *Protestant Churches*, p. 250.
59. Z. Swift Holbrook, "Professor Herron's Impressionism," *Bibliotheca Sacra* 52 (July 1895):563.
60. *Dictionary of American Biography*, 8: 504.
61. Rainsford to Gladden, January 26, 1900, Washington Gladden Papers, Box 4.
62. Pioneer and prophet of the Social Gospel, Josiah Strong achieved national fame in 1885 with the publication of *Our Country*, a volume that outlined many of the basic tenets of social Christianity. In his second work, *The New Era* (New York: Baker and Taylor, 1893) he joined Herron and others spokesmen of the Social Gospel in prodding the nation to clean up the slums, the "putrefying sores" of the city.
63. Gladden, *Recollections*, pp. 30–91.
64. Gladden to Bowen, May 22, 1863, Washington Gladden Papers, Box 1.
65. Gladden to Abbott, November 3, 1874, Washington Gladden Papers, Box 1. In his *Recollections*, p. 235, Gladden used the analogy of a policy shop.
66. Gladden, *Recollections*, pp. 249–250.
67. "Eulogy" (unpublished sermon), Washington Gladden Papers, Box 58.
68. "Trade Unionism" (unpublished sermon), Washington Gladden Papers, Box 58.
69. Reinhold Niebuhr in Robert D. Cross, ed., Walter Rauschenbusch, *Christianity and the Social Crisis* (New York: Harper Torchbooks, 1964), p. xx.
70. Ibid., p. xviii.
71. Ibid, p. 238.
72. Walter Rauschenbusch, *A Theology for the Social Gospel* (New York: Macmillan Co., 1918), p. 184.

73. Correspondence with Professor Robert T. Handy, author of *The Social Gospel in America*. "The New Apostolate" appears in that volume, pp. 331–337.

74. Rauschenbusch, *A Theology*, p. xiv.

75. Robert D. Cross in his introduction to a reprint of *Christianity and the Social Crisis* (New York: Harper Torchbooks, 1964), p. xvii.

76. Ibid., 414–422.

77. See Gabriel, *American Democratic Thought*, p. 280. "When Rauschenbusch contemplated in his imagination that Kingdom of God destined, one day, to become an earthly reality, he saw that it was nothing else than the democratic dream come true."

78. Thomas Hamilton, "Social Optimism and Pessimism in American Protestantism," *Public Opinion Quarterly* 6 (Summer 1942): 280–283.

79. G. Frederick Wright, "Ministers and Mobs," *Bibliotheca Sacra* 49 (October 1892): 676–681.

80. *People*, May 2, 1899, cited in Quint, *The Forging of American Socialism*, p. 126.

81. James Bryce, *The American Commonwealth* (Chicago: Charles H. Sergel and Co., 1891), 2: 582.

82. "Christian Socialism," *Nation*, May 25, 1893, pp. 381–382.

83. Thomas F. Gossett, *Race: The History of an Idea in America* (Dallas: Southern Methodist University Press, 1963), pp. 176–197.

84. Martin Luther King, Jr., *Strength to Love* (New York: Harper & Row, 1963), pp. 168.

85. Shailer Mathews, "The Significance of the Church to the Social Movement," *The American Journal of Sociology* 4 (March 1899): 620.

11

Rhetoric in the Higher Criticism Controversy

THOMAS H. OLBRICHT

In the waning years of the nineteenth century a discussion previously isolated in the classrooms and studies of scholars broke over into the American pulpit, the dinner conversation, and sidewalk debate. Already at the beginning of that century scholars on the continent, in England, and in America were developing modes of criticism for Biblical literature.[1] In the vocabulary of the times, these efforts were divided into lower criticism, concerned with the textual accuracy of varying manuscript traditions; and higher criticism, which scrutinized the literary characteristics of Biblical books, their authorship and sources, and their historical backgrounds. The public excitement was primarily sparked by higher criticism, for conclusions reached by the higher critics challenged such assumptions as the Mosaic authorship of the first five books of the Old Testament, and the Gospels as eye-witness biographies of Jesus.

The debate over the Bible was one facet of a many sided theological protest and reform. Other conflicts involved evolution, the inspiration of the Scriptures, the virgin birth of Jesus, the miracles, the second coming of Christ, and church involvement in social reform.[2] The controversy over higher criticism is significant in its own right and worthy of special consideration; but considered from the perspective of a historical movement, must take its place in conjunction with these other disputes. By the 1910s those who favored what in their view was the traditional outlook rallied around the term "fundamentalism." Those who welcomed new understandings accepted "liberalism" as a label.[3]

This essay traces the clash over higher criticism in popular oral discourse from 1875 to 1900. It is the examination of rhetoric in one strand of a movement in the manner proposed by Leland M. Griffin.[4]

CLOUDS ON THE HORIZON

To appreciate the furor over higher criticism, we must scrutinize the existential situation of American religious persons in the last quarter of the nineteenth century. After the Civil War strong intellectual winds began blowing from Europe, challenging long-held American views and methodologies. In time, American religion found itself in an identity crisis. Responses were various. Some openly sought revision and welcomed cutting adrift from the past. Others, threatened by the innovations, systematized and hardened the older ways as they understood them. Still others resolved the crisis by positions between these two extremes.

To attain a degree of empathy with nineteenth-century man caught in these conflicts we may recount the agonizing of William Newton Clarke as set forth in *Sixty Years with the Bible*.[5] Clarke's intellectual struggles were representative of many others in the last half of the century.[6] Clarke was brought up in his ministerial father's home in which Bible readings were a daily fare and through which he inculcated a deep loyalty for the Bible as God's word. By the end of the century he had moved from a traditional understanding of the Scriptures to an open acceptance of the Bible as seen through the eyes of higher criticism.[7]

Clarke's first challenges came from the older tradition of American Deism.[8] In 1856 when Clarke was fifteen, he engaged in conversation with a young man who mentioned a number of contradictions in the Bible. These revolved about specific items in the Scriptures after the manner of Thomas Paine and Ethan Allen, American popularizers of Deism.[9] Clarke turned to books in his father's library. These replied to alleged contradictions, but not those advanced by Clarke's interlocutor. Clarke could not resolve the contradictions, but he was undisturbed. The climate in which he lived was one of warm, loving belief in the Bible as the Word of God. But times were changing.

Already at the middle of the nineteenth century, science commanded the attention of intellectuals. Before long it would capture the imagination of the proverbial man in the street. Geology was making considerable headway at this time. Clarke relates that while studying geology in a secondary school some of his young associates lost their confidence in the Scriptures.[10] He himself stood firm, but redirected some of his thinking. He now decided that the days of the Genesis account of creation should be understood as long geological periods rather than as standard twenty-four hour days. But others would not concede to these new concepts of physical origin, and constructed apologies for the literal six days of creation.[11]

But the most severe scientific challenge to nineteenth century Christian orthodoxy was evolution. Darwin's *The Origin of Species*, published in 1859, created turmoil on both sides of the Atlantic.[12] The first impact of evolution was made upon Clarke in 1862 when he was assigned the task of presenting the views of Herbert Spencer to a group of ministers. He reports,

I did not accept the evolutionary idea I encountered there . . . Here was my objection: I knew from the Bible what was the method of God in creating the world and man, and it was not the method Spencer proclaimed as the actual one. The doctrine was in contradiction to the Scriptures, and that stood as reason enough for leaving it aside.[13]

A few years later Clarke reversed his position, and observed ". . . my experience with it is interesting, and worth recording, because it was precisely the reproduction in miniature of the experience of the Christian world in those first years of evolutionary doctrine."[14]

Evolutionary explanations particularly challenged long-held theological positions. Furor in the churches over evolution was reaching its peak when, in the early nineties, views of Genesis held by the higher critics and influenced by evolution began to filter into the churches. The result was the compounding of the anxieties of the orthodox.

The acknowledged leader in these new approaches to Genesis was a German Biblical scholar named Julius Wellhausen (1844–1918). His Seminal work, *Prolegomena to the History of Ancient Israel* appeared in Germany in 1878 and in English translation in 1885.[15] Wellhausen argued that the Pentateuch consisted of four documents interlaced by an editor (redactor) some time in the second century B.C. The documents were labeled "Jahwist," "Eloist," "Priestly," and "Deuteronomic," and often identified by the first letters of these names.[16] This meant, to the irritation of many believers, that Moses could not have authored these books. By the time Wellhausen's views were widely disseminated in the 1890s those who adhered to the old ways were compelled to defend Genesis on two fronts. Actually higher criticism was as destructive to orthodox understandings of other sections of the Old Testament and the New Testament. But in the popular mind, because evolution and higher criticism cast doubt specifically upon this book, Genesis became the focus of controversy. T. Dewitt Talmage put it sermonically. "The infidel hurls the chief force of his caricature and vulgarity at the first book of the Bible."[17]

In the mind of the most religious persons these literary developments were an attack on the inspiration of the Scriptures.[18] Even persons whose minds were open to new vistas found it painful to break away from long-cherished affirmations on Biblical inspiration.[19] But these new conclusions challenged statements which hithertofore had been taken as fact, for example, Jesus' reference to a Pentateuchal source as Mosaic. One of the revisions necessitated by these new insights was the doctrine of inspiration. So Clarke wrote:

. . . no new theories of inspiration have been formed lately: the theories that stand in theological books are old ones, discredited by later knowledge of the Bible . . . We are able now to take the Bible as it is, and listen to its testimony, without first proving by a doctrine of inspiration that it must be listened to.[20]

From this new vantage point Clarke argued that a view of inspiration which began with whatever is found in Scripture could accommodate whatever the critics discovered, whether evolution or documents.

It was not until the late 1880s that Clarke first gave serious attention to higher criticism.[21] Earlier he had dealt with individual questions, but had not as yet considered a total system after the manner of Wellhausen.[22] Biblical criticism entered America as early as Joseph S. Buckminster (1784–1812) in the Unitarian tradition, and somewhat later with Moses Stuart (1780–1852) who was Congregational.[23] But it was not until the early nineties that heresy trials of various seminary professors made higher criticism headline news. On the popular front, just like Clarke, many Americans were taking up the question for the first time.

The higher-criticism controversy in America resulted from American scholars embracing German views. Various Americans studied in Germany before the Civil War. Edward Everett received a doctorate at Gottingen in 1817 and George Bancroft in 1820. Everett became a statesman and Bancroft a historian, thus exerting little influence on American Biblical scholarship.[24] The influence of people like Charles Hodge of Princeton who studied at Halle in 1827–28, and Irah Chase of Newton Theological Seminary who was there in 1823–24, however, was more permanent.[25] American Biblical scholars kept abreast of German developments during the mid-century years.[26] After the war a flood of American students matriculated at German universities. In 1860 there were 77 Americans in German philosophical faculties; in 1880, 173; in 1891, 446; in 1892, 383; in 1895, 422; and in 1898, 397.[27] Charles A. Briggs (1841–1913) sometimes accredited with introducing higher criticism to America, received his training in Germany.[28] Crawford Howell Toy (1836–1919) of Harvard University, studied in Berlin. His colleague, David Gordon Lyon, took his Ph.D. at Leipzig in 1882. Both men were of Southern Baptist backgrounds. They taught at Harvard following their denomination's rejection of their critical views.

The higher criticism debate in the theological journals preceded the public eruption by about a decade. In 1880 a new theological journal—*The Presbyterian Review*—appeared under the editorship of Archibald A. Hodge and Charles A. Briggs. The two editors represented opposite views on higher criticism, Princeton scholars opposing (Hodge was a professor there) and those at Union Theological Seminary, as well as others, supporting. The journal opened its pages to debate on criticism of the Pentateuch, the verbal inspiration of the Scriptures, and the critical theories of Wellhausen. The dispute proceeded amicably at first, but relations declined, and that along with financial problems brought the demise of the journal in 1889.[29] Other journals also entered the fray, especially *Bibliotheca Sacra*.[30]

By the 1890s, what had been a relatively quiet scholarly dispute, erupted into overt polemics. Those who envisioned a new day in which theology would embrace the scientific turn of mind called for major revisions. They encouraged scholars and leaders to aggressively air out the churches. They predicted a glorious future for the church once freed of its stodgy past. Others viewed these developments with great alarm. They feared an undermining of the fundamentals of the Christian faith, especially belief in the Scriptures as the inspired Word of God. In the 1890s higher criticism became the storm center of the attack.

THE SHOWERS COMMENCE

To ascertain the rhetorical strategies in the early years of controversy (1875–1890) we shall scrutinize oral presentations of Robert Ingersoll, T. DeWitt Talmage, and Henry Ward Beecher. In popular circles Ingersoll was noted for his radical attitudes toward the Bible. Talmage represented a somewhat enlightened, if not flamboyant, orthodoxy. Beecher hewed out a mediating position from a popular, though not scholarly, standpoint.

In the decades of the seventies and eighties Ingersoll kept the American pulpit busy answering his attacks on the Scriptures.[31] A major bone of contention was Ingersoll's widely delivered and printed lecture "Some Mistakes of Moses." Ingersoll printed his own version in 1879 with these remarks:

The lecture was never written and consequently never delivered twice the same. On several occasions it was reported and published without consent, and without revision. All these publications were grossly and glaringly incorrect. As published, they have been answered several hundred times, and many of the clergy are still engaged in the great work. To keep these revered gentlemen from wasting their talents on the mistakes of reporters and printers, I concluded to publish the principal points in all my lectures on this subject.[32]

One of the most famous pulpit responses was a series of six sermons by T. DeWitt Talmage, of the Central Presbyterian Church in Brooklyn, in early 1882.[33] Large audiences were present. The sermons were also printed in about three thousand weekly newspapers.[34] Ingersoll believed the sermons so influential he published his response in interview form in a book of 350 pages.[35]

Both speakers tacitly assumed that Ingersoll was prosecuting a well-ensconced orthodoxy for its misdeeds. Talmage heralded himself and his auditors as defendants and pleaded not guilty. Nevertheless it is apparent that Talmage was troubled by the inroads of scientific views among his constituency. Ingersoll astutely observed:

A few years ago, Science endeavored to show that it was not inconsistent with the Bible. The tables have been turned, and now, Religion is endeavoring to prove that the Bible is not inconsistent with Science.[36]

Ingersoll aggressively sought to steer his hearers away from orthodox commitments in respect to Scriptures. Talmage stood with the majority who felt committed in some degree to the Bible as the Word of God. These opposing roles obviously affected rhetorical strategies.

Ingersoll elicited common agreement with his hearers as he commenced, but because of his position he could not long maintain this rapprochement.[37] At a point when he turned to unpopular views he changed to satire and ridicule. Talmage, in contrast, assumed an audience that shared his views. His strategy was to invoke religious opinions held by most middle-class Americans. The different strategies obviously resulted from the relationship of speaker, ideas, and audience, for the speakers themselves were much alike in temperament and style.

Both Ingersoll and Talmage exhibited a flair for popular eloquence that eschewed complexity and words unfamiliar to the typical audience. At times they burst forth in emotive energy punctuated by short phrases and parallelisms. Both were specific in words and concepts. Talmage related numerous personal incidents, some of which identified directly, others analogically to his points. He was more direct and personal. Ingersoll was analytical, relying much more on historical perspective. Both minimized rigorous structuring, motivated by popular interest rather than logical interrelationships.[38]

We turn now to the speeches themselves to examine the strategies in detail. We are not simply interested in arguments. We want to discover the rhetorical strategies involved in the precursory stages of the movement. For that reason we must scrutinize the arguments in the order in which they unfold.

Robert Ingersoll

Ingersoll commenced his remarks by commending intellectual freedom. He rightly assumed that he held this commitment in common with his auditors. Upon that agreement he launched an attack on the religious status quo. The greatest contemporary detriments to freedom he charged are the orthodox clergy and a superstitious adherence to Scriptures. Clergymen, he declared, are employed so as to be true to their clients rather than open to new truth. Specifically he cited the requirement of Andover Seminary that the faculty affirm the same confession of faith every five years. Since some of his auditors would dispute the thrust of this point, Ingersoll employed ridicule.

The professors, for the most part, are ministers who failed in the pulpit and were retired to the seminary on account of their deficiency in reason and their excess of faith. As a rule, they know nothing of this world, and far less of the next; but they have the power of stating the most absurd propositions with faces solemn as stupidity touched by fear.[39]

The ministers themselves received similar treatment being identified as less than manly.[40] Despite this vicious attack, Ingersoll remained in proximity to his audience by calling for a new ministry whose concern would be to escape the "evils of this world instead of the next."[41] The sort of ministry he envisioned, in fact, anticipated the social gospel movement which commenced later in the decade. While not all would agree, Ingersoll struck a responsive chord with several of the kind who attended his lectures. A nascent movement begins slowly, winning a few at a time.

The restraint on freedom which drew most of Ingersoll's attention, however, was a superstitious adherence to Scriptures. Early in his lecture Ingersoll frankly declared that Moses was not the author of the Pentateuch. This was a radical declaration for the man on the street, but by no means new.[42] He dwelt at length in setting out two conflicting accounts of creation; the first in Genesis 1–2:4a, and the second 2:4b–25. In the hypothesis of Wellhausen these were the Priestly and the Jahwist accounts respectively. But it is not obvious that Ingersoll drew on Wellhausen. He apparently was more concerned to disabuse popular audiences of orthodox views, than to disseminate current scholarship. Ingersoll cited the well-known popular British commentators Adam Clarke,[43] Matthew Henry,[44] Alexander Cruden,[45] and Thomas Scott,[46] rather than the German commentators who impressed scholars. Ingersoll shrewdly realized that audiences such as his responded to these household names rather than those of Wellhausen, Briggs, or Driver. He cited these popular commentators—to establish that even they recognized difficulties, and advanced elaborate explanations for embarrassing statements in the Scriptures. At the same time he relished pointing out how the explanations of these commentators contradicted each other. Scholars dwell at length on literary matters. Ingersoll recognized that laymen soon tire of concerns so abstract.

Ingersoll now turned to the more vivid charge that the Scriptures are both primitive and immoral. In providing a structure for Ingersoll's accusations we can do no better than follow Talmage's summary.

I have read many of the complaints made concerning the Scriptures, and I classify all the complaints under four heads:

The Bible is an impure book, the Bible is a cruel book, the Bible is a contradictory book, the Bible is an unscientific book.[47]

Ingersoll titled a section of his lecture "Faith in Filth." He charged that since everyone knows of the moral filth in the Bible he need not be specific. He professed to be too embarrassed to read such passages in public.[48] The honest person should admit the Bible's true character and desist from Bibliolatry.

Would it not be far better to admit that the Bible was written by barbarians in a barbarous, coarse and vulgar age? Would it not be safer to charge Moses with vulgarity, instead of God? Is it not altogether more probable that some ignorant Hebrew should write the vulgar words?[49]

Ingersoll did not propose banning the Bible, but did request that "Every foolish and immodest thing should be expunged . . ."

Ingersoll centered upon the conquest of Canaan in alleging cruelty in the Old Testament. Assuming common acquaintance with the story, he appealed to compassion.

If the bible be true, God commanded his chosen people to destroy men simply for the crime of defending their native land. They were not allowed to spare trembling and white-haired age, nor dimpled babes clasped in the mothers' arms. They were ordered to kill women, and to pierce, with the sword of war, the unborn child.[50]

He compared this destruction of human lives with that of Indians who killed a pioneer mother defending her children in a frontier cabin. He anticipated that none of his auditors would identify the Indians as agents of God, so why the Israelites?

In taking up contradictions, Ingersoll moved into the arena of the Biblical critics. He dwelt, however, not on the problems discussed by scholars, but those more immediately obvious to a popular audience. A lengthy portion of the lecture focused on Genesis 1:1–2:3 and the seven days of creation. Then in the next section Ingersoll quoted Genesis 2:4b-23 and schematically compared the order of creation in the two chapters. As to differences, he noted: "In the second account, man was made *before* the beasts and fowls. If this is true, the first account is false."[51] From Exodus he discussed the two accounts of the giving of the law. He charged that Exodus 20 and 34 are actually two tellings of the same event, yet chapter 34 says nothing of the golden calf or the breaking of the tables of stone. He concluded: "Both of these stories cannot be true, and yet both must be believed."[52]

True to the age in which he lived, Ingersoll spent considerable time pointing to ways in which the Pentateuch is unscientific. In that age Science was widely heralded by persons of all persuasions. He dwelt mostly on scientific inaccuracies readily grasped by an unsophisticated audience. Only rarely did he refer to the publications of well-known scientists.[53] A typical approach to what Ingersoll called scientific illiteracy in Genesis is his discussion of "dry land."

Certainly the writer of this did not have any conception of the real form of the earth. He could not have known anything of the attraction of gravitation. He must have regarded the earth as flat and supposed that it required considerable force and power to induce the water to leave the mountains and collect in the valleys . . . And all this happened before a ray had left the quiver of the sun, before a glittering beam had thrilled the bosom of a flower, and before the Dawn with trembling hands had drawn aside the curtains of the East and welcomed to her arms the eager god of Day.[54]

In effect, Ingersoll charged that any modern man of common sense knows more about these matters than did the author of Genesis. Those who take science seriously, he declared, admit that the Bible is not inspired with respect to astronomy, geology, botany, zoology, or any other science.

In matters of fact, the Bible has ceased to be regarded as a standard. Science has succeeded in breaking the chains of theology.[55]

If for no other reason than its scientific primitiveness, modern man should throw off the strangle hold of the Bible and become free.

In his rhetorical strategy Ingersoll sought popular consent. He did not muster rigorous arguments or line up the experts. He did little which would excite scholars, whether scientists or Biblical critics. Unfortunately for Ingersoll the man in the street held emotional attachments to the Bible. But through his lectures Ingersoll changed the attitudes of some auditors and paved the way for future revisions.

T. DeWitt Talmage

Talmage reflected the views of middle-class America. He knew it. He realized that rhetorical strategy required him to wave middle-class flags with respect to the Bible. He was not compelled to marshall cogent arguments; which fortunately, coincided admirably with his temperament. His reason for replying to Ingersoll was not that he feared Ingersoll would empty the churches by his great persuasive powers. Ingersoll would deter Christianity, he declared, "like a Switzerland insect floating through the air impeding an Alpine avalanche."[56]

I preach these sermons for the benefit of individuals. There are young men who through his teachings have given up their religion and soon after gave up their morals. Infidel teachings triumphant would fill all the penitentiaries, and the gambling hells and houses of shame on the continent—on the planet . . . My fear is not that Christianity in general shall be impeded, but I want to persuade these young men to get aboard the train instead of throwing themselves across the tracks.

Talmage spent more time, as this comment suggests, depicting the calamities about to befall those persuaded by Ingersoll, than in rebutting his charges. He likely did not dissuade many who delighted in Ingersoll's lectures, but he confirmed churchgoers in their cherished opinions.

It was not until the fifth sermon, "Slanders Against the Bible," that Talmage took up, one at a time, Ingersoll's charges against the Bible. In prior sermons Talmage was quite cognizant of Ingersoll's claims, but not through orderly rebuttal. In the first three, Talmage chiefly defended the Bible against scientific illiteracy.[57] He was astute in taking up this matter first since the younger set calling for revision was doing so in the name of science. But let's follow the fourfold categories proposed by Talmage.

In the third sermon: "Captious Criticism" Talmage answered the charge of immorality in the Bible. He had worked at length on the scientific repercussions of the long day of Joshua and the story of Jonah. Suddenly, about a third of the way through the sermon he changed direction. "Then, too, I have heard it asserted that the Bible is full of indecencies."[58] He admitted Ingersoll's charge that some parts of the Bible are too vulgar for the pulpit or the family circle. He responded that not all the Bible was designed to be read in public. These parts should be read in private, just as books in a physician's office. A physician's books are pure, but not suitable for family reading. The reason these parts are there, Talmage argued, is so as to create a healthy disgust and horror of sin. But no one ever became impure through Bible reading, and the morals are obviously higher where it is read than where it is not such as in Madras and Peking.[59] These responses, given Talmage's audience, are clever, but do little to reflect on these materials from the standpoint of Biblical theology.

Talmage faced up to the cruelty in the Bible in the fifth sermon. He simply countered that no one ever became cruel through Bible reading. In fact, he asserted, the opposite is the case. ". . . all the institutions of mercy were founded by Bible readers."[60] He cited examples including institutions established by George Peabody and Florence Nightingale.

As to contradictions in the Bible, Talmage completely ignored those discussed by Ingersoll. He perhaps felt most of his hearers could handle the charges, or that an answer would be too long and involved. Regardless, his response was the statement of John Mill that in 30,000 different Bible readings there is not one important contradiction.[61] Obviously this was not a cogent reply, for Mill was concerned with variant textual readings, not contradictions of the sort pinpointed by Ingersoll. A second response was more to the point. The Bible has had several different writers in a number of ages, he explained, but there is an amazing agreement "in the great cardinal doctrines of the Bible." But even this observation did not refute head-on the concrete problems advanced by Ingersoll.

As to the charge that the Bible is unscientific, the topic on which he spent the majority of his time, Talmage contended that there is no contest between Science and revelation; it only appears so because of mistaken views about the purpose of the Bible. Geological and astronomical discoverers complement rather than contradict the Bible, for "you are not compelled to believe that the world was made in six of our days."[62] Furthermore, the critics are nit-pickers, if not ignorant of true science. Ingersoll had shown that in Genesis, light was created on Monday and the sun on Thursday. Talmage exclaimed, "Here the infidel plaintiff shows his geological and chemical and astronomical ignorance."[63] Any schoolboy knows, he continued, there can be light without the sun; that vapors around the earth may have prevented the sun from getting through to the earth until Thursday; that the astronomers Brewster and Herschel hold that the sun is not light but rather that light is the atmosphere floating around it and that there are other sources of light in the universe—for example, the Aurora Borealis. Only the final observation seems either one of substance or a response to Ingersoll. On occasion Talmage employed ridicule, but not with the frequency of Ingersoll. As Talmage tells it, had Ingersoll been in a high school science class, the teacher would have said, "Boy, go down to the foot and be in disgrace for your stupidity!"[64]

Talmage hoped to turn the tables on Ingersoll by showing that several statements about the universe in the Bible are amazingly accurate according to the discoveries of modern science. He offered a number of instances in the second sermon "The Folly of Infidelity." Isaiah knew about the orbiting of the earth, Job knew about trade winds, Solomon was familiar with the circulation of the blood, Nahum described streetcars, and Job knew of electrical communication such as the telegraph.[65] Furthermore, many scientists feel perfectly comfortable with the Bible, for example, Herschel, Keppler, and Newton.[66] He admitted, however, that a few such as Mill, Darwin, and Tyndall were not so disposed.

Talmage managed clever counters, but for the most part, his refutation was weak because it was supported by neither solid biblical nor scientific erudition. His best responses were quick and pungent. He seldom sustained a long chain of thought. Like Ingersoll he knew the pulse of a popular audience, especially of contemporary American churchgoers. He was an astute rhetorician even though he failed in clarifying or adding materially to the issues. But then this stage of a controversy or moment is characterized by imprecision.

Henry Ward Beecher

A third approach, perhaps best labeled "mediating", was that of Henry Ward Beecher.[67] He saw himself as a spokesman for the church. His reading was wide, but not definitive. He served as a front man, directing professional and moneyed persons to newly adjusted opinions. His views on the Bible, as compared with Wellhausen, seem near those of the orthodox. But he laid the groundwork so that informed laypersons moved with less agony to more radical conclusions.

From the autumn to the spring months of 1878–79, the same year that Ingersoll published "Some Mistakes of Moses," Beecher delivered a series of Sunday evening lectures on the first part of the Old Testament. The lectures did not appear in print, however, until 1892.[68] Beecher's purpose was at least twofold. First of all he sought to emphasize the message of the books. But second, he sought to present the Old Testament in such a manner that it became palatable to an enlightened person of the time.

For the general purpose of bringing home especially the more ancient of the Hebrew Scriptures to your consideration and your confidence, unembarrassed by the theories which have been given and which turn the Bible very largely into a book of disputes, I purpose, in this series of Sunday evening lectures, first, to discuss somewhat the meaning of "inspiration," as applied to this source of our faith, and then to go over with you the chief historical books of the Old Testament, trying to find what there is in them for us of the modern day.[69]

Beecher was the sort of preacher the crowds flocked to hear, but these lectures incorporate few attention getting devices, nor are they particularly arresting stylistically, especially when compared with Talmage and Ingersoll. Beecher proceeded under the assumption—and with justification—that current doctrines of inspiration were the largest single obstacle to widespread acceptance of biblical criticism.[70] His first lecture was therefore on the subject of inspiration. In it he anticipated later objections which might arise because of specific critical observations.

As Beecher sized it up, the difficulty with current views was that they came not "out of the Word of God, but out of their own idea of the action of God upon the human soul."[71] For a correct doctrine of inspiration "we must go humbly to the Word of God and see how it is made up, and ask what the facts are, and then out of the facts form a theory of inspiration . . ."[72] For Beecher, the Bible was not basically a book of "revelations;" but a book written by inspired writers. He defined inspiration as "a divine influence that quickens the faculties of men."[73]

In the sermon on inspiration Beecher set forth eight items prerequisite to framing such a doctrine. Three are of particular significance.

First, Beecher argued that an adequate theory of inspiration must accommodate the fact that biblical authors incorporated existing records into the Scriptures.[74] Genesis, he professed, was compiled from "several then existing records of things." He offered no delineation of these records, however. Second, he declared that certain incidental facts in the Bible are from the "errant operation of the human mind." He explicitly rejected the infallibility of the Scriptures. "It is destructive of any theory of the inspiration of the Bible to claim that every word and letter which it contains is infallibly correct."[75] But despite minor miscues, Beecher held that the theology of the Scriptures is from God. Third, he believed the Bible had unity, but unlike that commonly conceived. The Bible was variegated in the manner of Winchester Cathedral which has five distinct periods of architecture yet comprised "a unit which is admirable."[76] He believed the unity of Scripture to be so strong that even should a book be declared inauthentic—which he thought unlikely—the whole would not be affected. By his eight claims, three of which we have noticed, Beecher sought to pave the way for conclusions advanced by higher critics.

In the third sermon, "The Book of Beginnings" Beecher offered his main observations on Biblical criticism. He first presented a panoramic view of the Pentateuch, then took up the controversial matters of authorship and composition. He assured the congregation that whatever the outcome of scholarly debate—the details of which he did not present—the message of God remains intact. Matters of authorship and literary composition are, in the final analysis, unimportant. As to his own conclusions he declared:

> The result of my mind is about this, that these books were very largely produced by Moses or under his direction; either compiled—as the first twelve chapters; or, as the subsequent chapters, formed from legends, traditional histories, or other material, giving the same sequences, accounts of the patriarchs down to his own time, and then adding his own personal history, and the history of the different tribes and of their wanderings until they came to the Promised Land.
>
> I have no doubt that the substantial basis of the books was from the hand of Moses, or that they were written by some clerk or Levite under his direction.[77]

Beecher's use of "legend" for these early accounts would upset the orthodox, but he is still a considerable distance from Wellhausen who held that these materials were from 300 to 1000 years later than Moses.[78] What Beecher means becomes clear when he refers to the story of Adam and Eve in the garden as legendary or allegorical.[79] Beecher did not present advanced or even well-informed positions, but he opened a number of minds to the possibility of the more radical paths of the scholars a decade later.

In the germinal stages of the higher criticism controversy, popular speakers struggled superficially with concepts already argued at depth by scholars. At first these matters were ill defined, if not confusing. Various Americans were aware of these new modes of thought, but they had not as yet captured the popular imagination. Even Ingersoll recognized that it was not rhetorically astute to bore his auditors with scholarly positions for which they had little appetite. In less than a decade, however, the issues sharpened, requiring more precise and detailed argumentation. The speakers in this first wave were precursors for the more technically trained who emerged when the controversy reached the crisis stage.

THE DELUGE BREAKS FORTH

In the last decade of the nineteenth century higher criticism came into its own as a major issue. For some ten years American academicians had carried on debates in scholarly journals, especially over the Wellhausian documentary hypothesis.[80] By the 1890s heresy trials in various denominations brought the finer details of the controversy into public domain.[81] At this time an occasional Sunday sermon embarked upon an erudite discussion of detailed arguments.[82] There were also public lectures of various sorts, indicating some hardening in the controversy, and a new stage in the movement. In these discourses a different sort of rhetoric emerged. In order to assess the new situation we shall examine lectures by Charles A. Briggs, William Henry Green, and George Plattenburg.

Charles A. Briggs

Briggs, appointed to the chair in Biblical Theology at Union Theological Seminary, January 20, 1891, was no doubt a leader among those who sought to gain acceptance for higher criticism in America. His inaugural lecture, "The Authority of Holy Scripture," became a focal point for controversy. At the time when he gave the lecture he was under considerable suspicion, not only for his views on higher criticism, but also for his objections to the American Revised Version of the Old Testament. He was also involved in a polemic with conservative Presbyterian theologians over whether they or he had departed from the Westminster Confession. Because of the charged atmosphere, Briggs decided to give an innocuous scholarly discourse on Biblical geography, the speciality of Edward Robinson for whom the chair was named.[83] But the donor for the chair, who was also president of Union's board, argued that the occasion called for a defense of the school, the donor, and of Briggs himself.[84] Briggs therefore intentionally popularized his lecture and spoke so pointedly that when it was over, his friends felt compelled to apologize. According to Loetscher, the religious press "was almost unanimous in condemning Dr. Briggs' inaugural."[85] The war of words over the lecture did much to bring to a head opposing views and the delineation of positions.

Briggs did not immediately take up higher criticism since, faithful to his title, his thematic emphasis was the authority of the Scriptures. But the presuppositions for which he argued laid the groundwork for higher criticism as he envisioned it. The discipline at stake was biblical theology, not biblical criticism.[86]

Even though the lecture is "popular," Briggs is more the professor than the preacher. The discourse is carefully structured and closely reasoned. But the language is lively and occasional illustrations sustain audience attention. While the speech was delivered at the seminary, the intent was to give it wide distribution in print. As Briggs composed the address he probably had the reader more in mind than the immediate audience. Despite Loetscher's comments to the contrary, the lecture shows a studied effort on Brigg's part to bring his auditors from their long ingrained views to his.[87] This is especially apparent as one examines the structure of the address. But those who hoped for a conciliatory statement were, of course, disappointed. Briggs was straightforward in setting out his views, which could not fail but alienate myriad churchmen.

Briggs commenced the address by identifying a common ground on which he and his auditors could agree. The age, he declared, searched for authority because of the uncertainty of the times. He was quite willing to grant that Christianity rested upon authority, the prevailing types being the Church, reason, and the holy Scripture. Clearly Briggs had Protestants in mind in designing his remarks. Protestants, he suggested, recognized only the authority of the Scriptures. To them the authority of the church seemed Romish, and the authority of reason, Deistic. Briggs suggested that this bias gave neither reason nor the church their due. He did not mean to leave the impression that the Church and reason were equal with the Scriptures, though that was the way he was widely interpreted. Later, the weight assigned to the Scriptures is apparent, "We are now face to face with Biblical Theology. Here, if anywhere, the Divine authority will be found."[88] Briggs actually hoped to show that while all three forms of authority are viable, each is subject to abuse. At first glance the strategy seems excellent, but feedback indicated that the result was confusion rather than persuasion. Unfortunately, most of Briggs' auditors, at least, for purposes of polemics, assigned less value to reason and the church than Briggs' argument demanded.

After identifying strengths and weaknesses of authority in reason and the Church, Briggs turned to the Scriptures. He hoped his auditors agreed that just as authority in the other realms carried potential dangers, so also the authority of the Scriptures. In fact, he offered six points of potential danger: 1) superstition about the Scriptures, 2) the doctrine of verbal inspiration, 3) the concern for authenticity of authors, 4) the affirmation of inerrancy, 5) an improper view of natural law, and 6) the viewing of prophecy as minute prediction. As he took up the barriers, Briggs made little direct reference to biblical criticism, but in each instance, conservative positions were premises from which critical conclusions were rejected.

The order of the barriers shows Briggs' rhetorical acuity. His age uniquely battled superstition, so he shrewdly commenced with this point. What Briggs accomplished through structural priority, however, he sometimes lost by injudicious lucidity. In ridiculing misplaced adoration of the Bible he charged, "It will not stop a bullet any better than a mass-book. . . . It will not guard a home from fire half so well as holy water."[89] Briggs was obviously clever, but unfortunately for him, most mainstream Protestants would have been turned off by what in their way of thinking was an outlandish comparison. The most controversial of the six barriers was Briggs' rejection of inerrancy. He did well to take up this topic in fourth position so as not to alienate his auditors at the beginning and end.

In the third section, comprising more than half the whole, Briggs set forth the content of biblical theology. He advanced three divisions: A. The Religion of the Bible, B. The Faith of the Bible, and C. Biblical Ethics. His main concern was to contrast biblical theology with the conservative theology of his detractors. In section B, for example, he argued that in biblical theology the sanctification of many persons continues after death.[90] Remarks such as these added to the furor caused by the address. In a technical sense one should distinguish between higher criticism and Biblical theology though obviously conclusions affirmed on the one influence positions taken on the other. But in popular American thinking the views of the Germans in both biblical theology and higher criticism were radical and both were attacked under the odious label "higher criticism."

If one were to judge by the response, the lecture was a dismal failure, except in New York. The lecture was given on January 20, 1891. In May, the General Assembly of the Presbyterian Church, with which Union was then affiliated, voted 449 to 60 to uphold a committee recommendation that the election of Professor Briggs to the chair of Biblical theology be vetoed.[91] The considerations were not just the lecture but also numerous books published by Briggs.[92] The lecture, however, became the focus of the higher criticism controversy both in the press and in the pulpit.

Briggs hoped through this lecture to secure new support for revisions he felt necessary, and which he visualized on the horizon. With a new day in mind he ended the lecture by expressing confidence that in time to come all three forms of authority would be assigned their proper role and a correct understanding of the Bible emerge. Unfortunately, Briggs' premises were too radical and too intertwined with the emotional commitments of mainstream Protestants to carry the day. His platform called for a new Protestant identity which many viewed as a threat. But growing numbers were being won. In another thirty years almost all the professors in the major seminaries in America had embraced if not surpassed Briggs' views on Biblical criticism.

William Henry Green

Sometime in 1891 or early 1892, William Henry Green, Professor of Old Testament literature at Princeton Theological Seminary, gave an address at the "Marble Church," in New York, titled, "The Anti-Biblical Higher Criticism."[93] Green had for some years opposed higher criticism in the scholarly journals and was one of Briggs' chief antagonists. Green was chairman of the Old Testament committee of the American Bible revision, which work Briggs openly criticized. He was also elected moderator of the General Assembly of the Presbyterian Church in May 1891, the same

Assembly which vetoed Briggs' professorial chair.[94] Soon after delivering his address in the Marble Church, Green revised it in an enlargened version and published it in *The Presbyterian Quarterly*.[95] A wider audience for the lecture was thus secured, just as with Briggs' inaugural lecture.

Green took little time for rhetorical amenities before plunging into the perils of higher criticism. He sought to identify with the congregation by declaring in introductory remarks that the Bible is what the church has always believed it to be because of its "marvellous miracles," and "accurately fulfilled prophecies."[96] Very little strategy is obvious in respect to structure or style, though specific arguments are often phrased so as to elicit audience support. Since the topic created so much excitement at the time, and since Green both spoke and wrote for an audience who agreed with him, his singular attention to the arguments seems justified.

Green identified as the crux of the dispute the fact that he held as crucial the Mosaic authorship of the Pentateuch while the higher critics did not. He could not conceive how these materials were inspired if authored by anyone other than Moses. Green discussed certain arguments of Briggs' lecture, but likely not as direct refutation. He was more exercised by the larger higher criticism movement. On various occasions he identified positions but seldom by naming persons. He referred to Briggs once, but probably had in mind positions found in Briggs' books.[97]

Green's chief claim was that, despite higher criticism, attributed authorship does matter. Biblical criticism is essential, but destructive when undercutting authorship authenticity.[98] The only way for the Pentateuch to be God's inspired Word is that Moses be author. A document, he declared, is valid only insofar as its attributed source is authenticated. If Moses is the author of the Pentateuch, the historical truth of the books is beyond controversy. Green, interestingly, did not argue that the Pentateuch claims Mosaic authorship, but rather he cites Jesus in the New Testament as the basis for this claim.[99] The critical position, he declared, proposes four authors for the Pentateuch but in turn relinquishes the advantage of Moses' authority, for nothing about them is known. The documentary hypothesis places these authors three to nine hundred years after the events. Obviously Moses as a contemporary would supply far greater credibility. The whole question, Green declared, is larger than the critics like to make out, namely, that they are simply questioning inspiration in small details. He admitted that parts of the histories were written centuries after the events, but the authors such as Moses and Ezra used documents, whereas no such claim is made for the four authors from whom the Pentateuch is said to be compiled.[100]

Green argued at length that the composition of the Pentateuch proposed by the higher critics undercut its accuracy as history, and if not accurate history, how can it be inspired? He also questioned the approach to separating the documents. The literary critics assume the documents are identifiable by differences of style and diction. Green shows how these delineations are fraught with perils.[101] The four document hypothesis is constructed in such a manner, Green declared, so as to imply the untrustworthiness of the documents as well as the editor who brought them together. He showed that when critics discover two similar events, for example, Abraham's statement that Sarah is his sister, they assume different accounts of a singular occurrence. The critic thus proceeds to reconstruct what really happened by putting aside the differences. The assumption is that only the details shared in common by the accounts are valid. A strange doctrine of inspiration results, Green contended, if we are to accommodate contradictory embellishments.

If these Pentateuchal documents, as they describe them, were inspired, it must have been in a very peculiar sense. It is not a question of inerrancy, but of wholesale mutual contradiction which quite destroys their credit as truthful histories.[102]

Furthermore, as the critics tell it, even the editors are implicated for they added and deleted materials according to their interests and whims. The result is that one cannot even be certain that what the critics sort out as the four documents is what was originally written. If all these uncertainties obtain, then asks Green,

Must we not say that the history of the Mosaic age, if this be the only way of arriving at it, rests upon a quicksand? and that nothing of any consequence can be certainly known regarding it?[103]

For these reasons Green felt justified in calling higher criticism "Anti-biblical Criticism."[104]

Green concludes by requesting notice of how much in abeyance the critics leave matters important to faith. Under such circumstances how is it possible for higher criticism to "encourage faith in Scriptures and a reverent submission to its authority"?

Green located the crux of the American dispute in a remarkable way. He did so in a manner which challenged scholars, yet which enabled nonspecialists to follow the arguments. Green represented the positions of the critics justly without making spurious claims such as accusing them of scepticism in disguise. He did not belittle their commitment to Christianity, but argued that they themselves were not fully aware of the implications of their positions.[105] Green met the critical positions head on.

In some cases later scholarship modified its claims along lines proposed by Green, though not likely as the result of his rebuttal.

At this stage of the higher criticism movement both experts and laypersons evinced an intense interest in the details of the argument. The doors for communication are still open though feelings are running high. The persons of the various presuppositions still speak with each other. Positions are still being clarified and minds won over.

George Plattenburg

Interest in the documentary hypothesis was not restricted to the eastern seaboard. In 1890 George Plattenburg, a Christian Church minister, presented a lecture, "Who Wrote the Pentateuch?" to a group of churchmen at the Missouri Christian Lectures.[106] The annual lectures began in 1881 and were hosted by a different church each year. The 1890 lectureship was held at the church in Marshall, Missouri, of which Plattenburg was minister.[107] Discussion of Biblical criticism could be found in Christian Church journals as early as 1880. Three years before the Plattenburg address, George W. Longan published an article in *The Christian-Evangelist* (a St. Louis journal) advocating the documentary hypothesis.[108] Longan's article created some stir, but no great rancor.[109] Plattenburg opposed higher criticism, but without mentioning proponents in his own fellowship.[110] He identified several critics by name, but all were German, British, or Dutch.

Plattenburg's lecture, because of the absence of attention getting devices, presupposes an audience intensely interested in the topic.[111] Not all those present agreed with Plattenburg's conclusions, but the majority did.[112] He commenced the lecture by setting forth the documentary view of the origin of the Pentateuch. He did this lucidly and fairly, citing statements from proponents of the hypothesis. After about five minutes he turned to disagree with these "anti-traditionalists" as he called them. He focused more on the developmental view of Israel's religion than on the documentary hypothesis, but failed to make this distinction since in his time the two were thought to go hand in hand.[113]

The address was essentially an attack on the thesis that Israel's religion shows progressive development. A typical position of the higher critics was that early Israel affirmed a primitive polytheism which she gradually cast off until reaching the apex of theology in the ethical monotheism of the great prophets. It was further assumed that various vestiges of these developments could be found in the Old Testament itself. Plattenburg first responded by citing Deuteronomy 6:4 as proof of the one God idea in early Israel. The point was telling for those who dated Deuteronomy as early as

Moses, but the critics placed it much later. Plattenburg was usually more careful however, to rebut the critics on their own grounds. His second charge was that there is no evidence for any religion developing from a primitive to a higher form.[114] Third, he charged that evolutionary development ejects the supernatural from history. He further contended that the religion of Israel was not a straight line of growth, but action and reaction.[115] The reactions were not pressing ahead to new truths, as the critics required, but a return to the old ones.[116] Fifthly, Plattenburg argued that monotheism appeared in the early days of Israel. In fact, it could be found in Egypt in 3000 B.C. Therefore, it is not surprising that a group, such as the Israelites, left Egypt with monotheistic beliefs. As a sixth argument, Plattenburg observed that some critics think the various names for God show development. He declared that divine names were employed biblically in such a manner so they cannot be catalogued chronologically. The work on the names is not scientific, he declared, despite the critics, since conclusions are established by rearranging the data to make it come out right. He also objected to the minute scraps of documents professed as identifiable.[117]

A major argument of Plattenburg was that internal evidence in the Old Testament itself indicates that law codes existed in Israel before the days of Josiah and Ezra. The point is telling since Wellhausen and others argued that major law codes in Israel were all compiled after 600 B.C. He first claimed that the book of Joshua presupposes the existence of Mosaic law. But on this point the critics denied the essential historicity of Joshua. He also noted that as reported in the histories, laws were present in the days of David and the prophets. Furthermore, the book of Ezra indicates that law codes existed before his time. Plattenburg's implication, though inexplicit, was that if Old Testament documents presuppose ancient law codes, then despite Wellhausen they go all the way back to Moses.

Plattenburg ended his lecture by citing both the Old and New Testaments in support of the Mosaic authorship of the Pentateuch. He was aware that the Pentateuch nowhere claims the whole for Mosaic authorship, but he cites the New Testament as conclusive proof. If one accepts the self claims of Scriptures, and Americans traditionally did, then Plattenburg's proof was forceful. But higher critics themselves were not always impressed with internal authorship claims.

CONCLUSIONS

By 1875 news began to filter to church members that scholars were at work reconstructing traditional views of the Scriptures. Sermons in the ten years following gave recognition, but superficially, to the disputes going on in academe. Popular discourses were more designed to win adherents or comfort the troubled, than ascertain what truths might reside in these new approaches to the Bible. But by 1890, several had been won to higher criticism so that disputants could easily be located on either side. By this time too, the issues had become more clearly delineated. In this new stage more and more persons were familiar with the intricate arguments. Audiences were now prepared to sit through detailed discussions, and preachers explored these matters in depth. After a few years the lines hardened. Soon religious leaders ceased communicating. Even scholars sealed themselves off from each other. These conditions prevailed until the rise of neo-orthodoxy and biblical theology in the early forties.[118] The movements for and against higher criticism crystallized, resulting in modernist and fundamentalists camps. After the turn of the century, pulpit discussion of these critical matters once again became cursory and superficial. Neither side felt an obligation to communicate with the other, nor prolong the earlier disputes.

NOTES

1. For the standard German histories see the bibliography in Hans W. Frei, *The Eclipse of Biblical Narrative* (New Haven: Yale University Press, 1974).
2. The famous Presbyterian Five Points of the "Portland Deliverance," (1892) made clear these concerns. See also Sydney E. Ahlstrom's monumental *A Religious History of the American People* (New Haven: Yale University Press, 1972), pp. 763–824.
3. These are umbrella terms covering smaller groupings. See Ahlstrom, *Religious History*, p. 788.
4. "The Rhetoric of Historical Movements," *Quarterly Journal of Speech* 38 (April 1952): 184–188. Griffin identifies three stages in a movement: (1) the period of inception when men are becoming dissatisfied with their environment and begin using speech to attempt a change, (2) a period of rhetorical crisis when the balance between those favoring the change and those opposing it is disturbed by a radical change in the rhetorical strategy by one side or the other, (3) a period of consummation when it succeeds or fails and then comes to an end. Only the first two stages of the higher criticism movement are discussed here.
5. (New York: Charles Scribner's Sons, 1917). Clarke (1841–1912) a Baptist, was minister in several churches in the northeast, then professor of New Testament Interpretation, Baptist Theological Seminary, Toronto 1883, and Professor of Christian Theology, Colgate Seminary 1890–1912.
6. Ahlstrom, *Religious History*, p. 788.
7. See also Clifford E. Clarke, Jr., "The Changing Nature of Protestantism in

Mid-nineteenth Century America: Henry Ward Beecher's Seven Lectures to Young Men," *Journal of American History* 57 (1971): 832–846.

8. Clarke, *Sixty Years*, pp. 18–20.

9. Thomas Paine, *The Age of Reason* (Boston: Thomas Hall, 1794) and Ethan Allen, *Reason, The Only Oracle of Man: or a Compendious System of Natural Religion* (Bennington, Vt., 1784). See also Herbert Monfort Morais, *Deism in Eighteenth Century America* (New York: Columbia University Press, 1934).

10. Clarke, *Sixty Years*, pp. 31ff. John Bascom's *Science, Philosophy, and Religion* (New York: Scribners, 1871) shows the significance of science.

11. The interest is obvious in the journals, e.g. William W. Patton, "The Tendency of Scientific Men to Skepticism," *Methodist Quarterly Review* 44 (Jan. 1862): 541–560; Andrew P. Peabody, "The Bearing of Modern Scientific Theories on the Fundamental Truths of Religion," *Bibliotheca Sacra*, 21 (1864): 710–724; and C. H. Hitchcock, "The Relations of Geology to Theology," 24 (1867): 429–481.

12. The articles on evolution in the religious periodicals are almost inexhaustible. Among them are Frederic Gardiner, "Darwinism," *Bibliotheca Sacra* 29 (1872): 240–288; George D. Armstrong, "Darwin and Darwinism," *Presbyterian Quarterly* 3 (1889): 334–351; and W. J. Wright, "A Generation of Darwinism," 7 (1893): 223–241.

13. Clarke, *Sixty Years*, pp. 56 f.

14. Ibid.

15. Julius Wellhausen, *Prolegomena to the History of Ancient Israel*, (Edinburgh: Adam & Charles Black, 1885).

16. Wellhausen dated the Jahwistic source in the 9th century B.C., the Eloistic in the 8th century, and the Priestly in the 5th. The position of Wellhausen is essentially that affirmed by Old Testament scholars today.

17. T. DeWitt Talmage, "The Folly of Infidelity," *500 Selected Sermons* (Grand Rapids: Baker Book House, 1956), 4:40. Cf. Ira V. Brown, "The Higher Criticism Comes to America, 1880–1900," *Journal of the Presbyterian Historical Society* 38 (December, 1960): 195, "Higher Criticism and the theory of evolution went hand in hand, and both were kin to the idea of progress."

18. Clarke returned to the subject repeatedly. See *Sixty Years*, pp. 59–63, 133, 196–200.

19. See Charles Hodge, *Systematic Theology* (New York: Charles Scribner's Sons, 1873), 1:152, for a standard statement on inspiration. See also J. H. Thayer, *The Change of Attitude Towards the Bible* (Boston: Houghton Mifflin and Co., 1891). Cf. I. P. Warren, "The Inspiration of the Old Testament," *Bibliotheca Sacra*, 41 (1884): 310–326.

20. Clarke, *Sixty Years*, p. 198. See also p. 178 for the way Clarke characterizes the Bible.

21. Ibid., pp. 173 ff.

22. Wellhausen, *History of Ancient Israel*, pp. 188–192. For Wellhausen the prophets stood higher theologically than the law which was a later development.

23. In 1811 Buckminster was appointed Dexter Lecturer on Biblical Criticism at Harvard, but died before he could take up the position. In 1807 he brought back 3000 volumes of European books on the Bible and Biblical criticism. Jerry Wayne Brown, *The Rise of Biblical Criticism in America*, 1800–1870 (Middletown: Wesleyan University Press, 1969), pp. 19–26. Stuart (1780–1852) taught at rival Andover Seminary and was generally conservative, but read German works and was open to the new studies. Jerry W. Brown, pp. 94–110.

24. Ibid., pp. 35–44. Both Everett and Bancroft studied under Johann Gottfried Eichhorn (1752–1827) who is called the father of higher criticism, a term he popularized. For others who studied in Germany between 1815 and 1850 see H. M. Hinsdale, "Notes on the History of Foreign Influences upon Education in the United States," *Report of the Commissioner of Education 1897–98*, 1:591–629.

25. A. A. Hodge, *The Life of Charles Hodge* (New York: Charles Scribner's Sons, 1880), pp. 114 ff.

26. Notices in the journals show this. In *Bibliotheca Sacra* founded in 1844 by Andover Seminary prefessors one finds statistics of theological students in European Universities 2 (1845): 199–200 and teachers 4 (1847): 209–216. *The Methodist Quarterly Review* lists lectures in Berlin 32 (1851): 178–179 and information on German books and schools 31 (1849): 162–174 and 37 (1856): 305–309. Almost regular notices of the German Universities may be found in these journals.

27. Albert Bernhardt Faust, *The German Element in the United States* (Boston: Houghton Mifflin Co., 1909), 2:231.

28. Carl E. Hatch, *The Charles A. Briggs Heresy Trial* (New York: Exposition Press, 1969). The term "higher criticism" was not widely used in America until Briggs' time. He was at the forefront of the movement to secure its approval, but he by no means introduced the discipline as we have already shown. Briggs attended Union Theological Seminary 1861–63. In 1866 he went to Berlin where, after four years, he took a doctorate in Old Testament. He studied under Hengstenberg who, according to Briggs was "the last great champion of traditionalism in the Old Testament." Briggs further related that "Hengstenberg himself convinced him in his own lecture-room that he was defending a lost cause." Briggs soon yielded to the documentary view of the Hexateuch against his own desires because of the insuperable arguments. Charles Augustus Briggs, *The Higher Criticism of the Hexateuch* (New York: Charles Scribner's Sons, 1893), p. 62.

29. Lefferts A. Loetscher, *The Broadening Church* (Philadelphia: University of Pennsylvania, 1954), p. 39.

30. Samuel Ives Curtiss, "Sketches of Pentateuch Criticism," 41 (1884): 1–23; 660–697; 42 (1885): 291–326. Also "A Symposium on the Antediluvian narratives . . . Delitzsch, Haupt, Dillman," 159 (1883): 501–530.

31. Robert Green Ingersoll (1833–1899) was the self-educated son of a Congregational minister. He practiced law in Peoria, Washington, D.C. and New York. He was well known in the 1880s for his lectures against religion which drew enormous crowds. See Wayland Maxfield Parrish and Alfred Dwight

Huston, "Robert G. Ingersoll" in *A History and Criticism of American Public Address*. William Norwood Brigance, ed. (New York: McGraw-Hill, 1943), 1:363–386.

32. *The Works of Robert G. Ingersoll*, ed. Clinton P. Farrell (New York: The Ingersoll League, 1900), 2:vi. One such response was a collection of replies edited by J. B. McClure, *Mistakes of Ingersoll* (Chicago: Rhodes & McClure, 1879) in which various Chicago Churchmen reacted to the famous lecture.

33. T. DeWitt Talmage (1832–1902) attended the University of the City of New York, studied law for a time, then graduated from New Brunswick Seminary in 1856. When he commenced in Brooklyn, in 1869, 35 persons attended, but soon there were thousands.

34. At the height of Talmage's career his sermons were printed in 3500 papers. The sermons are in T. DeWitt Talmage, *The Brooklyn Tabernacle* (New York: Funk and Wagnalls 1884), pp. 93–120. They are delivered on successive Sunday Mornings from January 15– February 12, and on February 26, 1882. The pagination in this essay are to Talmage, *500 Selected Sermons*.

35. They appear in *The Works of Ingersoll*, 5:25–359. In the preface Ingersoll stated that his friends advised him not to pay any attention to the sermons, but after thinking the matter over he "became satisfied that my friends were mistaken. . . ." Ingersoll wrote this preface in April, 1882.

36. *Works of Ingersoll*, 2:242.

37. Parrish and Huston noted, "Ingersoll had three chief weapons of argument: ridicule, appeal to reason, and vehement assertation. Perhaps the greatest of these was ridicule." p. 378.

38. Parrish and Huston observe, "Ingersoll's speeches have no uniform plan of organization. Often they seem to have no plan at all but merely follow a loose chain of association . . ." p. 380. In "Some Mistakes of Moses" Ingersoll follows the six days of creation, then makes random comments through Genesis and Exodus and into Numbers.

39. *Works of Ingersoll*, 2:21, 22.

40. Ibid., 2:20.

41. Ibid., 2:23.

42. Ibid., 2:46. Thomas Hobbes (1588–1679) held that only those sections attributed to Moses were authored by him. Spinoza (1632–1677) and Spanish exegete Ibn Ezra (1092–1167) held that E:.ra wrote the Pentateuch.

43. Ibid., 2: 114, 115, 128. Clarke (1762–1832) a British Methodist published his famous commentary in 1810–26.

44. Henry (1662–1714) a Britisher wrote a commentary in 1708–10.

45. *Works of Ingersoll*, 2:218 ff. Cruden (1701–1770) a Scot best known for his concordance that appeared in 1737.

46. Ibid., 2: 115, 156. Scott (1747–1821) was a Britisher who published his *Holy Bible* in 1788–92.

47. Talmage, *500 Selected Sermons*, p. 83.

48. *Works of Ingersoll*, 2:176.

49. Ibid., 2:179.

50. Ibid., 2:253.

51. Ibid., 2:111, 112.
52. Ibid., 2: 232, 233.
53. He referred to geologists on the epochs of earth, but not by name. Later he cited names of persons who had enriched the insights on evolution: "Lamarck, Goethe, Darwin, Haeckel and Spencer . . ." Ibid., 2:96.
54. Ibid., 2:67, 68.
55. Ibid., 2: 242.
56. Talmage, *500 Selected Sermons*, p. 26.
57. See Talmage's account of talking with a man about his college student son in Cleveland. Ibid., p. 100.
58. Ibid., p. 60.
59. Ibid., p. 84.
60. Ibid., p. 85.
61. Ibid., p. 86. John Mill (1645-1707) a Britisher who did considerable work on the Greek text of the New Testament and as a New Testament Translator.
62. Ibid., p. 28.
63. Ibid., p. 29.
64. Ibid., p. 30.
65. Ibid., pp. 41-43.
66. Ibid., p. 87.
67. Beecher (1813-1887) was educated at Amherst and Lane Theological Seminary. Minister of Plymouth Church Brooklyn from 1847-1887. He was heralded as an advocate of evolution and scientific Biblical criticism. See Lionel Crooker, "Henry Ward Beecher," in *History and Criticism of American Public Address*, 1:270.
68. Henry Ward Beecher, *Bible Studies in the Old Testament* (New York: F. H. Revell, 1892). Concerning the sermons, T. J. Ellinwood wrote in the preface, "These lectures were not published immediately after their delivery because at that time a series of Mr. Beecher's morning sermons was being issued in his paper, *The Christian Union*; but, following my usual custom as reporter of his utterances, I preserved full stenographic notes of them." p. iii.
69. Ibid., p. 11.
70. Beecher did not use "higher criticism" apparently because the term was not as yet in the popular vocabulary.
71. Ibid., p. 11.
72. Ibid., p. 12.
73. Ibid., p. 14.
74. Ibid., p. 15.
75. Ibid., p. 16.
76. Ibid., p. 27.
77. Ibid., p. 50.
78. His claim sounds something like earlier fragmentary hypotheses, but even Alexander Geddes of Scotland in *Critical Remarks* (1800) denied Mosaic authorship.
79. Beecher, *Bible Studies*, p. 57.

80. Charles Farace, "The History of Old Testament Higher Criticism in the United States," (Ph.D. diss., University of Chicago, 1939).
81. See Loetscher, pp. 29–74.
82. Lyman Abbott in his *The Life and Literature of the Ancient Hebrews* (Boston: Houghton Mifflin Co., 1901) wrote, "I have followed the lines and used freely the material employed on the course of Sunday evening lectures on the Old Testament given in Plymouth Church, Brooklyn, N.Y., in the winter of 1896–97 . . ." p. vi.
83. For backgrounds see Loetscher, *Broadening Church*, pp. 48–53 and Carl E. Hatch, *The Charles A. Briggs Heresy Trial*.
84. Loetscher, *Broadening Church*, p. 51.
85. Ibid., p. 52.
86. C. A. Briggs, "The Authority of Holy Scripture," in *Inspiration and Inerrancy* (London: James Clarke & Co., 1891) p. 39.
87. Ibid., p. 51.
88. Ibid., p. 65.
89. Ibid., p. 49.
90. Ibid., p. 82.
91. Loetscher, *Broadening Church*, p. 54.
92. Especially *Whither? A Theological Question for the Times* (1899) and *Biblical Study, its Principles, Methods, and History* (1883).
93. *The Presbyterian Quarterly*, 6 (1892): 341–359. The church was a conservatively oriented Presbyterian congregation of which James David Burrell was minister. Green (1825–1900) graduated from Lafayette College, and received a B.D. at Princeton Seminary in 1846. He was professor of Old Testament at Princeton from 1851 until his death.
94. Loetscher, *Broadening Church*, pp. 53–55.
95. "The Anti-Biblical Higher Criticism," *The Presbyterian Quarterly* 6 (1892): 341.
96. Ibid.
97. Ibid., p. 345.
98. Ibid., p. 342.
99. Ibid., p. 343.
100. Old Testament scholars have increasingly argued that authors of the documents depended on earlier materials, some perhaps going back to the age of Moses and before. See John Bright, *A History of Israel*, 2nd ed. (Philadelphia: The Westminster Press, 1972), pp. 68–76.
101. Green "The Anti-Biblical," p. 349.
102. Ibid., p. 353 f.
103. Ibid., p. 357.
104. Ibid., p. 359.
105. Ibid., p. 358 f.
106. This lecture is found in J. W. Monser, et al., eds., *The Missouri Christian Lectures*, (St. Louis: Christian Publishing Company, 1892), pp. 84–130.
107. F. D. Powers, "Washington Letter," *Christian Standard*, 25 (July 26, 1890):

491. Cf. G. A. Hoffmann, "Missouri Christian Lectures," *The Christian-Evangelist*, (July 24, 1890): 473.

108. George W. Longan, "Higher Criticism," *The Christian-Evangelist* (Jan. 20, 1887): 36 f.

109. Anthony Ash, "Old Testament Studies in the Restoration Movement," *Restoration Quarterly* 9 (1966) pp. 216–228, and especially, "Part II: From 1887 to 1892;" 10 (1967) pp. 25–29.

110. Plattenburg (1828–1904) was born in Wellsburg, Va. He graduated from Bethany College, founded by Alexander Campbell, in 1851. He commenced preaching in 1855 and so spent the remainder of his years, mostly in Missouri. He read widely and apparently had some knowledge of German. Monser, *The Missouri Christian Lectures*, p. 96.

111. Powers in his *Christian Standard* report spent more time on the contents of Plattenburg's lecture than any of the others. p. 491.

112. G. A. Hoffmann, associate editor of *The Christian-Evangelist* spoke well of the lecture, but said that ". . . a few may not have at all times agreed with his conclusion." (July 24, 1890): 473. Hoffmann wished to foster an irenic climate for the subject.

113. See J. J. M. Roberts, "The Decline of the Wellhausen Reconstruction of Israelite Religion," *Restoration Quarterly*, 9 (1966): 229–240.

114. Monser, *The Missouri Christian Lectures*, p. 87.

115. Ibid., p. 89.

116. At this point Plattenburg refers to Bissell. Edwin Cone Bissell (1832–1894) in 1892 professor at McCormick Seminary in Chicago, wrote *The Pentateuch Its Origin and Structure* (New York: Charles Scribner's Sons, 1885).

117. Monser, *The Missouri Christian Lectures*, p. 96 f.

118. See Brevard S. Childs, *Biblical Theology in Crisis* (Philadelphia: Westminster Press, 1970).

V

THE INTELLECTUALS
TRY TO REVITALIZE
SOCIETY

12

The Protests of Writers and Thinkers

MARY GRAHAM

Politicians, literary figures, and reformers thronged to the lecture platform during the decade before and the decade after the American Civil War. Lyceums and library associations provided the audiences—and a supplementary income for many of the great and near-great. When the development of the railroads made it possible by 1858 to visit Chicago from New York without changing trains, almost three hundred lecturers advertised their willingness—even their eagerness—to spread before midwestern audiences their moralistic and cultural interests.

The Civil War brought a halt to such activities. Not long after the end of the war, however, James Redpath organized his Boston Lyceum Bureau in 1869. Lecturing revived and became a big business proposition.

From the many writers who frequented the lecture platform in the last three decades of the nineteenth century, four men were selected for special attention. All are better known for their writing than for their speaking, but it was their speaking—particularly their appearances on the lecture platform—that also commanded attention. The first is the universally known and almost universally admired Samuel L. Clemens, "Mark Twain." The second is George Washington Cable, a southern writer whose descriptions of Creole life in New Orleans brought him widespread attention in his own day. The third is Edward Bellamy, best remembered for his Utopian novel, *Looking Backward*. And last comes the prophet of San Francisco, the great single taxer Henry George.

What did these four great writers and speakers have in common? The answer is simple: they were far ahead of their times, and their imaginative thinking gave them widespread appeal. Mark Twain, the satirist, advocated women's rights, spoke against corruption in government, and was bitter in his opposition to imperialism. George Washington Cable had little influence on race relations in his own day, but in our times he is accepted as an early leader in the fight for civil rights. Edward Bellamy's *Looking Backward* is still widely read, and during the 1930s Bellamy Clubs flourished in the West. Urban renewal owes much to Henry George, whose theories of taxation play their part in providing recreation and other centers for blighted areas. One cannot say that the four men were practical men in the usual sense of the word, but it can be argued that men of vision and imagination are the real leaders of reform and change.

SAMUEL L. CLEMENS

In the early autumn of 1869 Samuel L. Clemens ("Mark Twain") became a hundred-dollar man for the Boston Lyceum Bureau of James Redpath. Former printer, steamboat pilot, soldier, miner, and newspaper reporter, Twain had already achieved a national reputation before he joined Redpath. Letters to the Sacramento *Union* from the Sandwich Islands, to the *New York Tribune* from the Quaker City-Holy Land tour, and from Washington to the *New York Tribune*, *Post*, and *Herald*, coupled with stories in *Harper's* and his famous *Jumping Frog* (published as a book in 1867), established him as a humorous author. Lecturing in California, New York, and Brooklyn had given him confidence in facing an audience and charming it into submission.[1]

All that he was to write, except for his return to the Mississippi River of his boyhood, was to be merely an expression and consolidation of his life on the frontier and its culmination in San Francisco. His ability to relate tall tales, his travel reports, his knowledge of human nature, his humor, and his ability to observe and report accurately were shown in his writings in San Francisco and Sacramento.[2] By 1866, when he left California for the first time, "the frontier, having completed him, was done with him forever."[3]

The same frontier also molded his lecturing activities. His famous speech on the Sandwich Islands, first delivered in San Francisco on October 2, 1866, was to be his basic lecture. In the same period he established his methods of publicizing his lectures, his drawling delivery, his informality on the platform, and his extravagant methods of travel.[4]

Eager to establish himself in literary circles and anxious to earn money, Twain began his lecturing career after returning to New York from San Francisco in 1866. His final lecture tour was in 1873, when he delivered "Our Fellow Savages of the Sandwich Islands" and "Roughing It" before enthusiastic English audiences.

Twain's first lecture tour after he deserted California was the tour of 1868–1869. Most of his engagements came by his own efforts or through the booking of the Western Library Association of Dubuque, Iowa. His subject: "The American Vandal Abroad"[5] was based on his forthcoming book *Innocents Abroad*. In this lecture he gently chided the American traveler who was not elaborately educated, cultivated and refined, and gilded and filigreed with the ineffable graces of the first society.[6] He ended with a moral, as he always did if requested. On this occasion he advised Americans to travel because travel liberalized them. Since *Innocents Abroad* had been published by the end of the season, he never used the lecture again. It had served its purpose.

The winter of 1869–70 found Twain on the lyceum circuit once more, but under the Redpath management. His lecture was his old favorite: "The Sandwich Islands," now usually called "Our Fellow Savages of the Sandwich Islands."[7] Originally the lecture had grown out of his travel letters to the Sacramento *Union*. First delivered in San Francisco, it was sometimes savage and coarse in its humor. Revised for this tour, its satirical tone was less savage, particularly in its treatment of missionaries.[8] The season was most successful, but Twain wanted no more of the confining and lonely life of the lecture circuit. He wrote to Redpath, saying that he was out of the field permanently.

He kept his vow for one year. In late July, 1871, dissatisfied with his connections on the *Buffalo Express* and needing money for his move to Hartford, he agreed with Redpath that he would lecture during the winter of 1871–72. The season was to prove to be his "most detestable campaign." He attempted to write two lectures, one of which: "Artemus Ward,"[9] he used for about six weeks. In sheer desperation he wrote "Roughing It,"[10] a synopsis of his soon-to-be published book by the same name. It was a natural choice, for he was reading proof at the time. Certainly the lecture was successful. And it enabled him to advertise his book quite openly. In Grand Rapids, he "informed his audience that he had a book in press, a book of six hundred pages, the style the same as in *Innocents Abroad*, splendidly illustrated, and costing only . . . but he wasn't canvassing for the book. No, only if they wished it, he could read from forty to fifty pages of it from memory, or indeed the whole 600 pages."[11]

Although Redpath pleaded with him to lecture during the winter of 1872–73, Twain had other plans. He left the United States for England on August 31, hoping to gather material for a book similar to *Innocents Abroad* and to secure a copyright for *Roughing It*. Amid the social activity he arranged with George Dolby, the English impresario, for a brief series of lectures. In October he gave his old favorite: "Our Fellow Savages of the Sandwich Islands." On December 9 he changed to his new lecture: "Roughing It On The Silver Frontier." Both were rewritten for the English audience, particularly the second, as he realized that the English knew little, if anything, about Nevada.[12] Reviews and comments were laudatory, praising the vast amount of information as well as the delivery and humor.[13]

Upon his return from England, Twain informed Redpath that he would under no circumstances ever return to the lecture circuit. In reality he had decided while on tour with "An American Vandal Abroad" "that the platform would do as an occasional money-maker in an emergency, but he didn't want it for his lifework."[14] He disliked the traveling, the hotels, and, most of all, the loneliness. Such a resolution did not mean that he never spoke in public again, for Twain was a compulsive talker. From this time on, however, he chose the occasion, the time, and the audience. His books and his reputation as a humorous speaker gave him all the occasions he desired.

Twain did go on two more tours, but not as a lecturer; as a reader of his own works. The establishment of his own publishing house and the forthcoming publication of *The Adventures of Huckleberry Finn* prompted him to arrange a joint tour with George Washington Cable under the auspices of J. B. Pond for the winter of 1884–85. The plan was that Twain would read from *Huckleberry Finn*, to be published in February, 1885, and Cable would relate selections from his Creole stories and novels. They performed more than a hundred times in eighty different cities during the four-month season. Twain's share of the profits was approximately $15,000.[15]

Ten years elapsed before he was compelled to go once more on tour. Bankruptcy of his publishing house in 1894 and the financial disaster with the Paige typesetter before that had forced him to live in Europe after 1890. With complete disaster facing him Twain planned a world tour, which took him to Australia, New Zealand, South Africa, and England. He again chose readings from his books, although he wove the readings together and called it "The Morals Lecture." By this time he had memorized and perfected more than seventy-five stories with which to vary his programs. The tour and the book, *Following the Equator*, which followed, enabled him to pay his debts, and he was a free man once more. Twain never lectured for payment again.

Although some, including J. G. Holland,[16] criticized Twain's lectures as being only humorous and not worthy of presentation on lyceum programs, an examination of the lectures shows that if one should eliminate the stories and other humorous lines, much information would remain. Descriptions of lands visited are certainly more definite and more beautiful than the moralistic travelogues of Ike Marvel, George William Curtis, and Bayard Taylor, so popular in the 1850s.

Nor was Twain's humor on the platform so barbed and pointed as in his books. Realizing that many of his lectures were given in churches or were sponsored by Y.M.C.A.s, he had no wish to offend his sponsors or his audiences.

One of Twain's great contributions to the reform of the lecture circuit was his recognition that the platform demanded a different style from that of the written word. As a result he always wrote his speeches, then memorized them. Adapting them to the audience, he constantly reworked his materials.[17]

Writing to his wife after attending a Chicago dinner in honor of Ulysses S. Grant, Twain said, "I heard four speeches which carried away all my wits and made me drunk with enthusiasm. When I look at them in print they didn't seem the same—their still sentences seem rather the prize dead forms of a ghost—Lord, there's nothing like the human organ to make words live and throb, and lift the hearer to the full attitudes of their meaning."[18]

The drawling voice, the dead-pan expression, the ambling walk, the self-introductions, all added to Twain's popularity. Those who have seen the performances of Hal Holbrook can testify to their power. Most important of all, nevertheless, was Twain's use of the pause, to him the most delicate and important part of telling a story.[19] As he used it and perfected his presentation, his audiences "simmered," not only at the manner, but also at the "throw-away" lines criticizing some event or issue of his times.[20] It is difficult at some points to be certain whether he is serious or not. And many of his criticisms, of course, varied from audience to audience and from time to time.

And so Twain became one of the most popular lecturers of his own "Gilded Age." Before the Civil War lecturers frequently spoke of morals or travel abroad or criticized English literature. During the Civil War reformers became popular. Now, with Redpath showing the way, the lyceum became more varied. Even musical events were included. Twain played his role in this reform of the lecture system by making humor popular and respectable. No longer was it necessary to feel that laughter was not useful.

Twain rarely spoke for payment after the British tour of 1872–73. But he did not cease to be interested in politics and social criticism. Elected to membership in the Monday Evening Club of Hartford in 1871, he read papers criticizing many aspects of American life, often expressing views not shared by its members. In addition he became extremely popular as an after-dinner speaker. And his interest in politics and government made him active in Republican politics. Government always was a serious business with Mark Twain.

From 1873 to 1885 Twain made few speeches, for these years were the period of his greatest artistic productivity. In addition he struggled to become a successful businessman, eager to make money for his expensive household. Most Americans shared this desire. His own publishing house, the Paige typesetter fiasco, and his consuming interest in all mechanical innovations led to his financial downfall. Convinced that he could live more cheaply abroad, he moved his family to Europe in 1877, remaining there until 1901.

Yet he was conscious throughout this period that his world was not going well, as *The Gilded Age* and *A Connecticut Yankee in King Arthur's Court* demonstrate. Fully aware that his main skill was writing, Twain spoke mainly on after-dinner occasions. His long absence from America also prevented him from stating his positions on the public platform, although his writings made him well-known as a critic of the evils of his age. As a matter of fact, he disliked professional reformers, saying that they often confused reform with force, calling it diplomacy.[21] He continued, however, to speak and write concerning the evils of his "Gilded Age" more than any other author of his time.[22]

The popularization of humor on the lecture platform was only one of Twain's innovations. He did not look to Europe for inspiration, as did many American authors who considered Europe to be the prime center of culture and cultivation. His speeches on the lyceum circuit were about America and Americans. On his reading tours he used stories from the South, West, and North.

Twain likewise cherished his pride as an American. Speaking in 1889 on "Foreign Critics" in an after-dinner speech, he declared that the American Revolution had planted the seed that brought on the French Revolution and improved freedom and liberty in England.[23] Appearing at the Lotos Club on November 12, 1893, he praised the Americans traveling in Europe, finding "that nearly all preserved their Americanism."[24] And he meant America and not any one section. Addressing the first annual dinner of the New England Society in Philadelphia on December 20, 1881, in one of his typically humorous toasts he mocked the pride of those descended from the Puritans, insisting that the Puritans were a hard lot and that most Americans came from mixed stock. He ended by emphasizing that New England virtues could not be improved upon "except having them born in America."[25] He never deviated from this belief.

Devotion to American interests led Twain to join those authors who were advocating reform of copyright laws. Soon after the publication of *A Connecticut Yankee in King Arthur's Court*, he went to Washington and lobbied for a revision of the copyright law in behalf of American writers.[26] He returned to the task in 1906, appearing before a congressional committee and presenting a well-organized case.[27]

On the whole few events in American life escaped Mark Twain's attention. As early as 1881, in a paper before the Hartford Monday Evening Club, he delivered a paper, including these remarks:

All that we require of a voter is that he shall be forked, wear pantaloons instead of petticoats, and bear a more or less humorous resemblance to the reported image of God . . . We brag of our universal, unrestricted suffrage; but we are shams after all, for we restrict when we come to the women.[28]

He repeated this viewpoint in 1901 before the annual meeting of the Hebrew Technical School for Girls.[29]

Improvement in the conditions of the southern freedman did not claim much of Twain's attention at this time. In all probability he acquiesced in the assumption that the lot of the Negro would improve with the times. To individual needs, however, he responded with his customary generosity. At Hartford he once gave a lecture composed of readings from his works before the African Methodist Church, permitting only Negroes to attend. On two other occasions he organized readings for the benefit of Father Hawley who labored with Negroes in Hartford.[30] On his return from his long stay abroad he spoke on "Taxes and Morals" on behalf of Tuskegee Institute, implying therein his approval of Booker T. Washington's views concerning the education of the Negro.[31]

In fact Twain was not much interested in the South as a region. He assumed that the nation was a unity. Not until February 11, 1900, did he mention the Civil War except in a humorous way. Introducing Colonel Watterson at a celebration of Lincoln's birthday in 1901,[32] he ended by saying:

We are here to honor the birthday of the greatest citizen, and the noblest and the best, after Washington, that this land or any other has yet produced. The old wounds are healed; you and we are brothers again; you testify by honoring the two of us, once soldiers of the Lost Cause and foes of your great and good leader—we are now indistinguishably fused together and namable by one common great name—Americans.[33]

Only one great reform movement of the late nineteenth century—the regulation of business—did not receive Mark Twain's endorsement on the platform. Three reasons seem to account for this omission. In the first place, he believed wholeheartedly in capitalism and in the right of every man to succeed by his own efforts. Business enthralled him. He had been a publisher and had financed the Paige typesetter. Second, he had been rescued from bankruptcy caused by these ventures by Henry H. Rogers, one of the chief architects of Standard Oil. Rogers and Andrew Carnegie became his friends, and he demonstrated his loyalty to them. Third, Mark

Twain lived mainly in Europe from 1887 to 1901, apart from the controversy.

As a matter of fact Twain knew little about laboring conditions in mills and mines and less concerning the vast profits accruing to their owners. He recognized the need of labor to organize as early as March 23, 1886. In a paper read before the Hartford Monday Evening Club he concluded his speech by saying that when all trades unite, the nation would see to it that there is fair play, work, hours, and wages.[34] Although advocating the eight-hour day in 1899, he had little conception of conditions among the poor. Not until 1901 did he even visit a settlement house.

Political reform obsessed Mark Twain throughout his long life. Ambivalent about the right to vote, sometimes favoring equality of voting rights and on other occasions stating that suffrage should be restricted, he likewise fluctuated in his attitude toward the press. He poked fun at the working press in his lecture "Roughing It."[35] His attitude had changed by 1873. In a paper presented to the Monday Evening Club he castigated the press for bad reporting, editorializing in the news columns, and lying journalists. He ended by saying:

I have a vague idea that there is too much liberty of the press in this country, and that through the absence of all wholesome restraint the newspaper has become in a large degree a national curse and will probably damn the Republic yet.[36]

Twain blamed the press for not reporting the widespread evils of government. He knew, however, that the disease was endemic. As a member of the "Third House" in California he had scored corruption in that state's legislature. He continued the fight in Hartford. Although personally idolizing President Grant, Twain nevertheless recognized that the federal government reeked with corruption. Part of the disease, he thought, was due to universal suffrage. The "damned human race" accounted for the remainder.

But Mark Twain believed in being active in politics. He campaigned vigorously for James Garfield in 1880, having satisfied himself that Garfield was "sound" on the tariff and the elimination of graft.[37] Presiding at a dinner in Boston after the election, he gloated over the results, saying, "The most important part of the victory was the election of Republican sheriffs . . . officers and criminals [were] on opposite sides!"[38] He supported Grover Cleveland in 1884 for the same reason, again making speeches for his chosen candidate.[39]

On his return to New York in 1900, Twain turned his attention to corruption in municipal government. Speaking before the St. Nicholas Society on December 6, 1900, he chastised the venality of the local government with savage satire. Sentences such as "you have the best municipal government in the world—the purest and the most fragrant" were frequent.[40] He continued his attack, gentler this time, before the City Club Dinner on January 4, 1901.[41] He campaigned vigorously against the Croker machine, making speeches and joining a parade when Croker was defeated.[42]

The Cleveland campaign forced Twain to reconsider his position on party loyalty. Reared in the Whig tradition, he joined the Republican Party on his arrival in the East. Doubts about Republican idealism assailed him after 1880, and the nomination of Blaine in 1884 compelled him to bolt the party in 1884. He became a mugwump and eloquently defended his position in vigorous campaign speeches.[43] Later that year he read a serious paper, "Consistency," before the Monday Evening Club, outlining and explaining his thoughts. Among other things, he said:

I am persuaded—convinced—that this idea of consistency—unchanging allegiance to Party—has lowered the manhood of the whole nation—pulled it down and dragged it in the mud.[44]

At the City Club dinner on January 4, 1901, he satirized regular party members by proposing an Anti-Doughnut Party, saying:

Now it seems to me that an Anti-Doughnut Party is just what is wanted in the present emergency. I would have the Anti-Doughnut felt in every city and hamlet and school district in this state and in the United States.[45]

The Spanish-American War impressed Twain at first as a noble cause. The treaty with the Philippines and his glimpse of the British Colonies in Africa and Asia, however, made him a strong anti-imperialist. On reaching America he stated his views candidly. Introducing young Winston Churchill to his first lecture audience in December, 1900, he could not resist saying, "I think that England sinned when she got herself into South Africa just as we have sinned in getting into a similar war in the Philippines."[46] A month earlier Twain praised the United States for supporting the Boxers in China.[47] Speeches were not enough. Vitriolic letters from Mark Twain flowed to the newspapers. He attempted to intercede at the State Department, maintaining that the Philippine's treaty should not be signed. And he refused to vote in 1904, so great was his feeling against American imperialism.

As one looks back over Mark Twain's long life, one perceives that he supported most of the reform movements of his times. In many ways he resembled a bumblebee, lighting on one interest and dropping it until a later time. He organized no reform movements, for he knew that authorship was his main career.

In a letter to Andrew Lang, he insisted that he had never "tried in even one single instance to help cultivate the cultivated classes. I was not equipped for it, either by native gifts or training. And I never had any ambition in that direction, but always hunted for bigger game—the masses."[48]

Current affairs interested him; long-range reforms he did not clearly understand. He put it this way in 1900: "The Twentieth Century is a stranger to me—I wish it well but my heart is all for my own century. I took 65 years of it—but if I had known as much about it as I know now I would have taken the whole of it."[49]

GEORGE WASHINGTON CABLE

The reading tour of Mark Twain and George Washington Cable in 1884–85 was for the former an easy way to earn money for his varied business enterprises; for Cable it was the financial and literary pinnacle of his long career. A southern writer, depicting Creole life in New Orleans, Cable had published four volumes by 1883. The fifth, *Dr. Senier*, appeared during the tour. His literary reputation was at least equal to that of Mark Twain. According to the *Critic*'s list of "forty immortals," published in 1884, Cable was ranked fifth, while Twain was fourteenth.[50]

Both men were accomplished readers. During the four-month tour, newspaper notices indicate that their humor was well received.[51] Twain went on to greater fame, while Cable gradually sank into obscurity because he possessed less creativity as a novelist and devoted most of his time to reform activities.

Cable, the foremost local-color novelist of the 1870s and 1880s, was self-educated. A son of slaveholders, orphaned at fourteen, a Confederate soldier, bookkeeper, reporter, and census computer, he observed the brawling city of New Orleans with keen eyes. He had seen slavery, Reconstruction, and the return of the Democrats to power. He pondered over the scene but said little until the early 1880s. In the meantime he wrote his stories and novels and developed his convictions.

A strict Presbyterian, Cable firmly believed in fighting evil. He expressed his attitude toward reform in "My Politics," writing:

It is my politics that a man *belongs* to the community in which he lives to whatever extent he can serve it, consistently with the fact of equal moment that he belongs to the nation and the human race to the extent of his power to serve them.[52]

Cable, an inveterate joiner, found his dictum easy to fulfill. This dismayed friends and editors who wished him to devote his time to his writing.

Prison reform was the first issue Cable felt free to discuss publicly in New Orleans and later throughout the South. A member of a grand jury in 1881, Cable had investigated the jails of New Orleans. On his eastern trips to visit editors and relatives he studied the prisons of Hartford, Boston, and New York. Successfully organizing a Permanent Prisons and Reform Association, he wrote and spoke for the closing of the local insane asylum, for the relocation of the orphans' home, and for complete municipal regulation of prison management.[53]

Impressed with the amount of reform still needed, Cable, with the assistance of Dr. I. T. Payne, sent questionnaires to all the parishes of Louisiana, requesting information about their penal institutions. He also queried various officials in the southern states on the same question. He discovered the practice of leasing convicts as laborers to private contractors, discussing his discoveries before the Congregational Club of New York on March 26, 1883. Because of this activity Cable was invited to address the National Conference of Charities and Corrections at the annual meeting in Louisville on September 26, 1883.

Cable's speech (a carefully written manuscript) proved him to be a masterful polemicist. Opening with a brief description of an ideal prison, he employed statistics and varied contrasts to recount the horrors of the convict-lease system. In an objective manner he presented rates of escape, death rates, and the ultimate effects upon society, referring to reports of prison officials. His main appeals were for justice, decency, and the public good.[54]

Cable's two-hour address was well received in most quarters. The report in Henry Matterson's *Louisville Courier Journal* said in part:

Mr. Cable is the ablest writer the South has had since Poe, and ranks as a novelist with Harrells and James . . . his paper lasted for two hours, and it is safe to say that during that time not a man but kept his eyes fixed upon the speaker. It is needless to say that the Southern author received an ovation.[55]

Editorials in the *New York Times* and *Tribune* were likewise laudatory.

Disliking his routine tasks in New Orleans, Cable by 1880 had decided to earn his livelihood by means of *belles-lettres*. For the next five years he wrote, lectured, and began to give readings from his own books. Although he was usually in debt, this did not trouble him unduly. His lectures on prison reform had made him famous, and he had become the best-known author in the Deep South. Early in 1884, however, he made two decisions that were to alienate him from his own region: First, he decided to move his family to the North because he needed to be closer to his publishers and his booking agent. The second decision—to speak out clearly on the subject of civil rights for the Negro—was more fatal to his reputation in the South.

Cable had made tentative steps in this direction as early as 1881. In an address delivered before the New Orleans Sunday School Association on April 4, 1881, he attacked the idea of class, declaring that "God does not judge people by classes any more than he saves them by classes."[56]

In the following year Cable delivered the commencement address at the University of Mississippi on June 28.[57] Carefully explaining that slavery and the plantation system had separated the South from most nineteenth-century thought and literature, he insisted that the region had broken with human progress. Pleading with the audience to rejoin the nation, he said:

There is a newly-coined name . . . the New South. It is a term only fit to indicate a transitory condition. What we want—what we ought to have in view—is the No South! . . . I trust that the time is not far away when anyone who rises before you and addresses you as "Southern" shall be stared at as the veriest Rip Van Winkle that the times can show.[58]

He ended his address by declaring that the caste system must be eliminated and that "all are to rule." His words were not challenged by the press.

Commendation greeted his commencement address at the University of Louisiana (later Tulane) on June 18, 1883. On this occasion Cable pleaded that young writers be given freedom to write openly about "their own state, possibly their own neighborhood without fear of undue criticism."[59]

Pleased with the acceptance of the two speeches, Cable decided that the time was ripe for an open discussion of Negro civil rights. He chose the commencement ceremonies at the University of Alabama on June 18, 1884, for a statement of his views. He spoke in favor of free public education for the Negro and against segregation in public accommodations. The press of Alabama unanimously disapproved.[60]

Believing that the question of civil rights needed national discussion and having kept his resolution to speak in the South before he stated his position in the North, Cable now felt free to accept an invitation from the American Social Service Association to address its annual meeting at Saratoga, New York, on September 11, 1884.[61] The manuscript speech, divided into ten parts, took two hours to deliver. Tracing the historical background and describing the situation in the South, Cable then attacked segregated transportation facilities,[62] discrimination in the courts and prisons,[63] and separation of the races in the schools.[64] The essay was published in the January, 1885, issue of *The Century Magazine*.

Even Cable had not foreseen the violence of the reaction in the South. Newspapers reviled him. He received almost one hundred letters calling him a traitor. The *Century* was deluged with complaints.[65] Undaunted by the furor, the editors of the *Century* asked Henry W. Grady to reply to the article. Grady's answer, "In Plain Black and White," insisted that the Negro was inferior in all ways but happy.[66] Cable's reply: "The Silent South," defending his position on civil rights, appeared five months later.[67] The dialogue pleased Cable, for he believed that the problem could be solved only if men felt free to discuss it.

During the next five years, Cable delivered about fifteen addresses and published as many articles espousing his cause. In Madison, Wisconsin, on October 29, 1885, he discussed the freedman's vote. Four months later, in New York City, he indicted northerners who did not favor education for Negroes. Addressing various groups in New England in 1886, he reminded his audiences that the entire nation shared the responsibility for slavery and its evil consequences. Late in November, 1888, he pleaded for opportunities for the Negro to use his vote. Nor was the church immune from his attacks. He asked the churches to accept Negroes as members.[68] Cable did not publish these speeches separately but incorporated them into a speech delivered before the Massachusetts Club in Boston on Washington's Birthday, 1890.[69] Granting the sincerity of most southerners, he maintained that a pure government depended on equal protection of citizens by public officials.

Cable attempted to speak in the South only once after the publication of his paper, "The Freedman's Case In Equity." Invited to give the literary commencement address at Vanderbilt University on June 14, 1887, Cable visited and traveled throughout the South. Mr. Pond, his agent, attempted to arrange a tour for Cable's readings but was unsuccessful except for readings given in Fayetteville and Chattanooga. Cable's address: "Faith of Our Fathers" delivered in Fayetteville and at Vanderbilt, was fairly well received, although most newspapers advised him not to advocate his cause in the South.[70] During this same period Cable conducted a large correspondence among southern sympathizers, requesting information about new restrictive laws. Many responded who did not wish to have their names associated with civil rights. Among them was Booker T. Washington.[71]

Nor did Cable alter his position when he spoke before Negro audiences. He urged them to vote, to organize, to educate themselves, and to support their own institutions.[72]

Cable's last speech on civil rights for Negroes was given before the Massachusetts Club in 1890. From this time on he separated himself so completely from the cause that he was not asked to be a sponsor of the

National Association for the Advancement of Colored People when it was founded in 1909.

Cable's main appeals throughout his crusade were for understanding and justice. His own character and earnestness aided his cause. He considered himself a moderate; for he never contended that the Negro was equal to the white man, nor did he ever ask for social equality of the races.

Was Cable's long crusade a failure? Perhaps. In the first place he was far ahead of his times. Men still struggle in behalf of his ideas. Secondly, he lacked full compassion for the oppressed.

Devoted to literature, admiring prominent people, he was incapable of understanding a class of people whom he considered to be inferior. Thirdly, he was a rigid person whom more worldly men found difficult to like or communicate with. As Mark Twain said, "You know that when it comes to moral honesty, limpid innocence, and utterly blameless piety, the apostles were mere policemen to Cable."[73] Nor did his physical appearance aid his cause. He never weighed more than 110 pounds. His nasal tenor voice did not carry conviction, although he took voice lessons throughout his public career and carried a trumpet, on which he practiced to develop his lung capacity.

Cable's failures, however, did not stifle his interest in reform. He conducted Bible classes in *The Busy Man's Bible* in 1891.[74] Organizing Home Culture Clubs in Northampton, he often spoke on literary topics before these groups, although he had little comprehension of the needs of factory employees.[75]

Again Cable retired to writing stories and novels; but he discovered that his interest in polemics had made imaginative writing almost impossible. Never out of debt to his publishers, he earned his precarious livelihood from long reading tours and small royalties. In the later years of his life he was dependent on his daughters and a gift from Andrew Carnegie.

EDWARD BELLAMY

New England and particularly Boston, so vibrant with ideas before the Civil War, seemed in many ways to lose its vitality in the 1870s and 1880s. Emerson, Longfellow, Motley, and Dana were dead; Whittier had retired; Holmes and Lowell were past their prime. As William Dean Howells realized, Boston authors had become local writers. Howells, believing in human equality, scandalized by vast differences between rich and poor, and sickened by political corruption, now felt that New England no longer was interested in political reform, democracy, or new industrial problems.[76]

Edward Bellamy's Utopian novel, *Looking Backward*, published in 1888, aroused Howell's enthusiasm. At last someone in New England envisaged the modern world much as he saw it. Ten thousand copies of *Looking Backward* were sold in 1888; 200,000 by 1890, about a million in the 1890s.[77] Based on the concept of the brotherhood of man and a socialistic form of government, the novel appealed to political reformers, to the economically depressed, and to advocates of social change.

Bellamy, son of a poor but well-educated family, student at Union College and in Germany, reporter in New York City, spent most of his adult life as editor and novelist in Springfield and Chicopee Falls, Massachusetts.[78] His early novels, written in the tradition of Hawthorne, did not forecast the radicalism of *Looking Backward*. Not only does the novel instruct the reader in the advantages of a new co-operative commonwealth and in the evils of competitive capitalism; it also exposes the weaknesses of private business, inefficiency in production, and the futility and misery experienced by rich and poor. Bellamy paints the glories of a co-operative system achieved without revolution, giving material prosperity to all, and promoting an enlarged and vital spiritual well-being. More successfully than any other novelist, Bellamy carried "our American democratic ideology over from politics into economics."[79]

Shortly after the publication of *Looking Backward*, prominent intellectuals in Boston suggested that steps be taken to promote Bellamy's program. Although he had not written the novel as a political tract, he was delighted to have his ideas discussed. As a result, the first Nationalist Club was organized in Boston in September, 1888. By January of 1890 there were 44 clubs in 14 states; in February, 1890, the clubs numbered 165.[80] After 1892 they declined rapidly as the theosophists and Bellamy drew apart and as other movements, such as populism, offered an easier and more direct program.

Bellamy made few speeches in his lifetime. He gave two before his local lyceum, others before the First Nationalist Club of Boston. This club was a friendly audience, since its members included William Dean Howells, Lucy Stone, Thomas Wentworth Higginson, Hamlin Garland, and Cyrus Field Willard.[81]

Bellamy's first speech, on "Plutocracy or Nationalism," was delivered at Tremont Temple on May 31, 1889, before 2,000 adherents to his cause. On this occasion he developed his economic argument. Attacking the competitive system, he maintained that it was non-Christian, did not make for the survival of the fit, was wasteful in production, and distributed work unfairly. He further argued that no return to the competitive world was possible for the poor or middle class. Outlining his ideal of a national government as a stock company for all citizens, he stated that his proposed socialistic society gave true economic equality, was evolutionary in method, and protected the weak, particularly women and children.[82]

The second address, "Nationalism—Principles and Purposes," was presented at the Nationalist Club anniversary in December 1889. Stating his premise that wealth is power, Bellamy proceeded to argue that equality had disappeared from American life because of the concentration of wealth, which in turn produced political corruption, inhuman contrasts of want and luxury, monopolies, and degradation of small businessmen and farmers.

Pleading for equality of all citizens, Bellamy then advocated the nationalization of railroads, telephone and telegraph services, express companies, and the mining of coal. In addition he asked for municipal ownership of lighting, heating, and street cars.

Bellamy offered his military organization of society as a remedy for such political and social inequality. He suggested that all services to the state be graded, that promotions be made only from the lower ranks, that no discharges be made without cause, that child labor be abolished, and that immigration from abroad be regulated. He further advocated absolute equality for women, temperance, and public ownership of all property.[83]

Both speeches aroused enthusiasm in his elitist audience. Indeed, Bellamy had a slightly condescending and custodial attitude toward the laboring man.[84] Certainly he hoped that his novel would be read by intellectuals. Much of his appeal lay in his wide knowledge of industrial conditions in America. He had seen the cotton and woolen mills of New England, the horrible working conditions, the immigrants, and extensive child labor.[85]

Bellamy's delivery also aided his cause. He read his manuscripts in an informal manner, but he spoke with "dignity and force, the deep chest tones of his pleasing voice slightly raised above conversational pitch."[86]

Invitations to speak came from other Nationalist clubs. For reasons of health, however, he was unable to accept them. Editing the *Nationalist* and *The New Nation* kept him in touch with the clubs, although he was well aware that he had never planned a political movement. He felt incapable of organizing a campaign.

Bellamy died in 1898 of tuberculosis. The Nationalist Clubs disappeared as other men advocated different methods of reform. But his novel *Looking Backward*, the basis of his speeches, initiated a Utopian debate that dominated much of the liberal reform movement until the close of the century.

HENRY GEORGE, THE PROPHET OF SAN FRANCISCO

Henry George was in many respects the most prominent American speaking for economic and social reform in the 1880s and 1890s. Unlike

Edward Bellamy, George possessed an analytical and speculative mind, a deep devotion to Jeffersonian principles of government, a distaste for socialism, and a fervid faith in the brotherhood of man and the fatherhood of God. Editorials, magazine articles, books and some 800 speeches advocated social and economic change. For many Americans and Englishmen, Henry George's ideas were a restatement in applied economics of the Declaration of Independence.[87]

George, man of many occupations, arrived in California in 1857. Gold prospector, printer, reporter, and editor, he studied and read extensively, particularly in economics and politics. A man of the frontier, he observed with growing horror land speculation and the special favors sought by the railroads.[88] Visiting New York on business, he witnessed extreme poverty, child labor, and slums. On his return to San Francisco he had determined his future. As Parrington says, "He removed economic theory from the academic world and set it in the thick of political conflict."[89]

Essentially George believed that progress and poverty were interrelated, that the problem was world-wide, and that land monopoly was the main cause of poverty. These views were expressed in his principal works: *Progress and Poverty* in 1879, *Social Problems* in 1872, and *Protection of Free Trade* in 1886.[90]

George, however, had developed his economic and social views during the 1870s. Numerous editorials, pamphlets, and speeches expressed his fundamental ideas and contributed to the development of his style. The ideas were original, based on observation and personal experience. As he said in one early speech:

For the study of political economy you need no special knowledge, no extensive library, no costly laboratory. You do not even need text-books nor teachers, if you will but think for yourselves. All that you need is care in reducing complex phenomena to their elements, in distinguishing the essential from the accidental, and in applying the simple laws of human action with which you are familiar. Take nobody's opinion for granted; "try all things: hold fast that which is good." In this way, the opinions of others will help you by their suggestions, elucidations, and corrections; otherwise they will be to you but as words to a parrot.[91]

After the publication of *Progress and Poverty*, George spent the remainder of his active career speaking and writing for land reform, not only in America, but also in Great Britain and Australia.

George's original contribution to economics was his theory of land taxation. He firmly believed that if land alone were taxed, whether the land was used or not, the problems of poverty would be solved. And poverty, to the Prophet of San Francisco, was a crime. Until 1888 George was indefinite in his statement concerning the methods of taxation; after that he spoke and wrote of "the single tax."

Henry George gained his early reputation in the British Isles. Visiting Ireland soon after *Progress and Poverty* was published, he allied himself with the movement for Irish land reform.[92] Returning in 1883–84, he again advocated land reform before the Scottish and English Land Reform Unions he helped to organize. His campaigns were highly successful, particularly in Scotland, although they aroused bitterness among the landowners, who talked of "confiscation." On the other hand, he attracted the interest of the early Fabians, John Ruskin, George Bernard Shaw, Randolph Churchill, and academic audiences at Oxford and Cambridge.[93]

The Prophet returned to England in 1888 to speak once more about land taxation and land reform. By now he was known as a single-tax man. Although he aroused great audiences and spoke for many of his usual reforms, the abolition of child labor, the elimination of poverty, and the rights of man to enjoy the fruits of his labor, George was no longer popular with the Socialists. They recognized that he did not share their position on controls of production, state ownership, or unionization. But they welcomed him to their platforms because he promoted the cause of reform.[94]

George's success in the British Isles led to the earlier acceptance of his ideas among the intellectuals in the United States than would otherwise have happened. By 1886, according to Henry J. Rose, he had "reached the peak of his career as a personal symbol of reform"[95] Occasional lectures in New England, New York, and Brooklyn were not successful financially, although, along with his writings, they enhanced his reputation.

In 1886, backed by labor unionists, Socialists, and reformers, George was nominated as an independent candidate for mayor of New York City. In his acceptance speech he reiterated his main theme—that land, and only land, should be taxed:

We propose to put that tax on land exclusive of improvements, so that a man who is holding land vacant will have to pay as much for it as if he was using it, just upon the same principle that a man who goes to a hotel and hires a room and takes the key and goes away would have to pay as much for it as if he occupied the room and slept in it. In that way we propose to drive out the dog in the manger who is holding from you what he will not use himself. We propose in that way to remove this barrier and open the land to the use of labor in putting up buildings for the accommodation of the people of the city.[96]

Using this basic tenet, he elaborated upon crowded slums,[97] and child labor.[98] He also told his large audiences that the resulting taxes would provide "public accommodations, playgrounds, schools, and facilities for recreation."[99] His campaign was vigorous. George made as many as five appearances in one evening. He lost the election to the regular Democrat, Abram Hewitt, but outdistanced the Republican, Theodore Roosevelt.[100] From that time, however, George's programs became a factor in American politics, the Anti-Poverty League was formed, the weekly *Standard* was established, and labor's political activities were increased.[101]

While George participated in two more elections, most of his energy until his death in 1896 was devoted to writing. Two lecture tours in Texas and the Midwest and a round-the-world tour were undertaken, not only for money, but also to promulgate his life-long belief that the single tax levied equally upon land would solve the problem of poverty and prevent the exploitation of labor.

Henry George often appeared on platforms with Socialists. Nevertheless, he did not believe in socialism.

We should leave the whole of the value produced by individual exertion to the individual. We should respect the rights of property not to any limited extent, but fully. We should leave to him who produces wealth, to him whom the title of the producer passed, all that wealth. No matter what its form, it belongs to the individual.[102]

Fabians recognized that George's aims were different from theirs but did not fight the distinctions, because they realized that his ethical, logical, and emotional appeal also carried weight with the people. So, also, did many American liberals.

George came to believe that laboring men should organize and form unions. Accepting the nomination for the mayoral election in 1886 was the first major step. In 1894 he spoke before a labor-union meeting held in Cooper Union to protest Cleveland's action in sending troops to quell the great railroad strike. He spoke against restricted union membership, compulsory arbitration, and strikes.[103] He favored union membership but did not speak for special privileges for unions, for he believed in justice and equality for all citizens.

Free trade was another great intellectual passion of Henry George. Although his book on the subject was not published until 1886, George believed in free trade from the beginning. As early as 1877 he said that the tariff increased the price of bringing goods from abroad. His last speech in San Francisco in 1890 shows that his attitude had not changed during the years. He said:

Bring almost any article of wealth to this country from a foreign country, and you are confronted at once with a tax. It is not from a common-sense standpoint a stupid thing, if we want more wealth—if the prosperous country is the country that increases in wealth, why in Heaven's name should we put up a barrier against the men who want to bring wealth into this country.[104]

As a matter of fact George advocated many reforms during his career. He spoke in favor of the Australian ballot. He helped organize anti-poverty leagues, various land-reform institutions, and single-tax societies. He attacked churches and religious groups because they seemed afraid to disapprove of slums, poverty, child labor, and the exploitation of the needy.

The main basis for all of his agitation was his firm and unaltering devotion to the Jeffersonian tradition of equal freedom for all. Speaking at the California Theatre in San Francisco on July 4, 1887, he said:

The assertion of the equal rights of all men to life, liberty, and the pursuit of happiness is the assertion of the right of each to the fullest, freest exercise of all his faculties, limited only by the equal right of every other. It includes freedom of person and security of earnings, freedom of trade and capital, freedom of conscience and speech and the press. It is the declaration of the same equal rights of all human beings to the enjoyment of the bounty of the Creator—to light and air, to water and to land. It asserts these rights to be inalienable—as the direct grant of the Creator to each human being.[105]

Over and over George appealed to all who favored freedom. His appeals resembled much that Ralph Waldo Emerson had written earlier in the century.

Although Henry George organized no great and lasting movement, he made a profound impression upon his times and influenced the economic thought of many today. The Fabians and the Liberal Party in England advocated land taxation, which became a part of the famous Lloyd George Budget of 1909. Russians and Scandinavians were influenced by George. In the United States his great followers were Tom Johnson, Father McGlynn, and Hamlin Garland. In some cities, such as New York, organizations still conduct classes and distribute leaflets promoting George's ideas.

The deeper influences may be said to be three in number. As Barker says:

The participation of free governments in the processes of social justice is now accepted everywhere as policy to be maintained. A desire for world-wide free trade recurs in our day; and many believe that a greater equality among the people of the earth, of access to its resources, would increase mankind's hope for mankind.[106]

In addition to his original ideas three other elements contributed to George's success, the first being his own character. He was a man not overly interested in financial success, he was generous in aiding causes, and he was sincere in his convictions. Men from all walks of life admired these traits, as the outpouring at his funeral and the published testimonials proved. In the second place, George's style was simple but eloquent. Using few statistics, he employed the allegory, the descriptive story (such as the one about Robinson Crusoe) in a masterly fashion. His sentences were short and direct. His delivery also made it easy to accept his message. In the early years he read from a manuscript and was rather ineffective with audiences.[107] Later he came to feel that "verbal preparation may prevent one from making poor speeches, but it also prevents one's reaching high levels. The few instances of inspiration to which one may rise if he speaks extemporaneously more than compensate for all his failures."[108]

CONCLUSION

Twain, Cable, Bellamy and George were all reformers; all were natural writers; yet they were unwilling to confine themselves to the printed page, using their reputations as writers to appeal even more intimately to the masses through the spoken word from the lecture platform. Still, to attempt a synthesis of four intellectuals with such diverse backgrounds is impossible. They came from different parts of the country and pursued different issues and problems, championing different reforms. Cable and Bellamy lived in New England but did not know each other. Mark Twain and Henry George knew the United States from coast to coast and the world as well. All four were vitally concerned with intellectual pursuits during the late nineteenth century. The serious humorist, the southern civil-rights agitator, the Utopian dreamer, and the economic prophet, each with his own peculiar rhetorical flairs, added to the ferment of protest with his own special brand of reform.

NOTES

1. Justin Kaplan, *Mr. Clemens and Mark Twain. A Biography* (New York: Simon and Schuster, 1968). The best biography of Twain, particularly of the period after 1868.
2. Bernard DeVoto, *Mark Twain's America* (Boston: Houghton Mifflin Co., 1967), pp. 3-78.
3. DeLancy Ferguson, *Mark Twain Man and Legend* (Indianapolis and New York: Russell and Russell, 1943), p. 112. Excellent for early period.
4. Paul Fatout, *Mark Twain on the Lecture Circuit* (Bloomington: Indiana University Press, 1960), pp. 33–86. Fred W. Lorch, *The Trouble Begins at Eight* (Ames: Iowa State University Press, 1966), pp. 3–67.
5. Lorch, *Trouble*, pp. 284–297. This version seems to be the most complete.

6. Ibid., pp. 285–288.
7. Ibid., pp. 274–285.
8. Ibid., p. 277.
9. Ibid., p. 297–304.
10. Ibid., pp. 304–321.
11. Ibid., pp. 121–122.
12. Ibid., pp. 141–146.
13. Howard J. Baetzhold, *Mark Twain and John Bull* (Bloomington: Indiana University Press, 1970), pp. 18–19.
14. Ferguson, *Mark Twain*, p. 144.
15. Lorch, *Trouble*, pp. 161–182. For Cable's reaction, see Arlin Turner, *Mark Twain and George W. Cable: The Record of a Literary Friendship.* (East Lansing, Michigan: Michigan State University Press, 1960).
16. Josiah G. Holland, "Lecture Brokers and Lecture Breakers," *Scribner's Monthly* 2 (March 1871): 560–561; "Triflers on the Platform," *Scribner's Monthly* 3 (February 1876).
17. Lorch, *Trouble*, pp. 211–243.
18. *Mark Twain's Letters*, ed. Albert Bigelow Paine (New York: Harper and Brothers, 1917), 1: 370–371.
19. "How To Tell A Story," *The Writings of Mark Twain*, ed. Albert Bigelow Paine (New York: Harper and Brothers, 1917), 18: 263–271.
20. *Mark Twain's Speeches* with an Introduction by Albert Bigelow Paine. (New York: Harper and Brothers, 1923), pp. 26–82.
21. Lorch, *Trouble*, pp. 232–235.
22. Edward Wagenknect, *Mark Twain, The Man and His Work* (Norman: University of Oklahoma Press, 1963), pp. 150–163.
23. *Mark Twain's Speeches*, pp. 150–153.
24. Ibid., p. 163.
25. Ibid., p. 86–92.
26. Louis J. Budd, *Mark Twain, Social Philosopher* (Bloomington: Indiana University Press, 1962), p. 110.
27. *Mark Twain's Speeches*, pp. 323–329.
28. *Mark Twain on the Damned Human Race*, ed. Janet Smith (Clinton, Mass.: The Colonial Press, 1962), p. 230.
29. *Mark Twain's Speeches*, pp. 222–224.
30. Albert Bigelow Paine, *Mark Twain, A Biography*, 3 vols. (New York: Harper and Brothers, 1912), 1: 474–75; 540–541.
31. *Mark Twain's Speeches*, pp. 276–280.
32. Ibid., pp. 228–231.
33. Ibid., p. 231.
34. Paul J. Carter, Jr., "Mark Twain and the American Labor Movement," *New England Quarterly* 30 (1957): 382–388.
35. Lorch, *Trouble*, pp. 316–318.
36. *Mark Twain's Speeches*, pp. 46–52.
37. Paine, *Mark Twain, A Biography*, 2: 691; 694.

38. Budd, *Mark Twain*, p. 82. ˌ
39. *Mark Twain's Speeches*, pp. 113–116.
40. Ibid., p. 217.
41. Ibid., pp. 218–221.
42. Paine, *Mark Twain, A Biography*, 3: 1145–1147.
43. Ibid., 2: 780–781.
44. *Mark Twain's Speeches*, p. 126.
45. Ibid., p. 221.
46. *Mark Twain-Howells Letters*, ed. Henry Nash Smith and William M. Gibson (Cambridge: Harvard University Press, Belknap Press, 1960), 2: 724.
47. *Mark Twain's Speeches*, pp. 211–213.
48. *Mark Twain-Howells Letters*, 2: 588.
49. *Mark Twain's Notebook*, ed. Albert Bigelow Paine (New York: Harper and Brothers, 1935), p. 372.
50. Philip Butcher, *George Washington Cable* (New York: Twayne Publishers, 1962), p. 165.
51. Fatout, *Mark Twain on the Circuit*, pp. 204–231.
52. George W. Cable *The Negro Question: A Selection of Writings on Civil Rights in the South*, ed. Arlin Turner (Garden City: Doubleday & Co., 1958), p. 19.
53. Arlin Turner, *George W. Cable* (Durham: Duke University Press, 1956), pp. 123–129.
54. George W. Cable, "The Convict Lease System in the Southern States," *Century Magazine* 27 (February 1884): 582–599.
55. Turner, *George W. Cable*, p. 144.
56. Cable, *The Negro Question*, p. 38.
57. Ibid., pp. 40–50.
58. Ibid., pp. 47–48.
59. Turner, *George W. Cable*, pp. 158–159.
60. Ibid., pp. 158–159.
61. Cable, *The Negro Question*, pp. 54–82.
62. Ibid., pp. 50–76.
63. Ibid., pp. 76–78.
64. Ibid., pp. 78–80.
65. Turner, *George W. Cable*, pp. 194–207.
66. Henry W. Grady, "In Plain Black and White," *Century Magazine* 29 (April 1885): 909–17.
67. Cable, *The Negro Question*, pp. 83–131.
68. Turner, *George W. Cable*, pp. 244–248.
69. Cable, *The Negro Question*, pp. 236–271.
70. Ibid., p. 133.
71. Philip Butcher, "George W. Cable and Booker T. Washington," *Journal of Negro Education* 17 (February 1948): 464.
72. Cable, *The Negro Question*, pp. 170–184.
73. Paine, *Mark Twain: A Biography*, 2: 443.

74. Butcher, *George W. Cable*, p. 111.
75. Philip Butcher, *George W. Cable; The Northampton Years* (New York: Columbia University Press, 1959). Best study of Cable's last years, pp. 72–91.
76. Van Wyck Brooks, *New England Indian Summer* (New York: E. P. Dutton & Co., 1940), pp. 513–519.
77. Charles H. Madison, *Critics and Crusaders, A Century of American Protest* (New York: Henry Holt and Co., 1947), p. 146.
78. Arthur E. Morgan, *Edward Bellamy* (New York: Columbia University Press, 1944), pp. 3–200.
79. "Fiction and Social Debate," *Literary History of the United States*. ed. Robert E. Spiller et al. (New York: Macmillan Co., 1953), p. 991.
80. John Hope Franklin, "Edward Bellamy and The Nationalist Movement," *New England Quarterly* 11 (December 1938): 739–772.
81. Morgan, *Edward Bellamy*, pp. 249–251.
82. Edward Bellamy, *Edward Bellamy Speaks Again* (Kansas City: The Peerage Press, 1937), pp. 33–51.
83. Ibid., pp. 53–71.
84. Richard Hofstadter, *Anti-Intellectualism in American Life* (New York:Vintage Press, 1963), p. 292.
85. Morgan, *Edward Bellamy*, pp. 204–222.
86. Ibid, p. 253.
87. Edward J. Rose, *Henry George* (New York: Twayne Publishers, 1968), p. 19. Best biography for the later part of his life.
88. Charles A. Barker, *Henry George* (New York: Oxford University Press, 1935), pp. 72–160. Best biography for the earlier life of Henry George.
89. Vernon Louis Parrington, *Main Currents in American Thought* (New York: Harcourt, Brace, & Company, 1927–30) Vol. 3 *The Beginnings of Critical Realism*, p. 26.
90. Rose, *Henry George*, pp. 60–89; Barker, *Henry George*, pp. 205–315.
91. Henry George, *The Study of Political Economy* (New York: The Robert Schalkenbach Foundation), p. 13.
92. Elwood P. Lawrence, *Henry George in the British Isles* (East Lansing: Michigan State University Press, 1957), pp. 13–24.
93. Ibid., pp. 26–50.
94. Ibid., pp. 51–60.
95. Rose, *Henry George*, p. 119.
96. Charles W. Lomas, *The Agitator in American Society* (Englewood Cliffs, N.J.: Prentice-Hall, 1968), p. 57.
97. Ibid., pp. 55–56.
98. Ibid., pp. 57–58.
99. Ibid., p. 57.
100. For a complete study of this campaign, see Louis Post and Fred Leubascher, *An Acount of the George-Hewitt Campaign* (New York: Reprint ed. The Robert Schalkenbach Foundation, 1886).
101. Rose, *Henry George*, pp. 122–123.

102. *The Writings of Henry George*, ed. Henry George, Jr., 10 Vols. (New York: Doubleday and McClure, 1898–1901), 8:313.
103. Ibid., 8: 335–348.
104. Ibid., 8: 306.
105. Ibid., 8: 173.
106. Barker, *Henry George*, p. 635.
107. Charles W. Lomas, "Kearney and George: The Demagogue and the Prophet," *Speech Monographs* 28 (March 1961): 50–59.
108. Louis F. Post, *The Prophet of San Francisco* (New York: Vanguard Press, 1930), p. 63.

13

The Platform and Public Thought

JAMES H. McBATH

The voices of protest and reform found a ready audience from lecture platforms during the closing decades of the century. Commentators on nineteenth-century American life commonly referred to the platform as a national institution. "The stump-speaker is the father of American civilization," said Oliver Wendell Holmes in his lecture that introduced the 1852 season at Broadway Tabernacle in New York City.[1] Dr. Holmes added, "That lecturing has succeeded in establishing itself as a fifth estate, there can be no doubt." Other observers of contemporary society noted our zest for the public lecture. "The custom of organising Lyceums, and of employing lecturers," observed Charles Dickens, "has long been in vogue in some parts of the United States. . . . But, in recent years, the occasional custom has grown into a universal national 'institution.' Now it would be difficult to find a community, counted by thousands, without its established system of lecturing."[2] In 1869, the editor of the *New York Tribune* opined that "when the historian of a later day comes to search out the intellectual antecedents of his modern society, he will devote an interesting chapter to the rise and progress of ideas as illustrated in the institution of the public lecture."[3]

The social and intellectual ferment that characterized post-Appomatox America found expression on hundreds of platforms. These platforms facilitated the widespread sharing of ideas needed to shape the course of public policy. They were, as well, powerful agencies for the transmission and popularization of knowledge. Speakers addressed themselves to a national audience—vast, scattered, diverse, and mobile—whose dominant characteristic was its shift from rural to urban settings. The census of 1880

320

showed that approximately three-fourths of the 50,000,000 inhabitants lived on open land or in towns of less than 4,000 population. In 1890 only one out of three citizens was an urban dweller. By 1900 the city had become dominant. But the transition was substantive as well as physical, bringing with it a variety of new problems affecting the quality of life. In this dynamic environment the platform was a prime instrument for public communication and social melioration as well as an indispensable agency in the nationalization of American culture.

LYCEUM

The organized public platform in this country had its beginning in a meeting of farmers and mechanics organized in 1826 by Josiah Holbrook in Millbury, Massachusetts. With Holbrook vigorously promoting local institutes for popular education, his lyceum idea was copied in hundreds and then thousands of communities. By 1834 a vast network had been established, involving county, state, and even a national organization. In Massachusetts in 1839, for example, Horace Mann reported that there were 137 lyceums with an average weekly attendance of 32,698.[4] Expenses for the local lyceum were small—the cost of a hall, doorkeeper, a few advertisements, and a modest fee, if any, for the lecturer.[5]

During the 1840s and 1850s the lyceum movement flourished as it responded to the buoyant optimism, humanitarianism, and idealism that gave rise to reform movements in education, temperance, women's rights, and especially anti-slavery. George William Curtis expressed the general view that heightened feeling over anti-slavery reform stimulated public interest in lecturing: "The singular success of the lyceum lecture of that time was due, undoubtedly, to two causes—the simultaneous appearance of a remarkable group of orators, and their profound sympathy with the question which absorbed the public mind."[6] Wendell Phillips, John B. Gough, and Henry Ward Beecher (regarded by James B. Pond as "the great triumvirate of lecture kings") led a lyceum roster that included Edward Everett Hale, Oliver Wendell Holmes, James Russell Lowell, Horace Greeley, Ralph Waldo Emerson, George W. Curtis, Charles Sumner, William Lloyd Garrison, Horace Mann, Thomas Wentworth Higginson, Susan B. Anthony, and other makers of mid-century opinion. Audiences also were introduced to the rustic humor of Artemus Ward, Josh Billings, and Petroleum V. Nasby. Inevitably the lecturers who prospered in the East came westward with the railroads that spread across the Alleghenies to the Mississippi Valley. By 1860 the lecture movement, which still bore the name "lyceum," had assumed national dimensions.

During the war years lectures on cultural subjects were largely supplanted by discussion of paramount domestic issues. "The profound interest of the time," commented the editor of *Harper's Weekly*, "will hardly suffer any speaker to wander far from some aspect of the condition of the country."[7] The subjects delivered to a western New York lyceum are probably representative of any lyceum program during the Civil War: "The Southern Whites," "The State of the Country," "The Probable Issues of the War," "The Way of Peace," "The National Heart," and "The Crisis of the Nation."[8] Political and reform themes were popular if they were cast in the language of patriotism. Humorous lecturers also gained favor during the later war period, providing variety in the standard fare of political oratory and offering brief diversions from the anxieties of war.

The lyceum system revived quickly after the Civil War. With the coming of peace in the spring of 1865 "the public mind, released from the long strain of the southern conflict, was hungry for this form of entertainment and instruction. . . ."[9] Not only had the war years created an appetite for diversion; they also had shaped a new social milieu with questions demanding understanding and resolution. The lyceum also received impetus from the introduction of the lecture bureau. Mainly responsible for professionalizing the platform was James Redpath, a journalist best known for his abolitionist writings, who in 1868 organized the Boston Lyceum Bureau.[10] Observing the need of an agency for the booking of lectures, Redpath established a small office in Boston for the purpose of handling administrative details for any lecturer willing to share 10 percent of his fee. This innovation released lecturers from the tedious routine of booking arrangements and provided a dependable clearing house for lecture committees. Lyceum bureaus simultaneously made lecturing more attractive to public figures and provided them national audiences by compressing extensive tours into feasible itineraries. A galaxy of lecturers, including men of letters as well as politicians and reformers, crisscrossed America. Between 1833 and 1881 Emerson gave 1,469 (and possibly as many as 1,602) lectures in at least 22 states.[11] During his experience as a lecturer between 1842 and 1886, John B. Gough, it was estimated, traveled 450,000 miles to deliver 8,606 addresses before more than nine million persons.[12] In the years 1875 to 1887 Henry Ward Beecher "delivered 1,261 lectures in every state in the Union except Arizona and New Mexico, covering approximately 300,000 miles."[13] For ten years Frances Willard averaged one speech a day.[14] During her tour of 1883 she delivered temperance addresses in capital cities of all the states and territories except Idaho and Arizona. Wendell Phillips was perhaps the most active of American lecturers, espousing anti-slavery and reform and, later, speaking on literary and scientific subjects. He repeated his famous lecture on "The Lost Arts" for forty-five years.[15]

The bureaus also encouraged an influx of lecturers from abroad. Just as Dickins's tour of 1867 motivated James Redpath to devise a comprehensive plan for lecture booking, the existence of the bureau stimulated arrangements with foreign lecturers. British celebrities were especially in demand, and they came in increasing numbers in the 1870s and 1880s. Dickens and Thackeray were followed, in 1870–71, by Thomas Hughes and A. J. Mundella. Edmund Yates, James Anthony Froude, George MacDonald, Emily Faithfull, John Tyndall, and Professor J. H. Pepper (with his scientific demonstrations) came in 1872–73 to be followed the next season by Charles Bradlaugh (in the first of his three winter tours), Wilkie Collins, Gerald Massey, Charles Kingsley, Edward Jenkins, and R. A. Proctor. "It has become quite the fashion for whoever is best and brightest in England to come to America," said the *New York Tribune* of February 18, 1874. In succeeding years a stream of prominent Britons continued to appear before American audiences. Oscar Wilde's lecture tour of 1882 lasted from January to his departure in late December. Herbert Spencer visited New York in the fall of 1882, though he declined offers for an extended tour. Matthew Arnold arrived on October 13, 1883, to lecture some seventy times on "Literature and Science," "Numbers," and "Emerson." In 1891–92 Sir Edward Arnold offered his literary lectures and readings to audiences from Boston to Minneapolis. Henry Drummond presented his famous series on the "Ascent of Man" at Lowell Institute in 1893 and stayed to repeat them at Lake Chautauqua. Arthur Conan Doyle came in October 1894, and gave forty readings.

A corps of Irish speakers also visited the United States, usually to appeal for political and financial support for their embattled land. Michael Davitt, the "Father of the Land League," came from Ireland to address American audiences first in 1878 and, again, in 1880, 1882, and 1886. John Dillon arrived in 1880, while Justin McCarthy returned in 1886 to discuss the prospects of home rule. Charles Parnell landed in New York on January 2, 1880, to initiate a speaking tour through eighteen states, where he delivered more than one hundred addresses.[16]

Besides providing a rostrum for their talents and special interests, the commercial circuit offered lecturers inviting financial rewards. Lecturers of established reputation usually received from $75 to $125 for each appearance. "I lecture every night, except Sundays," wrote Bayard Taylor in 1874, "and receive an average of $110 a night. My engagements this season . . . are 112."[17] Lions of the platforms earned more. Joseph Cook called for $250. Emerson, wishing to avoid an engagement in Cincinnati, set his price at $300 and was promptly accepted. Carl Schurz received $200. Mrs. Scott-Siddons easily commanded $250.[18] Anna Dickinson's tours took her to "from one hundred to 150 different cities a season at fees ranging from $150 to $400 a night."[19] George William Curtis, at the height of his career, received $200 to $350 a lecture. Henry Ward Beecher, Robert Ingersoll, and T. Dewitt Talmage were available for $500 per engagement. In 1872 lecture fees reached a new ceiling when Redpath paid the first one-thousand-dollar fee to Beecher for one lecture in the Boston Music Hall.[20] John B. Gough, with fees ranging between $200 and $500, averaged $260 for 2,080 lectures on temperance between 1862 and 1870. During the last decade of his life, Gough's annual income from lecturing was never less than $30,000.[21] In 1875 Theodore Tilton earned $30,000 for delivering 217 lectures.[22] Now organized on a sound financial and administrative basis, the lyceum movement flourished as it catered to a voracious national interest in reform, religious re-emphasis, and entertainment.

Mark Twain, whose lecture career spanned forty years, was a candid reporter on the everyday business of a lyceum bureau:

In every town there was an organization of citizens who occupied themselves in the off season, every year, in arranging for a course of lectures for the coming winter; they chose their platform people from the Boston Lecture Agency list and they chose according to the town's size and ability to pay the prices. The course usually consisted of eight or ten lecturers. All that was wanted was that it should pay expenses; that it should come out with a money balance at the end of the season was not required. Very small towns had to put up with fifty-dollar men and women, with one or two second-class stars at a hundred dollars each as an attraction; big towns employed hundred-dollar men and women altogether and added John B. Gough or Henry Ward Beecher or Anna Dickinson or Wendell Phillips as a compelling attraction; large cities employed this whole battery of stars.[23]

What seems to have been a typical lyceum of the period was one described as it operated in the 1880s in a small New England town. Max Bennett Thrasher recalled that Mary A. Livermore came three times to the town, as did the Fisk Jubilee Singers. Single appearances were made by Lyman Abbott, a leading exponent of the Social Gospel; George Kennan, the Siberian traveler; Robert J. Burdette, the "Hawkeye Humorist"; Judge Albion W. Tourgee, an Ohioan who had lived in the South for years after the war; B. K. Bruce, the Negro Senator from Mississippi; Will Carleton, who declaimed, among his other works, "Over the Hill to the Poorhouse"; Joseph Cook, the Arctic explorer; Belva Lockwood, Equal Rights Party candidate for President in 1884 and 1888; and General Lew Wallace.[24]

But the Gilded Age did not sustain its interest in the lyceum platform. "There is a general complaint this year," observed an editor of *Scribner's* in 1871, "throughout that portion of the country in which the 'lecture system' has become an institution, that the usual courses of lecturers and of intellectual entertainments grouped with lectures have been un-remunerative."[25] Widespread economic stresses of the early seventies (repercussions of the Panic of 1873 lasted until 1878) doubtless also contributed to decreased lyceum attendance. Just after the opening of the 1874 season James Redpath wrote to his friend William Cooper Howells:

The lecture season this winter is very dull all over the country, and the same is true of every kind of amusement; for the people begin to feel the effects of the last year's panic, and are everywhere economizing. They seem to have conceived the wicked and absurd theory that it is easier to do without lectures and concerts than pork and beans; and in consequence of this abominable heresy, I do not think I shall be able to make as much money as I expected.[26]

That same year, 1874, Redpath sold his Boston agency to Major James B. Pond, who later opined that the postwar period of lyceum prosperity had ended by 1877.[27] Pond attributed dwindling interest in the lyceum to a scarcity of good lecturers, noting that Charles Sumner had died, Emerson was "worn out," Curtis was busy as editor of *Harper's Weekly*, Gough's voice had failed him, Douglass had become Minister to Haiti, Beecher's reputation was compromised by scandal, and Anna Dickinson had deserted the lecture platform for the stage.[28] Moreover, there was a waning interest in the declamations of women's rights lecturers, who had "told all there was to say" on the subject. With no dominating reform issue to fire the public imagination, as abolition had done in the 1850s, it seemed to many that "the old causes were dead and forgotten, and no new ideal has arisen to rally the minds of the younger men."[29] Magazines and newspapers were beginning to provide "almost everything to be said on the subjects of progress, genius, education, reform, and entertainment"[30] (and, Pond might have added, at far less cost than courses offered by the commercial bureaus). After a decade of postwar acceptance and prosperity the lyceum now encountered competition as well as changing public expectations. "People got tired of being instructed when they simply wanted to be amused," commented the *New York Tribune*'s editor, "and after a while even the most noted names failed to arouse more than a languid enthusiasm."[31] The annual *Tribune Index* reflected a flagging interest in public lecturing, listing 107 lectures in 1875, 64 in 1877, 54 in 1880, 28 in 1885, and 8 in 1887. The *New York Times Index* listed 113 reports for 1878, 86 for 1880, 46 for 1885, and in 1886 dropped the category "Lecturers and Addresses" from the *Index*. Not until the prosperous closing years of the century did lyceum lectures regain their popularity. In December 1897, the humorist Robert J. Burdette wrote a friend: "The season has been a busy one for me. In all my twenty-one years on the platform I never had such houses. Night after night they have seated the stage, packed the standing room, and then turned people away. It's great business."[32] By the early

1900s over 150 bureaus were in operation, the half dozen largest each booking more than three thousand dates every winter.[33]

COOPER UNION

Conspicuously successful among platforms of the post-Civil War decades was that of Cooper Union in New York City. Founded by Peter Cooper, a wealthy manufacturer known for his philanthropies, the Cooper Union for the Advancement of Science and Art was dedicated on November 2, 1859. Reflecting Cooper's wishes, the trustees announced a plan to elevate the working classes of New York through instruction in "the branches of knowledge which are practically applied in their daily occupations"; in personal hygiene; in social and political science; and by training "addressed to the eye, the ear, and the imagination, with a view to furnish a reasonable and healthy recreation to the working classes after the labors of the day."[34] To achieve these purposes the Union established instructional departments to offer such classes as mathematics, chemistry, mechanical drawing, and design, as well as a library, an art gallery, and a debating society. Enrollment in the classes, beginning with about 2,000 students in 1859, reached more than 5,000 in 1900.

Peter Cooper had become convinced during the lyceum movement of the 1840s that lectures were effective instruments for informal instruction and that workingmen, unaccustomed to reading, might more readily learn useful knowledge from lecturers. In his deed of trust Cooper appended a recommendation that instruction in social and political science should be emphasized through "free public lectures for the people,"[35] an institutional policy that was adopted in 1863. Five years later the trustees broadened the subject matter to include technology, physical and natural science, literature, art, and travel. The Saturday Night Free Lectures became a popular permanent feature of the Union. By the time of Cooper's death in 1883, 290 instructional lectures had been offered on the Saturday programs, including 86 in physical science; 47 in social and political science; 60 in zoology, anatomy, and hygiene; 42 in travel and archaeology; 21 in art; 17 in literature and literary readings.[36] Most of the lectures were presented by professors from New York City colleges and universities or from other eastern schools. Abram Hewitt, Cooper's son-in-law, who arranged the programs, was authorized to pay up to $50 expenses for each lecture. Many of the faculty from nearby schools, pleased to participate in the new program for adult education, did not request compensation.

Although free educational lectures became a mainstay of its program, Cooper Union is better known for the public platform on which speakers, independent of Union sponsorship, addressed audiences on the compass of contemporary popular concerns. On other than Saturday nights the Great Hall was available to any responsible person or group that could furnish rent of $250 and provide a bond to cover possible damage. Interested mainly in a community-service tradition, Peter Cooper did not attempt to develop a lyceum reputation for the Union by sponsoring (or even encouraging) lecture courses that featured the star professionals. Although the Great Hall was available and sometimes was used for lyceum engagements, the lyceum did not play a prominent role in the Cooper Union tradition. When towering figures of the lyceum world—Wendell Phillips, Henry Ward Beecher, John B. Gough, and Anna Dickinson—appeared at Cooper Union, they did not come as commercial attractions; they came as advocates for causes with which they were identified.

Cooper's liberal booking policy, coupled with the size of the lecture room, soon established the Great Hall as a favorite meeting place in New York City. Political leaders, for example, mounted the Cooper Union platform in every presidential campaign from 1860 through the end of the century. In 1864, with the country sighing for peace, Lincoln's reelection was by no means assured. The demonstration by War Democrats pledging support for his policies, just a week before the election, was regarded as one of the crucial events of the campaign.[37] The 1872 campaign found the administration of President Grant attacked by Liberal Republican Senators Lyman Trumbull and Carl Schurz; Roscoe Conkling vigorously defended Grant's conduct in office. Early in 1876 Peter Cooper presided over a mass meeting of workers held to spread the gospel of Greenbackism; several months later, a grateful Greenback Party nominated Cooper as its candidate for President. In the fall of 1876 the "bloody shirt" was waved at Republican rallies by James G. Blaine and Robert G. Ingersoll. "Recollect, my friends," exclaimed Ingersoll to an approving audience,

that it was the Democratic Party that did these devilish things when the great heart of the North was filled with agony and grief. Recollect that they did these things when the future of your country and mine was trembling in the balance of war; recollect that they did these things when the question was liberty, or slavery and perish; recollect that they did these things when your brothers, husbands, and dear ones were bleeding and dying on the battlefields of the South, lying there alone at night, the blood slowly oozing through the wounds of death. . . . Recollect that the Democracy did these things when those dear to you were in the prison pens, with no covering at night except the sky, with no food but what the worms refused, and with no friends except insanity and death.[38]

During the 1872 campaign Republican high-tariff advocates Thomas B. Reed, John Sherman, and Chauncey Depew praised the protective

McKinley Act. The "free silver" campaign of 1896 drew champions of the gold standard and bimetallism. Listeners also heard a reasoned denunciation of federal interference in state labor affairs by Illinois Governor John P. Altgeld.[39] Abraham Lincoln's celebrated appearance of February 1860, was one of four by men later elected to the presidency (the others were Grant, Roosevelt, and Cleveland).

Leaders of social protest found the Great Hall an ideal setting for their public meetings. Peter Cooper's sympathy for wage earners was widely known; the Great Hall was available to all and at low cost. The Union's location in lower East Side New York made it easily accessible to working class constituencies (and not so inviting to patrons of the lyceum). Contemporary news reports frequently mentioned Cooper Union as the scene of activities for economic and political reform. Socialists and anarchists, usually unable to rent other meeting halls, found no prohibition to radical assemblies at Cooper Union. Anti-Tweed Ring agitation found its main expression in a series of mass meetings conducted in the Great Hall during 1871–72.[40] It was the scene of mass sympathy meetings for the railroad strikes of 1877 and 1894 and the Knights of Labor rally in 1890. In 1895 the American Federation of Labor held its national convention in the Great Hall. Over the years Samuel Gompers, Terence V. Powderly, Eugene V. Debs, and J. Keir Hardie spoke in the Great Hall; so did Marxian socialist Daniel DeLeon and Johann Most, the country's leading anarchist. Between 1863 and 1896 the New York newspapers carried accounts of more than 60 occasions when audiences were addressed by labor spokesmen of all shades of opinion.

The spectrum of topics that interested antebellum audiences was heard in the Great Hall. John H. Surratt in 1870 described his part in Booth's plot to abduct President Lincoln; Victoria Woodhull advocated free love in 1872 after exposing infidelities of the Reverend Henry Ward Beecher; Theodore Tilton, plaintiff in the Beecher case, concluded in July 1875, drew cheers "when with impassioned eloquence, he made indirect references to his recent troubles";[41] and the redoubtable Beecher began an 18,500-mile lecture tour, his most extensive, with "Evolution and Revolution" on January 6, 1883.[42] The Irish free-land cause was espoused by Michael Davitt while the Indian's story of broken treaties and government abuse was told by Chief Lewis Downing of the Cherokees and Chief Red Cloud of the Sioux. In single-tax agitation during 1886 and 1890 Henry George advocated the community-land-ownership doctrine. Religious activity found Dwight L. Moody and General William Booth conducting evangelistic services in 1883 and 1894. Crusades for temperance and women's rights, led by legendary orators of the movements, often were launched by mass meetings in the Great Hall.[43]

The Great Hall could seat 2,500, but some reports estimate larger audiences by 500 persons. When seats were filled, the overflow audience would crowd the aisles, pressing near the platform. Important Cooper Union addresses were reported in the more than a dozen daily newspapers of New York City and by telegraphic news services whose stories were dominated by New York events. The principal agency for cooperative newsgathering was the New York Associated Press, controlled by a parent group of New York newspapers. In 1880 the association provided news reports to 350 member newspapers; by 1898 the number had grown to 708.[44] Eastern newspapers routinely published columns of all types of New York news. Its immediate and absentee audience constituted for Cooper Union speakers a sizable national forum.

Unlike the deliberately nonpartisan disputations at Lake Chautauqua, discussion on controversial subjects at Cooper Union was usually confined to one side of a question. Pro and con arguments occurred only in presidential campaign speaking (with Republican voices dominant) and in speechmaking relating to conduct of the Civil War and Reconstruction. That many important subjects failed to stir up even the froth of controversy may seem surprising, since agitational rhetoric tends to be strident and provocative. But the explanation is to be found not so much in the popular issues that found expression in the Great Hall as in the policy of its management. Advocates of moral and social reform gravitated to Cooper Union because they were welcome there, while spokesmen for the orthodoxy may have felt constraint in using a forum so available to the opposition. Although Peter Cooper made his hall accessible to all causes and movements, he assumed no responsibility for the representation of opposing points of view. Still, Cooper did provide a free and influential platform for reformers grappling with fearful issues created by the urban and industrial revolutions.

CHAUTAUQUA

If by the early 1870s lecturers were losing their lyceum audiences, the peripatetic speakers found another major platform at the newly organized Chautauqua Assembly near Jamestown, New York. Equally fortuitous was the opportunity for year-round lecturing; the lyceum thrived from September through the winter, while Chautauqua convened during the summer months.

Chautauqua was founded in 1874 by John Heyl Vincent, editor of the *Sunday School Journal* and other Methodist Sunday-school periodicals, and later a Methodist bishop, and Lewis Miller, a businessman and prominent Methodist layman. Both men had particular interest in the advanced training of Sunday-school workers, which they decided to pursue through a short, outdoor summer assembly. Vincent recalled:

For many years while in the pastorate and in my special efforts to create a general interest in the training of Sunday School teachers and officers I held in all parts of the country institutes and normal classes after the general plan of secular educators. In this work I had the sympathy and cooperation of Mr. Lewis Miller of Akron, O., an energetic and aggressive Sunday School worker, . . . and it was at his suggestion that I consented to take one of my Sunday School institutes to Chautauqua. I gave it the name of "assembly" to distinguish it from the ordinary Sunday School conventions and institutes. . . . The camp meeting management at Fairpoint on the shores of Lake Chautauqua . . . allowed us to use their ground for two weeks in August, 1874.[45]

The decision to conduct the opening session at Lake Chautauqua was based on the suitability and availability of the location. There was no connection between the assembly and the Methodist camp meeting that owned the property. "Sometime during the summer of next year," reported the newspaper of nearby Jamestown, New York, "a national Sunday School convention is to be held, and Dr. Vincent hearing of Fair Point and the Camp Meeting came here to ascertain if it was a suitable place for such a meeting. He was delighted with the grounds, and yesterday, at a meeting of the Executive Committee, presented a proposition to call the National S. S. Association for 1874 at Fair Point."[46]

The Assembly held its initial session from August 4 to 18, 1874, with Miller as chairman and Vincent as head of instruction. Their program allowed little time for frivolity or dawdling by the lakeshore.

At the first Assembly there were twenty-two lectures on the theory and practice of Sunday-school work; seven upon the authority of the Bible; nine sectional primary meetings; six intermediate; six seniors', superintendents', and pastors' meetings; eight conductors' conferences; twenty-five meetings of normal sections; two teachers' meetings; two model Sunday-schools; four Bible readings; three praise services; two immense children's meetings; six sermons, and other meetings of minor note; also prayer meetings, vesper services and temperance addresses.[47]

The program for the second Sunday School Assembly, August 3 to 17, 1875 resembled that of the first summer. Chautauqua's evolution from a training school for Sunday-school teachers into a popular educational institution began with the 1876 session, which was extended to three weeks and added a scientific congress, a temperance conference, and a church congress. Vincent, sensing the intellectual ferment of the seventies, began what was to become a progressive enlargement of purpose and program.

The original plan of the Sunday School Assembly at Fair Point has developed into something much larger and more complete as an educational agency than was at first contemplated. It was a Sunday-school Institute at first. It is now putting on the form and employing the methods of a much more comprehensive institution. It is a summer school in the interest of Religion, Temperance and Science as well of Biblical instruction. It aims in its new development to serve the cause of Social and of Religious Reform. It has an educational, a reformatory and an ecclesiastical purpose.[48]

Chautauqua was thus transformed gradually into a popular assembly embracing a wide range of secular interests. The Assembly's formal work was carried out through three contemporary educational innovations: summer classes, home reading and correspondence study, and university extension.[49] The Chautauqua Literary and Scientific Circle was formed in 1878 to offer a four-year course of home readings. Eight thousand members joined the first class; eighteen years later the enrollment had reached 240,000. Collegiate instruction by correspondence began in 1883 with the College of Liberal Arts chartered by the State of New York to grant the usual academic degrees. By 1895 the system of summer instruction, conducted by William Rainey Harper and a distinguished resident faculty, included courses organized into Schools of Arts and Sciences, Pedagogy, Sacred Literature, Expression, Music, Physical Education, and Practical Arts. Even after his appointment as president of the new University of Chicago, Harper continued to serve as principal of Chautauqua's College of Liberal Arts. He adapted many of Chautauqua's educational ideas to the requirements of formal higher education.[50]

By the 1890s Vincent's brief conference for Sunday-school teachers had become a summer-long festival of education, culture, and entertainment.

The program for this season shows 130 important lectures and addresses, of which 30 are illustrated, 10 musical recitals, 20 concerts and entertainments by musicians and readers, 2 superb tableaux, 4 evenings of fireworks, illuminations and illuminated fleets, 2 prize matches, besides baseball matches, bicycle and athletic exhibitions, and other minor entertainments without number. And this list of lectures does not include those by Dr. Harper and other members of the College faculty, any of the Missionary or Women's Club lectures and addresses, any of the Round Tables, Girls' Club or Boys' Congress meetings; nor are the band concerts or services of songs included. . . . The list, in fact, includes only the more noteworthy lectures and entertainments, and to all of them no admission fee is charged except the regular gate fee.[51]

Such summer programs had for years led local reporters to speak wonderingly of "the regular tread-mill work and course of study" and of "lectures and concerts in distracting numbers."[52]

A principal feature of the annual assemblies was the platform, on which appeared prominent lecturers and speakers of the day, attracting a representative national audience. Although New York, Pennsylvania, and Ohio were most heavily represented, listeners came from every state.[53] By 1885 Chautauqua was playing host to as many as 100,000 visitors—a cross section of Protestant, middle-class America who sustained the churches, supported the educational renaissance, and supplied the impetus for many social reforms of the day. Enthusiastically and repeatedly they filled the amphitheater, which could comfortably seat nearly eight thousand people, to hear addresses regardless of speaker or subject. The schedule for a typical two-month season included 130 major lectures and addresses.[54] No charge was made for attendance at events in the amphitheater other than the gate fee. Season tickets, which also included admission to lectures, concerts, and educational activities, were $5; tickets for the week were $1 in July and $2 in August, while the daily tariff was 25 cents and 40 cents.[55]

While summer visitors listened at Chautauqua, the speeches they heard were accorded a national audience through the assembly's daily newspaper and press accounts sent regularly to leading newspapers. Often publishing verbatim reports of more than one hundred lectures a year, including all major addresses, Chautauqua's newspaper gained a substantial reading public. In 1881 about 50,000 copies were sent through the mails;[56] by 1884 this number had more than doubled.[57] From the beginning the nation's press was well represented at the summer assemblies. As early as 1878 no less than 38 newspapers had correspondents at Chautauqua, sending dispatches to their newspapers in New York, Pennsylvania, Ohio, Michigan, Illinois, Indiana, Missouri, and Louisiana.[58] To newspapers unable to maintain regular correspondents at the assembly, Chautauqua provided daily telegraphic reports.

Most of the issues agitating contemporary America were discussed at length by spokesmen for differing points of view. Chautauqua's conception of its responsibility to maintain a free platform accounted for its manifest attention to issues of current controversy. Within a single season the visitor might hear evolutionists and fundamentalists, protectionists and free traders, bimetallists and gold-standard advocates, suffragists and antifeminists, defenders of Darwinism and exponents of socialism. Even reformers with unsettling propositions for societal change were accorded a fair hearing in the amphitheater. No Chautauquan doubted that "every great message to humanity with the stamp of genuineness upon it gets at some time or other a hearing from the big rostrum."[59] To those who resented this deliberate impartiality the assembly leadership explained that it was "the duty and pleasure of Chautauqua to invite to this place the leaders of all forward movements in order that the people may judge of their merits after the case has been presented."[60] Advocates of one position were often followed within a few days by spokesmen for the other side. Formal debates were frequently arranged—for example, women's suffrage (1881 and 1892), regulation of trusts and monopolies (1889), and free silver (1893).

The speeches on controversial questions of the times delivered at Chautauqua provide an index to the popular issues and public opinions of the age. Chautauqua addresses, for instance, mirrored a swelling popular sentiment that the church must adjust itself and its message to the impact of scientific and Darwinian thought as well as to the rise of an urban, industrial society. Chatauqua lecturers, too, reflected the mounting interest of the period in women's suffrage, temperance and prohibition, and the rights of the Negro. It was on the assembly grounds that the Women's National Christian Temperance Union was organized in 1874, just a week after John B. Gough had addressed the largest audience of the first season.[61] Susan B. Anthony, Anna Howard Shaw, Frances Willard, Carrie Chapman Catt, and Booker T. Washington were in the front ranks of Chautauqua lecturers who spoke for moral, social, or political reform. In the realm of politics, the appeal of A. H. Colquitt, Governor of Georgia, for restoration of national unity, Theodore Roosevelt's espousal in 1890 and 1894 of civil-service reform, and Josiah Strong's declaration of the mission of the ascendant Anglo-Saxon race—all were pronouncements of men caught up in currents of post-Appomatox thought. When Washington Gladden denounced private monopolistic power and Richard T. Ely appraised the merits of socialism, they were reflecting significant public attitudes, just as was Russell Conwell when he preached a gospel of wealth and stewardship. Conwell's four speeches at Chautauqua were variations of a common theme of Christianized capitalism: "A Jolly Earthquake" (1886), "Looking Downward" (1890), "The Angel's Lily" (1893), and "Acres of Diamonds" (1898).

While Henry Drummond defended the evolutionary hypothesis in his famous "Ascent of Man" series in 1893, T. DeWitt Talmage described the "Absurdities of Evolution." Carrie Chapman Catt and Anna Howard Shaw upheld women's suffrage, but Horace Bushnell and John Buckley, editor of the *Christian Advocate*, objected (as did Bishop Vincent, who also opposed the involvement of women in politics). When Washington Gladden criticized trusts and monopolies, George Gunton applauded them.[62] Richard T. Ely urged government intervention in economic affairs; but William Graham Sumner supported *laissez faire* capitalism, arguing that "you can get no equality except upon the level of the lowest" and that any effort to create a different situation would mean "survival of the unfittest."[63] Other questions exciting platform controversy dealt with the status of the Negro, the single tax, and free silver. Still, the most vigorous clashes were evoked by discussions of the relation of science and the evolutionary hypothesis to religion and by argument on the role of government in national economic life.

While interest in social, economic, and political issues of the day was great, more impressive quantitatively were sermons and lectures on religious, cultural, and educational subjects. These speeches dealt with a variety of cultural and informative topics: personal improvement and success, travel experiences, history, literature, philosophy and psychology, science, and educational methods.

The record of public speechmaking for the 1895 season was typical: 17 courses of lectures; 10 sermons; 34 Biblical and religious lectures; 22 historical and biographical lectures; 32 lectures on literature and art; 10 pedagogical lectures; 10 scientific lectures; 23 sociological and economical lectures; 5 lectures on music; 25 miscellaneous lectures on such subjects as "Ships of Old," "A Lesson in Delsarte," and "The Nicaragua Canal"; and 24 illustrated lectures bearing such titles as "Denmark and the Danes," "Central Africa," "In and About Shakespeare's Home," and "Memories of the Lyceum" (presented by J. B. Pond).[64]

Chautauqua invited to its platform many of the foremost lecturers of the day to deliver single speeches, series of lectures, or to participate in formal debates. Approximately 850 speakers delivered more than 2,000 lectures, addresses, and sermons during the last quarter of the nineteenth century. Most speakers were drawn from university faculties and the ministry. Of the handful of foreign speakers the majority came from the British Isles and were drawn from rosters of the lecture bureaus that also supplied the lyceums.

At the end of the nineteenth century Chautauqua had changed from a religious encampment in rustic surroundings to a small city with public parks, a water and power system, hotels and boarding-houses, municipal buildings, and the many halls needed to house its cultural and educational activities. Whereas lectures were delivered out-of-doors in 1874, they subsequently were presented in several permanent structures, the largest of which would seat nearly eight thousand listeners.

While the Chautauqua Assembly continued to sponsor burgeoning educational and cultural activity, other summer institutes calling themselves "chautauquas" were established throughout the country (often by persons who had visited the New York institution). These permanent assemblies, not to be confused with tent or circuit chautauquas launched by Keith Vawter and J. Roy Ellison in 1904, patterned themselves after the original institution. By 1900 nearly four hundred such assemblies were in operation. Iowa led the nation with 60, followed by 40 in Illinois, 25 in

Ohio, and 20 in Indiana.[65] The New York assembly liked to contemplate a maternal relationship with scattered offspring; but beyond inspiration and endorsement there was no organic connection between the Chautauqua Assembly and community platforms bearing the same name. The latter groups conducted annual summer programs featuring lectures, sermons, dramatic readings, and musical entertainment as the home institution did, though usually for briefer periods.

OTHER PROMINENT PLATFORMS

Several platforms, renowned in American history, served special cultural functions during the last quarter of the nineteenth century. Faneuil Hall, celebrated as the "Cradle of Liberty," was used as a forum only sporadically after the Civil War. Infrequent use of the hall is probably explained less by its modest size and location in Boston's market district than by the policy governing use of the hall. Even today, though open to public meetings, Faneuil Hall may not be used for commercial purposes. Admission may not be charged for any scheduled events. The stipulation against admission fees discouraged use of the hall for lyceum engagements. Faneuil Hall for nearly a century has been more a public monument than a popular forum.

If Boston's Ford Hall, established in 1906, is outside the boundaries of this study, the Lowell Institute qualifies in several respects. Founded in 1839 to provide annual courses of lectures, the Lowell Institute platform continues to this day. Its record of activity up to the turn of the century was impressive:

From December 31, 1839, to January, 1898, there have been given under the auspices of the Lowell Institute four hundred and twenty-seven regular courses of lectures,— or four thousand and twenty separate lectures; these, with those repeated, bring the number to four thousand three hundred and twenty-five,—all absolutely free lectures, prepared by the best minds of the age, and representing the highest developments in all the various departments of science, literature, and art.[66]

The season of 1881–82 was typical. Speakers, their topics, and number of lectures were: Edward A. Freeman, "The English People in Their Homes" (6); Gamaliel Bradford, "Modern Europe, Social and Political" (12); Professor Simon Newcomb, "History of Astronomy" (12); James Bryce, "Past and Present of the Greek and Turkish East" (8); Professor Edward S. Morse, "Japan" (12); Edward B. Drew, "China" (6); James F. Clarke, "The Comparative Theology of Ethnic and Catholic Religions" (12); Hjalmar H. Boyesen, "The Icelandic Saga Literature" (6); and Horace E. Scudder,

"Childhood in Literature and Art" (6). Inspection of annual programs for the period 1870–1898 reveals similar emphasis upon ideas, places, and literature. Contemporary problems and issues seldom were discussed at Lowell Institute.

OVERVIEW

The platforms of the lyceum, Chautauqua, and Cooper Union provided significant opportunities for public discourse. For face-to-face communication these organized platforms are unrivaled in American history, challenged only by the circuit chautauquas of the early 1920s whose listeners numbered nearly twelve million each summer. During the period 1875–1900 lyceum lecturers annually reached a national audience of more than five million persons, while the New York Chautauqua Assembly and proliferating local chautauquas added greatly to these numbers by the end of the century.

The audiences of the lyceum, Chautauqua, and Cooper Union were exposed to the range of contemporary social, political, and intellectural currents. Inevitably the platform reflected as well as shaped popular attitudes and taste. "An American lecture," remarked George William Curtis, "is a brisk sermon upon the times."[67] Yet the lyceum, with its commercial base, came to include a fair share of "inspirational" speechmaking and genteel vaudeville. Chautauqua, with highly structured organization and determinedly serious motivation, held steadfastly to its original purpose. In content Chautauqua more nearly resembled Holbrook's lyceum ideal than did the later lyceum resemble its forerunner. After 1900 the circuit chautauquas borrowed more from the lyceum than from the pioneer institution at Lake Chautauqua.

The period saw a professionalization of the lecture field as booking agencies were created to satisfy a ravenous popular interest in speakers and readers. Lecturing became a lucrative profession, and bureaus vied for platform attractions to compete for public attention. In an age without radio or television, film or national theatre, the lyceum and chautauqua were synonymous with education, entertainment, and culture. Until well into the twentieth century, the platform was the sole vehicle for mass spoken communication. The nature of American thought prior to 1900 was largely determined by the extensive symbol-sharing facilitated by writers and speakers, who comprised the media of their day for public discussion. Of his lecturing experience, Carl Schurz would reflect, "I saw what I might call the middle-class culture in process of formation."[68]

The traveling lecturers made distinctive contributions to the nationalization of American culture. Radiating from urban centers to address distant audiences, the speakers gave information and ideas a common currency, elevated the level of public deliberation, and, at the same time, helped to shape the national language. Even the nation's literature "became accessory to the spoken word," observed Daniel Boorstin. "The most distinctive, most influential, and most successful forms of the new American literature were expressions in print of spoken American."[69] The contemporary social and intellectual climate was to a remarkable degree the product of interaction between a small army of public speakers and their audiences.

NOTES

1. The event is reported in the *New York Herald*, October 29, 1852, p. 8.
2. "Lyceums and Lecturing in America," *All the Year Round* 5 (March 4, 1871): 317.
3. *New York Tribune*, December 18, 1869, p. 6.
4. "Third Annual Report," Massachusetts State Board of Education, *Common School Journal* 3 (1840): 77.
5. Account books of the famous Concord Lyceum of 1851 record that papers were presented by Ralph Waldo Emerson, Henry David Thoreau, William Ellery Channing, Wendell Phillips, and Oliver Wendell Holmes. Emerson made four appearances without payment. Thoreau and Channing also did not accept fees. Phillips received $10 to discuss "The Lost Arts" and Holmes was paid $15 for his paper on "Love of Nature." Reproduced in Kenneth Walter Cameron, ed., *The Massachusetts Lyceum During the American Renaissance* (Hartford, Conn.: Transcendental Books, 1969), pp. 103–104.
6. "Editor's Easy Chair," *Harper's Monthly* 74 (April 1887): 824. See also, *Harper's Monthly* 40 (May 1870): 921. However, as lecturers traveled west, they found audiences less willing to hear discussions of abolitionism. For example: "At a time when the East was using the platform for reform propaganda, it was used in Iowa to make life more pleasant and refined. Only after the Civil War did the reform element arise and center popular interest in the speeches of Douglass, Phillips, and Anna Dickinson." Hubert H. Hoeltje, "Notes on the History of Lecturing in Iowa, 1855–1885," *Iowa Journal of History and Politics* 25 (January 1927): 112.
7. "The Lyceum," 7 (October 31, 1863): 691.
8. Mark Lee Luther, "The Bygone Lyceum," *The Dial* 25 (November 1, 1898): 292.
9. John Haynes Holmes, *The Life and Letters of Robert Collyer, 1823–1912* (New York: Dodd, Mead and Company, 1917), 2: 82.
10. Two other organizations had booked lecturers earlier than Redpath's agency. The Associated Western Literary Societies were operating in Detroit by 1855. In 1866 the American Literary Bureau was formed in New York with Colonel Edward G. Parker as its head. Four years later the Associated Western Literary

Societies were absorbed by the American Literary Bureau. See Hoeltje, "Notes on History," pp. 120–130.

11. William Charvat, "A Chronological List of Emerson's American Lecture Engagements," *Bulletin of the New York Public Library* 64 (1960): 494.

12. *Standard Encyclopedia of the Alcohol Problem*, ed. Ernest H. Cherrington (Westerville, Ohio: American Issue Publishing Co., 1925), 3: 1127.

13. James B. Pond, *Eccentricities of Genius* (New York: Dillingham Co., 1900), p. 125. Pond's rambling, anecdotal account of a quarter-century of lyceum booking is a goldmine of information about platform personalities.

14. *New York Times*, February 18, 1898, p. 1.

15. "No doubt it was an exaggeration to say he gave it over two thousand times and that it netted him $150,000." Oscar Sherwin, *Prophet of Liberty: The Life and Times of Wendell Phillips* (New York: Bookman Associates, 1958), p. 645.

16. Wayne C. Minnick, "Parnell in America," *Speech Monographs* 20 (March 1953): 40. Parnell, as "a representative of the Irish people," was invited to address Congress and did so on February 2, 1880.

17. Letter to Martha Kimber, November 29, 1874, in *The Unpublished Letters of Bayard Taylor in the Huntington Library*, ed. John R. Schultz (San Marino, California: Huntington Library, 1937), p. 183.

18. E. P. Powell, "The Rise and Decline of the New England Lyceum," *New England Magazine* 11 (February 1895): 730.

19. Giraud Chester, *Embattled Maiden: The Life of Anna Dickinson* (New York: Putnam, 1951), p. 89.

20. Luther, "The Bygone Lyceum," p. 291. Gross receipts, fortunately, exceeded $3,000.

21. A considerable improvement over Gough's first year of lecturing: "In three hundred and sixty-five days I gave three hundred and eighty-three addresses, and received from them one thousand and fifty-nine dollars,—out of which I paid all expenses; traveled six thousand eight hundred and forty miles. . . ." See *Autobiography and Personal Recollections of John B. Gough with Twenty-six Years' Experience as a Public Speaker* (Springfield, Mass.: Bill, Nichols & Co., 1869), p. 160.

22. *New York Tribune*, November 4, 1876, p. 9.

23. Samuel L. Clemens, *The Autobiography of Mark Twain*, ed. Charles Neider (New York: Harper & Brothers, 1959), p. 175. In the fall of 1868 Twain joined Redpath as a hundred-dollar lecturer.

24. "Is the Mission of the Lecture Platform Ended?" *New England Magazine* 15 (October 1896): 210–220.

25. Josiah G. Holland, "Lecture Brokers and Lecture-Breakers," *Scribner's Monthly* (Century) 1 (March 1871): 560–561. Cf. Dixon Wecter, ed., *Mark Twain to Mrs. Fairbanks* (San Marino, California: Huntington Library, 1949), pp. 145–146.

26. Letter dated November 12, 1874. Huntington Library Ms. 27597.

27. Pond, *Eccentricities of Genius*, p. 543.

28. "The Lyceum," *Cosmopolitan* 20 (April 1896): 597–598.

29. Van Wyck Brooks, *New England: Indian Summer, 1865–1915* (New York: E. P. Dutton & Co., Inc., 1950), p. 189.

30. Pond, "The Lyceum," p. 601.

31. *New York Tribune*, November 9, 1884, p. 6.

32. Quoted in Clara B. Burdette, *Robert J. Burdette: His Message* (Philadelphia: John C. Winston Company, 1922), p. 160.

33. Anna L. Curtis, "A Brief History of the Lyceum," in A. Augustus Wright, ed., *Who's Who in the Lyceum* (Philadelphia: Pearson Brothers, 1906), p. 31. "In fact," said Paul Pearson, "almost every State in the Union sustains at least one hundred Lyceum courses." See "The Modern Lyceum, Its Growth and Mission," *Lippincott's Magazine* 76 (December 1905): 744.

34. *First Annual Report of the Trustees of the Cooper Union of the Advancement of Science and Art for the Year Ending December 31, 1859* (New York, 1860), p. 9.

35. Edward C. Mack, *Peter Cooper: Citizen of New York* (New York: Duell, Sloan and Pearce, 1949), p. 258.

36. The estimate is from Richard A. Ek, "A Historical Study of the Speechmaking at Cooper Union, 1859–1897," Ph.D. dissertation, Southern California 1964, pp. 76–79. Ek's study is a valuable account of Cooper Union's speaking activity.

37. *New York Herald*, November 2, 1864, p. 5.

38. *New York Times*, September 12, 1876, p. 2. The editor commended the speech as "a bold, logical, eloquent, and fair statement of the political situation."

39. Altgeld's speech of October 17, 1896 was delivered before "the largest crowd in the history of the famous Cooper Union." *The World* (New York), October 18, 1896, p. 1.

40. Principal speaker at a concluding meeting of the agitation was William Cullen Bryant, who had been chairman for Lincoln's Cooper Union appearance. The elderly Bryant issued a call for united action against civic corruption to "a highly respectable audience of about two thousand high-toned reformers who were too awfully respectable to cheer or whistle." See *New York Herald*, September 24, 1872, p. 3.

41. Tilton's lecture, "The Problem of Life," attracted a partisan audience, including many women. *New York Times*, September 30, 1875, p. 5.

42. Beecher's theme was the essential harmony between Christianity and evolutionary theory. See *New York World*, January 7, 1883, p. 2.

43. On December 6, 1866, for example, suffrage advocates meeting at Cooper Union established the Citizens' Equal Rights Association, forerunner to the National Woman Suffrage Association. See *New York Herald*, December 7, 1866, p. 7.

44. See Frank Luther Mott, *American Journalism: A History, 1690–1960*. 3d ed. (New York: Macmillan Co., 1962), pp. 304–305; and Robert W. Jones, *Journalism in the United States* (New York: E. P. Dutton & Co., 1947), pp. 402–403.

45. "The Autobiography of Bishop Vincent," *Northwestern Christian Advocate* 58 (July 6, 1910): 847. The assembly's beginning and early years are also recounted in John H. Vincent, *The Chautauqua Movement* (Boston: Chautauqua Press, 1886).

46. *Jamestown Daily Journal*, August 13, 1873, p. 4.

47. *Chautauqua Assembly Daily Herald*, May 10, 1877, p. 2.

48. "Who Are Welcome to Chautauqua," *Chautauqua Assembly Daily Herald*, June 15, 1876, p. 2.

49. The academic program is described in the *Chautauqua Year-Book for 1895* (Chautauqua, New York, 1895).

50. This relationship is discussed in the chapter "Chautauqua Goes to Chicago," in Joseph E. Gould, *The Chautauqua Movement* (New York: State University of New York, 1961), pp. 55–71. Richard J. Storr also describes relations between the institutions: "In 1898, Harper tried unsuccessfully to bring parts of Chautauqua within the orbit of the University. He proposed to move to Chicago the headquarters of the Chautauqua Reading and Scientific Circles and two publishing enterprises working under contract with Chautauqua and, according to one version of the plan, to associate them with University Extension and the University Press." *Harper's University: The Beginnings* (Chicago: University of Chicago Press, 1966), pp. 327–328.

51. *Chautauqua Assembly Herald*, August 5, 1892, p. 1. William James found the program magnificent but overwhelming, exclaiming after a week at Chautauqua in the early 1890s: "Ouf! What a relief! Now for something primordial and savage, even though it were as bad as an Armenian massacre, to set the balance straight again." See *Talks to Teachers on Psychology* (New York: Henry Holt & Co., 1899), p. 270.

52. *The Democrat* (Olean, N.Y.), August 18, 1881, p. 1.

53. In 1881, for example, more than forty railroad companies advertised the sale of excursion tickets to Chautauqua. *Chautauqua Assembly Herald*, July 30, 1881, p. 8.

54. *Chautauqua Assembly Herald*, August 5, 1892, p. 1.

55. Herbert B. Adams, "Chautauqua: A Social and Educational Study," U. S. Commissioner of Education, *Report for 1894–95*, 1: 992. Not a profit-making institution, Chautauqua's expenditures often matched receipts. For discussion of finances, see Adams, pp. 994–995.

56. *Chautauqua Assembly Herald*, June 1881, p. 1.

57. Ibid., July 1884, p. 1.

58. Ibid., August 7, 1878, p. 5.

59. *Jamestown Evening Journal*, August 10, 1898, p. 5.

60. George E. Vincent, *Chautauqua Assembly Herald*, July 14, 1900, p. 1. Vincent, son of Chautauqua's co-founder, later was president of the University of Minnesota.

61. *Jamestown Daily Journal*, August 8, 1874, p. 4.

62. Several days after Gladden's lecture series on "Social Facts and Forces," Gunton, editor of the *Social Economist*, rose to refute Gladden's charge that concentrated economic power had unfavorable social consequences. Gladden, hearing Gunton's speech, challenged him to a formal debate. See *Chautauqua Assembly Herald*, August 27, 1889, pp. 2–3.

63. *Chautauqua Assembly Herald*, August 14, 1886, p. 2. Sumner spoke in the Ampitheater on August 11.

64. *Chautauqua Year-Book for 1895*, pp. 37–44.

65. Anna L. Curtis, "A Brief History of the Lyceum," p. 33. Some 600 community

chautauquas were in operation in 1908. See *Lyceumite and Talent* 7 (November 1908): 17.

66. Harriette Knight Smith, *The History of the Lowell Institute* (Boston: Lamson, Wolffe & Co., 1898), p. 29.
67. "Editor's Easy Chair," *Harper's Monthly* 24 (1861–62): 266.
68. *The Reminiscences of Carl Schurz* (New York: The McClure Co., 1907) 2: 158.
69. *The Americans: The National Experience* (New York: Vintage Books, 1965), p. 307.

CONTRIBUTORS

J. Harold Beaty, pastor of the Christ United Methodist Church, Memphis, Tennessee. He completed his dissertation at Florida State University under the direction of Wayne C. Minnick.

Paul H. Boase, Professor of Interpersonal Communication at Ohio University and Director of the School.

Betty Boyd Caroli, Professor of History, Kingsborough Community College of the City University of New York.

Paul Crawford, Emeritus Professor of Speech at Northern Illinois University.

Richard Doolen, former Associate Professor of History at Ohio University and presently Assistant Director of the Bentley Historical Library at the University of Michigan.

Donald H. Ecroyd, Professor of Speech, Temple University.

Mary Graham, Emeritus Professor of Speech at Brooklyn College.

Robert G. Gunderson, Professor of Speech Communication and of History at Indiana University.

Charles W. Lomas, Emeritus Professor of Communications Studies at the University of California, Los Angeles.

James McBath, Professor of Speech Communication and Chairman of the Department at the University of Southern California.

Frances McCurdy, Emeritus Professor of Speech at the University of Missouri.

Richard Murphy, Emeritus Professor of Speech Communication at the University of Illinois.

Thomas H. Olbricht, Professor of Speech and Homiletics, Abiline Christian College.

Lindsey S. Perkins, Associate Professor (retired) Brooklyn College, City University of New York.

Gregg Phifer, Professor of Speech and Department Chairman at Florida State University.

Malcolm O. Sillars, Professor of Speech and Dean of the College of Humanities, University of Utah.

Robert W. Smith, Professor of Speech, Alma College.

Donald K. Springen, Associate Professor of Speech at Brooklyn College, City University of New York.

INDEX